STUDENT SOLUTIONS MANUAL

Charles T. Horngren
Stanford University

George Foster
Stanford University

Srikant M. Datar
Stanford University

Howard D. Teall
Wilfrid Laurier University

COST ACCOUNTING
A Managerial Emphasis

Second Canadian Edition

Prentice Hall Canada Inc.
Scarborough, Ontario

ISBN 0-13-040129-3

Acquisitions Editor: Samantha Scully
Senior Developmental Editor: Lesley Mann
Production Editor: Nicole Mellow
Production Coordinator: Deborah Starks

Original English Language edition published by Prentice-Hall, Inc.,
Upper Saddle River, New Jersey
Copyright © 2000

7   04 03 02

Printed and bound in Canada.

TABLE OF CONTENTS

PREFACE
TO THE SECOND CANADIAN EDITION

This Student Solutions Manual provides solutions to even-numbered questions, exercises, and problems from *Cost Accounting*, Second Canadian Edition. This material is provided for students who would like to check their own solutions to assigned problems or for students who want to do extra problems. Clearly the purpose of providing these solutions is not to enable students to avoid the conscientious preparation of homework. While some students may want to put themselves at a disadvantage by not doing their assignments, this book has been provided for the benefit of those students who desire a better understanding of the subject of cost accounting.

If you have any questions or comments about *Cost Accounting* or this manual, please forward them to:

The Editor
Cost Accounting, 2nd Cdn. Ed.
edit_phch@prenhall.com

CHAPTER 1
THE ACCOUNTANT'S ROLE IN THE ORGANIZATION

1-2 **Management accounting** measures and reports financial as well as other types of information that assists managers in fulfilling the goals of the organization. **Financial accounting** focuses on external reporting that is guided by generally accepted accounting principles.

1-4 The business functions in the value chain are:

- **Research and development**—the generation of, and experimentation with, ideas related to new products, services, or processes.
- **Design of products, services, and processes**—the detailed planning and engineering of products, services, or processes.
- **Production**—the coordination and assembly of resources to produce a product or deliver a service.
- **Marketing**—the process by which individuals or groups (a) learn about and value the attributes of products or services and (b) purchase those products or services.
- **Distribution**—the mechanism by which products or services are delivered to the customer.
- **Customer service**—the support activities provided to customers.

1-6 Uses of feedback in a management control system include:

- Changing goals
- Searching for alternative means of operating
- Changing methods for making decisions
- Making predictions
- Changing operations
- Changing the reward system

1-8 Yes. Drucker is advocating that accountants do more than scorekeeping, which is often interpreted as being a "cop on the beat" or a watchdog. It is also essential that accountants emphasize their attention-directing and problem-solving functions.

1-10 The SMAC is the Society of Management Accountants of Canada. The CMA (Certified Management Accountant) is the professional designation for management accountants and financial executives. It demonstrates that the holder has passed the admission criteria and demonstrated the competency of technical knowledge required by the SMAC and its provincial societies.

1-12   Steps to take when established written policies provide insufficient guidance are:

(a)   discuss problem with the immediate superior (except when it appears that the superior is involved).
(b)   clarify relevant concepts by confidential discussion with an objective advisor.

If (a) and (b) and other avenues do not resolve the situation, resignation from the organization should be considered.

1-14   Yes, management accountants have customers just as companies have customers who purchase or use their products or services. Management accountants provide information and advice to many line and staff people in the organization and to various external parties. It is essential that they provide information and advice that line and staff customers and external parties view as timely and relevant.

1-16   (10 min.) **Management accountants and customer focus.**

1.   Line managers are the primary customers of the management accounting function. Line managers in each of the six business function areas (R&D, design, production, marketing, distribution, and customer service) use management accounting information in their decisions.

2.   Line managers rely on the continued support of management accountants to justify their budgets and headcount approvals. If these line managers do not find the information provided both relevant and timely, management accountants will not receive the resources necessary to continue fulfilling their potential contributions. This is similar to Ford not being able to retain its customers if it does not continue to satisfy (and even exceed) their expectations as to the reliability and performance of Ford motor vehicles.

1-18 (15 min.) **Major purposes of accounting systems.**

1.   The three major purposes are:

(a) Routine internal reporting for the decisions of managers.
(b) Nonroutine internal reporting for the decisions of managers.
(c) External reporting to investors, government authorities, and other outside parties on the organization's financial position, operations, and related activities.

2.   Note: In part 2 of the required for 1-18, it should read "Identify a major purpose served by each of the above five reports prepared by Barnes and Noble's management accounting group."

   1. (c)
   2. (a)
   3. (b)
   4. (c)
   5. (c)

3.   1. (a) Planning—decision by shareholder about whether to purchase more stock in Barnes and Noble (B&N).
       (b) Control—decision by bank whether B&N has maintained financial ratios specified in loan agreements.
     2. (a) Planning—decision to increase or decrease local marketing support.
       (b) Control—decision on whether recent sales promotion led to an increase in revenues.
     3. (a) Planning—decision about whether or not to expand B&N's Internet lines of business.
       (b) Control—decision by VP of New Business Development on the performance of an analyst.
     4. (a) Planning—decision on which books to include in a special chat-room site.
       (b) Control—decision by publisher to pay additional bonuses to authors due to their book being on a bestseller list.
     5. (a) Planning—decision by B&N on the amount and type of insurance to purchase next year.
       (b) Control—decision by insurance company to approve a cash payment to B&N.

1-20 (15 min.) **Value chain and classification of costs, pharmaceutical company.**

Cost Item	Value Chain Business Function
a.	Design
b.	Marketing
c.	Customer service
d.	Research and development
e.	Marketing
f.	Production
g.	Marketing
h.	Distribution

1-22 (15 min.) **Scorekeeping, attention-directing, and problem-solving.**

Because the accountant's duties are often not sharply defined, some of these answers might be challenged.

a. Scorekeeping
b. Attention directing
c. Scorekeeping
d. Problem solving
e. Attention directing
f. Attention directing
g. Problem solving
h. Scorekeeping, depending on the extent of the report
i. This question is intentionally vague. The give-and-take of the budgetary process usually encompasses all three functions, but it emphasizes scorekeeping the least. The main function is attention directing, but problem solving is also involved.
j. Problem solving

1-24 (15 min.) **Changes in management and changes in management accounting.**

Change in Management Accounting	Key Theme in New Management Approach
a.	Total value-chain analysis
b.	Key success factors (quality) or Total value-chain analysis
c.	Dual external/internal focus
d.	Continuous improvement
e.	Customer satisfaction is priority one

1-26 (20-30 min.) **Responsibility for analysis of performance.**

This problem raises plenty of thought-provoking questions. Unfortunately, there are no pat answers. The generalizations about these relationships are difficult to formulate.

1.   Apparently, the controller's performance-analysis staff have not won the confidence or respect of Whisler and other line officers. Whisler regards these accountants as interlopers who are unqualified for their analytical tasks on two counts: (a) the task is Whisler's, not the accountants'; and (b) Whisler better understands his own problems. It is unlikely that the controller's performance-analysis staff has maintained a day-to-day relationship with line personnel in Division C.

2.   Phillipson should point out that the work is being done by her performance-analysis staff in order to enable Whisler to better concentrate on his other work. The detailed analyses by her staff should help Whisler better understand and improve his own performance.

   Furthermore, Phillipson should point out that Whisler would need his own divisional accounting staff in order to prepare the necessary analysis of performance if Phillipson's group did not support him. More uniform reporting formats and procedures and more objective appraisals potentially could occur if the performance-analysis staff remains as part of the corporate controller's group.

3.   Two approaches within the existing organization reporting relationships would be:
   (a)   Placing higher priority on having her performance-analysis staff view the division personnel as important customers and actively seeking out ways to increase customer satisfaction.
   (b)   Encouraging greater use of teams in which division personnel and corporate control personnel are members. Hopefully, mutual respect will increase by this close interaction.

A more extreme approach would be to change the organization's reporting relationships and staff assignments. For example, each division manager could have his or her own performance-analysis staff member as part of the plant controller's group.

1-28 (15 min.) **Planning and control decisions; Internet company.**

1.   Planning decisions at WebNews.com focus on organizational goals, predicting results under various alternative ways of achieving those goals, and then deciding how to attain the desired goal. For example, WebNews.com could have the objective of revenue growth to gain critical mass or it could have the objective of increasing operating income. Many Internet companies in their formative years make revenue growth (and subscriber growth) their primary goal.

Control focuses on (a) deciding on, and taking actions that implement the planning decision, and (b) deciding on performance evaluation and the related feedback that will help future decision making.

2.   **Planning decisions**
    a.   Decision to raise monthly subscription fee
    c.   Decision to upgrade content of online services
    e.   Decision to decrease monthly subscription fee

Control decisions
    b.   Decision to inform existing subscribers about the rate of increase—an implementation part of control decisions
    d.   Demotion of VP of Marketing—performance evaluation and feedback aspect of control decisions

1-30 (30 min.) **Software procurement decisions, ethics.**

1. Companies with "codes of conduct" frequently have a "supplier clause" that prohibits their employees from accepting "material" (in some cases, any) gifts from suppliers. The motivations include:

(a) Integrity/conflict of interest. Suppose Michaels recommends that a Horizon 1-2-3 product subsequently be purchased by Mexa. This recommendation could be because he felt he owed them an obligation as his trip to the Cancun conference was fully paid by Horizon.

(b) The appearance of a conflict of interest. Even if the Horizon 1-2-3 product is the superior one at that time, other suppliers likely will have a different opinion. They may believe that the way to sell products to Mexa is via "fully-paid junkets to resorts." Those not wanting to do business this way may down-play future business activities with Mexa even though Mexa may gain much from such activities.

Some executives view the meeting as "suspect" from the start given the Caribbean location and its "rest and recreation" tone.

2. <u>Pros of attending user meeting</u>

(a) Able to learn more about the software products of Horizon.
(b) Able to interact with other possible purchasers and get their opinions.
(c) Able to influence the future product development plans of Horizon in a way that will benefit Mexa. An example is Horizon's subsequently developing software modules tailored to food product companies.
(d) Saves Mexa money. Visiting suppliers and their customers typically costs money whereas Horizon is paying for the Cancun conference.

<u>Cons of Attending</u>
(a) The ethical issues raised in requirement 1.
(b) Negative moral effects on other Mexa employees who do not get to attend the Cancun conference. These employees may reduce their trust and respect for Michaels' judgment, arguing he has been on a "supplier-paid vacation."

1-30 (cont'd)

Conditions on Attending Which Mexa Might Impose

(a)   Sizable part of time in Cancun has to be devoted to business rather than recreation.

(b)   Decision on which Mexa executive attends is <u>not</u> made by the person who attends (this reduces the appearance of a conflict of interest).

(c)   Person attending (Michaels) does not have final say on purchase decision (this reduces the appearance of a conflict of interest).

(d)   Mexa executives only go when a new major purchase is being contemplated (to avoid the conference becoming a regular "vacation").

A Conference Board publication on <u>Corporate Ethics</u> asked executives about a comparable situation:

- 76% said Mexa and Michaels face an ethical consideration in deciding whether to attend.
- 71% said Michaels should not attend as the payment of expenses is a "gift" within the meaning of a credible corporate ethics policy.

3.   <u>Pros of having a written code</u>

The Conference Board outlines the following reasons why companies adopt codes of ethics

(a)   Signals commitment of senior management to ethics.

(b)   Promotes public trust in the credibility of the company and its employees.

(c)   Signals the managerial professionalism of its employees.

(d)   Provides guidance to employees as to how difficult problems are to be handled. If adhered to, employees will avoid many actions that are unethical or appear to be unethical.

(e)   Drafting of the policy (and its redrafting in the light of ambiguities) can assist management in anticipating and preparing for ethical issues not yet encountered.

<u>Cons of having a written code</u>

(a)   Can give appearance that all issues have been covered. Issues not covered may appear to be "acceptable" even when they are not.

(b)   Can constrain the entrepreneurial activities of employees. Forces people to always "behave by the book."

(c)   Cost of developing code can be "high" if it consumes a lot of employee time.

CHAPTER 2
AN INTRODUCTION TO COST TERMS AND PURPOSES

2–2 **Cost assignment** is a general term that encompasses both (1) tracing accumulated costs to a cost object, and (2) allocating accumulated costs to a cost object.
Cost tracing is the assigning of direct costs to a chosen cost object.
Cost allocation is the assigning of indirect costs to a chosen cost object.
The relationship between these terms is as follows:

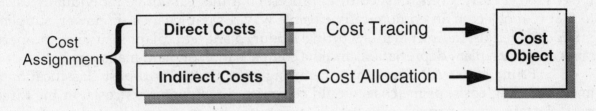

2–4 Managers believe that costs that are traced to a particular cost object are more accurately assigned to that cost object than are allocated costs. Managers prefer to use more accurate costs in their decisions.

2-6 Cost reduction efforts frequently focus on:

1.   doing only value-added activities, and
2.   efficiently managing the use of the cost drivers in those value-added activities.

2–8 **A variable cost** is a cost that changes in total in proportion to changes in the quantity of a cost driver.
A **fixed cost** is a cost that does not change in total despite changes in the quantity of a cost driver.

Suppose the cost object is a Ford motor vehicle. A dashboard is a variable cost of the motor vehicle. The annual lease of the plant in which the vehicle is assembled illustrates a fixed cost for that year.

2–10 A unit cost is computed by dividing some total cost (the numerator) by some number of units (the denominator). In many cases the numerator will include a fixed cost that will not change despite changes in the number of units to be assembled. It is erroneous in those cases to multiply the unit cost by volume changes to predict changes in total costs at different volume levels.

2–12 No. Service sector companies have no inventories and, hence, no inventoriable costs.

2–14   **Direct materials costs:** The acquisition costs of all materials that eventually become part of the cost object (say, units finished or in process) and that can be traced to that cost object in an economically feasible way. Acquisition costs of direct materials include freight-in (inward delivery) charges, sales taxes, and custom duties.

        Direct manufacturing labour costs: The compensation of all manufacturing labour that is specifically identified with the cost object (say, units finished or in process) and that can be traced to the cost object in an economically feasible way. Examples include wages and fringe benefits paid to machine operators and assembly-line workers.

        Indirect manufacturing costs: All manufacturing costs considered to be part of the cost object (say, units finished or in process) but that cannot be individually traced to that cost object in an economically feasible way. Examples include power, supplies, indirect materials, indirect manufacturing labour, plant rent, plant insurance, property taxes on plants, plant depreciation, and the compensation of plant managers.

        Prime costs: All direct manufacturing costs. In the two-part classification of manufacturing costs, prime costs would comprise direct materials costs. In the three-part classification, prime costs would comprise direct materials costs and direct manufacturing labour costs.

        Conversion costs: All manufacturing costs other than direct materials costs.

2-16   (10 min.) Total costs and unit costs.

1.   Total cost, $4,000. Unit cost per person, $4,000 ÷ 500 = $8.00

2.   Total cost, $4,000. Unit cost per person, $4,000 ÷ 2,000 = $2.00

3.   The main lesson of this problem is to alert the student early in the course to the desirability of thinking in terms of total costs rather than unit costs wherever feasible. Changes in the number of cost driver units will affect <u>total</u> variable costs but not <u>total</u> fixed costs. In our example, it would be perilous to use either the $8.00 or the $2.00 unit cost to predict the total cost because the total costs are not affected by the attendance. Instead, the student association should use the $4,000 total cost. Obviously, if the musical group agreed to work for, say $4.00 per person, such a unit variable cost could be used to predict the total cost.

2-18 (15 min.) **Computing and interpreting unit manufacturing costs.**

1.

	Supreme	Deluxe	Regular
Direct materials costs	$ 84.00	$ 54.00	$ 62.00
Direct manuf. labour costs	14.00	28.00	8.00
Indirect manuf. costs	42.00	84.00	24.00
Total manuf. costs	$140.00	$166.00	$ 94.00
Kilograms produced	80	120	100
Cost per kilogram	$1.7500	$1.3833	$0.9400

2.   The unit costs in requirement 1 includes $20 million worth of indirect manufacturing costs that are fixed irrespective of changes in the volume of output per month, while the remaining variable indirect manufacturing costs change with the production volume. Given the unit volume changes for August 2000, the use of unit costs from the past month at a different unit volume level (both in aggregate and at the individual product level) will yield incorrect estimates of total costs in August 2000.

2-20   (15 min.) **Cost drivers and the value chain.**

1.

Business Function Area	Representative Cost Driver
A. Research and Development	Number of patents filed with government agency
B. Design of Products/Processes	Hours spent designing tamper-proof bottles
C. Production	Hours Tylenol packing line in operation
D. Marketing	Minutes of television advertising time on "60 Minutes"
E. Distribution	Number of packages shipped
F. Customer Service	Number of calls to toll-free customer phone line

2.

Business Function Area	Representative Cost Driver
A. Research and Development	– Hours of laboratory work – Number of new drugs in development
B. Design of Products/Processes	– Number of focus groups on alternative package designs – Hours of process engineering work
C. Production	– Number of units packaged – Number of tablets manufactured
D. Marketing	– Number of promotion packages mailed – Number of sales personnel
E. Distribution	– Weight of packages shipped – Number of supermarkets on delivery route
F. Customer Service	– Number of units of a product recalled – Number of personnel on toll-free customer phone lines

2–22 (15-20 min.) **Variable costs and fixed costs.**

1.   Variable cost per tonne of beach sand mined:

      Subcontractor $80 per tonne
      Government tax   50 per tonne
      Total $130 per tonne

    Fixed costs per month:
      0 to 100 tonnes of capacity per day   = $150,000
      101 to 200 tonnes of capacity per day = $300,000
      201 to 300 tonnes of capacity per day = $450,000

2.

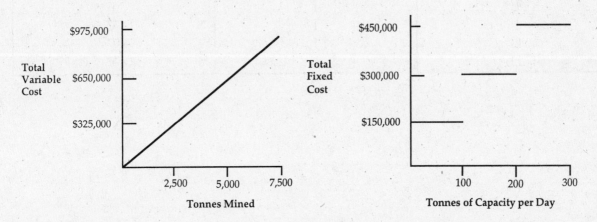

The concept of relevant range is potentially relevant for both graphs. However, the question does not place restrictions on the unit variable costs. The relevant range for the total fixed costs is from 0 to 100 tonnes; 101 to 200 tonnes; 201 to 300 tonnes, and so on. Within these ranges, the total fixed costs do not change in total.

3.

Tonnes Mined Per Day	Tonnes Mined Per Month	Fixed Unit Cost Per Tonne	Variable Unit Cost Per Tonne	Total Unit Cost Per Tonne
(1)	(2) = (1) × 25	(3) = FC ÷ (2)	(4)	(5) = (3) + (4)
(a) 180	4,500	$300,000 ÷ 4,500 = $66.67	$130	$196.67
(b) 220	5,500	$450,000 ÷ 5,500 =$81.82	$130	$211.82

The unit cost for 220 tonnes mined per day is $211.82, while for 180 tonnes it is only $196.67. This difference is caused by the fixed cost increment from 101 to 200 tonnes being spread over an increment of 80 tonnes, while the fixed cost increment from 201 to 300 tonnes is spread only over an increment of 20 tonnes.

2-24   (15-20 min.)   **Classification of costs, merchandising sector.**

Cost object: Video section of store

Cost variability: With respect to changes in the number of videos sold

 There may be some debate over classifications of individual items. Debate is more likely as regards cost variability.

Cost Item	D or I	V or F
A	D	F
B	I	V
C	D	V
D	D	F
E	I	F
F	I	V
G	I	F
H	D	V

2-26   (20-30 min.) Inventoriable costs vs. period costs.

1.   *Manufacturing-sector companies* purchase materials and components and convert them into different finished goods.

   Merchandising-sector companies purchase and then sell tangible products without changing their basic form.

   Service-sector companies provide services or intangible products to their customers—for example, legal advice or audits.

   Only manufacturing and merchandising companies have inventories of goods for sale.

2.   *Inventoriable costs* are all costs of a product that are regarded as an asset when they are incurred and then become cost of goods sold when the product is sold. These costs for a manufacturing company are included in work-in-process and finished goods inventory (they are "inventoried") to build up the costs of creating these assets.

   Period costs are all costs in the income statement other than cost of goods sold. These costs are treated as expenses of the period in which they are incurred because they are presumed not to benefit future periods (or because there is not sufficient evidence to conclude that such benefit exists). Expensing these costs immediately best matches expenses to revenues.

3.   (a) Mineral water purchased for resale by Loblaw—inventoriable cost of a merchandising company. It becomes part of cost of goods sold when the mineral water is sold.

   (b) Electricity used at a GE assembly plant—inventoriable cost of a manufacturing company. It is part of the manufacturing overhead that is included in the manufacturing cost of a refrigerator finished good.

   (c) Amortization on Excite's computer equipment—period cost of a service company. Excite has no inventory of goods for sale and, hence, no inventoriable cost.

   (d) Electricity for Loblaw's store aisles—period cost of a merchandising company. It is a cost that benefits the current period and is not traceable to goods purchased for resale.

   (e) Depreciation on GE's assembly testing equipment—inventoriable cost of a manufacturing company. It is part of the manufacturing overhead that is included in the manufacturing cost of a refrigerator finished good.

   (f) Salaries of Loblaw's marketing personnel—period cost of a merchandising company. It is a cost that is not traceable to goods purchased for resale. It is presumed not to benefit future periods (or at least not to have sufficiently reliable evidence to estimate such future benefits).

   (g) Water consumed by Excite's engineers—period cost of a service company. Excite has no inventory of goods for sale and, hence, no inventoriable cost.

   (h) Salaries of Excite's marketing personnel—period cost of a service company. Excite has no inventory of goods for sale and, hence, no inventoriable cost.

2-28 (30-40 min.) **Cost of goods manufactured.**

Canseco Company
Schedule of Cost of Goods Manufactured for the Year Ended December 31, 2000
(in thousands)

Direct materials costs:		
Beginning inventory, Jan. 1, 2000	$22,000	
Purchases of direct materials	75,000	
Cost of direct materials available for use	97,000	
Ending inventory, Dec. 31, 2000	26,000	
Direct materials used		$ 71,000
Direct manufacturing labour costs		25,000
Indirect manufacturing costs:		
Indirect manufacturing labour costs	$15,000	
Plant insurance	9,000	
Amortization—plant building and equipment	11,000	
Repairs and maintenance—plant	4,000	39,000
Manufacturing costs incurred during 2000		135,000
Add beginning work in process inventory, Jan. 1, 2000		21,000
Total manufacturing costs to account for		156,000
Deduct ending work in process inventory, Dec. 31, 2000		20,000
Cost of goods manufactured		$136,000

2.
Canseco Company
Income Statement for the Year Ended December 31, 2000
(in thousands)

Revenues		$300,000
Cost of goods sold:		
Beginning finished goods, Jan. 1, 2000	$ 18,000	
Cost of goods manufactured (Requirement 1))	136,000	
Cost of goods available for sale	154,000	
Ending finished goods, Dec. 31, 2000	23,000	131,000
Gross margin		169,000
Operating costs:		
Marketing, distribution, and customer-service	$ 93,000	
General and administrative	29,000	122,000
Operating income		$ 47,000

2-30 (15-20 min.) **Interpretation of statements.**

1.   The schedule in 2-29 can become a Schedule of Cost of Goods Manufactured and Sold simply by including the beginning and ending finished goods inventory figures in the supporting schedule, rather than directly in the body of the income statement. Note that the term <u>cost of goods manufactured</u> refers to the cost of goods brought to completion (finished) during the accounting period, whether they were started before or during the current accounting period. Some of the manufacturing costs incurred are held back as costs of the ending work in process; similarly, the costs of the beginning work in process inventory become a part of the cost of goods manufactured for 2000.

2.   The sales manager's salary would be charged as a marketing cost as incurred by both manufacturing and merchandising companies. It is basically an operating cost that appears below the gross margin line on an income statement. In contrast, an assembler's wages would be assigned to the products worked on. Thus, the wages cost would be charged to Work in Process and would not be expensed until the product is transferred through Finished Goods Inventory to Cost of Goods Sold as the product is sold.

3.   The direct-indirect distinction can be resolved only with respect to a particular cost object. For example, in defence contracting, the cost object may be defined as a contract. Then, a plant supervisor's salary may be charged directly and wholly to that single contract.

4.   Direct materials used   = $320,000,000 ÷ 1,000,000 units = $320 per unit
       Amortization   = $ 80,000,000 ÷ 1,000,000 units = $ 80 per unit

5.   Direct materials unit cost would be unchanged at $320. Amortization unit cost would be $80,000,000 ÷ 1,200,000 = $66.67 per unit. Total direct materials costs would rise by 20% to $384,000,000, whereas total amortization would be unaffected at $80,000,000.

6.   Unit costs are averages, and they must be interpreted with caution. The $320 direct materials unit cost is valid for predicting total costs because direct materials is a variable cost; total direct materials costs indeed change as output levels change. However, fixed costs like amortization must be interpreted quite differently from variable costs. A common error in cost analysis is to regard all unit costs as one—as if all the total costs to which they are related are variable costs. Changes in output levels (the denominator) will affect <u>total</u> variable costs, but not <u>total</u> fixed costs. Graphs of the two costs may clarify this point; it is safer to think in terms of total costs rather than in terms of unit costs.

2-32 (15-20 min.) **Interpretation of statements.**

1. The schedule in 2-31 can become a Schedule of Cost of Goods Manufactured and Sold simply by including the beginning and ending finished goods inventory figures in the supporting schedule, rather than directly in the body of the income statement. Note that the term cost of goods manufactured refers to the cost of goods brought to completion (finished) during the accounting period, whether they were started before or during the current accounting period. Some of the manufacturing costs incurred are held back as costs of the ending work in process; similarly, the costs of the beginning work in process inventory become a part of the cost of goods manufactured for 2000.

2. The sales manager's salary would be charged as a marketing cost as incurred by both manufacturing and merchandising companies. It is basically an operating cost that appears below the gross margin line on an income statement. In contrast, an assembler's wages would be assigned to the products worked on. Thus, the wages cost would be charged to Work in Process and would not be expensed until the product is transferred through Finished Goods Inventory to Cost of Goods Sold as the product is sold.

3. The direct-indirect distinction can be resolved only with respect to a particular cost object. For example, in defence contracting, the cost object may be defined as a contract. Then, a plant supervisor's salary may be charged directly and wholly to that single contract.

4. Direct materials used = $105,000,000 ÷ 1,000,000 units = $105 per unit
   Amortization   = $ 9,000,000 ÷ 1,000,000 units = $9 per unit

5. Direct materials unit cost would be unchanged at $105. Amortization unit cost would be $9,000,000 ÷ 1,500,000 = $6 per unit. Total direct materials costs would rise by 50% to $157,500,000 ($105 × 1,500,000). Total amortization cost of $9,000,000 would remain unchanged.

6. Unit costs are averages, and they must be interpreted with caution. The $105 direct materials unit cost is valid for predicting total costs because direct materials is a variable cost; total direct materials costs indeed change as output levels change. However, fixed costs like amortization must be interpreted quite differently from variable costs. A common error in cost analysis is to regard all unit costs as one—as if all the total costs to which they are related are variable costs. Changes in output levels (the denominator) will affect total variable costs, but not total fixed costs. Graphs of the two costs may clarify this point; it is safer to think in terms of total costs rather than in terms of unit costs.

2–34 (20-25 min.) **Finding unknown balances.**

Let G = given, I = inferred

	CASE 1	CASE 2
Step 1: Use gross margin formula		
Revenues	$ 32,000 G	$31,800 G
Cost of goods sold	A 20,700 I	20,000 G
Gross margin	$11,300 G	C $11,800 I
Step 2: Use schedule of cost of goods manufactured formula		
Direct materials used	$ 8,000 G	$ 12,000 G
Direct manufacturing labour costs	3,000 G	5,000 G
Indirect manufacturing costs	7,000 G	D 6,500 I
Manufacturing costs incurred	18,000 I	23,500 I
Add beginning work in process, 1/1	0 G	800 G
Total manufacturing costs to account for	18,000 I	24,300 I
Deduct ending work in process, 12/31	0 G	3,000 G
Cost of goods manufactured	$18,000 I	$21,300 I
Step 3: Use cost of goods sold formula		
Beginning finished goods inventory, 1/1	$ 4,000 G	4,000 G
Cost of goods manufactured	18,000 I	21,300 I
Cost of goods available for sale	22,000 I	25,300 I
Ending finished goods inventory, 12/31	B 1,300 I	5,300 G
Cost of goods sold	$20,700 I	$20,000 G

For case 1, do steps 1, 2 and 3 in order.

For case 2, do steps 1, 3 and then 2.

2–36 (30 min.) **Comprehensive problem on unit costs, product costs.**

1. If 2 kilograms of direct materials are used to make each unit of finished product, 100,000 units × 2 kg, or 200,000 kg, were used at $0.70 per kilogram of direct materials ($140,000 ÷ 200,000 kg). Therefore, the ending inventory of direct materials is

$$2,000 \text{ kg} \times \$0.70 = \$1,400$$

2.

	Manufacturing Costs for 100,000 units		
	Variable	Fixed	Total
Direct materials costs	$140,000	$ –	$140,000
Direct manufacturing labour costs	30,000	–	30,000
Plant energy costs	5,000	–	5,000
Indirect manufacturing labour costs	10,000	16,000	26,000
Other indirect manufacturing costs	8,000	24,000	32,000
Cost of goods manufactured	$193,000	$40,000	$233,000

Average unit manufacturing cost: $233,000 ÷ 100,000 units
                                      = $2.33 per unit

Finished goods inventory in units: $= \dfrac{\$20,970 \text{ (given)}}{\$2.33 \text{ per unit}}$
                                       = 9,000 units

3.   Units sold in 2000   = Beginning inventory + Production – Ending inventory
                           = 0 + 100,000 – 9,000 = 91,000 units

Selling price per unit in 2000   = $436,800 ÷ 91,000
                                   = $4.80 per unit

2–36 (cont'd)

4.

Revenues (91,000 units sold × $4.80)		$436,800
Cost of units sold:		
Beginning finished goods, Jan. 1, 2000	$ 0	
Cost of goods manufactured	233,000	
Cost of goods available for sale	233,000	
Ending finished goods, Dec. 31, 2000	20,970	212,030
Gross margin		224,770
Operating costs:		
Marketing, distribution, and customer-service costs	162,850	
Administrative costs	50,000	212,850
Operating income		$ 11,920

Note: Although not required, the full set of unit variable costs are:

Direct materials costs	$1.40	⎫
Direct manufacturing labour costs	0.30	⎪
Plant energy costs	0.05	⎬ per unit manufactured
Indirect manufacturing labour costs	0.10	⎪
Other indirect manufacturing costs	0.08	⎭
Marketing, distribution, and customer-service costs	1.35	⎬ per unit sold

2-38 (25-30 min.) **Revenue and cost recording and classifications, ethics.**

1. Concerns include:

(a) Total payments made by Canadian Outfitters do not "appear" to be adequately described. Elements of "total compensation" appear to be:
* $12 million payment to Jeans West in Caribe
* $4.8 million payment to Jeans West subsidiary in Switzerland
*   Assistance with life insurance plans for "Jeans West executives at rates much more favourable than those available in Caribe"

One possible motivation for restricting the payment in the Caribe to $12 million is to avoid showing higher profits in Caribe. A second motivation could be that the Swiss subsidiary is siphoning to Jeans West senior executives revenues that should be paid to Jeans West. This could arise if the Jeans West Swiss subsidiary is "owned" by the senior executives of Jeans West rather than being a 100% subsidiary of Jeans West.

The Conference Board in <u>Corporate Ethics Practices</u> (1992) has a discussion case where several Latin American distributors ask a U.S. company for some payments to be made to a Swiss bank account because "local taxes are confiscatory and the local exchange rates make it very difficult to achieve profitable results." A survey of over 200 executives recommended:

*   Deny the request because what is unethical in one country cannot be ethical in another   90%

*   Accede to the request because it does not violate the local distributors' standard business practices   10%

Those in the 10% included comments such as "we must play by the local rules," "it is arrogant to suggest home ethics are superior to local ethics," and "I'm not sure we can force our view of right and wrong on the whole world." Canadian Outfitters could have faced an ultimatum from Jeans West that part of the payment be sent to Switzerland and have been told "that everybody does it in Caribe."

The assistance with the insurance plans is in the grey area. If Jeans West is willing to accept a lower price in return for C.O. assisting with the insurance plans, it may be a judicious economic decision by C.O. C.O. is not hurt economically in this scenario. The concern is whether C.O. is assisting the senior executives in diverting "de facto payments" to themselves.

(b) Product design costs of C.O. include $4.8 million for "own product design." It is stated that the Director of Product Design views it "as an 'off-statement' item that historically he has no responsibility for nor any say about" and that "to his knowledge, Jeans West uses only C.O. designs with either zero or minimal changes." It may be that the $4.8 million payment is a hidden payment made to avoid Caribe taxation. However, the result is incorrect classification of product design costs at C.O.

2–38 (cont'd)

(c)   Jeans West receives from C.O. the margin between $16.8 million ($12 million + $4.8 million) and the $3.0 million payment for denim—i.e., $13.8 million. Note that C.O. can assist Jeans West to meet the 25% ratio of "domestic labour costs to total costs." Charging $6.00 million for denim and receiving $19.8 million for jeans will result in the same $13.8 million margin, but will mean Jeans West will not meet the 25% test as total costs will now be $13 million instead of $10 million. C.O. has to ensure it takes an arm's length approach to supply contracts and purchase contracts or else it may be accused by the Caribe government of assisting Jeans West to avoid local taxes.

Note: Some students will ask whether Jeans West should be able to classify employee fringe benefits as domestic labour costs. This is not Roberts' domain since she is Controller of C.O. Her concern with the Caribe tax rebate is whether C.O. is being "pressured" to adjust its billing amounts to facilitate Jeans West having a ratio of "domestic labour costs to total costs" exceeding 25%. If you want to discuss this issue, point out that labour fringe benefits are typically an integral part of labour costs. Hence, if they can be traced, Jeans West is justified by including them in domestic labour costs.

2.   There are a variety of ethical issues relating primarily to competence and integrity that Roberts faces:

(a)   Is C.O. assisting Jeans West to avoid income taxes in Caribe either
   • by funnelling $4.8 million to a Swiss company rather than to Jeans West in Caribe, or
   • by understating both the $3.0 million denim supply cost and the $16.8 total revenue amount?

(b)   Is C.O. assisting senior executives of Jeans West to enrich themselves at the expense of the shareholders of Jeans West?

(c)   Are the accounting records of C.O. properly reflecting the underlying activities?

3.   Steps Roberts could take include:

(a)   Seeking further information on why the $4.8 million payment is being made to the Swiss subsidiary. This should be done first internally and then by speaking to Jeans West executives.

(b)   Ensure product design costs at C.O. reflect actual product design work. So-called "off-statement" items should be eliminated if no adequate explanation can be given for them.

(c)   Ensure C.O. personnel follow any company guidelines about supplier relations or customer relations. There is nothing inherently wrong with assisting Jeans West to negotiate a better insurance package for its executives. The concern is whether developing a "too cozy" relationship will lead to more questionable practices being overlooked.

CHAPTER 3
COST-VOLUME-PROFIT RELATIONSHIPS

3–2   The assumptions underlying the CVP analysis outlined in Chapter 3 are:

1. Changes in the level of revenues and costs arise only because of changes in the number of product (or service) units produced or sold.
2. Total costs can be divided into a fixed component and a component that is variable with respect to the level of output.
3. The behaviour of total revenues and total costs is linear (straight-line) in relation to output units within the relevant range.
4. The unit selling price, unit variable costs, and fixed costs are known.
5. The analysis either covers a single product or assumes that a given revenue mix of products will remain constant as the level of total units sold changes.
6. All revenues and costs can be added and compared without taking into account the time value of money.

3–4   **Contribution margin** is computed as revenues minus all costs that vary with respect to the output level.

Gross margin is computed as revenues minus cost of goods sold.

Contribution-margin percentage is the total contribution margin divided by revenues.

Variable-cost percentage is the total variable costs (with respect to units of output) divided by revenues.

Margin of safety is the excess of budgeted revenues over breakeven revenues.

3-6   Breakeven analysis denotes the study of the breakeven point, which is often only an incidental part of the relationship between cost, volume, and profit. Cost-volume-profit analysis is a more comprehensive term than breakeven analysis.

3-8   An increase in the income tax rate does not affect the breakeven point. Operating income at the breakeven point is zero and thus no income taxes will be paid at this point.

3–10   Examples include:

Manufacturing—substituting a robotic machine for hourly wage workers.

Marketing—changing a sales force compensation plan from a percentage of sales dollars to a fixed salary.

Customer service—hiring a subcontractor to do customer repair visits on an annual retainer basis rather than a per visit basis.

3-12   Operating leverage describes the effects that fixed costs have on changes in operating income as changes occur in units sold and hence in contribution margin. Knowing the degree of operating leverage at a given level of sales helps managers calculate the effect of fluctuations in sales on operating incomes.

3-14 A company with multiple products can compute a breakeven point by assuming there is a constant mix of products at different levels of total revenue.

3–16 (10 min.) **CVP analysis computations.**

	Revenues	Variable Costs	Fixed Costs	Total Costs	Operating Income	Contribution Margin	Contribution Margin %
a.	$2,000	$ 500	$300	$ 800	$1,200	$1,500	75.0%
b.	2,000	1,500	300	1,800	200	500	25.0%
c.	1,000	700	300	1,000	0	300	30.0%
d.	1,500	900	300	1,200	300	600	40.0%

3-18 (15-20 min.) **CVP analysis, changing revenues and costs.**

1.
USP = 8% × $1,000 = $80
UVC = $35 ($17 + $18)
UCM = $45
FC   = $22,000 a month

(a) $Q = \dfrac{FC}{UCM} = \dfrac{\$22,000}{\$45}$
     = 489 tickets (rounded up)

(b) $Q = \dfrac{FC + TOI}{UCM} = \dfrac{\$22,000 + \$10,000}{\$45}$
     $= \dfrac{\$32,000}{\$45}$
     = 712 tickets (rounded up)

2.
USP = $80
UVC = $29 ($17 + $12)
UCM = $51
FC   = $22,000 a month

(a) $Q = \dfrac{FC}{UCM} = \dfrac{\$22,000}{\$51}$
     = 432 tickets (rounded up)

(b) $Q = \dfrac{FC + TOI}{UCM} = \dfrac{\$22,000 + \$10,000}{\$51}$
     $= \dfrac{\$32,000}{\$51}$
     = 628 tickets (rounded up)

3-20 (20 min.) CVP exercises.

	Revenues	Variable Costs	Contribution Margin	Fixed Costs	Budgeted Operating Income
Orig.	$10,000,000ᴳ	$8,200,000ᴳ	$1,800,000	$1,700,000ᴳ	$100,000
1.	10,000,000	8,020,000	1,980,000	1,700,000	280,000
2.	10,000,000	8,380,000	1,620,000	1,700,000	(80,000)
3.	10,000,000	8,200,000	1,800,000	1,785,000	15,000
4.	10,000,000	8,200,000	1,800,000	1,615,000	185,000
5.	10,800,000	8,856,000	1,944,000	1,700,000	244,000
6.	9,200,000	7,544,000	1,656,000	1,700,000	(44,000)
7.	11,000,000	9,020,000	1,980,000	1,870,000	110,000
8.	10,000,000	7,790,000	2,210,000	1,785,000	425,000

ᴳ stands for given.

3-22 (10-15 min.) CVP, income taxes.

1. Operating income = Net income ÷ (1 − tax rate)
   = $84,000 ÷ (1 − 0.40) = $140,000

2. Contribution margin − Fixed costs = Operating income
   Contribution margin − $300,000 = $140,000
   Contribution margin = $440,000

3. Revenues − 0.80 Revenues = Contribution margin
   0.20 Revenues = $440,000
   Revenues = $2,200,000

4. Breakeven point = Fixed costs ÷ Contribution margin percentage
   Breakeven point = $300,000 ÷ 0.20
   = $1,500,000

3–24 (10 min.) **CVP, margin of safety.**

1.
$$\text{Breakeven point} = \frac{\text{Fixed costs}}{\text{Contribution margin percentage}}$$

$$\text{Contribution margin percentage} = \frac{\$400,000}{\$1,000,000} = 0.40$$

2.
$$\text{Contribution margin percentage} = \frac{\text{Selling price} - \text{Variable cost per unit}}{\text{Selling price}}$$

$$0.40 = \frac{\text{USP} - \$12}{\text{USP}}$$

$$0.40\ \text{USP} = \text{USP} - \$12$$

$$0.60\ \text{USP} = \$12$$

$$\text{USP} = \$20$$

3.

Revenues, 80,000 units × $20	$1,600,000
Breakeven revenues	1,000,000
Margin of safety	$ 600,000

3-26 (30 min.) **CVP, sensitivity analysis**

1. USP = $30.00 × (1 − 0.30 margin to bookstore)
        = $30.00 × 0.70 = $21.00

    UVC = $ 4.00   variable production and marketing cost
          $\underline{\quad 3.15\quad}$ variable author royalty cost (0.15 × $30.00 × 0.70)
          $\underline{\$\ 7.15}$

    UCM = $21.00 − $7.15 = $13.85

    FC = $ 500,000   fixed production and marketing cost
         $\underline{3,000,000}$ up-front payment to Washington
         $\underline{\$3,500,000}$

Exhibit 3-26A shows the PV graph.

Exhibit 3-26A
PV Graph for Media Publishers

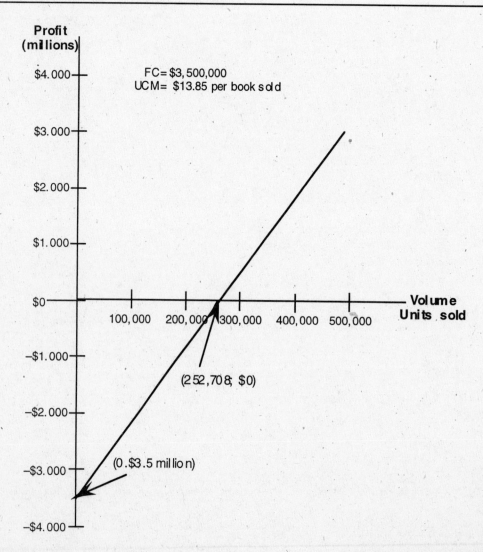

3-26 (cont'd)

2. (a) $\dfrac{\text{Breakeven}}{\text{number of units}} = \dfrac{FC}{UCM}$

$= \dfrac{\$3,500,000}{\$13.85}$

$= 252{,}708$ copies sold (rounded)

(b) Target OI $= \dfrac{FC + OI}{UCM}$

$= \dfrac{\$3,500,000 + \$2,000,000}{\$13.85}$

$= \dfrac{\$5,500,000}{\$13.85}$

$= 397{,}112$ copies sold (rounded)

3. (a) Decreasing the normal bookstore margin to 20% of the listed bookstore price of \$30 has the following effects:

USP $= \$30.00 \times (1 - 0.20)$
$= \$30.00 \times 0.80 = \$24.00$

UVC $= \$\,4.00$ variable production and marketing cost
$\underline{+\ 3.60}$ variable author royalty cost $(0.15 \times \$30.00 \times 0.80)$
$\$\,7.60$

UCM $=$ $\$24.00 - \$7.60 = \$16.40$

$\dfrac{\text{Breakeven}}{\text{number of units}} = \dfrac{FC}{UCM}$

$= \dfrac{\$3,500,000}{\$16.40}$

$= 213{,}415$ copies sold (rounded)

The breakeven point decreases from 252,708 copies in requirement 2 to 213,415 copies.

(b) Increasing the listed bookstore price to \$40 while keeping the bookstore margin at 30% has the following effects:

USP $= \$40.00 \times (1 - 0.30)$
$= \$40.00 \times 0.70 = \$28.00$

UVC $= \$\,4.00$ variable production and marketing cost
$\underline{+\ 4.20}$ variable author royalty cost $(0.15 \times \$40.00 \times 0.70)$
$\$\,8.20$

UCM $= \$28.00 - \$8.20 = \$19.80$

3-26 (cont'd)

$$\text{Breakeven number of units} = \frac{\$3,500,000}{\$19.80}$$

$$= 176,768 \text{ copies sold (rounded)}$$

The breakeven point decreases from 252,708 copies in requirement 2 to 176,768 copies.

3-28 (30 min.) **Revenue mix, new and upgrade customers.**

	New Customers	Upgrade Customers
USP	$210	$120
UVC	90	40
UCM	120	80

Let S = Number of upgrade customers

$1.5S$ = Number of new customers

Revenues – Variable costs – Fixed costs = Operating income

$[\$210\,(1.5S) + \$120S] - [\$90\,(1.5S) + \$40S] - \$14,000,000 = OI$

$\$435S - \$175S - \$14,000,000 = OI$

Breakeven point is 134,616 units when OI = 0

$\$260S$	=	$\$14,000,000$
S	=	53,846 (rounded)
$1.5S$	=	<u>80,770</u>
		<u>134,616</u>

Check

Revenues ($210 × 80,770; $120 × 53,846)	$23,423,220
Variable costs ($90 × 80,770; $40 × 53,846)	<u>9,423,140</u>
Contribution margin	14,000,080
Fixed costs	<u>14,000,000</u>
Operating income	$\cong \$\qquad 0$

2. When 200,000 units are sold, mix is:

New customers	120,000
Upgrade customers	80,000

Revenues ($210 × 120,000; $120 × 80,000)	$34,800,000
Variable costs ($90 × 120,000; $40 × 80,000)	<u>14,000,000</u>
Contribution margin	20,800,000
Fixed costs	<u>14,000,000</u>
Operating income	<u>$ 6,800,000</u>

3-28 (cont'd)

3.   (a) $[\$210S + \$120S] - [\$90S + \$40S] - \$14,000,000 = OI$

$$330S - 130S = \$14,000,000$$
$$200S = \$14,000,000$$
$$S = 70,000$$
$$S = \underline{70,000}$$
$$\underline{140,000} \text{ units}$$

Check

Revenues ($210 × 70,000; $120 × 70,000)	$23,100,000
Variable costs ($90 × 70,000; $40 × 70,000)	9,100,000
Contribution margin	14,000,000
Fixed costs	14,000,000
Operating income	$ 0

(b) $[\$210(9S) + \$120S] - [\$90(9S) + \$40S] - \$14,000,000 = OI$

$$2,010S - 850S = \$14,000,000$$
$$1,160S = \$14,000,000$$
$$S = 12,069 \text{ (rounded)}$$
$$9S = \underline{108,621}$$
$$\underline{120,690} \text{ units}$$

Check

Revenues ($210 × 108,621; $120 × 12,069)	$24,258,690
Variable costs ($90 × 108,621; $40 × 12,069)	10,258,650
Contribution margin	14,000,040
Fixed costs	14,000,000
Operating income	$\cong \$$ 0

As Zapo increases its percentage of new customers, which have a higher contribution margin than upgrade customers, the number of units required to breakeven decreases:

	New Customers	Upgrade Customers	Breakeven Point
Requirement 3(a)	50%	50%	140,000
Requirement 1	60%	40%	134,616
Requirement 3(b)	90%	10%	120,690

3-30 (20 min.) **Gross margin and contribution margin.**

1. Cost of Goods Sold $1,600,000
    Fixed Manufacturing Costs   500,000
    Variable Manufacturing Costs $1,100,000

    Variable manufacturing costs per unit = $1,100,000 ÷ 200,000 = $5.50 per unit

2. Total marketing and distribution costs $1,150,000
    Variable marketing and distribution (200,000 × $5)   1,000,000
    Fixed marketing and distribution costs $ 150,000

3. Selling price   = $2,600,000 ÷ 200,000 units = $13 per unit

$$\frac{\text{Contribution margin}}{\text{per unit}} = \frac{\text{Selling}}{\text{price}} - \frac{\text{Variable}}{\substack{\text{manufacturing} \\ \text{costs per unit}}} - \frac{\text{Variable marketing}}{\substack{\text{and distribution} \\ \text{costs per unit}}}$$

$$= \$13 - \$5.50 - \$5.00 = \$2.50$$

$$\text{Operating income} = \left(\frac{\text{Contribution margin}}{\text{per unit}} \times \frac{\text{Sales}}{\text{quantity}}\right) - \frac{\text{Fixed manufacturing}}{\text{costs}} - \frac{\text{Fixed marketing}}{\substack{\text{and distribution} \\ \text{costs}}}$$

$$= (\$2.50 \times 230,000) - \$500,000 - \$150,000$$

$$= -\$75,000$$

Foreman has confused gross margin with contribution margin. He has interpreted gross margin as if it were all variable, and interpreted marketing and distribution costs as all fixed. In fact, the manufacturing costs, subtracted from sales to calculate gross margin, and marketing and distribution costs contain both fixed and variable components.

4. Breakeven point in units $$= \frac{\text{Fixed manufacturing, marketing and distribution costs}}{\text{Contribution margin per unit}}$$

$$= \frac{\$650,000}{\$2.50} = 260,000 \text{ units}$$

Breakeven point in revenues = 260,000 × $13 = $3,380,000.

3-32 (15-20 min.)   **Appendix, uncertainty, CVP.**

1.   King pays Foreman $2 million plus $4 (25% of $16) for every home purchasing the pay-per-view. The expected value of the variable component is:

Demand (1)	Payment (2) = (1) × $4	Probability (3)	Expected payment (4) = (2) × (3)
100,000	$ 400,000	0.05	$ 20,000
200,000	800,000	0.10	80,000
300,000	1,200,000	0.30	360,000
400,000	1,600,000	0.35	560,000
500,000	2,000,000	0.15	300,000
1,000,000	4,000,000	0.05	200,000
			$1,520,000

The expected value of King's payment is $3,520,000 ($2,000,000 fixed fee + $1,520,000).

2.   USP = $16
       UVC = $ 6 ($4 payment to Foreman + $2 variable cost)
       UCM = $10
       FC   = $2,000,000 + $1,000,000 = $3,000,000

$$Q = \frac{FC}{UCM}$$
$$= \frac{\$3,000,000}{\$10}$$
$$= 300,000$$

If 300,000 homes purchase the pay-per-view, King will break even.

3–34 (10 min.) **CVP, movie production.**

1. Fixed costs = $5,000,000 (production cost)
    Unit variable cost = $0.20 per $1 revenue (marketing fee)
    Unit contribution margin = $0.80 per $1 revenue

    (a) Breakeven point in revenues = $\dfrac{\text{Fixed costs}}{\text{Unit contribution margin per \$1 revenue}}$

    $$= \dfrac{\$5,000,000}{\$0.80}$$

    $$= \$6,250,000$$

    (b) Royal Rumble receives 62.5% of box-office receipts. Box-office receipts of $10,000,000 translate to $6,250,000 in revenues to Royal Rumble.

2.
Revenues, 0.625 × $300,000,000	$187,500,000
Variable costs, 0.20 × $187,500,000	37,500,000
Contribution margin	150,000,000
Fixed costs	5,000,000
Operating income	$145,000,000

3–36 (20-30 min.) **CVP, shoe stores.**

1. In number of pairs:

$$\frac{\text{Fixed costs}}{\text{Contribution margin per pair}} = \frac{\$360,000}{\$9.00} = 40,000 \text{ pairs}$$

In revenues:

$$\frac{\text{Fixed costs}}{\text{Contribution margin \% per dollar}} = \frac{\$360,000}{100\% - 70\%} = \$1,200,000$$

2.

Revenues, $30 × 35,000	$1,050,000
Variable costs, $21 × 35,000	735,000
Contribution margin	315,000
Fixed costs	360,000
Operating income (loss)	$ (45,000)

An alternative approach is that 35,000 units is 5,000 units below the breakeven point and the unit contribution margin is $9.00:

$9.00 × 5,000 = $45,000 below the breakeven point

3. Fixed costs: $360,000 + $81,000 = $441,000
    Contribution margin per pair = $10.50

    (a) Breakeven point in units $= \dfrac{\$441,000}{\$10.50} = 42,000$ pairs

    (b) Breakeven point in revenues = $30 × 42,000 = $1,260,000

4. Fixed costs = $360,000
    Contribution margin per pair = $8.70

    (a) Breakeven point in units $= \dfrac{\$360,000}{\$8.70} = 41,380$ pairs (rounded up)

    (b) Breakeven point in revenues = $30 × 41,380 = $1,241,400

3–36 (cont'd)

5. Breakeven point = 40,000 pairs
    Store manager receives commission on 10,000 pairs.
    Cost of commission = $0.30 × 10,000 = $3,000

Revenues, $30 × 50,000		$1,500,000
Variable costs:		
Cost of shoes	$975,000	
Sales commission	75,000	
Manager commission	3,000	1,053,000
Contribution margin		447,000
Fixed costs		360,000
Operating income		$ 87,000

An alternative approach is 10,000 units × $8.70 = $87,000.

3–38 (10-20 min.) **Sensitivity and inflation (continuation of 3-37).**

1.
Revenues, $30 × 48,000	$1,440,000	
$18 × 2,000	36,000	$1,476,000
Variable costs:		
Goods sold $19.50 × 50,000	975,000	
Commission, 5% × $1,476,000	73,800	1,048,800
Contribution margin		427,200
Fixed costs		360,000
Operating income		$ 67,200

An alternative approach is:

Contribution margin on 48,000 pairs × $9.00	$432,000
Deduct negative contribution margin on unsold pairs,	
2,000 × [$18.00 − ($19.50 + $.90* commission)]	4,800
Contribution margin	427,200
Fixed costs	360,000
Operating income	$ 67,200

*5% of $18.00 = $.90

2. Optimal operating income, given perfect knowledge, would be the $432,000 contribution computed above, minus $360,000 fixed costs, or $72,000.

3–38 (cont'd)

3.   The point of indifference is where the operating incomes are equal. Let X = unit cost per pair that would produce the identical operating income of $67,200. Then:

$$
\begin{aligned}
48{,}000[\$30.00 - (X + \$1.50)] - \$360{,}000 &= \$67{,}200 \\
48{,}000(\$28.50 - X) - \$360{,}000 &= \$67{,}200 \\
\$1{,}368{,}000 - 48{,}000X - \$360{,}000 &= \$67{,}200 \\
48{,}000X &= \$940{,}800 \\
X &= \$19.60
\end{aligned}
$$

Therefore, any rise in purchase cost in excess of $19.60 per pair increases the operating income benefit of signing the long-term contract.

In a short-cut solution you could take the $4,800 difference between the "ideal" operating income (of $72,000) at the current cost per pair and the operating income under the contract (of $67,200) and divide it by 48,000 units to get 10 cents per pair difference.

3-40 (30 min.) Choosing between compensation plans, operating leverage.

1.   Variable cost of goods sold as a percentage of revenues $= \dfrac{\$11{,}700{,}000}{\$26{,}000{,}000} = 45\%$

Let breakeven revenues be denoted by $R, then

$$
\$R = \dfrac{\text{Variable manuf.}}{\text{costs}} + \dfrac{\text{Fixed manuf.}}{\text{costs}} + \dfrac{\text{Variable marketing}}{\text{costs}} + \dfrac{\text{Fixed marketing}}{\text{costs}}
$$

$R = \$0.45R + \$2,870,000 + \$0.18R + \$3,420,000$

$$
\begin{aligned}
\$R - \$0.45R - \$0.18R &= \$2{,}870{,}000 + \$3{,}420{,}000 = \$6{,}290{,}000 \\
\$0.37R &= \$6{,}290{,}000 \\
R &= \$6{,}290{,}000 \div 0.37 = \$17{,}000{,}000
\end{aligned}
$$

2.   With its own sales force, Marston's fixed marketing costs would increase to $3,420,000 + $2,080,000 = $5,500,000.
Variable cost of marketing = 10% of Revenues

Let breakeven revenues be denoted by $R, then

$R = \$0.45R + \$2,870,000 + \$0.10R + \$5,500,000$

$$
\begin{aligned}
\$R - \$0.45R - \$0.10R &= \$2{,}870{,}000 + \$5{,}500{,}000 = \$8{,}370{,}000 \\
0.45R &= \$8{,}370{,}000 \\
R &= \$8{,}370{,}000 \div 0.45 = \$18{,}600{,}000
\end{aligned}
$$

3–40 (cont'd)

3.

	Using Sales Agents	Employing Own Sales Staff
Revenues	$26,000,000	$26,000,000
Variable manufacturing costs		
$26,000,000 × 0.45; 0.45	11,700,000	11,700,000
Variable marketing costs		
$26,000,000 × 0.18; 0.10	4,680,000	2,600,000
Contribution margin	9,620,000	11,700,000
Fixed costs		
Fixed manufacturing costs	2,870,000	2,870,000
Fixed marketing costs	3,420,000	5,500,000
Total fixed costs	6,290,000	8,370,000
Operating income	$ 3,330,000	$ 3,330,000

$$\text{Degree of operating leverage} = \frac{\text{Contribution margin}}{\text{Operating income}} \quad \frac{\$9,620,000}{\$3,330,000} = 2.89 \quad \frac{\$11,700,000}{\$3,330,000} = 3.51$$

The calculations indicate that at sales of $26,000,000, a percentage change in sales and contribution margin will result in 2.89 times that percentage change in operating income if Marston continues to use sales agents and 3.51 times that percentage change in operating income if Marston employs its own sales staff. The higher contribution margin per dollar of sales and higher fixed costs gives Marston more operating leverage, that is greater benefits (increases in operating income) if revenues increase but greater risks (decreases in operating income) if revenues decrease.

4. Variable costs of marketing   = 15% of Revenues
    Fixed marketing costs   = $5,500,000

Denote the revenues required to earn $3,330,000 of operating income by $R, then

$$\text{Operating income} = \text{Revenues} - \frac{\text{Variable}}{\text{manuf. costs}} - \frac{\text{Fixed}}{\text{manuf. costs}} - \frac{\text{Variable}}{\text{marketing costs}} - \frac{\text{Fixed}}{\text{marketing costs}}$$

$$\$3,330,000 = \$R - \$0.45R - \$2,870,000 - \$0.15R - \$5,500,000$$

$$\$3,330,000 + \$2,870,000 + \$5,500,000 = \$R - \$0.45R - \$0.15R$$
$$\$11,700,000 = \$0.40R$$
$$R = \$11,700,000 \div 0.40 = \$29,250,000$$

3-42 (30 min.) **Multi-product breakeven, decision making.**

1. Breakeven point in 2000 (units) $= \dfrac{\text{Fixed Costs}}{\text{Unit Contribution Margin}} = \dfrac{\$495,000}{\$50 - \$20} = 16,500$ units

   Breakeven point in 2000 (in revenues) $= 16,500$ units $\times \$50 = \$825,000$ in sales revenues

2. Breakeven point in 2001 (in units)

   Evenkeel expects to sell 3 units of Evenflo for every 2 units of Ridex in 2001, so consider a bundle consisting of 3 units of Evenflo and 2 units of Ridex.

   Unit Contribution Margin from Evenflo $= \$50 - \$20 = \$30$

   Unit Contribution Margin from Ridex $= \$25 - \$15 = \$10$

   The contribution margin for the bundle is

   ($\$30 \times 3$ units of Evenflo) + ($\$10 \times 2$ units of Ridex) = $\$110$

   So bundles to be sold to breakeven $= \dfrac{495,000}{\$110} = 4,500$ bundles

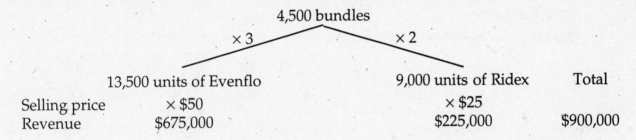

	13,500 units of Evenflo	9,000 units of Ridex	Total
Selling price	$\times \$50$	$\times \$25$	
Revenue	$\$675,000$	$\$225,000$	$\$900,000$

3. Contribution margin percentage in 2000 $= \dfrac{\text{Unit contribution margin in 2000}}{\text{Unit selling price in 2000}}$

   $= \dfrac{\$30}{\$50} = 60\%$

   Contribution margin percentage in 2001 $= \dfrac{\text{Unit contribution margin on bundle in 2001}}{\text{Selling price of bundle in 2001}}$

   $= \dfrac{\$110}{(3 \times \$50) + (2 \times \$25)} = \dfrac{\$110}{\$200} = 55\%$

The breakeven point in 2001 increases because fixed costs are the same in both years but the contribution margin generated by each dollar of sales revenue at the given product mix decreases in 2001 relative to 2000.

4.   Despite the breakeven sales revenue being higher, I would advise Andy Minton to *accept* Glaston's offer. The breakeven points per se are irrelevant because I do not expect Evenkeel *to operate in the region of the breakeven dollars.* By accepting Glaston's offer, Andy has the ability to sell all the 30,000 units of Evenflo he expects to sell in 2001 and make more sales of Ridex to Glaston *without incurring any more fixed costs.*

Profits in 2001 with and without Ridex are expected to be as follows:

	2001 without Ridex	2001 with Ridex
Sales	$1,500,000[1]	$2,000,000[2]
Variable costs	600,000[3]	900,000[4]
Contribution margin	900,000	1,100,000
Fixed costs	495,000	495,000
Operating profit	$ 405,000	$ 605,000

[1] $50 × 30,000 units

[2] $50 × 30,000 units + $25 × 20,000 units

[3] $20 × 30,000 units

[4] $20 × 30,000 units + $15 × 20,000 units

3-44 (25 min.) **CVP analysis, decision making.**

1.

Unit selling price	$105
Variable manufacturing costs per unit	45
Variable marketing and distribution costs per unit	10
Contribution margin per unit	$ 50

Fixed manufacturing costs	$ 800,000
Fixed marketing and distribution costs	600,000
Total fixed costs	$1,400,000

$$\text{Breakeven point in units} = \frac{\text{Total fixed costs}}{\text{Contribution margin per unit}} = \frac{\$1,400,000}{\$50} = 28,000 \text{ units}$$

Breakeven point in revenues = 28,000 units × $105 per unit = $2,940,000

2.   Tocchet's current operating income is as follows:

Revenues, $105 × 40,000	$4,200,000
Variable costs, $55 × 40,000	2,200,000
Contribution margin	2,000,000
Fixed costs	1,400,000
Operating income	$ 600,000

Let the fixed marketing and distribution costs be $F. We calculate $F when operating income = $600,000 and the selling price is $99.

$$
\begin{aligned}
(\$99 \times 50,000) - (\$55 \times 50,000) - \$F &= \$600,000 \\
\$4,950,000 - \$2,750,000 - \$F &= \$600,000 \\
\$F &= \$4,950,000 - \$2,750,000 - \$600,000 = \$1,600,000
\end{aligned}
$$

Hence the maximum increase in fixed marketing and distribution costs for which Tocchet will prefer to reduce the selling price is $200,000 ($1,600,000 – $1,400,000).

3.   Let the selling price be $P.

We calculate $P for which, after increasing fixed manufacturing costs by $100,000 to $900,000 and variable manufacturing cost per unit by $2 to $47, operating income = $600,000

$$
\begin{aligned}
\$40,000\,P - (\$47 \times 40,000) - (\$10 \times 40,000) - \$900,000 - \$600,000 &= \$600,000 \\
\$40,000\,P - \$1,880,000 - \$400,000 - \$900,000 - \$600,000 &= \$600,000 \\
\$40,000\,P &= \$600,000 + \$1,880,000 + \$400,000 + \$900,000 + \$600,000 \\
\$40,000\,P &= \$4,380,000 \\
P &= \$4,380,000 \div 40,000 = \$109.50
\end{aligned}
$$

Tocchet will consider adding the new features provided the selling price is at least $109.50 per unit.

3-46 (15-25 min.) **Nonprofit institution.**

1. Let Q = Number of patients

$$\text{Revenues} - \text{Variable costs} - \text{Fixed costs} = 0$$
$$\$400,000 - \$400Q - \$150,000 = 0$$
$$\$400Q = \$400,000 - \$150,000$$
$$Q = \$250,000 \div \$400$$
$$Q = 625 \text{ patients}$$

2. $$\text{Revenues} - \text{Variable costs} - \text{Fixed costs} = 0$$
$$\$360,000 - \$400Q - \$150,000 = 0$$
$$\$400Q = \$360,000 - \$150,000$$
$$Q = \$210,000 \div \$400$$
$$Q = 525 \text{ patients}$$

The reduction in service is more than the 10% reduction in the budget. Without restructuring operations, the quantity of service units must be reduced 16% (from 625 to 525 patients) to stay within the budget.

3. Let Y = Drug prescriptions per patient

$$\$360,000 - 625Y - \$150,000 = 0$$
$$625Y = \$210,000$$
$$Y = \$336$$

Percentage drop: $(\$400 - \$336) \div \$400 = 16\%$

Regarding requirements 2 and 3, note that the decrease in service can be measured by a formula:

$$\% \text{ reduction in service} = \frac{\% \text{ budget change}}{\% \text{ variable cost}}$$

The variable cost percentage is $(\$400 \times 625) \div \$400,000 = 62.5\%$

$$\% \text{ reduction in service} = \frac{10\%}{62.5\%} = 16\%$$

This is a challenging question that covers both Chapters 2 and 3. One or both cases can be used as an examination question.

(All answers are in thousands of $)

Income Statement	Case 1		Case 2	
Revenues	$100		$100	
Cost of goods sold:				
Beginning finished goods, 1/1	0		5	
Cost of goods manufactured	75	(G)	80	(U)
Cost of goods available for sale	75		85	
Ending finished goods, 12/31	0		5	
Cost of goods sold	75		80	
Gross margin	25		20	
Operating costs*				
Variable	13	(K)**	15	(T)
Fixed	2	(J)	10	
Operating costs	15		25	
Operating income (loss)	$ 10	(L)	$ (5)	

*   Operating costs include marketing, distribution, customer service, and administrative costs.
** Total variable costs of:
$70,000 - (G - I) \text{ or}$
$70,000 - (\$75,000 - \$18,000) = \$13,000$

(All answers are in thousands of $)

Cost of Goods Manufactured	Case 1		Case 2	
Direct materials costs:				
Beginning inventory, 1/1	$12		$20	
Purchases of direct materials	15		50	
Direct materials available for use	27		70	
Ending inventory, 12/31	5		30	(W)
Direct materials used	22	(H)	40	
Direct manufacturing labour costs	30		15	
Manufacturing overhead costs:				
Variable costs	5		5	(X)
Fixed costs	18	(I)	20	
Manufacturing overhead costs	23		25	

3–48 (cont'd)

	Case 1	Case 2
Total manufacturing costs incurred during year	75	80
Add beginning work in process, 1/1	0	9
Total manufacturing costs to account for	75	89
Deduct ending work in process, 12/31	0	9
Cost of goods manufactured	$75 (G)	$80 (U)

Breakeven Computations

	Case 1	Case 2
Total costs	$ 90	$105 **
Fixed manufacturing overhead	18	20
Fixed marketing, distribution, customer service, and administrative costs	2 (J)*	10
Total fixed costs	20	30
Total variable costs	70	75
Total revenue	100	100 **
Total contribution margin	30	25 (V)***
Contribution margin percentage	30%	25%
Breakeven point in dollars	$ 67 *	$120 (Y)

*The $67,000 figure is rounded in the tabulation; it should be $66,667.

$$\$66,667 \times .30 = \$20,000 \text{ total fixed costs}$$
$$\$20,000 - \$18,000 = \$ 2,000$$

**If the loss is $5,000, total costs are $100,000 + $5,000 = $105,000
***100 – 75 = 25

3-50 (15 min.) **Appendix, CVP under uncertainty.**

1. Both products have the same unit contribution margin:

Unit contribution margin $=$ Selling price per unit $-$ Variable costs per unit
$= \$10 - \$8 = \$2$

$$\text{Breakeven point} = \frac{\text{Fixed costs}}{\text{Unit contribution margin}}$$

$$= \frac{\$400,000}{\$2}$$

$= 200,000$ units for each product

2. The expected demand for the two umbrellas is:

Event	Emerald Green		Shocking Pink	
(1) Demand	(2) Probability	(1) × (2) Units	(3) Probability	(1) × (3) Units
50,000	0.0	-	0.1	5,000
100,000	0.1	10,000	0.1	10,000
200,000	0.2	40,000	0.1	20,000
300,000	0.4	120,000	0.2	60,000
400,000	0.2	80,000	0.4	160,000
500,000	0.1	50,000	0.1	50,000
	1.0		1.0	
Expected demand		300,000 units		305,000 units

Expected operating income of Emerald Green umbrellas:
$\$2(300,000) - \$400,000 = \$200,000$
Expected operating income of Shocking Pink umbrellas:
$\$2(305,000) - \$400,000 = \$210,000$

The shocking pink umbrellas should be chosen because they have the higher expected operating income.

3. The expected operating income from the two products would be identical. If the choice criterion is to maximize expected operating income, the company will be indifferent between emerald green and shocking pink umbrellas. However, assume that management considers risk factors. Emerald green umbrellas, for example, have a 10% chance of selling only 100,000 units, which would result in a net operating loss of $200,000. Also, there is a 30% chance that sales of emerald green will exceed 300,000 units. If this event happens, the operating income of emerald green umbrellas will be higher than the operating income of shocking pink umbrellas

The expected values are important, but the dispersion of the probability distribution is also important. Normally, the wider the dispersion, the greater the risk. Knowledge of the entire probability distribution helps management assess the risk before reaching a decision.

3-52 (30 min.) **Ethics, CVP analysis.**

1. Contribution margin percentage $= \dfrac{\text{Revenues} - \text{Variable costs}}{\text{Revenues}}$

$$= \dfrac{\$5,000,000 - \$3,000,000}{\$5,000,000}$$

$$= \dfrac{\$2,000,000}{\$5,000,000} = 40\%$$

Breakeven revenues $= \dfrac{\text{Fixed costs}}{\text{Contribution margin percentage}}$

$$= \dfrac{\$2,160,000}{0.40} = \$5,400,000$$

2. If variable costs are 52% of revenues, contribution margin percentage equals 48% (100% − 52%).

Breakeven revenues $= \dfrac{\text{Fixed costs}}{\text{Contribution margin percentage}}$

$$= \dfrac{\$2,160,000}{0.48} = \$4,500,000$$

3.
Revenues	$5,000,000
Variable costs (0.52 × $5,000,000)	2,600,000
Fixed costs	2,160,000
Operating income	$ 240,000

4.   Incorrect reporting of environmental costs with the goal of continuing operations is unethical. The management accountant could consider the following issues:

Competence
Clear reports using relevant and reliable information should be prepared. Preparing reports on the basis of incorrect environmental costs in order to make the company's performance look better than it is violates competence standards. It is unethical for Bush not to report environmental costs in order to make the plant's performance look good.

Integrity
The management accountant has a responsibility to avoid actual or apparent conflicts of interest and advise all appropriate parties of any potential conflict. Bush may be tempted to report lower environmental costs to please Lemond and Woodall and save the jobs of his colleagues. This action, however, violates the responsibility for integrity.

3-52 (cont'd)

Objectivity
The management accountant should require that information should be fairly and objectively communicated and that all relevant information should be disclosed. From a management accountant's standpoint, underreporting environmental costs to make performance look good would violate the standard of objectivity.

Bush should indicate to Lemond that estimates of environmental costs and liabilities should be included in the analysis. If Lemond still insists on modifying the numbers and reporting lower environmental costs, Bush should raise the matter with one of Lemond's superiors. If after taking all these steps, there is continued pressure to understate environmental costs, Bush should consider resigning from the company and not engage in unethical behaviour.

CHAPTER 4
JOB COSTING

4-2 In a *job-costing system* costs are assigned to a distinct unit, batch, or lot of a product or service. In a *process-costing system*, the cost of a product or service is obtained by using broad averages to assign costs to masses of similar units.

4-4 The seven steps in job costing are (1) identify the chosen cost object or job, (2) identify the direct costs of the job, (3) select the cost-allocation base(s) to use for allocating indirect costs to the job, (4) identify the indirect costs associated with each cost-allocation base, (5) compute the rate per unit of each cost-allocation base used to allocate indirect costs to the job, (6) compute the indirect costs allocated to the job, and (7) compute the total cost of the job by adding all direct and indirect costs assigned to it.

4-6 Three major source documents used in job-costing systems are (1) job cost record or job cost sheet, a document that records and accumulates all costs assigned to a specific job, (2) materials requisition record, a document used to charge job cost records and departments for the cost of direct materials used on a specific job, and (3) labour-time record, a document used to charge job cost records and departments for labour time used on a specific job.

4-8 Two reasons for using six-month or annual budget periods are:
  a. The numerator reason—the longer the time period, the less the influence of seasonal patterns, and
  b. The denominator reason—the longer the time period, the less the effect of variations in output levels on the allocation of fixed costs.

4-10 An accounting firm can use job cost information (a) to determine the profitability of individual jobs, (b) to assist in bidding on future jobs, and (c) to evaluate professionals who are in charge of managing individual jobs.

4-12 Debit entries to Work-in-Process Control represent increases in work in process. Examples of debit entries are: (a) direct materials used (credit to Materials Control), (b) direct manufacturing labour billed to job (credit to Wages Payable Control), and (c) manufacturing overhead allocated to job (credit to Manufacturing Overhead Allocated).

4-14 A service company might use budgeted costs rather than actual costs to compute direct labour rates because it may be difficult to trace some costs to jobs as they are completed.

4-16   (20 min.) **Actual costing, normal costing, manufacturing overhead.**

1.
$$\text{Budgeted manufacturing overhead rate} = \frac{\text{Budgeted manufacturing overhead costs}}{\text{Budgeted direct manufacturing labour costs}}$$

$$= \frac{\$1,750,000}{\$1,000,000} = 1.75 \text{ or } 175\%$$

$$\text{Actual manufacturing overhead rate} = \frac{\text{Actual manufacturing overhead costs}}{\text{Actual direct manufacturing labour costs}}$$

$$= \frac{\$1,862,000}{\$980,000} = 1.9 \text{ or } 190\%$$

2.   Costs of Job 626 under actual and normal costing follow:

	Normal Costing	Actual Costing
Direct materials	$ 40,000	$ 40,000
Direct manufacturing labour costs	30,000	30,000
Manufacturing overhead costs		
$30,000 × 1.75; $30,000 × 1.90	52,500	57,000
Total manufacturing costs of Job 626	$122,500	$127,000

3.
$$\text{Total manufacturing overhead allocated under normal costing} = \text{Actual manufacturing labour costs} \times \text{Budgeted overhead rate}$$

$$= \$980,000 \times 1.75$$
$$= \$1,715,000$$

$$\text{Underallocated manufacturing overhead} = \text{Actual manufacturing overhead costs} - \text{Manufacturing overhead allocated}$$

$$= \$1,862,000 - \$1,715,000 = \$147,000$$

There is no under- or overallocated overhead under actual costing because overhead is allocated under actual costing by multiplying actual manufacturing labour costs and the actual manufacturing overhead rate. This, of course, equals the actual manufacturing overhead costs. All actual overhead costs are allocated to products. Hence, there is no under- or overallocated overhead.

4.   Actual costing reflects the actual results incurred, while normal costing reflects expectations of the amount the overhead should be. Normal costing can be done in advance and thus can be used in pricing and planning decisions.

4-18 (20-30 min.) **Job costing, accounting for manufacturing overhead, budgeted rates.**

1.   An overview of the product costing system is:

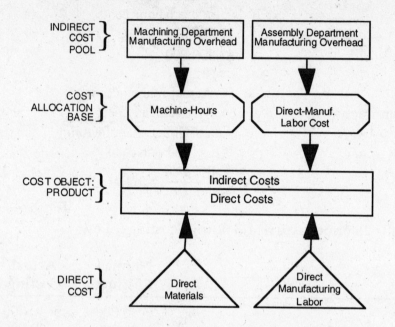

Budgeted manufacturing overhead divided by allocation base:

Machining overhead: $\dfrac{\$1,800,000}{50,000}$ = $36 per machine-hour

Assembly overhead: $\dfrac{\$3,600,000}{\$2,000,000}$ = 180% of direct manuf. labour costs

2.   Machining overhead, 2,000 hours × $36 $72,000
Assembly overhead, 180% of $15,000   27,000
Total manufacturing overhead allocated to Job 494 $99,000

3.

	Machining	Assembly
Actual manufacturing overhead	$2,100,000	$ 3,700,000
Manufacturing overhead allocated,		
55,000 × $36	1,980,000	
180% of $2,200,000		3,960,000
Underallocated (Overallocated)	$ 120,000	$ (260,000)

4-20 (20-30 min.) **Computing indirect-cost rates, job costing.**

1.

a.

	Budgeted Fixed Indirect Costs	Budgeted Hours	Budgeted Fixed Indirect Cost Rate Per Hour	Budgeted Variable Indirect Cost Rate Per Hour	Budgeted Total Indirect Cost Rate Per Hour
Jan.-March	$50,000	20,000	$ 2.50	$10	$12.50
April-June	50,000	10,000	5.00	10	15.00
July-Sept.	50,000	4,000	12.50	10	22.50
Oct.-Dec.	50,000	6,000	8.33	10	18.33
b.	$200,000	40,000	$ 5.00	$10	$15.00

2a.   All four jobs use 10 hours of professional labour time. The only difference in job costing is the indirect cost rate. The quarterly-based indirect job cost rates are:

Hansen: $(10 \times \$12.50)$ = $125.00
Kai: $(6 \times \$12.50) + (4 \times \$15.00)$ = $135.00
Patera: $(4 \times \$15.00) + (6 \times \$22.50)$ = $195.00
Stevens: $(5 \times \$12.50) + (2 \times \$22.50) + (3 \times \$18.33)$ = $162.50

	Hansen	Kai	Patera	Stevens
Revenues, $65 × 10	$650	$650	$650	$650.00
Direct costs, $30 × 10	300	300	300	300.00
Indirect costs	125	135	195	162.50
Total costs	425	435	495	462.50
Operating income	$225	$215	$155	$187.50

b.   Using annual-based indirect job cost rates, all four customers will have the same operating income:

Revenues, $65 × 10 $650
Direct costs, $30 × 10   300
Indirect costs, $15 × 10   150
Total costs   450
Operating income $200

3.   All four jobs use 10 hours of professional labour time. Using the quarterly-based indirect cost rates, there are four different operating incomes as the work done on them is completed in different quarters. In contrast, using the annual indirect cost rate all four customers have the same operating income. All these different operating income figures for jobs with the same number of professional labour-hours are due to the allocation of fixed indirect costs.

4-20 (cont'd)

An overview of the Tax Assist job costing system is:

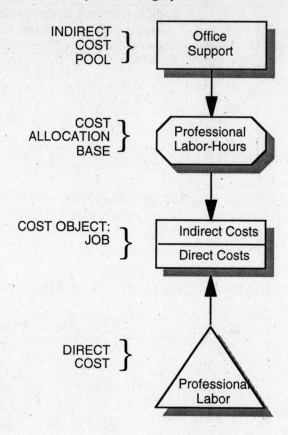

4-22 (20 min.) **Job costing, journal entries, and source documents. (Continuation of 4-21)**

The analysis of source documents and subsidiary ledgers follows:

1. a. Approved invoice
   b. dr. Materials record, "received" column

2. a. Materials requisition record
   b. dr. Job cost records
   cr. Materials record, "issued" column

3. a. Materials requisition record
   b. dr. Department overhead cost records, appropriate column
   cr. Materials record, "issued" column

4. a. Summary of time records or daily time analysis. This summary is sometimes called a *labour cost distribution summary*.
   b. dr. Job cost records
   dr. Department overhead cost records, appropriate columns for various classes of indirect labour

5. a. Special authorization from the responsible accounting officer
   b. dr. Department overhead cost records, appropriate columns

6. a. Various approved invoices and special authorizations
   b. dr. Department overhead cost records, appropriate columns

7. a. Use of an authorized budgeted manufacturing overhead rate
   b. dr. Job cost record

8. a. Completed job cost records
   b. dr. Finished goods records
   cr. Job cost record

9. a. Approved sales invoice
   b. dr. Customers' accounts (or Cash)
   cr. Sales ledger, if any

10. a. Costed sales invoice
    b. cr. Finished goods records

11. a. Special authorization from the responsible accounting officer
    b. Subsidiary records are generally not used for these entries

4-24 (10–15 min.) **Accounting for manufacturing overhead.**

1. Budgeted manufacturing overhead rate $= \dfrac{\$7,000,000}{200,000}$

   $= \$35$ per machine-hour

2. Work-in-Process Control   6,825,000

        Manufacturing Overhead Allocated   6,825,000

   (195,000 machine-hours × \$35 = \$6,825,000)

3. \$6,825,000 – \$6,800,000 = \$25,000 overallocated, an insignificant amount.

   Manufacturing Overhead Allocated   6,825,000

        Manufacturing Overhead Control   6,800,000

        Cost of Goods Sold   25,000

4-26 (20–30 min.) **Job costing; actual, normal, and variation of normal costing.**

1. Actual direct cost rate for professional labour = \$58 per professional labour-hour

$$\text{Actual indirect cost rate} = \frac{\$744,000}{15,500 \text{ hours}} = \$48 \text{ per professional labour-hour}$$

$$\text{Budgeted direct cost rate for professional labour} = \frac{\$960,000}{16,000 \text{ hours}} = \$60 \text{ per professional labour-hour}$$

$$\text{Budgted indirect cost rate} = \frac{\$720,000}{16,000 \text{ hours}} = \$45 \text{ per professional labour-hour}$$

	(a) Actual Costing	(b) Normal Costing	(c) Variation of Normal Costing
Direct-Cost Rate	\$58 (Actual rate)	\$58 (Actual rate)	\$60 (Budgeted rate)
Indirect-Cost Rate	\$48 (Actual rate)	\$45 (Budgeted rate)	\$45 (Budgeted rate)

2.

	(a) Actual Costing	(b) Normal Costing	(c) Variation of Normal Costing
Direct Costs	\$58 × 120 = \$ 6,960	\$58 × 120 = \$ 6,960	\$60 × 120 = \$ 7,200
Indirect Costs	48 × 120 = 5,760	45 × 120 = 5,400	45 × 120 = 5,400
Total Job Costs	\$12,720	\$12,360	\$12,600

All three costing systems use the actual professional labour time of 120 hours. The budgeted 110 hours for the Montreal Expos audit job is not used in job costing. However, Chirac may have used the 110-hour number in bidding for the audit.

The actual costing figure of \$12,720 exceeds the normal costing figure of \$12,360, because the actual indirect-cost rate (\$48) exceeds the budgeted indirect-cost rate (\$45). The normal costing figure of \$12,360 is less than the variation of normal costing (based on budgeted rates for direct costs) figure of \$12,600, because the actual direct-cost rate (\$58) is less than the budgeted direct-cost rate (\$60).

Although not required, the following overview diagram summarizes Chirac's job-costing system.

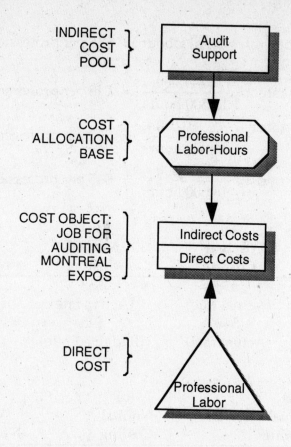

4-28 (20–30 min) **Job costing; accounting for manufacturing overhead, budgeted rates.**

1. An overview of the job-costing system is:

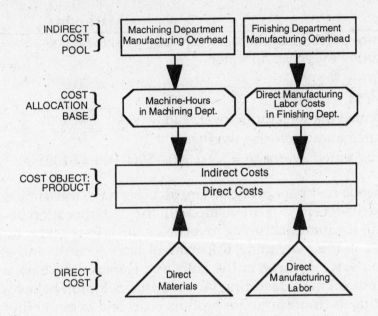

2. Budgeted manufacturing overhead divided by allocation base:
    a.   Machining Department:

$$\frac{\$10,000,000}{200,000} = \$50 \text{ per machine-hour}$$

    b.   Finishing Department:

$$\frac{\$8,000,000}{\$4,000,000} = 200\% \text{ of direct manufacturing labour costs}$$

3. Machining overhead, $50 × 130 hours $6,500
    Finishing overhead, 200% of $1,250   2,500
    Total manufacturing overhead allocated $9,000

4. Total costs of Job 431:
    Direct costs:

Direct materials —Machining Department	$14,000	
—Finishing Department	3,000	
Direct manufacturing labour —Machining Department	600	
—Finishing Department	1,250	$18,850

    Indirect costs:

Machining overhead, $50 × 130	$6,500	
Finishing overhead, 200% of $1,250	2,500	9,000
Total costs		$27,850

The per-unit product cost of Job 431 is $27,850 ÷ 200 units = $139.25 per unit

4-28 (cont'd)

5.   The point of this part is (a) to get the definitions straight and (b) to underscore that overhead is allocated by multiplying the actual amount of the allocation base by the budgeted rate.

	Machining	Finishing
Manufacturing overhead incurred (actual)	$11,200,000	$7,900,000
Manufacturing overhead allocated		
220,000 hrs. × $50	11,000,000	
200% of $4,100,000		8,200,000
Underallocated manufacturing overhead	$ 200,000	
Overallocated manufacturing overhead		$ 300,000
Total overallocated overhead = $300,000 – $200,000 = $100,000		

6.   A homogeneous cost pool is one where all costs have the same or a similar cause-and-effect or benefits-received relationship with the cost-allocation base. Solomon likely assumes that all its manufacturing overhead cost items are not homogeneous. Specifically, those in the Machining Department have a cause-and-effect relationship with machine-hours, while those in the Finishing Department have a cause-and-effect relationship with direct manufacturing labour costs. Solomon believes that the benefits of using two cost pools (more accurate product costs and better ability to manage costs) exceed the costs of implementing a more complex system.

4-30 (25-30 min.) **Job costing with two direct- and two indirect-cost categories, law firm. (Continuation of 4-29)**

Although not required, the following overview diagram is helpful in understanding Keating's job-costing system.

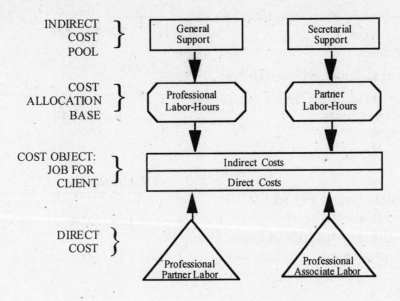

1.

	Professional Partner Labour	Professional Associate Labour
Budgeted compensation per professional	$200,000	$80,000
Budgeted hours of billable time per professional	1,600	1,600
Budgeted direct-cost rate	$125 per hour*	$50 per hour†

*Can also be calculated as $\dfrac{\text{Total budgeted partner labour costs}}{\text{Total budgeted partner labour-hours}} = \dfrac{\$200,000 \times 5}{1,600 \times 5} = \dfrac{\$1,000,000}{8,000} = \$125$

†Can also be calculated as $\dfrac{\text{Total budgeted associate labour costs}}{\text{Total budgeted associate labour-hours}} = \dfrac{\$80,000 \times 20}{1,600 \times 20} = \dfrac{\$1,600,000}{32,000} = \$50$

2.

	General Support	Secretarial Support
Budgeted total costs	$1,800,000	$400,000
Budgeted quantity of allocation base	40,000 hours	8,000 hours
Budgeted indirect cost rate	$45 per hour	$50 per hour

4-30 (cont'd)

3.

	Richardson		Punch	
Direct costs:				
Professional partners, $125 × 60; 30	$7,500		$3,750	
Professional associates, $50 × 40; 120	2,000		6,000	
Direct costs		$ 9,500		$ 9,750
Indirect costs:				
General support, $45 × 100; 150	4,500		6,750	
Secretarial support, $50 × 60; 30	3,000		1,500	
Indirect costs		7,500		8,250
Total costs		$17,000		$18,000

4.

	Richardson	Punch
Single direct - Single indirect (from Prob. 4-29)	$12,000	$18,000
Multiple direct - Multiple indirect (from requirement 3 of Prob. 4-30)	17,000	18,000
Difference	$5,000 undercosted	No change

The Richardson and Punch jobs differ in their use of resources. The Richardson job has a mix of 60% partners and 40% associates, while Punch has a mix of 20% partners and 80% associates. Thus, the Richardson job is a relatively high user of the more costly partner-related resources (both direct partner costs and indirect partner secretarial support). The refined-costing system in Problem 4-30 increases the reported cost in Problem 4-29 for the Richardson job by 41.7% (from $12,000 to $17,000).

4-32 (40–55 min.) Overview of general ledger relationships.

1. & 3. An effective approach to this problem is to draw T-accounts and insert all the known figures. Then, working with T-account relationships, solve for the unknown figures (here coded by the letter X for beginning inventory figures and Y for ending inventory figures).

Materials Control

X	15,000	(1)	70,000
Purchases	85,000		
	100,000		70,000
Y	30,000		

Work-in-Process Control

X		10,000	(4)	305,000
(1) DM	70,000			
(2) DL	150,000			
(3) Overhead	90,000	310,000		
		320,000		305,000
(a)		5,000		
(c)		3,000		
Y		23,000		

Finished Goods Control

X	20,000	(5)	300,000
(4)	305,000		
	325,000		300,000
Y	25,000		

Cost of Goods Sold

(5)	300,000	(d)	6,000

Manufacturing Department Overhead Control

	85,000	(d)	87,000
(a)	1,000		
(b)	1,000		

Manufacturing Overhead Allocated

(d)	93,000	(3)	90,000
		(c)	3,000

4-32 (cont'd)

Manufacturing overhead cost rate = $90,000 \div $150,000 = 60\%$

Wages Payable Control		
	(a)	6,000

Various Accounts		
	(b)	1,000

2. Adjusting and closing entries:

(a) Work-in-Process Control 5,000
     Manufacturing Department Overhead Control 1,000
          Wages Payable Control 6,000
     To recognize payroll costs

(b) Manufacturing Department Overhead Control 1,000
          Various accounts 1,000
     To recognize miscellaneous manufacturing overhead

(c) Work-in-Process Control 3,000
          Manufacturing Overhead Allocated 3,000
     To allocate manufacturing overhead

Note: Students tend to forget entry (c) entirely. Stress that a budgeted overhead allocation rate is used consistently throughout the year. This point is a major feature of this problem.

(d) Manufacturing Overhead Allocated 93,000
          Manufacturing Department Overhead Control 87,000
          Cost of Goods Sold 6,000
     To close manufacturing overhead accounts and over-allocated overhead to cost of goods sold

4-32 (cont'd)

An overview of the product-costing system is:

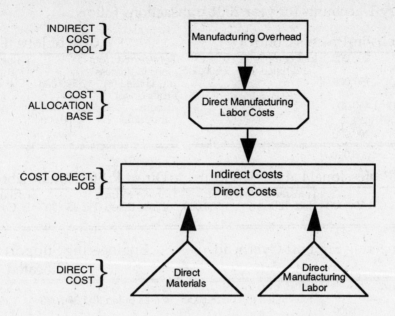

3. See the answer to 1.

4-34 (30 min.) **General ledger relationships, under- and overallocation, service industry.**

1. Summary T-accounts for year 2001 transactions follow.

Jobs-in-Process Control

1-1-2000	200,000	Jobs completed	
Actual direct		and billed (6)	2,500,000
costs (1)	150,000		
Prof. labour			
allocated (4)	1,450,000*		
Supp.overhead			
allocated (5)	1,200,000†		
12-31-2001	500,000		

Cost of Jobs Billed

Transferred from		Engineering	
Jobs in Process		support costs	
and billed (6)	2,500,000	overalloc. (8)	20,000
Professional			
labour			
underalloc. (7)	50,000		

Direct Professional Labour Control

Actual prof.		Transfer to Cost of	
labour costs (2)	1,500,000	Jobs Billed (7)	1,500,000

Direct Professional Labour Allocated

Transfer to Cost		Allocated to WIP	
of Jobs Billed (7)	1,450,000	Control (4)	1,450,000*

Engineering Support Overhead Control

Actual support		Transfer to Cost of	
overhead		Jobs Billed (8)	1,180,000
costs (3)	1,180,000		

Engineering Support Overhead Allocated

Transfer to Cost		Allocated to WIP	
of Jobs Billed (8)	1,200,000	Control (5)	1,200,000†

Cash Control

Direct cash costs (1)	150,000	
Prof. labour costs (2)	1,500,000	
Support overhead		
costs (3)	1,180,000	

*$50 per hour × 29,000 hours = $1,450,000

†80% × professional labour costs = 80% × $1,500,000 = $1,200,000

2. Operating income for 2001 is as follows:

Revenues	$2,800,000
Cost of jobs billed	
($2,500,000 + $50,000 – $20,000)	2,530,000
Operating income	$ 270,000

4-36 (30 min.) **Allocation and proration of manufacturing overhead.**

1. Although not required, an overview of the product costing system follows:

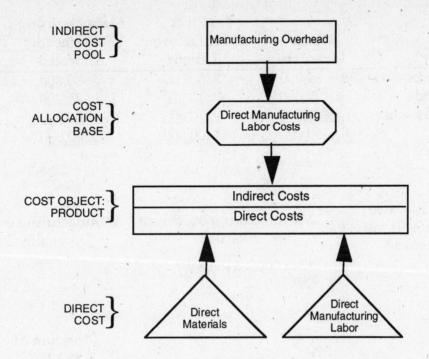

$$\text{Budgeted manufacturing overhead cost rate} = \frac{\text{Budgeted manufacturing overhead costs}}{\text{Direct manufacturing labour costs}}$$

$$= \frac{\$252,000}{\$420,000} = \$0.60 \text{ per direct manufacturing labour dollar}$$

The Work-in-Process inventory breakdown at the end of 2001 for Jobs 1768B and 1819C is:

	Job 1768B	Job 1819C	Total
Direct materials (given)	$22,000	$ 42,000	$ 64,000
Direct manufacturing labour (given)	11,000	39,000	50,000
Manufacturing overhead allocated,			
60% × DML dollars	6,600	23,400	30,000
Total manufacturing costs	$39,600	$104,400	$144,000

The finished goods inventory at the end of 2001 is $156,000 (given). A direct manufacturing labour cost of $40,000 implies a budgeted manufacturing overhead costs component of $24,000.

The COGS is $1,600,000 (given). The total direct manufacturing labour of $400,000 implies direct manufacturing labour in COGS of $310,000 ($400,000 − $11,000 − $39,000 − $40,000). Hence, manufacturing overhead allocated in COGS is 60% × $310,000 = $186,000. Direct materials in COGS is $1,104,000 ($1,600,000 − $310,000 − $186,000).

4-36 (cont'd)

The summary account information is:

	Direct Materials	Direct Manufacturing Labour	Manufacturing Overhead Allocated	Total
Work in process	$ 64,000	$ 50,000	$ 30,000	$ 144,000
Finished goods	92,000	40,000	24,000	156,000
Cost of goods sold	1,104,000	310,000	186,000	1,600,000
Total	$1,260,000	$400,000	$240,000	$1,900,000

2.

$$\text{Overallocated manufacturing overhead} = \text{Manufacturing overhead allocated} - \text{Manufacturing overhead incurred}$$

$$= \$240,000 - \$186,840$$
$$= \$53,160$$

3a.

Account	End-of-Year Balance (before Proration) (1)			Proration of $53,160 Overallocated Manuf. Overhead (2)	End-of-Year Balance (after Proration) (3)=(1)+(2)
Work in process	$ 144,000	(144/1,900 =	7.58%)	$(4,030)	$ 139,970
Finished goods	156,000	(156/1,900 =	8.21%)	(4,364)	151,636
Cost of goods sold	1,600,000	(1,600/1,900 =	84.21%)	(44,766)	1,555,234
Total	$1,900,000		100.00%	$(53,160)	$1,846,840

b.

Account	End-of-Year Balance (before Proration)	Allocated Overhead in End-of-Year Balance (before Proration)		Proration of $53,160 Overallocated Manufacturing Overhead	End-of-Year Balance (after Proration)
Work in process	$ 144,000	$ 30,000	(12.5%)	$(6,645)	$ 137,355
Finished goods	156,000	24,000	(10.0%)	(5,316)	150,684
Cost of goods sold	1,600,000	186,000	(77.5%)	(41,199)	1,558,801
Total	$1,900,000	$240,000	100.0%	$(53,160)	$1,846,840

4-36 (cont'd)

4. The COGS amount when the overallocated overhead is immediately written off to COGS is $1,546,840 (see below) compared with $1,555,234 in 3(a) and $1,558,801 in 3(b). Thus, with a lower COGS, there is a higher operating income.

Account	End-of-Year Balance (before Proration)	Proration of $53,160 Overallocated	End-of-Year Balance (after Proration)
Work in process	$ 144,000	$ 0	$ 144,000
Finished goods	156,000	0	156,000
Cost of goods sold	1,600,000	(53,160)	1,546,840
Total	$1,900,000	$(53,160)	$1,846,840

4-38 (25 min.) Job costing, accounting for overhead costs, budgeted rates.

1. $$\text{Budgeted overhead rate} = \frac{\text{Budgeted overhead costs}}{\text{Budgeted direct labour costs}} = \frac{\$1,200,000}{\$1,500,000} = 80\%$$

Jefferson allocates overhead costs at 80% of direct labor costs or $0.80 per direct labour dollar.

2.

$$\begin{array}{l}\text{Overhead} \\ \text{allocated to Job 101} \\ \text{as of } 1/31/2001\end{array} = 0.80 \times \begin{array}{l}\text{Actual direct labour} \\ \text{costs of Job 101}\end{array} = 0.80 \times \$50,000 = \$40,000$$

$$\begin{array}{l}\text{Overhead} \\ \text{allocated to Job 104} \\ \text{as of } 2/28/2001\end{array} = 0.80 \times \begin{array}{l}\text{Actual direct labour} \\ \text{costs of Job 104}\end{array} = 0.80 \times \$40,000 = \$32,000$$

3. $$\begin{array}{l}\text{Overhead allocated to} \\ \text{jobs in February}\end{array} = 0.80 \times \text{Actual direct labour costs in February}$$

$$= 0.80 \times \$120,000 = \$96,000$$

Actual overhead costs incurred in February = $102,000
Underallocated overhead costs = $102,000 − $96,000 = $6,000

4. To calculate Cost of Jobs Billed for February 2001 of $400,000 we make entries to the Jobs-in-Process Control, Cost of Jobs Billed, Overhead Costs Control, and Overhead Costs Allocated T-accounts.

4-38 (cont'd)

Jobs-in-Process Control

1-31-2001	$120,000*	Costs of jobs completed and billed (2)	394,000
Direct materials	150,000		
Direct labour	120,000		
Overhead costs allocated (1)	96,000		
2-28-2001	92,000†		

Cost of Jobs Billed

Cost of jobs completed and billed	(2) 394,000	
Underallocated overhead costs	(3) 6,000	

Overhead Costs Control

Overhead costs for February	102,000	Transfer to Cost of Jobs Billed (3)	102,000

Overhead Costs Allocated

Transfer to Cost of Jobs Billed (3) 96,000		Overhead costs allocated in February (1)	96,000

*Cost of Job A21 = Direct materials + Direct labour + Overhead allocated
  = $30,000 + $50,000 + $40,000 = $120,000
†Cost of Job A24 = Direct materials + Direct labour + Overhead allocated
  = $20,000 + $40,000 + $32,000 = $92,000

Cost of jobs completed and billed from Jobs-in-Process Control account can be calculated by plugging for the missing number in Jobs-in-Process Control account, $120,000 + $150,000 + $120,000 + $96,000 − $92,000 = $394,000

Cost of Jobs Billed is also increased by the underallocated overhead costs of $6,000.

Hence, Cost of Jobs Billed for February 2001 = $394,000 + $6,000 = $400,000.

CHAPTER 5
ACTIVITY-BASED COSTING AND ACTIVITY-BASED MANAGEMENT

5-2 Overcosting may result in competitors entering a market and taking market share for products that a company erroneously believes are low-margin or even unprofitable.

Undercosting may result in companies selling products on which they are in fact losing money, when they erroneously believe them to be profitable.

5-4 An activity-based approach focuses on activities as the fundamental cost objects. It uses the cost of these activities as the basis for assigning costs to other cost objects such as products, services, or customers.

5-6 The purpose for computing a product cost is to determine whether unit costs should be based on total manufacturing costs in all or only some levels of the cost hierarchy. Inventory valuation for financial reporting requires *total* or only some manufacturing costs (all levels of the hierarchy) to be expressed on a per output-unit basis. In contrast, for cost management purposes, the cost hierarchy need not be unitized, as units of output is not the cost driver at each level in the hierarchy.

5-8 Four decisions for which ABC information is useful are:
(1) pricing and product mix decisions,
(2) cost reduction and process improvement decisions,
(3) design decisions, and
(4) planning and managing activities

5-10 "Tell-tale" signs that indicate when ABC systems are likely to provide the most benefits are:
1. Significant amounts of indirect costs are allocated using only one or two cost pools.
2. All or most indirect costs are identified as output-unit-level costs (i.e., few indirect costs are described as batch-level, product-sustaining, or facility-sustaining costs).
3. Products make diverse demands on resources because of differences in volume, process steps, batch size, or complexity.
4. Products that a company is well suited to make and sell show small profits, whereas products that a company is less suited to produce and sell show large profits.
5. Complex products appear to be very profitable, and simple products appear to be losing money.
6. Operations staff have significant disagreements with the accounting staff about the costs of manufacturing and marketing products and services.

5-12 No, ABC systems apply equally well to service companies such as banks, railroads, hospitals, and accounting firms, and to merchandising companies such as retailers and distributors.

5-14 Increasing the number of indirect-cost pools does NOT guarantee increased accuracy of product, service, or customer costs. If the existing cost pool is already homogeneous, increasing the number of cost pools will not increase accuracy. If the existing cost pool is not homogeneous, accuracy will increase only if the increased cost pools themselves increase in homogeneity vis-a-vis the single cost pool.

5-16 (30 min.) **Cost smoothing or peanut butter costing, cross-subsidization.**

1. Cost smoothing or peanut butter costing is a costing approach that uniformly assigns the cost of resources to customers when the individual customers use those resources in a nonuniform way. The reunion dinner averages the costs across all five people. These five people differ sizably in what they consume.

2.

Diner	Entree	Dessert	Drinks	Total
Armstrong	$27	$8	$24	$59
Gonzales	24	3	0	27
King	21	6	13	40
Poffo	31	6	12	49
Young	15	4	6	25
Average	$23.60	$5.40	$11.00	$40.00

The average-cost pricing will result in each person paying $40.

	Amount Over- or Undercosted
Accurately costed person	
• King, $40 – $40	$ 0
Undercosted people	
• Armstrong, $40 – $59	$(19)
• Poffo, $40 – $49	$(9)
Overcosted people	
• Gonzales, $40 – $27	$ 13
• Young, $40 – $25	$ 15

Yes, Young's complaint is justified. He is "overcharged" $15. He could point out likely negative behaviours with this approach to costing. These include:

a. It can lead some people to order the most expensive items because others will "subsidize" their extravagance.

b. It can lead to friction when those who dine economically are forced to subsidize those who dine extravagantly. At the limit, some people may decide not to attend the reunion dinners.

Likely benefits of this approach are:

a. it is simple, and

b. it (purportedly) promotes a group atmosphere at the dinner.

5-16 (cont'd)

3.   Each one of the costs in the data is directly traceable to an individual diner. This makes it straightforward to compute the individual cost per diner. Examples where this is not possible include:

- A plate of hors d'oeuvres is shared by two or more diners
- A loaf of garlic bread is shared by two or more diners
- A bottle of mineral water or wine is shared by two or more diners

Each of these items cannot be directly traced to only one diner.

Some possible behaviours if each person pays for his or her own bill are:

   a.   Some people may reduce their ordering of more expensive items because they will not be subsidized by other diners.

   b.   May encourage some potential diners to attend who otherwise would have stayed away.

   c.   May encourage a person "trying to impress others with his or her success" to order the most expensive items.

5-18 (25 min.) **Cost hierarchy, ABC, distribution.**

1. Total distribution costs (given), $2,130,000

$$\text{Distribution cost per case under existing system} = \frac{\text{Total distribution costs}}{\text{Total cases of specialty and regular wine shipped}} = \frac{\$2,130,000}{200,000} = \$10.65 \text{ per case}$$

	Regular		Specialty	
	Total (1)	Per Case (2) = (1) ÷ 120,000	Total (3)	Per Case (4) = (3) ÷ 80,000
Distribution costs				
$10.65 × 120,000; $10.65 × 80,000	$1,278,000	$10.65	$852,000	$10.65

2a. Promotional activity—distributor-level costs because these costs do not depend on the number of cases shipped or the number of batches in which the cases are shipped. An amount of $8,000 is incurred for each of Sonoma's distributors.

Order-handling costs—batch-level costs because these costs are incurred each time a customer places an order regardless of the number of cases ordered. These costs total $300 per order.

Freight distribution costs—Unit-level costs because a cost of $8 is incurred on freight for each case shipped.

2b.

	Regular		Specialty	
	Total (1)	Per Case (2) = (1) ÷ 120,000	Total (3)	Per Case (4) = (3) ÷ 80,000
Distribution costs of freight				
$8 × 120,000 cases	$ 960,000	$8.00		
$8 × 80,000 cases			$ 640,000	$8.00
Ordering costs				
$300 × 10 orders/year × 10 distr.	30,000	0.25		
$300 × 20 orders/year × 30 distr.			180,000	2.25
Promotion costs				
$8,000 × 10 distributors	80,000	0.67		
$8,000 × 30 distributors			240,000	3.00
Total costs	$1,070,000	$8.92	$1,060,000	$13.25

5-18 (cont'd)

3.   The existing costing system uses cases shipped, a unit-level cost driver, as the only cost allocation base for distribution costs. As a result, the distribution cost per case is the same for specialty and regular wines ($10.65). In fact, specialty wines use distribution resources more intensively than regular wines: (a) Sonoma spends $8,000 on promotional activity at each distributor independent of cases sold. Specialty wine distributors sell fewer cases a year than regular wine distributors. As a result the promotional cost per case of wine sold is higher for specialty wines than for regular wines. (b) Sonoma's cost per order is $300 regardless of the number of cases sold in each order. Because specialty wine distributors order fewer cases per order, the ordering costs per case are higher for specialty wines than for regular wines.

The existing costing system undercosts distribution costs per case for specialty wines and overcosts distribution costs per case for regular wines.

Sonoma's management can use the information from the ABC system to make better pricing and product mix decisions, to reduce costs by eliminating processes and activities that do not add value, to identify and evaluate new designs that reduce the activities demanded by various products, to reduce the costs of doing various activities, and to plan and manage activities.

5-20 (15 min.) **Alternative allocation bases for a professional services firm.**

1.

Client	Direct Professional Time			Support Services		Amount Billed to Client
	Rate per Hour	Number of Hours	Total	Rate	Total	
(1)	(2)	(3)	(4) = (2) × (3)	(5)	(6) = (4) × (5)	(7) = (4) + (6)
WINNIPEG DOMINION						
Wolfson	$500	15	$7,500	30%	$2,250	$ 9,750
Brown	120	3	360	30	108	468
Anderson	80	22	1,760	30	528	2,288
						$12,506
TOKYO ENTERPRISES						
Wolfson	$500	2	$1,000	30%	$300	$1,300
Brown	120	8	960	30	288	1,248
Anderson	80	30	2,400	30	720	3,120
						$5,668

2.

Client	Direct Professional Time			Support Services		Amount Billed to Client
	Rate per Hour	Number of Hours	Total	Rate per Hour	Total	
(1)	(2)	(3)	(4) = (2) × (3)	(5)	(6) = (3) × (5)	(7) = (4)+(6)
WINNIPEG DOMINION						
Wolfson	$500	15	$7,500	$50	$ 750	$ 8,250
Brown	120	3	360	50	150	510
Anderson	80	22	1,760	50	1,100	2,860
						$11,620
TOKYO ENTERPRISES						
Wolfson	$500	2	$1,000	$50	$ 100	$1,100
Brown	120	8	960	50	400	1,360
Anderson	80	30	2,400	50	1,500	3,900
						$6,360

	Requirement 1	Requirement 2
Winnipeg Dominion	$12,506	$11,620
Tokyo Enterprises	5,668	6,360
	$18,174	$17,980

Both clients use 40 hours of professional labour time. However, Winnipeg Dominion uses a higher proportion of Wolfson's time (15 hours), which is more costly. This attracts the highest support-services charge when allocated on the basis of direct professional labour costs.

3.   Assume that the Wolfson Group uses a cause-and-effect criterion when choosing the allocation base for support services. You could use several pieces of evidence to determine whether professional labour costs or hours is the driver of support-service costs:

a.   *Interviews with personnel*. For example, staff in the major cost categories in support services could be interviewed to determine whether Wolfson requires more support per hour than, say, Anderson. The professional labour costs allocation base implies that an hour of Wolfson's time requires 6.25 ($500 ÷ $80) times more support-service dollars than does an hour of Anderson's time.

b.   *Analysis of tasks undertaken for selected clients*. For example, if computer-related costs are a sizable part of support costs, you could determine if there was a systematic relationship between the percentage involvement of professionals with high billing rates on cases and the computer resources consumed for those cases.

5-22 (30 min.) Department indirect-cost rates as activity rates. (Continuation of 5-21)

1.

	2001 Variable MOH Costs	Total Driver Units	Rate
Design-CAD	$ 39,000	390	$100 per design-hour
Engineering	29,600	370	$ 80 per engineer-hour
Production	240,000	4,000	$ 60 per machine

2.

	United Motors	Holden Motors	Leland Vehicle
Design			
$100 × 110; 200; 80	$11,000	$ 20,000	$ 8,000
Engineering			
$80 × 70; 60; 240	5,600	4,800	19,200
Production			
$60 × 120; 2,800; 1,080	7,200	168,000	64,800
Total	$23,800	$192,800	$92,000

3.

		United Motors	Holden Motors	Leland Vehicle
a.	Department rate (Exercise 5-22)	$23,800	$192,800	$92,000
b.	Plantwide rate (Exercise 5-21)	9,258	216,020	83,322
	Ratio of (a) ÷ (b)	2.57	0.89	1.10

The three contracts differ sizably in the way they use the resources of the three departments. The percentage of total driver units in each department is:

Department	United Motors	Holden Motors	Leland Vehicle
Design	28%	51%	21%
Engineering	19	16	65
Production	3	70	27

The United Motors contract uses only 3% of total machines-hours in 2001, yet uses 28% of CAD design-hours and 19% of engineering hours. The result is that the plantwide rate, based on machine-hours, will greatly underestimate the cost of resources used on the United Motors contract. Hence, the 157% increase in indirect costs assigned to the United Motors contract when department rates are used.

In contrast, the Holden Motors contract uses less of design (51%) and engineering (16%) than of machine-hours (70%). Hence, department rates will report lower indirect costs than does a plantwide rate.

5-24 (30 min.) **ABC, product costing at banks, cross-subsidization.**

1.

	Robinson	Skerrett	Farrel	Total
Revenues				
Spread revenue on annual basis				
(3% × ; $1,100, $800, $25,000)	$ 33	$ 24	$750.0	$ 807.0
Monthly fee charges				
($20 ×; 0, 12, 0)	0	240	0.0	240.0
Total revenues	33	264	750.0	1,047.0
Costs				
Deposit/withdrawal with teller				
$2.50 × 40; 50; 5	100	125	12.5	237.5
Deposit/withdrawal with ATM				
$0.80 × 10; 20; 16	8	16	12.8	36.8
Deposit/withdrawal on prearranged basis:				
$0.50 × 0; 12; 60	0	6	30.0	36.0
Bank cheques written				
$8.00 × 9; 3; 2	72	24	16.0	112.0
Foreign currency drafts				
$12.00 × 4; 1; 6	48	12	72.0	132.0
Inquiries				
$1.50 × 10; 18; 9	15	27	13.5	55.5
Total costs	243	210	156.8	609.8
Operating income	$(210)	$ 54	$593.2	$ 437.2

The assumption that the Robinson and Farrel accounts exceed $1,000 every month and the Skerrett account is less than $1,000 each month means the monthly charges apply only to Skerrett.

One student with a banking background noted that in this solution 100% of the spread is attributed to the "borrowing side of the bank." He noted that often the spread is divided between the "borrowing side" and the "lending side" of the bank.

2. Cross-subsidization across individual Premier Accounts occurs when profits made on some accounts are offset by losses on other accounts. The aggregate profitability on the three customers is $437.20. The Farrel account is highly profitable ($593.20), while the Robinson account is sizably unprofitable.

FIB should be very concerned about the cross-subsidization. Competition likely would "understand" that high-balance low-activity type accounts (such as Farrel) are highly profitable. Offering free services to these customers is not likely to retain these accounts if other banks offer higher interest rates. Competition likely will reduce the interest rate spread FIB can earn on the high-balance low-activity accounts they are able to retain.

5-24 (cont'd)

3.   Possible changes FIB could make are:
    a.   Offer higher interest rates on high-balance accounts to increase FIB's competitiveness in attracting and retaining these accounts.
    b.   Introduce charges for individual services. The ABC study reports the cost of each service. FIB has to decide if it wants to price each service at cost, below cost, or above cost. If it prices above cost, it may use advertising and other means to encourage additional use of those services by customers.

5-26   (30 min.)   ABC, product cost cross-subsidization (continuation of 5-25).

1.   Direct costs
        Direct materials $150,000
    Indirect costs
        Product support   983,000
    Total costs $1,133,000

Cost per kilogram of
potato cuts (for either the   = $\dfrac{\$1,133,000}{1,000,000}$
retail or the institutional
market)

                              = $1.133

2.

	Retail Potato Cuts		Institutional Potato Cuts	
Direct costs				
Direct materials	$135,000		$15,000	
Packaging	180,000	$ 315,000	8,000	$23,000
Indirect costs				
Cleaning				
$0.120 × 700,000	108,000			
$0.120 × 100,000			12,000	
Cutting				
$0.24 × 900,000 hours	216,000			
$0.15 × 100,000 hours			15,000	
Packaging				
$0.48 × 900,000	432,000			
$0.12 × 100,000		756,000	12,000	39,000
		$1,071,000		$62,000
Total costs		900,000		100,000
Kilograms produced		$1.19		$0.62
Costs per kilogram				

Note: The total costs of $1,133,000 ($1,071,000 + $62,000) are the same as those in requirement 1.

5-26 (cont'd)

3. There is much evidence of product-cost cross-subsidization.

	Retail	Institutional
Current system	$1.133	$1.133
ABC system	$1.190	$0.620

Assuming the ABC numbers are more accurate, retail is undercosted by approximately 5% ($1.133 ÷ $1.19 = 0.95), while institutional is overcosted by 83% ($1.133 ÷ $0.620 = 1.83).

The current system assumes each product uses all the activity areas in a homogeneous way. This is not the case. Institutional sales use sizably less resources in the cutting area and the packaging area. The percentage of total costs for each cost category are:

	Retail	Institutional	Total
Direct costs			
Direct materials	90.0%	10.0%	100.0%
Packaging	95.7	4.3	100.0
Indirect costs			
Cleaning	90.0	10.0	100.0
Cutting	93.5	6.5	100.0
Packaging	97.3	2.7	100.0
Units produced	90.0%	10.0%	100.0%

PEI can use the revised cost information for a variety of purposes:

a. *Pricing/product emphasis decisions.* The sizable drop in the reported cost of institutional potatoes makes it possible that PEI was overpricing potato products in this market. It lost the bid for a large institutional contract with a bid 30% above the winning bid. With its revised product cost dropping from $1.133 to $0.620, Idaho could have bid much lower and still made a profit. An increased emphasis on the institutional market appears warranted.

b. *Product design decisions.* ABC provides a road map as to how to reduce the costs of individual products. The relative components of costs are:

	Retail	Institutional
Direct costs		
Direct materials	12.6%	24.20 %
Packaging	16.8	12.90
Indirect costs		
Cleaning	10.1	19.35
Cutting	20.2	24.20
Packaging	40.3	19.35
Total costs	100.0%	100.00%

5-26 (cont'd)

Packaging-related costs constitute 57.1% (16.8% + 40.3%) of total costs of the retail product line. Design efforts that reduce packaging costs can have a big impact on reducing total unit costs for retail.

c.   *Process improvements.* Each activity area is now highlighted as a separate cost. The three indirect cost areas are over 60% of total costs for each product, indicating the upside from improvements in the efficiency of processes in these activity areas.

5-28   (20-25 min.)   **Activity-based costing, job-costing system.**

1.   An overview of the activity-based job-costing system is:

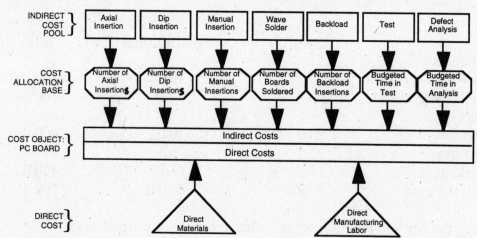

2.

Activity Area	Indirect Manufacturing Costs Allocated		
1. Axial insertion	0.08	× 45	= **3.60**
2. Dip insertion	0.25	× **24**	= 6.00
3. Manual insertion	**0.50**	× 11	= 5.50
4. Wave solder	3.50	× **1**	= 3.50
5. Backload	**0.70**	× 6	= 4.20
6. Test	90.00	× 0.25	= **22.50**
7. Defect analysis	**80.00**	× 0.10	= 8.00
Total			$53.30

Direct manufacturing costs:		
Direct materials	$75.00	
Direct manufacturing labour	15.00	$ 90.00
Indirect manufacturing costs:		
Manufacturing overhead (see above)		53.30
Total manufacturing costs		$143.30

5-28 (cont'd)

3. The manufacturing manager likely would find the ABC job-costing system useful in cost management. The seven indirect cost pools are systematically linked to the activity areas at the plant. Productivity measures can be developed that directly link to the management accounting system.

Marketing managers can use the ABC approach to help suggest ways for customers to reduce the cost of jobs on which they are bidding.

5-30 (20-25 min.) Job costing with multiple direct-cost categories, single indirect-cost pool, law firm (continuation of 5-29).

1. Panel B of the Solution Exhibit 5-29/5-30/5-31 presents the costing overview for the multiple direct/single indirect (MD/SI) approach.

2. Indirect costs = $7,000
Total professional labour-hours = 200 hours (104 hours on Widnes Coal + 96 hours on St. Helen's Glass)

Indirect cost allocated per professional labour-hour = $7,000 ÷ 200 = $35 per hour

3.

	Widnes Coal	St. Helen's Glass	Total
Direct costs:			
Direct professional labour,			
$70 × 104; 96	$ 7,280	$ 6,720	$14,000
Research support labour	1,600	3,400	5,000
Computer time	500	1,300	1,800
Travel and allowances	600	4,400	5,000
Telephones/faxes	200	1,000	1,200
Photocopying	250	750	1,000
Total direct costs	10,430	17,570	28,000
Indirect costs allocated,			
$35 × 104; 96	3,640	3,360	7,000
Total costs to be billed	$14,070	$20,930	$35,000

5-30 (cont'd)

4.

	Widnes Coal	St. Helen's Glass	Total
SD/SI Problem 5-29	$18,200	$16,800	$35,000
MD/SI Problem 5-30	14,070	20,930	35,000

The MD/SI (5-30) approach directly traces to the individual jobs $14,070 that is allocated in the SD/SI (5-29) approach on the basis of direct professional labour-hours. The averaging assumption implicit in the SD/SI (5-29) approach appears incorrect—for example, the St. Helen's Glass job has travel costs over seven times higher than the Widnes Coal case despite having lower direct professional labour-hours.

5-32 (30-40 min.) **Activity-based costing, merchandising.**

1.

	General Supermarket Chains	Drugstore Chains	"Mom and Pop" Single Stores	Total
Revenues[a]	$3,708,000	$3,150,000	$1,980,000	$8,838,000
Cost of goods sold[b]	3,600,000	3,000,000	1,800,000	8,400,000
Gross margin	$ 108,000	$ 150,000	$ 180,000	438,000
Other operating costs				301,080
Operating income				$ 136,920
Gross margin %	2.91%	4.76%	9.09%	

[a]($30,900 × 120); ($10,500 × 300); ($1,980 × 1,000)
[b]($30,000 × 120); ($10,000 × 300); ($1,800 × 1,000)

The gross margin of Figure Four Inc. was 4.96% ($438,000 ÷ $8,838,000). The operating income margin of Figure Four Inc. was 1.55% ($136,920 ÷ $8,838,000).

2.   The per-unit cost driver rates are:

1. Customer purchase order processing, $80,000 ÷ 2,000 = $40 per order
2. Line item ordering, $63,840 ÷ 21,280 = $ 3 per line item
3. Store delivery, $71,000 ÷ 1,420 = $50 per delivery
4. Cartons shipped, $76,000 ÷ 76,000 = $ 1 per carton
5. Shelf-stocking, $10,240 ÷ 640 = $16 per hour

3.   The activity-based costing of each distribution market for August 1999 is:

	General Supermarket Chains	Drugstore Chains	"Mom and Pop" Single Stores
1. Customer purchase order processing,			
($40 × 140; × 360; × 1,500)	$ 5,600	$14,400	$ 60,000
2. Line item ordering,			
[$3 × (140 × 14; 360 × 12; 1,500 × 10)]	5,880	12,960	45,000
3. Store delivery,			
($50 × 120, × 300, × 1,000)	6,000	15,000	50,000
4. Cartons shipped,			
[$1 × (120 × 300; 300 × 80; 1,000 × 16)]	36,000	24,000	16,000
5. Shelf-stocking,			
[$16 × (120 × 3; 300 × 0.6; 1,000 × 0.1)]	5,760	2,880	1,600
	$59,240	$69,240	$172,600

5-32 (cont'd)

The revised operating income statement is:

	General Supermarket Chains	Drugstore Chains	"Mom and Pop" Single Stores	Total
Revenues	$3,708,000	$3,150,000	$1,980,000	$8,838,000
Cost of goods sold	3,600,000	3,000,000	1,800,000	8,400,000
Gross margin	108,000	150,000	180,000	438,000
Operating costs	59,240	69,240	172,600	301,080
Operating income	$ 48,760	$ 80,760	$ 7,400	$ 136,920
Operating income margin	1.31%	2.56%	0.37%	1.55%

The rankings of the three markets are:

Using Gross Margin
1. Mom and Pop Single Stores   9.09%
2. Drugstore Chains   4.76%
3. General Supermarket Chains   2.91%

Using Operating Income
1. Drugstore Chains   2.56%
2. General Supermarket Chains   1.31%
3. Mom and Pop Single Stores   0.37%

The activity-based analysis of costs highlights how the "Mom and Pop" Single Stores use a larger amount of Figure Four resources per revenue dollar than do the other two markets. The ratios for the operating costs to revenues for the three markets are:

General Supermarket Chains	1.60%	($59,240 ÷ $3,708,000)
Drugstore Chains	2.20%	($69,240 ÷ $3,150,000)
Mom and Pop Single Stores	8.72%	($172,600 ÷ $1,980,000)

This is a classic illustration of the maxim that "all revenue dollars are not created equal."

4.   a.   *Choosing the appropriate cost drivers for each area.* The case gives a cost driver for each chosen activity area. However, it is likely that over time further refinements in cost drivers would occur. For example, not all store deliveries are equally easy to make, depending on parking availability, accessibility of the storage/shelf space to the delivery point, etc. Similarly, not all cartons are equally easy to deliver—their weight, size, or likely breakage component are factors that can vary across carton types.

     b.   *Developing a reliable database on the chosen cost drivers.* For some items, such as the number of orders and the number of line items, this information likely would be available in machine readable form at a high level of accuracy. Unless the delivery personnel have hand-held computers that they use in a systematic way, estimates of shelf-stocking time are likely to be unreliable. Advances in information technology likely will reduce problems in this area over time.

5-32 (cont'd)

    c.   *Deciding how to handle costs that may be common across several activities.* For example, (3) store delivery and (4) cartons shipped to stores have the common cost of the same trip. Some organizations may treat (3) as the primary activity and attribute to (4) only incremental costs. Similarly, (1) order processing and (2) line item ordering may have common costs.

    d.   *Choice of the time period to compute cost rates per cost driver.* Flair calculates driver rates on a monthly basis (August 1999). He may want to consider using longer time periods that may be less affected by seasonal or random variations in demand.

    e.   *Behavioural factors are likely to be a challenge to Flair.* He must now tell those salespeople who specialize in "Mom and Pop" accounts that they have been less profitable than previously thought.

5-34 (30 min.) Plantwide versus department overhead cost rates.

1.

	Amounts (in thousands)			
	Molding	Component	Assembly	Total
Manufacturing department overhead	$21,000	$16,200	$22,600	$59,800
Service departments:				
Power				18,400
Maintenance				4,000
Total estimated plantwide overhead				$82,200

Estimated direct manufacturing labour hours (DMLH):	
Molding	500
Component	2,000
Assembly	1,500
Total estimated DMLH	4,000

$$\text{Plantwide overhead rate} = \frac{\text{Estimated plantwide overhead}}{\text{Estimated DMLH}}$$

$$= \frac{\$82,200}{4,000} = \$20.55 \text{ per DMLH}$$

2.   The department overhead cost rates are shown in Solution Exhibit 5-34

3.   MumsDay Corporation should use department rates to allocate plant overhead to its products. A plantwide rate is appropriate when all products pass through the same processes, and all departments are similar. Departmental rates are appropriate when the converse is true. MumsDay's departments are dissimilar in that the Molding Department is machine-intensive and the other two departments are labour-intensive. Department rates better capture cause-and-effect relationships at MumsDay than does a plantwide rate.

5-34 (cont'd)

SOLUTION EXHIBIT 5-34

Departments (in thousands)

	Service		Manufacturing		
	Power	Maintenance	Molding	Component	Assembly
Departmental overhead costs	$18,400	$ 4,000	$21,000	$16,200	$22,600
Allocation of maintenance costs (direct method) $4,000 × 90/125, 25/125, 10/125		(4,000)	2,880	800	320
Allocation of power costs $18,400 × 360/800, 320/800, 120/800	(18,400)		8,280	7,360	2,760
Total budgeted overhead of manufacturing departments	$ 0	$ 0	$32,160	$24,360	$25,680
Allocation Base			875 MH	2,000 DMLH	1,500 DMLH
Budgeted Overhead Rate (Budgeted overhead ÷ Base)			$36.75/MH	$12.18/DMLH	$17:12/DMLH

5-36 (30-40 min.) **Activity-based costing, product cost cross-subsidization.**

The motivation for 5-36 came from "ABC Minicase: Let Them Eat Cake," *Cost Management Update* (Issue No. 31).

1. $$\text{Budgeted MOH rate in 2001} = \frac{\$210,800}{200,000 \text{ units}}$$

= $1.054 per one-kilogram unit of cake

	Raisin Cake		Layered Carrot Cake	
Unit direct manufacturing cost				
Direct materials	$0.600		$0.900	
Direct manufacturing labour	0.140	$0.740	0.200	$1.100
Unit indirect manufacturing cost				
Manufacturing overhead				
($1.054 × 1, 1)	$1.054	1.054	$1.054	1.054
Unit total manufacturing cost		$1.794		$2.154

2.

	Raisin Cake		Layered Carrot Cake	
Unit indirect manufacturing cost				
Direct materials	$0.600		$0.900	
Direct manufacturing labour	0.140	$0.740	0.200	$1.100
Unit indirect manufacturing cost				
Mixing ($0.04 × 5,8)	$0.200		$0.320	
Cooking ($0.14 × 2,3)	0.280		0.420	
Cooling ($0.02 × 3,5)	0.060		0.100	
Creaming/Icing ($0.25 × 0,3)	0.000		0.750	
Packaging ($0.08 × 3,7)	0.240	0.780	0.560	2.150
		$1.520		$3.250
Unit total manufacturing cost				

3. The unit product costs in requirements 1 and 2 differ only in the assignment of indirect costs to individual products. The assumed usage of indirect cost areas under each costing system is:

	Existing System		ABC System	
		Layered		Layered
	Raisin Cake	Carrot Cake	Raisin Cake	Carrot Cake
Mixing	50%	50%	38.5%	61.5%
Cooking	50	50	40.0	60.0
Cooling	50	50	37.5	62.5
Creaming/Icing	50	50	0.0	100.0
Packaging	50	50	30.0	70.0

5-36 (cont'd)

The ABC system recognizes the substantial difference in usage of individual activity areas between raisin cake and layered carrot cake. The existing costing system erroneously assumes equal usage of activity areas by a kilogram of raisin cake and a kilogram of layered carrot cake.

4. Uses of activity-based cost numbers include:

(a) Pricing decisions. BD can use the ABC data to decide on preliminary prices for negotiating with its customers. Raisin cake is currently overcosted, while layered carrot cake is undercosted. Actual production of layered carrot cake is 100% more than budgeted. One explanation could be the underpricing of layered carrot cake.

(b) Product emphasis. BD has more accurate product margins with ABC. BD can use this information for deciding which products to push (especially if there are production constraints).

(c) Product design. ABC provides a road map for how a change in product design can reduce costs. The percentage breakdown of total indirect costs for each product is:

	Raisin Cake	Layered Carrot Cake
Mixing	25.6% ($0.20/$0.78)	14.9% ($0.32/$2.15)
Cooking	35.9	19.5
Cooling	7.7	4.7
Creaming/Icing	0.0	34.9
Packaging	30.8	26.0
	100.0%	100.0%

BD can reduce the cost of either cake by reducing its usage of each activity area. For example, BD can reduce raisin cake's cost by sizably reducing its cooking time or packaging time. Similarly, a sizable reduction in creaming/icing will have a marked reduction in layered carrot cake costs.

(d) Process improvements. Improvements in how activity areas are configured will cause a reduction in the costs of products that use those activity areas.

(e) Cost planning and flexible budgeting. ABC provides a more refined model to forecast costs of BD and to explain why actual costs differ from budgeted costs.

5-38   (40-50 min.)   **Activity-based job costing, unit cost comparisons.**

1.

	Job Order 410		Job Order 411	
Direct manufacturing costs:				
Direct materials	$9,700		$59,900	
Direct manufacturing labour,				
$30 × 25; 375	750	$10,450	11,250	$ 71,150
Indirect manufacturing costs,				
$115 × 25; 375		2,875		43,125
Total manufacturing costs		$13,325		$114,275
Number of units		÷ 10		÷ 200
Unit manufacturing cost per job		$ 1,332.50		$ 571.375

2.

	Job Order 410		Job Order 411	
Direct manufacturing costs:				
Direct materials	$9,700		$59,900	
Direct manufacturing labour,				
$30 × 25; 375	750	$10,450	11,250	$71,150
Indirect manufacturing costs:				
Materials handling,				
$0.40 × 500; 2,000	200		800	
Lathe work,				
$0.20 × 20,000; 60,000	4,000		12,000	
Milling,				
$20.00 × 150; 1,050	3,000		21,000	
Grinding,				
$0.80 × 500; 2,000	400		1,600	
Testing,				
$15.00 × 10; 200	150	7,750	3,000	38,400
Total manufacturing costs		$18,200		$109,550
Number of units per job		÷ 10		÷ 200
Unit manufacturing cost per job		$ 1,820		$ 547.75

3.

	Job Order 410	Job Order 411
Number of units in job	10	200
Unit cost per job with prior costing system	$1,332.50	$571.375
Unit cost per job with activity-based costing	1,820.00	547.75

Job order 410 has an increase in reported cost of 36.6% [($1,820 − $1,332.50) ÷ $1,332.50] while Job order 411 has a decrease in reported cost of 4.1% [($547.75 − $571.375) ÷ $571.375].

A common finding when activity-based costing is implemented is that low-volume products have increases in their reported cost while high-volume products have decreases in their reported cost. This result is also found in requirements 1 and 2 of this problem.

The product costs figures computed in requirements 1 and 2 differ because:
(a)   the job orders differ in the way they use each of five activity areas, and
(b)   the activity areas differ in their indirect cost allocation bases (specifically, each area does not use the direct labour-hours indirect cost allocation base).

5-38 (cont'd)

The following table documents how the two jobs differ in the way they use each of the five activity areas included in indirect manufacturing costs:

Activity Area	Usage Based on Analysis of Activity Area Cost Drivers		Usage Assumed with Direct Labour-Hours as Application Base	
	Job Order 410	Job Order 411	Job Order 410	Job Order 411
Materials handling	20.0%	80.0%	6.25%	93.75%
Lathe work	25.0	75.0	6.25	93.75
Milling	12.5	87.5	6.25	93.75
Grinding	20.0	80.0	6.25	93.75
Testing	4.8	95.2	6.25	93.75

Areas where the differences in product cost figures might be important to Tracy Corporation include:

(a) *Product pricing and product emphasis*. The activity-based accounting approach indicates that Job order 410 is being undercosted while Job order 411 is being overcosted. Tracy Corporation may erroneously push Job 410 and deemphasize Job 411. Moreover, by its actions, Tracy Corporation may encourage a competitor to enter the market for Job order 411 and take market share away from itself.

(b) *Product design*. Product designers at Tracy Corporation likely will find the numbers in the activity-based costing approach more believable and credible than those in the existing system. In a machine-paced manufacturing environment, it is unlikely that direct labour-hours would be the major cost driver. Activity-based costing provides more credible signals to product designers about the ways the costs of a product can be reduced—for example, use fewer parts, require fewer turns on the lathe, and reduce the number of machine hours in the milling area.

An overview of the product-costing system is:

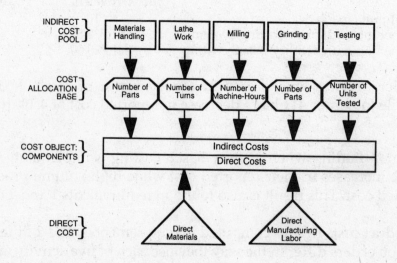

CHAPTER 6
MASTER BUDGET AND RESPONSIBILITY ACCOUNTING

6-2   The budgeting cycle includes the following elements:
   a.   Planning the performance of the organization as a whole as well as its subunits. The entire management team agrees as to what is expected.
   b.   Providing a frame of reference, a set of specific expectations against which the actual results can be compared.
   c.   Investigating variations from the plans. If necessary, corrective action follows investigation.
   d.   Planning again, considering feedback and changed conditions.

6-4   Budgeted performance is better than past performance for judging managers. Why? Mainly because inefficiencies included in past results can be detected and eliminated in budgeting. Also, new opportunities in the future, which did not exist in the past, may be ignored if past performance is used.

6-6   A company that shares its own internal budget information with other companies can gain multiple benefits. One benefit is better coordination with suppliers, which can reduce the likelihood of supply shortages. Better coordination with customers can result in increased sales as demand by customers is less likely to exceed supply. Better coordination across the whole supply chain can also help a company reduce inventories and thus reduce the costs of holding inventories.

6-8   A *rolling budget* is a budget or plan that is always available for a specified future period by adding a month, quarter, or year in the future as the month, quarter or year just ended is dropped. For example, a 12-month rolling budget for the March 2000 to February 2001 period becomes a 12-month rolling budget for the April 2000 to March 2001 period the next month, and so on.

6-10   The revenue budget is typically the cornerstone for budgeting because production (and hence costs) and inventory levels generally depend on the forecasted level of demand and revenue.

6-12   Cash budgeting is pivotal to a startup company because growth requires increasing amounts of cash flow, and without cash the business will not survive even with a strong profit potential.

6-14   Non-output-based cost drivers can be incorporated into budgeting by the use of activity-based budgeting (ABB). ABB focuses on the budgeted cost of activities necessary to produce and sell products and services. Non-output-based cost drivers, such as the number of part numbers, number of batches, and number of new products, can be used with ABB.

6-16 (15 min.) **Production budget (in units), fill in the missing numbers.**

	Model 101	Model 201	Model 301
Budgeted sales	180^G	193^c	867^G
Add target ending FGI	14^a	6^G	33^G
Total requirements	194^G	199^G	900^e
Deduct beginning FGI	11^G	8^G	45^f
Units to be produced	183^b	191^d	855^G

^{a} 194 – 180 = 14 ^{d} 199 – 8 = 191   G = given
^{b} 194 – 11 = 183 ^{e} 867 + 33 = 900
^{c} 199 – 6 = 193 ^{f} 900 – 855 = 45

6-18 (5 min.) **Direct materials budget.**

Direct materials to be used in production (bottles)	1,500,000
Add target ending direct materials inventory (bottles)	50,000
Total requirements (bottles)	1,550,000
Deduct beginning direct materials inventory (bottles)	20,000
Direct materials to be purchased (bottles)	1,530,000

6-20   (30 min.) Sales and production budget.

1.

	Selling Price	Units Sold	Total Revenues
1-litre bottles	$0.25	4,800,000[a]	$1,200,000
16-litre units	1.50	1,200,000[b]	1,800,000
			$3,000,000

[a] 400,000 × 12 months = 4,800,000

[b] 100,000 × 12 months = 1,200,000

2.

Budgeted unit sales (1-litre bottles)	4,800,000
Add target ending finished goods inventory	600,000
Total requirements	5,400,000
Deduct beginning finished goods inventory	900,000
Units to be produced	4,500,000

3.

$$\text{Beginning inventory} = \text{Budgeted sales} + \text{Target ending inventory} - \text{Budgeted production}$$

$$= 1,200,000 + 200,000 - 1,300,000$$

$$= 100,000 \text{ 16-litre units}$$

6-22   (15-20 min.) Revenue, production, and purchases budget.

1.   800,000 motorcycles × 400,000 yen = 320,000,000,000 yen

2.

Budgeted sales (units)	800,000
Add target ending finished goods inventory	100,000
Total requirements	900,000
Deduct beginning finished goods inventory	120,000
Units to be produced	780,000

3.

Direct materials to be used in production, 780,000 × 2	1,560,000
Add target ending direct materials inventory	30,000
Total requirements	1,590,000
Deduct beginning direct materials inventory	20,000
Direct materials to be purchased	1,570,000
Cost per wheel in yen	16,000
Direct materials purchase cost in yen	25,120,000,000

Note the relatively small inventory of wheels. In Japan, suppliers tend to be located very close to the major manufacturer. Inventories are controlled by just-in-time and similar systems. Indeed, some direct materials inventories are almost nonexistent.

6-24 (20-30 min.) **Activity-based budgeting.**

1.

	Soft Drinks	Fresh Produce	Packaged Food	Total
Ordering				
$90 × 14; 24; 14	$1,260	$2,160	$1,260	$4,680
Delivery				
$82 × 12; 62; 19	984	5,084	1,558	7,626
Shelf-stocking				
$21 × 16; 172; 94	336	3,612	1,974	5,922
Customer-support				
$0.18 × 4,600; 34,200; 10,750	828	6,156	1,935	8,919
	$3,408	$17,012	$6,727	$27,147

2.   An ABB approach recognizes how different products require different mixes of support activities. The relative percentage of how each product area uses the cost driver in each activity area is:

Activity Area	Soft Drinks	Fresh Produce	Packaged Food	Total
Ordering	26.9	46.2	26.9	100.0%
Delivery	12.9	66.7	20.4	100.0
Shelf-stocking	5.7	61.0	33.3	100.0
Customer-support	9.3	69.0	21.7	100.0

By recognizing these differences, FS managers are better able to budget for different unit sales levels and different mix of individual product-line items sold. Using a single cost driver (such as COGS) assumes homogeneity across product lines which does not occur at FS.

Other benefits cited by managers include: (1) better identification of resource needs, (2) clearer linking of costs with staff responsibilities, and (3) identification of budgetary slack.

6-26 (20 min.)   **Budgeting and behaviour.**

1. (a) Gain additional insight into the strategy of an organization. Exhibit 6-1 shows arrows pointing both ways between strategy analysis and long-term planning and short-term planning. Detailed analysis for budgeting can sometimes highlight strategy assumptions (such as cost levels and demand levels) that are not likely to hold.
    (b) Anticipate resource demands in a timely way. Budgeting can highlight working capital shortages, cash shortages, personnel shortages, and so on. Early warning signals can enable a company to take action to avoid having small problems become large problems.

    (c) Improve the communication level in an organization. The budgeting process itself can assist in having diverse groups gain a better understanding of how other groups affect their performance. Sharing budgets across organizations in a supply chain can help a company better meet end-point customer demand. Communication with suppliers can reduce parts shortages.

2. Factors to consider when preparing sales forecasts include:
    (a) Any constraining variables on sales. For example, if demand outstrips available productive capacity or a key component is in short supply, the sales forecast should be based on the maximum units that could be produced.
    (b) Information from customers about their new product developments and advertising plans.
    (c) Feedback from customers about satisfaction with a company's products vis-à-vis satisfaction levels for the products of competitors.
    (d) Likely new product releases by competitors or new entrants into a market.

6-28 (40 min.) **Budget schedules for manufacturer.**

1. Sales or Revenue Budget

	Executive Line	Chairperson Line	Total
Units sold	740	390	
Unit selling price	$1,020	$1,600	
Budgeted revenue	$754,800	$624,000	$1,378,80

2. Production Budget in Units

	Executive Line	Chairperson Line
Budgeted sales	740	390
Add budgeted ending f.g. inventory	30	15
Total requirements	770	405
Deduct beginning f.g. inventory	20	5
Budgeted production	750	400

3. Direct Materials Usage Budget (units):

	Oak Top	Red Oak Top	Oak Legs	Red Oak Legs	Total
Executive Line:					
1. Budgeted input per f.g. unit	16	–	4	–	
2. Budgeted production	750	–	750	–	
3. Budgeted usage	12,000	–	3,000	–	
Chairperson Line:					
4. Budgeted input per f.g. unit	–	25	–	4	
5. Budgeted production	–	400	–	400	
6. Budgeted usage	–	10,000	–	1,600	
Total direct materials usage (3+6)	12,000	10,000	3,000	1,600	
1. Beginning inventory	320	150	100	40	
2. Unit price (FIFO)	$18	$23	$11	$17	
3. Cost of DM used from beginning inventory	$5,760	$3,450	$1,100	$680	$10,990
4. Materials to be used from purchases	11,680	9,850	2,900	1,560	
5. Cost of DM in March	$20	$25	$12	$18	
6. Cost of DM purchased and used in March	$233,600	$246,250	$34,800	$28,080	542,730
Direct materials used (3+6)	$239,360	$249,700	$35,900	$28,760	$553,720

6-28 (cont'd)

Direct Materials Purchases Budget:

	Oak Top	Red Oak Top	Oak Legs	Red Oak Legs	Total
Budgeted usage	12,000	10,000	3,000	1,600	
Add ending inventory	192	200	80	44	
Total requirements	12,192	10,200	3,080	1,644	
Deduct beginning inventory	320	150	100	40	
Total DM purchases	11,872	10,050	2,980	1,604	
Purchase price (March)	$20	$25	$12	$18	
Total purchases	$237,440	$251,250	$35,760	$28,872	$553,322

4.   Direct Manufacturing Labour Budget

	Output Units Produced	Direct Manu. Labour-Hours per Output Unit	Total Hours	Hourly Rate	Total
Executive Line	750	3	2,250	$30	$ 67,500
Chairperson Line	400	5	2,000	$30	60,000
			4,250		$127,500

5.   Manufacturing Overhead Budget

Variable manufacturing overhead costs (4,250 × $35)	$148,750
Fixed manufacturing overhead costs	42,500
Total manufacturing overhead costs	$191,250

Total manufacturing overhead cost per hour

$$= \frac{\$191,250}{4,250} = \$45 \text{ per direct manufacturing labour-hour}$$

Fixed manufacturing overhead cost per hour

$$= \frac{\$42,500}{4,250}$$

$$= \$10 \text{ per direct manufacturing labour-hour}$$

6-28 (cont'd)

6.   Computation of unit costs of finished goods:

	Executive Line	Chairperson Line
Direct materials		
Oak top ($20 × 16,0)	$320	$ 0
Red oak top ($25 × 0,25)	0	625
Oak legs ($12 × 4,0)	48	0
Red oak legs ($18 × 0,4)	0	72
Direct manufacturing labour ($30 × 3,5)	90	150
Manufacturing overhead		
Variable ($35 × 3,5)	105	175
Fixed ($10 × 3,5)	30	50
Total manufacturing cost per unit	$593	$1,072

Ending Inventory Budget

	Cost per Unit	Units	Total
Direct Materials			
Oak top	$ 20	192	$ 3,840
Red oak top	25	200	5,000
Oak legs	12	80	960
Red oak legs	18	44	792
			10,592
Finished Goods			
Executive	593	30	17,790
Chairperson	1,072	15	16,080
			33,870
Total			$44,462

7.   Cost of Goods Sold Budget

Budgeted finished goods inventory, March 1, 2000 ($10,480 + $4,850)		$ 15,330
Direct materials used	$553,720	
Direct manufacturing labour	127,500	
Manufacturing overhead	191,250	
Cost of goods manufactured		872,470
Cost of goods available for sale		887,800
Deduct ending finished goods inventory, March 31, 2000		33,870
Cost of goods sold		$853,930

6-30 (60 min.) **Sensitivity analysis and changing budget assumptions.**

1.

	Chippo	Choco	Total
Revenues			
Chippo, $3 × 500,000	$1,500,000		$1,500,000
Choco, $3 × 500,000		$1,500,000	1,500,000
	1,500,000	1,500,000	3,000,000
Cost of goods sold			
Chocolate chips ($2 × 250,000[a]; $2 × 125,000[b])	500,000	250,000	750,000
Cookie dough ($1 × 250,000[a]; $1 × 375,000[b])	250,000	375,000	625,000
	750,000	625,000	1,375,000
Gross margin	$ 750,000	$ 875,000	$1,625,000
Gross margin percentage	50%	58.33%	54.17%

[a] Chippo: 500,000 × 0.50 = 250,000 chips; 500,000 × 0.50 = 250,000 dough
[b] Choco: 500,000 × 0.25 = 125,000 chips; 500,000 × 0.75 = 375,000 dough

2.

	Chippo	Choco	Total
Revenues			
Chippo, $2.60 × 500,000	$1,300,000		$1,300,000
Choco, $3.20 × 500,000		$1,600,000	1,600,000
	1,300,000	1,600,000	2,900,000
Cost of goods sold			
Chocolate chips	500,000	250,000	750,000
Cookie dough	250,000	375,000	625,000
	750,000	625,000	1,375,000
Gross margin	$ 550,000	$ 975,000	$1,525,000
Gross margin percentage	42.31%	60.94%	52.59%

Gross margin change from requirement 1:

Chippo: $\dfrac{\$550,000 - \$750,000}{\$750,000} = -26.7\%$ Total: $\dfrac{\$1,525,000 - \$1,625,000}{1,625,000} = -6.2\%$

Choco: $\dfrac{\$975,000 - \$875,000}{\$875,000} = 11.4\%$

3.

	Chippo	Choco	Total
Revenues			
Chippo, $3 × 400,000	$1,200,000		$1,200,000
Choco, $3 × 500,000		$1,500,000	1,500,000
	1,200,000	1,500,000	2,700,000
Cost of goods sold			
Chocolate chips ($2 × 200,000[a]; $2 × 125,000[b])	400,000	250,000	650,000
Cookie dough ($1 × 200,000[a]; $1 × 375,000[b])	200,000	375,000	575,000
	600,000	625,000	1,225,000
Gross margin	$ 600,000	$ 875,000	$1,475,000
Gross margin percentage	50%	58.33%	54.63%

Gross margin change from requirement 1:

Chippo: $\dfrac{\$600,000 - \$750,000}{\$750,000} = -20\%$

Choco: $\dfrac{\$875,000 - \$875,000}{\$875,000} = 0\%$

Total: $\dfrac{\$1,475,000 - \$1,625,000}{\$1,625,000} = -9.2\%$

[a] Chippo: 400,000 × 0.50 = 200,000 chips; 400,000 × 0.50 = 200,000 dough
[b] Choco: 500,000 × 0.25 = 125,000 chips; 500,000 × 0.75 = 375,000 dough

6-34 (30 min.) Cash budgeting.

1. Projected Sales

	May	June	July	August	September	October
Sales, Units	80	120	200	100	60	40
Sales, Dollars	$36,000	$54,000	$90,000	$45,000	$27,000	

Collections of Receivables

	May	June	July	August	September	October
From sales in:						
May			$10,800			
June			27,000	$16,200		
July			18,000	45,000	$27,000	
August				9,000	22,500	
September					5,400	
Total			$55,800	$70,200	$54,900	

Calculation of Payables

	May	June	July	August	September	October
Material and Labour Use, Units						
Budgeted production		200	100	60	40	
Direct materials						
Wood (board feet)		1,000	500	300	200	
Fiberglass (yards)		1,200	600	360	240	
Direct labour (hours)		1,000	500	300	200	
Disbursement of Payments						
Direct materials						
Wood			$30,000	$15,000	$9,000	
Fiberglass			6,000	3,000	1,800	
Direct labour			12,500	7,500	5,000	
Interest payment			150	150	150	
Variable OHD Calculation						
Variable OHD rate			$7	$7	$7	
OHD driver			500	300	200	
Variable OHD expense			$3,500	$2,100	$1,400	

6-34 (cont'd)

Cash Budget for the months of July, August, September 2001

	July	August	September
Beginning cash balance	$ 0	$(4,350)	$30,100
Add receipts:			
Collection of receivables	55,800	70,200	54,900
Total receipts	55,800	70,200	54,900
Total cash available	$55,800	$65,850	$85,000
Deduct disbursements:			
Material purchases	36,000	18,000	10,800
Direct labour	12,500	7,500	5,000
Variable costs	3,500	2,100	1,400
Fixed costs	8,000	8,000	8,000
Interest payments	150	150	150
Total disbursements	60,150	35,750	25,350
Ending cash balance	$(4,350)	$30,100	$59,650

2. Yes. Slopes will be in a position to pay off the $30,000 1-year note on October 1, 2001.

3. No. Slopes does not maintain a $10,000 minimum cash balance in July. It could encourage its customers to pay earlier by offering a discount. An alternate plan is to arrange additional short-term financing from the bank.

6-36 (15 min.) **Fixing responsibility.**

Note that the lost contribution margin of $1,000 is rarely accounted for in ordinary accounting systems. If measured at all, it would appear as an underachieved budgeted contribution margin; that is, actual would be less than budgeted by $1,000.

The essence of this case is to demonstrate the limitations of responsibility accounting and the futility of a "blame-setting" theme in implementing responsibility accounting.

The theory of responsibility accounting is straightforward—link each cost ultimately to the one person in the organization who has the most day-to-day influence over its total amount. Repair and maintenance costs provide one of the most difficult illustrations of implementing the theory. The total cost of the repair job, by itself, is the responsibility of the repair shop manager. The manager has the most influence over the total amount incurred at the instant of repair. However, in the eyes of many observers, the department is only an intermediate cost objective because it services other departments.

Most students will probably maintain that the utility department should bear the $2,600 cost because its failure to maintain specified clearances led to this incident. Some students will feel that the sanitation department should bear the extra costs above the $2,000 original proposal.

Decisions regarding these disputes are inherently contextual, so students should be properly uneasy about choosing a course of action for the controller. The controller has dealt with all parties before and will interact with them again and again, so he must measure the effects of his present decision against a whole series of decisions about the running of the control system. The key is to prevent a similar occurrence in this or other areas.

Given these precautions, the controller might avoid the issue of "fixing blame" by not charging any department (or by charging the controller's department). All the managers seem to have partial responsibility. The controller should learn from this incident and take action to:

1. Pinpoint responsibility for preventive maintenance of utility lines in the future. Decide how future costs should be allocated to provide the best set of coordinated goals and incentives.

2. Have a meeting of all department heads involved to improve mutual understanding of responsibilities.

6-38 (50-60 min.) **Comprehensive review of budgeting.**

1. **Schedule 1 : Revenue Budget**
   For the Year Ended December 31, 2000

	Units (Lots)	Selling Price	Total Sales
Lemonade	1,080	$9,000	$ 9,720,000
Diet Lemonade	540	8,500	4,590,000
Total			$14,310,000

2. **Schedule 2 : Production Budget in Units**
   For the Year Ended December 31, 2000

	Products	
	Lemonade	Diet Lemonade
Budgeted sales (Schedule 1)	1,080	540
Add target ending finished-goods inventory	20	10
Total requirements	1,100	550
Deduct beginning finished-goods inventory	100	50
Units to be produced	1,000	500

3. **Schedule 3A : Direct Materials Usage Budget in Units and Dollars**
    For the Year Ended December 31, 2000

	Syrup—Lemonade	Syrup—Diet Lemonade	Containers	Packaging	Total
Units of direct materials to be used for production of Lemonade (1,000 lots ×1)	1,000	–	1,000	1,000	
Units of direct materials to be used for production of Diet Lemonade (500 lots ×1)	–	500	500	500	
Total direct materials to be used (in units)	1,000	500	1,500	1,500	
Units of direct material to be used from beginning inventory (under FIFO)	80	70	200	400	
Multiply by cost per unit of beginning inventory	$ 1,100	$ 1,000	$ 950	$ 900	
Cost of direct materials to be used from beginning inventory (a)	$ 88,000	$ 70,000	$ 190,000	$ 360,000	$ 708,000
Units of direct materials to be used from purchases (1,000 – 80; 500 – 70; 1,500 – 200; 1,500 – 400)	920	430	1,300	1,100	
Multiply by cost per unit of purchased materials	$ 1,200	$ 1,100	$ 1,000	$ 800	
Cost of direct materials to be used from purchases (b)	$1,104,000	$473,000	$1,300,000	$ 880,000	3,757,000
Total costs of direct materials to be used [(a) + (b)]	$1,192,000	$543,000	$1,490,000	$1,240,000	$4,465,000

6-38 (cont'd)

4. **Schedule 3B : Direct Materials Purchases Budget in Units and Dollars**
   For the Year Ended December 31, 2000

	Syrup—Lemonade	Syrup—Diet Lemonade	Containers	Packaging	Total
Direct materials to be used in production (in units) from Schedule 3A	1,000	500	1,500	1,500	
Add target ending direct materials inventory in units	30	20	100	200	
Total requirements in units	1,030	520	1,600	1,700	
Deduct beginning direct materials inventory in units	80	70	200	400	
Units of direct materials to be purchased	950	450	1,400	1,300	
Multiply by cost/unit of purchased materials	$ 1,200	$ 1,100	$ 1,000	$ 800	
Direct materials purchase costs	$1,140,000	$495,000	$1,400,000	$1,040,000	$4,075,000

6-18

5. **Schedule 4 : Direct Manufacturing Labour Budget**
   For the Year Ended December 31, 2000

	Output Units Produced (Schedule 2)	Direct Manufacturing Labour Hours per Unit	Total Hours	Hourly Rate	Total
Lemonade	1,000	20	20,000	$25	$500,000
Diet Lemonade	500	20	10,000	25	250,000
Total			30,000		$750,000

6. **Schedule 5 : Manufacturing Overhead Costs Budget**
   For the Year Ended December 31, 2000

Variable manufacturing overhead costs:		
Lemonade [$600 × 2 hours per lot × 1,000 lots (Schedule 2)]		$1,200,000
Diet Lemonade [$600 × 2 hours per lot × 500 lots (Schedule 2)]		600,000
Variable manufacturing overhead costs		1,800,000
Fixed manufacturing overhead costs		1,200,000
Total manufacturing overhead costs		$3,000,000

Fixed manufacturing overhead per bottling hour = $1,200,000 ÷ 3,000 = $400. Note that the total number of bottling hours is 3,000 hours : 2,000 hours for Lemonade (2 hours per lot × 1,000 lots) plus 1,000 hours for Diet Lemonade (2 hours per lot × 500 lots).

7. **Schedule 6B : Ending Inventory Budget**
   December 31, 2000

	Units (Lots)	Cost per Unit (Lot)	Total	
Direct materials:				
Syrup for Lemonade	30	$1,200	$ 36,000	
Syrup for Diet Lemonade	20	1,100	22,000	
Containers	100	1,000	100,000	
Packaging	200	800	160,000	$318,000

	Units	Cost per Unit	Total	
Finished goods:				
Lemonade	20	$5,500*	$110,000	
Diet Lemonade	10	5,400*	54,000	164,000
Total ending inventory				$482,000

*From Schedule 6A below

Schedule 6A : Computation of Unit Costs of Manufacturing Finished Goods
For the Year Ended December 31, 2000

	Cost per Unit (Lot) or Hour of Input	Lemonade		Diet Lemonade	
		Inputs in Units (Lots) or Hours	Amount	Inputs in Units (Lots) or Hours	Hour
Syrup			$1,200		$1,100
Containers			1,000		1,000
Packaging			800		800
Direct manufacturing labour	$ 25	20	500	20	500
Variable manufacturing overhead*	600	2	1,200	2	1,200
Fixed manufacturing overhead*	400	2	800	2	800
Total			$5,500		$5,400

* Variable manufacturing overhead varies with bottling hours (2 hours per lot for both Lemonade and Diet Lemonade). Fixed manufacturing overhead is allocated on the basis of bottling hours at the rate of $400 per bottling hour calculated in Schedule 5.

8. ### Schedule 7 : Cost of Goods Sold Budget
For the Year Ended December 31, 2000

	From Schedule		Total
Beginning finished goods inventory, January 1, 2000	Given*		$ 790,000
Direct materials used	3A	$4,465,000	
Direct manufacturing labour	4	750,000	
Manufacturing overhead	5	3,000,000	
Cost of goods manufactured			8,215,000
Cost of goods available for sale			9,005,000
Deduct ending finished goods inventory, December 31, 2000	6		164,000
Cost of goods sold			$8,841,000

* Given in description of basic data and requirements (Lemonade, $5,300 × 100; Diet Lemonade, $5,200 × 50)

6-38 (cont'd)

9.   **Schedule 8 : Marketing Costs Budget**
For the Year ended December 31, 2000
Marketing costs, 12% × Sales, $14,310,000 $1,717,200

10.   **Schedule 9 : Distribution Costs Budget**
For the Year ended December 31, 2000
Distribution costs, 8% × Sales, $14,310,000 $1,144,800

11.   **Schedule 10 : Administration Costs Budget**
For the Year ended December 31, 2000
Administration costs
    10% × Cost of goods manufactured, $8,215,000 $821,500

12.   **Budgeted Income Statement**
For the Year ended December 31, 2000

Sales	Schedule 1		$14,310,000
Cost of goods sold	Schedule 7		8,841,000
Gross margin			5,469,000
Operating costs:			
Marketing costs	Schedule 8	$1,717,200	
Distribution costs	Schedule 9	1,144,800	
Administration costs	Schedule 10	821,500	
Total operating costs			3,683,500
Operating income			$ 1,785,500

6-40 (40-50 min.) **Cash budgeting.**

Itami Wholesale Co.
Statement of Budgeted Cash Receipts and Disbursements
For the Months of December 2000, and January 2001

	December 2000	January 2001
Cash balance, beginning	$ 10,000	$ 2,025
Add receipts:		
Collections of receivables (schedule 1)	235,900	285,800
Total cash available for needs (a)	245,900	287,825
Deduct disbursements:		
For merchandise purchases (schedule 2)	183,875	141,750
For variable costs (schedule 3)	50,000	25,000
For fixed costs (schedule 3)	10,000	10,000
Total disbursements (b)	243,875	176,750
Cash balance, end of month [(a) – (b)]	$ 2,025	$111,075

Enough cash should be available for repayment of the note on January 31, 2001.

Schedule 1: Collections of Receivables

Collections in	October	November	December	Total
December	$14,400[a]	50,000[b]		
		171,500[c]		$235,900
January		20,000[d]	60,000[e]	
			205,800[f]	$285,800

[a] 0.08 × $180,000 [b] 0.20 × $250,000 [c] 0.70 × $250,000 × 0.98
[d] 0.08 × $250,000 [e] 0.20 × $300,000 [f] 0.70 × $300,000 × 0.98

Schedule 2: Payments for Merchandise

	December	January
Target ending inventory (in units)	875 [a]	800 [c]
Add units sold (Sales ÷ $100)	3,000	1,500
Total requirements	3,875	2,300
Deduct beginning inventory (in units)	1,250 [b]	875
Purchases (in units)	2,625	1,425
Purchases in dollars (units × $70)	$183,750	$99,750

	December	January
Cash disbursements:		
For previous month's purchases at 50%	$ 92,000	$ 91,875
For current month's purchases at 50%	91,875	49,875
	$183,875	$141,750

[a] 500 units + 0.25($150,000 ÷ $100) [b] $87,500 ÷ $70 [c] 500 units + 0.25($120,000 ÷ $100)

6-40 (cont'd)

Schedule 3: Marketing, Distribution, and Customer Service Costs

Total annual fixed costs, $150,000, minus $30,000 amortization	$120,000
Monthly fixed cost requiring cash outlay	$ 10,000

$$\text{Variable cost ratio to sales} = \frac{\$400,000 - \$150,000}{\$1,500,000} = 1/6$$

December variable costs: 1/6 × $300,000 sales	=	$50,000
January variable costs: 1/6 × $150,000 sales	=	$25,000

6-42   (15 min.) **Budgetary slack and ethics.**

The use of budgetary slack, particularly if it has a detrimental effect on the company, may be unethical. In assessing the situation, the management accountant should consider the following:

Competence
Clear reports using relevant and reliable information should be prepared. Reports prepared on the basis of incorrect revenue or cost projections would violate the management accountant's responsibility for competence. Ford's and Granger's performances would appear to look better than they actually are because their performances are being compared with understated and unreliable budgets.

Integrity
Any activity that subverts the legitimate goals of the company should be avoided. Incorrect reporting of revenue and cost budgets could be viewed as violating the responsibility for integrity. The management accountant should communicate unfavourable as well as favourable information. Atkins will probably regard Ford's and Granger's behaviour as unethical because it is attempting to project their results in a favourable light.

Objectivity
The management accountant should require that information be fairly and objectively communicated and that all relevant information be disclosed. From a management accountant's standpoint, Ford and Granger are clearly violating both these precepts. For the various reasons cited above, Atkins should take the position that the behaviour described by Ford and Granger is unethical.

7-2   Sources of information about budgeted amounts include (a) past amounts, and (b) detailed engineering studies.

7-4   The key difference is the output level used to set the budget. A *static budget* is based on the level of output planned at the *start of the budget period*. A *flexible budget* is developed using budgeted revenues or cost amounts based on the level of output actually achieved in the budget period. The actual level of output is not known until the *end of the budget period*.

7-6   The steps in developing a flexible budget are:

Step 1:   Determine the budgeted selling price per unit, the budgeted variable costs per unit, and the budgeted fixed costs.

Step 2:   Determine the actual quantity of the revenue driver.

Step 3:   Determine the flexible budget for revenue based on the budgeted unit revenue and the actual quantity of the revenue driver.

Step 4:   Determine the actual quantity of the cost driver(s).

Step 5:   Determine the flexible budget for costs based on the budgeted unit variable costs and fixed costs and the actual quantity of the cost driver(s).

7-8   A manager should decompose the flexible-budget variance for direct materials into a price variance and an efficiency variance. The individual causes of these variances can then be investigated, recognizing possible interdependencies across these individual causes.

7-10   Direct materials price variances are often computed at the time of purchase while direct materials efficiency variances are often computed at the time of usage. Purchasing managers are typically responsible for price variances, while production managers are typically responsible for usage variances.

7-12   An individual business function, such as production, is interdependent with other business functions. Factors outside of production can explain why variances arise in the production area. For example.
   - poor design of products or processes can lead to a sizable number of defects, and
   - marketing personnel making promises for delivery times that require a large number of rush orders that create production-scheduling difficulties.

7-14 Variances can be calculated at the activity level as well as at the company level. For example, a price variance and an efficiency variance can be computed for an activity area.

7-16 (20-30 min.) **Flexible budget.**

	Actual Results (1)	Flexible-Budget Variances (2) = (1) − (3)	Flexible Budget (3)	Sales-Volume Variances (4) = (3)−(5)	Static Budget (5)
Units sold	2,800^G		2,800		3,000^G
Revenues	$313,600^a	5,600 F	$308,000^b	$22,000 U	$330,000^c
Variable costs	229,600^d	22,400 U	207,200^e	14,800 F	222,000^f
Contribution margin	84,000	16,800 U	100,800	7,200 U	108,000
Fixed costs	50,000^G	4,000 F	54,000^G	0	54,000^G
Operating income	$ 34,000	$12,800 U	$ 46,800	$ 7,200 U	$ 54,000

$12,800 U → Total flexible-budget variance

$ 7,200 U → Total sales-volume variance

$20,000 U → Total static-budget variance

^{a} $112 × 2,800 = $313,600
^{b} $110 × 2,800 = $308,000
^{c} $110 × 3,000 = $330,000
^{d} Given. Unit variable cost = $229,600 ÷ 2,800 = $82 per tire
^{e} $74 × 2,800 = $207,200
^{f} $74 × 3,000 = $222,000
^{G} Given

2. The key information items are:

	Actual	Budgeted
Units	2,800	3,000
Unit selling price	$ 112	$ 110
Unit variable cost	$ 82	$ 74
Fixed costs	$50,000	$54,000

The total static-budget variance in operating income is $20,000 U. There is both an unfavourable total flexible-budget variance ($12,800) and an unfavourable sales-volume variance ($7,200).

The unfavourable sales-volume variance arises solely because actual units manufactured and sold were 200 fewer than the budgeted 3,000 units. The unfavourable static-budget variance of $12,800 in operating income is due primarily to the $8 increase in unit variable costs. This increase in unit variable costs is only partially offset by the $2 increase in unit selling price and the $4,000 decrease in fixed costs.

7-18 (10 min.)   **Flexible budget.**

1.

Static-budget variance	=	Actual results	−	Static-budget amount
	=	$6,556,000	−	$3,150,000
	=	$3,406,000 F		

2.

Flexible-budget variance	=	Actual results	−	Flexible-budget amount
	=	$6,556,000	−	$6,930,000
	=	$ 374,000 U		

Sales-volume variance	=	Flexible-budget amount	−	Static-budget amount
	=	$6,930,000	−	$3,150,000
	=	$3,780,000 F		

3.

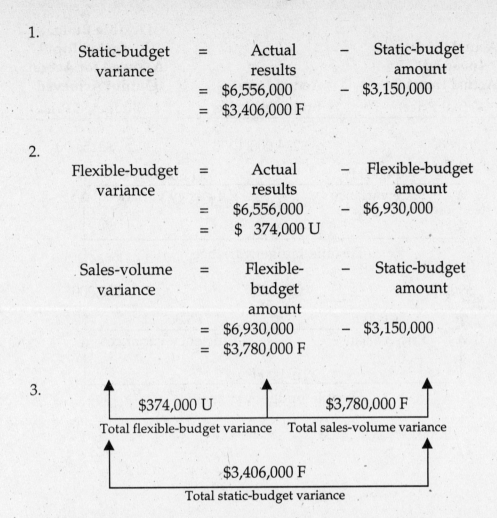

$374,000 U $3,780,000 F

Total flexible-budget variance   Total sales-volume variance

$3,406,000 F

Total static-budget variance

The total flexible-budget variance is $374,000 unfavourable. This arises because for the actual output level: (a) selling prices were lower than budgeted, or (b) variable costs were higher than budgeted, or (c) fixed costs were higher than budgeted, or (d) some combination of (a), (b), and (c) existed.

7-20 (15 min.) **Materials and manufacturing labour variances.**

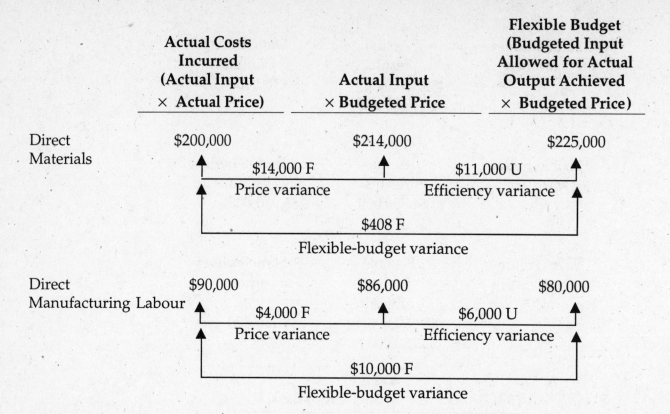

7-22 (30-40 min.)   **Comprehensive variance analysis.**

1.

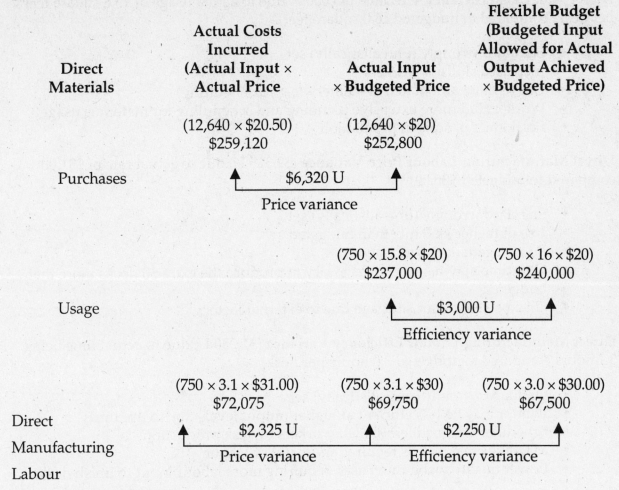

Direct Materials	Actual Costs Incurred (Actual Input × Actual Price	Actual Input × Budgeted Price	Flexible Budget (Budgeted Input Allowed for Actual Output Achieved × Budgeted Price)
	(12,640 × $20.50) $259,120	(12,640 × $20) $252,800	
Purchases	↑ $6,320 U ↑ Price variance		
		(750 × 15.8 × $20) $237,000	(750 × 16 × $20) $240,000
Usage		↑ $3,000 U ↑ Efficiency variance	
	(750 × 3.1 × $31.00) $72,075	(750 × 3.1 × $30) $69,750	(750 × 3.0 × $30.00) $67,500
Direct Manufacturing Labour	↑ $2,325 U ↑ Price variance	↑ $2,250 U ↑ Efficiency variance	

2.   **Direct Materials Price Variance** ($6,320 U, due to actual price of $20.50 exceeding budgeted price of $20.00)

- Standard wrongly (unrealistically) set
- Poor price negotiation
- Purchase of higher quality wood
- Materials price unexpectedly increased due to external shocks (e.g., a natural disaster in major forest areas)
- Purchased in smaller lot sizes than budgeted and did not get quantity discounts
- Change in supplier when lower-priced supplier went out of business

Direct Materials Efficiency Variance ($3,000 F, due to actual usage of 15.8 square feet per desk, compared to budgeted 16.0 square feet)

- Standard wrongly (unrealistically) set
- Increased skills of workers
- Use of more automated machinery (e.g., laser cutting)
- Workers did more extensive planning and scheduling for materials usage
- Economies of scale in production

Direct Manufacturing Labour Price Variance ($2,325 U, due to actual rate of $31.00 compared to budgeted $30.00)

- Standard wrongly (unrealistically) set
- Use of higher skill mix than budgeted
- Poor negotiations with labour
- Overtime may have been necessary to produce the extra 50 decks more than budgeted
- Unexpected labour shortage due to external factors

Direct Manufacturing Labour Efficiency Variance ($2,250 U, due to actual time being 3.1 hours compared to budgeted 3.0 hours per desk)

- Standard wrongly (unrealistically) set
- Labour may be less efficient at higher output levels due to tiredness
- Scheduler assigned less skilled workers to desk production
- Machine breakdowns required more use of labour
- Lower quality wood purchased requiring more labour input to finish desks

7-24 (25-30 min.) Flexible budget preparation and analysis.

1. Variance Analysis for Bank Management Printers for September 2000
   Level 1 Analysis

	Actual Results (1)	Static-Budget Variances (2) = (1) – (3)	Static Budget (3)
Units sold	12,000	3,000 U	15,000
Revenue	$252,000 [a]	$ 48,000 U	$300,000 [c]
Variable costs	84,000 [d]	36,000 F	120,000 [f]
Contribution margin	168,000	12,000 U	180,000
Fixed costs	150,000	5,000 U	145,000
Operating income	$ 18,000	$ 17,000 U	$ 35,000

$17,000 U

Total static-budget variance

2. Level 2 Analysis

	Actual Results (1)	Flexible-Budget Variances (2) = (1) – (3)	Flexible Budget (3)	Sales-Volume Variances (4) = (3) – (5)	Static Budget (5)
Units sold	12,000	0	12,000	3,000 U	15,000
Revenue	$252,000 [a]	$12,000 F	$240,000 [b]	$60,000 U	$300,000 [c]
Variable costs	84,000 [d]	12,000 F	96,000 [e]	24,000 F	120,000 [f]
Contribution margin	168,000	24,000 F	144,000	36,000 U	180,000
Fixed costs	150,000	5,000 U	145,000	0	145,000
Operating income	$ 18,000	$19,000 F	$ (1,000)	$36,000 U	$ 35,000

$19,000 F $36,000 U

Total flexible-budget variance   Total sales-volume variance

$17,000 U

Total static-budget variance

[a] 12,000 × $21 = $252,000
[b] 12,000 × $20 = $240,000
[c] 15,000 × $20 = $300,000
[d] 12,000 × $7 = $ 84,000
[e] 12,000 × $8 = $ 96,000
[f] 15,000 × $8 = $120,000

3. Level 2 analysis provides a breakdown of the static-budget variance into a flexible-budget variance and a sales-volume variance. The primary reason for the static-budget variance being unfavourable ($17,000 U) is the reduction in unit volume from the budgeted 15,000 to an actual 12,000. One explanation for this reduction is the increase in selling price from a budgeted $20 to an actual $21. Operating management was able to reduce variable costs by $12,000 relative to the flexible budget. This reduction could be a sign of efficient management. Alternatively, it could be due to using lower-quality materials (which in turn adversely affected unit volume).

7-26 (30 min.) **Flexible-budget variances for finance function activities.**

1.

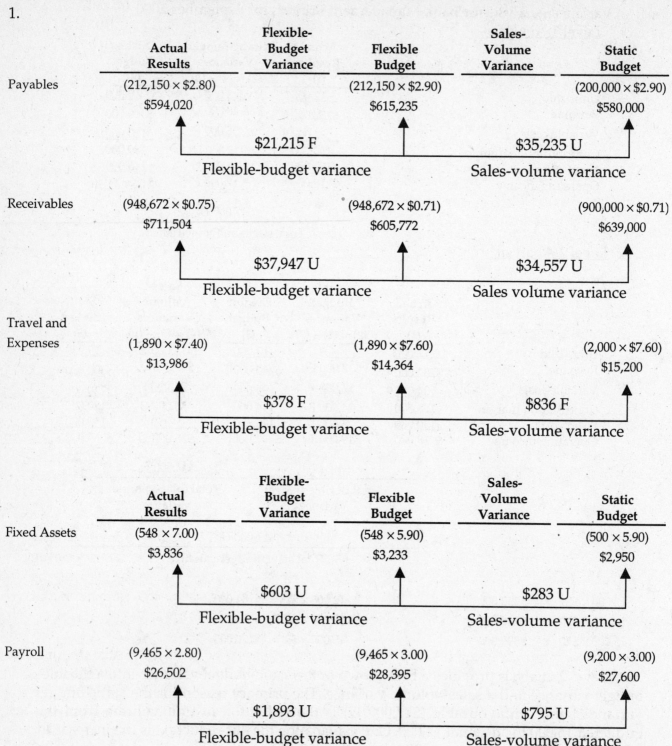

	Actual Results	Flexible-Budget Variance	Flexible Budget	Sales-Volume Variance	Static Budget
Payables	(212,150 × $2.80) $594,020	$21,215 F	(212,150 × $2.90) $615,235	$35,235 U	(200,000 × $2.90) $580,000
		Flexible-budget variance		Sales-volume variance	
Receivables	(948,672 × $0.75) $711,504	$37,947 U	(948,672 × $0.71) $605,772	$34,557 U	(900,000 × $0.71) $639,000
		Flexible-budget variance		Sales volume variance	
Travel and Expenses	(1,890 × $7.40) $13,986	$378 F	(1,890 × $7.60) $14,364	$836 F	(2,000 × $7.60) $15,200
		Flexible-budget variance		Sales-volume variance	
Fixed Assets	(548 × 7.00) $3,836	$603 U	(548 × 5.90) $3,233	$283 U	(500 × 5.90) $2,950
		Flexible-budget variance		Sales-volume variance	
Payroll	(9,465 × 2.80) $26,502	$1,893 U	(9,465 × 3.00) $28,395	$795 U	(9,200 × 3.00) $27,600
		Flexible-budget variance		Sales-volume variance	

7-26 (cont'd)

Comparison of the unit costs per finance activity are:

	Actual Cost	Budgeted Cost	(Actual Cost −Budgeted Cost) Budgeted Cost
Payables	$2.80	$2.900	−3.4%
Receivables	0.75	0.639	17.4%
Travel	7.40	7.600	−2.6%
Fixed Assets	7.00	5.90	15.7%
Payroll	2.80	3.00	−7.1%

Receivables are an output-level unit-driven activity. The unfavourable flexible-budget variance for receivables reflects the actual cost per remittance ($0.750) exceeding the budgeted amount ($0.71).

Changes in output levels show up as sales-volume variances. When actual volume exceeds the budgeted amount, the sales-volume variance is unfavourable for cost items. The sales-volume variance is favourable when actual output is less than the budgeted amount for cost items. The actual output level (948,000 deliveries/remittances) is less than the budgeted output level (1,000,000 deliveries/remittances). Hence, the sales-volume variance for costs is favourable for each of the three finance activities.

2. *Efficiency* measures the relative amount of inputs used to achieve a given level of output. *Effectiveness* measures the degree to which a predetermined objective or target is met.

The variances do not examine the extent to which the finance activities help Flowers.net achieve its objective(s). Suppose this objective is to maximize operating income. Chase would want to examine how, say, changes in the cost of processing travel visit reimbursements affects operating income. For example, what is the effect of delays or errors in processing travel reimbursements?

3. To further assess efficiency, the flexible budget variances should be separated into price and usage variances and monitored over time.

7-28 (30 min.) **Price and efficiency variances, journal entries.**

1. Direct materials and direct manufacturing labour are analyzed in turn:

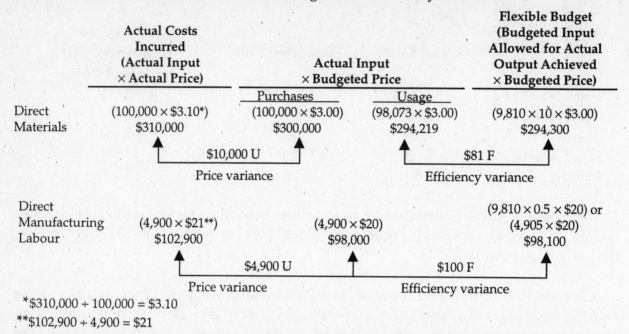

	Actual Costs Incurred (Actual Input × Actual Price)	Actual Input × Budgeted Price		Flexible Budget (Budgeted Input Allowed for Actual Output Achieved × Budgeted Price)
		Purchases	Usage	
Direct Materials	(100,000 × $3.10*) $310,000	(100,000 × $3.00) $300,000	(98,073 × $3.00) $294,219	(9,810 × 10 × $3.00) $294,300
		$10,000 U ← Price variance →	$81 F ← Efficiency variance →	
Direct Manufacturing Labour	(4,900 × $21**) $102,900	(4,900 × $20) $98,000		(9,810 × 0.5 × $20) or (4,905 × $20) $98,100
		$4,900 U ← Price variance →	$100 F ← Efficiency variance →	

*$310,000 ÷ 100,000 = $3.10
**$102,900 ÷ 4,900 = $21

Some students' comments will be immersed in conjecture about higher prices for materials, better quality materials, higher grade labour, better efficiency in use of materials, and so forth. A possibility is that approximately the same labour force is taking slightly less time with better materials and causing less waste and spoilage.

A key point in this problem is that all of these efficiency variances are likely to be insignificant. They are so small as to be nearly meaningless. Fluctuations about standards are bound to occur in a random fashion. Practically, from a control viewpoint, a standard is a band or range of acceptable performance rather than a single-figure measure.

2.
Materials Control	$300,000	
Direct Materials Price Variance	10,000	
Accounts Payable or Cash Control		$310,000
Work in Process Control	$294,300	
Materials Control		$294,219
Direct Materials Efficiency Variance		81
Work in Process Control	$98,100	
Direct Labour Price Variance	4,900	
Wages Payable Control		$102,900
Direct Labour Efficiency Variance		100

3.   The *purchasing point* is where responsibility for price variances is found most often. The *production point* is where responsibility for efficiency variances is found most often. Chemical Inc. may calculate variances at different points in time to tie in with these different responsibility areas.

7-30 (20-30 min.) **Materials and manufacturing labour variances, standard costs.**

1.   Direct Materials

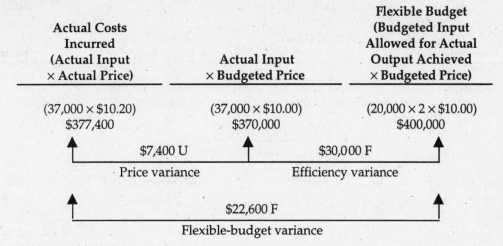

The unfavourable materials price variance may be unrelated to the favourable efficiency variance. For example, (a) the purchasing officer may be less skillful than assumed in the budget, or (b) there was an unexpected increase in materials price per square metre due to reduced competition. Similarly, the favourable materials efficiency variance may be unrelated to the unfavourable price variance. For example, (a) the production manager may have been able to employ higher-skilled workers, or (b) the budgeted time standards were set too loosely. It is also possible that the two variances are interrelated. The higher materials input price may be due to higher quality materials being purchased.

Direct Manufacturing Labour

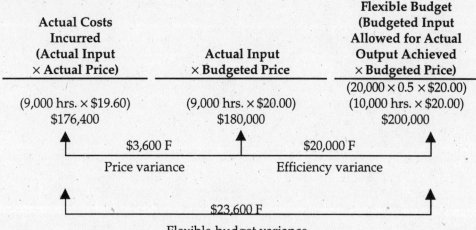

The favourable labour price variance may be due to (say) (a) a reduction in labour rates due to a recession, or (b) the standard being set without detailed analysis of labour compensation. The favourable labour efficiency variance may be due to (say) (a) more efficient workers being employed, or (b) a redesign in the plant enabling labour to be more productive.

7-30 (cont'd)

2.

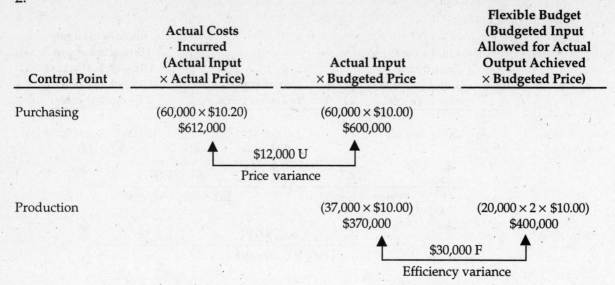

Control Point	Actual Costs Incurred (Actual Input × Actual Price)	Actual Input × Budgeted Price	Flexible Budget (Budgeted Input Allowed for Actual Output Achieved × Budgeted Price)
Purchasing	(60,000 × $10.20) $612,000	(60,000 × $10.00) $600,000	
		$12,000 U Price variance	
Production		(37,000 × $10.00) $370,000	(20,000 × 2 × $10.00) $400,000
		$30,000 F Efficiency variance	

7-32 (25 min.) **Flexible budget (continuation of 7-30 and 7-31).**

The manager's glee may be warranted, but the magnitude of the favourable variances may be deceptively large. Furthermore, if the manager had aimed at a scheduled production of 24,000 units, he or she may be troubled at the inability to attain that output target. A more detailed analysis underscores the fact that the world of variances may be divided into three general parts: price, efficiency, and what is labelled here as a sales-volume variance. Failure to pinpoint these three categories muddies the analytical task. The clearer analysis follows (in dollars):

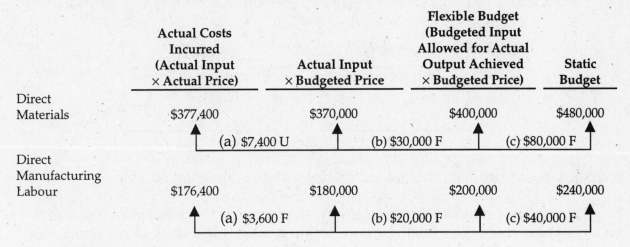

	Actual Costs Incurred (Actual Input × Actual Price)		Actual Input × Budgeted Price		Flexible Budget (Budgeted Input Allowed for Actual Output Achieved × Budgeted Price)		Static Budget
Direct Materials	$377,400		$370,000		$400,000		$480,000
		(a) $7,400 U		(b) $30,000 F		(c) $80,000 F	
Direct Manufacturing Labour	$176,400		$180,000		$200,000		$240,000
		(a) $3,600 F		(b) $20,000 F		(c) $40,000 F	

(a) Price variance
(b) Efficiency variance
(c) Sales-volume variance

The sales-volume variances are favourable here in the sense that less cost would be expected solely because the output level is less than budgeted. However, this is an example of how variances must be interpreted cautiously. The general manager may be incensed at the failure to reach scheduled production (it may mean fewer sales) even though the 20,000 units were turned out with supreme efficiency. Sometimes this phenomenon is called being efficient but ineffective, where effectiveness is defined as the ability to reach original targets and efficiency is the optimal relationship of inputs to any given outputs. Note that a target can be reached in an efficient or inefficient way; similarly, as this problem illustrates, a target can be missed but the given output can be attained efficiently.

7-34 (15 min.) **Professional labour efficiency and effectiveness (continuation of 7-33).**

1.

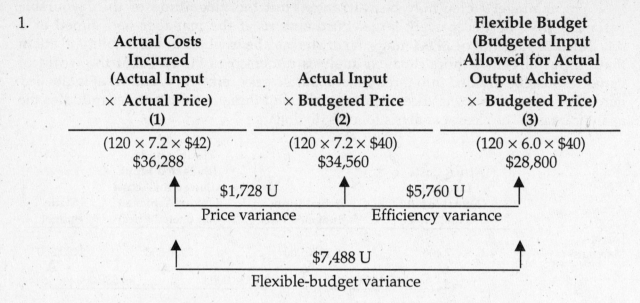

Actual Costs Incurred (Actual Input × Actual Price) (1)	Actual Input × Budgeted Price (2)	Flexible Budget (Budgeted Input Allowed for Actual Output Achieved × Budgeted Price) (3)
(120 × 7.2 × $42) $36,288	(120 × 7.2 × $40) $34,560	(120 × 6.0 × $40) $28,800

$1,728 U — Price variance $5,760 U — Efficiency variance

$7,488 U — Flexible-budget variance

Both the labour price and the labour efficiency variances are unfavourable.

2.   Effectiveness refers to the degree to which a predetermined objective or target is met. One objective of Meridian Finance for professional labour is to maximize loan-based revenue (1/2% of loans × # of loans). The professional staff has increased loans from a budgeted 90 to 120, a very sizable increase. Moreover the average loan amount increased from a budgeted $200,000 to $224,000. The result is an increase in revenues from a budgeted $1,000 per loan to $1,120 per loan.

With both a higher number of loans and a higher average amount per loan, there was an increase in the effectiveness of professional labour in November 2000.

7-36 (30-35 min.) **Flexible and static budgets, service company.**

1.

(in thousands)	Budgeted Amount per Revenue Dollar	Flexible-Budget Amounts		
Revenues		$9,000	$10,000	$11,000
Variable costs:				
Fuel	$0.10	900	1,000	1,100
Repairs and maintenance	0.01	90	100	110
Supplies and miscellaneous	0.02	180	200	220
Variable labour payroll	0.57	5,130	5,700	6,270
Variable costs	$0.70	6,300	7,000	7,700
Fixed costs:				
Supervision		200	200	200
Rent		200	200	200
Depreciation		1,600	1,600	1,600
Other fixed costs		200	200	200
Fixed costs		2,200	2,200	2,200
Total costs		8,500	9,200	9,900
Operating income		$ 500	$ 800	$ 1,100

2. Total costs per quarter = $2,200,000 + ($0.70 \times R)$
where R = total revenue dollars.

3.

(in thousands)	Actual Results (1)	Flexible-Budget Variances (2)=(1) – (3)	Flexible Budget (3)	Sales-Volume Variances (4) = (3) – (5)	Static Budget (5)
Revenues	$9,500	$ 0	$9,500	$500 U	$10,000
Variable costs	6,780	130 U	6,650	350 F	7,000
Contribution margin	2,720	130 U	2,850	150 U	3,000
Fixed costs	2,200	0	2,200	0	2,200
Operating income	$ 520	$130 U	$ 650	$150 U	$ 800

$130 U $150 U

Total flexible-budget variance   Total sales-volume variance

$280 U

Total static-budget variance

7-38 (30 min.) **Benchmarking, hospital cost comparisons.**

1.   Detailed cost studies of the kind developed by Market Insights can provide insight into one critical area of Horn's performance—that is, cost management.

Horn apparently believes in an "ask no questions" approach in relation to cost management. When an institution is running large deficits, this approach is totally unacceptable. (Even if surpluses were occurring, an "ask no questions" approach is not appropriate.) Horn is correct in noting that in many areas of hospital administration, it is not possible to have well-defined relationships between inputs and outputs. He is also correct in observing that "good output" is difficult to define. However, neither point means that he cannot learn from a study that shows the cost management skills of other hospitals doing similar operations to PUH.

2.   The main inference is that PUH has well-above-average cost levels. At the aggregate hospital level, its cost structure is 20% above the average cost. Even more disconcerting, it is over 70% more costly than hospitals E, C and J.

PUH is above average cost for five of the six diagnostic groups listed. Even more disconcerting is the magnitude of the difference between PUH and the 25th percentile for five of the six diagnostic groups:

	Ratio of PUH to 25th Percentile
Angina, chest pain	1.33
Asthma, bronchitis	1.48
Skin disorders, cellulitis	1.48
Renal failure & dialysis	1.81
Diabetes	1.81
Gastroenteritis	0.75

3.   Smith could use the MI benchmark cost report as an attention-directing mechanism. It provides some quantitative data to use with PUH managers when discussing cost management. The onus could be put on PUH managers to explain why their cost structure is so far above average.

Smith might also consider using the MI reports in subsequent performance evaluation of PUH managers. Targets could be set for the managers to reduce (say) the gap between PUH and the 25th percentile.

4.   Horn might make the following criticisms of the MI benchmark cost reports:
    (a)   The reports focus only on cost—they are "a cost accountant's view of the world."
    (b)   The reports rely on data hospitals submit to various regulatory bodies. These reports likely serve different purposes and hence may not be appropriate to use for cost comparisons.
    (c)   Cost accounting systems of hospitals are of highly variable quality. Horn probably would argue "garbage-in garbage-out" applies to this data.

7-38 (cont'd)

5.   Other factors include:
    (a)   The perceived (and actual) quality of service provided to patients.
    (b)   The success rate of operations.
    (c)   The morale of the doctors, nurses, and other staff.
Being a university hospital, other factors would also likely be important, including:
    (d)   The teaching ability of doctors at the hospital.
    (e)   The research record of doctors at the hospital.

7-40 (60 min.) **Comprehensive variance analysis, responsibility issues.**

1. (a) Actual selling price = $82.00
       Budgeted selling price = $80.00
       Actual sales volume = 4,850 units
       Selling price variance = (Actual Sales Price – Budgeted Sales Price) × Actual Units
       = ($82 – $80) × 4,850 = $9,700 Favourable
   (b) Development of Flexible Budget

	Budgeted Unit Amounts	Actual Volume	Flexible Budget Amount
Revenues	$80.00	4,850	$388,000
Variable costs			
DM–Frames	$ 2.20 × 3.00 6.60	4,850	32,010
DM–Lenses	3.10 × 6.00 18.60	4,850	90,210
Direct Labour	15.00 × 1.20 18.00	4,850	87,300
Total variable manufacturing costs			$209,520
Fixed manufacturing costs			75,000
Total manufacturing cost			284,520
Gross margin			$103,480

	Actual Results (1)	Flexible-Budget Variances (2)=(1)–(3)	Flexible Budget (3)	Sales - Volume Variance (4)=(3)–(5)	Static Budget (5)
Units sold	4,850		4,850		5,000
Revenues	$397,700	$ 9,700 F	$388,000	$ 12,000 U	$400,000
Variable costs					
DM–frames	37,248	5,238 U	32,010	990 F	33,000
DM–lens	100,492	10,282 U	90,210	2,790 F	93,000
Direct labour	96,903	9,603 U	87,300	2,700 F	90,000
Total variable costs	234,643	25,123 U	209,520	6,480 F	216,000
Fixed manuf. costs	72,265	2,735 F	75,000	0	75,000
Total costs	306,908	22,388 U	284,520	6,480 F	291,000
Gross margin	$ 90,792	$12,688 U	$103,480	$ 5,520 U	$109,000

(c) **Price and Efficiency Variances**

DM: Frames—Actual grams used = 3.20 per unit × 4,850 units = 15,520 grams
Price per gram = $37,248/15,520 = $2.40

DM: Lenses—Actual grams used = 7.00 per unit × 4,850 units = 33,950 grams
Price per gram = $100,492/33,950 = $2.96

Direct Labour—Actual labour hours = $96,903/14.80 = 6,547.5 hours
Labour hours per unit = 6,547.5/4,850 units = 1.35 hours per unit

	Actual Costs Incurred (Actual Input × Actual Price) (1)	Actual Input × Budgeted Price (2)	Flexible Budget (Budgeted Input Allowed for Actual Output × Budgeted Price) (3)
Direct Materials: Frames	(4,850 × 3.2 × $2.40) $37,248	(4,850 × 3.2 × $2.20) $34,144	(4,850 × 3.00 × $2.20) $32,010
	↑ $3,104 U Price variance	↑ $2,134 U Efficiency variance	↑
Direct Materials: Lenses	(4,850 × 7.0 × $2.96) $100,492	(4,850 × 7.0 × $3.10) $105,245	(4,850 × 6.00 × $3.10) $90,210
	↑ $4,753 F Price variance	↑ $15,035 U Efficiency variance	↑
Direct Manufacturing Labour	(4,850 × 1.35 × $14.80) $96,903	(4,850 × 1.35 × $15.00) $98,212.50	(4,850 × 1.20 × $15.00) $87,300
	↑ $1,309.50 F Price variance	↑ $10,912.50 U Efficiency variance	↑

7-40 (cont'd)

Frames:
Possible explanations for the price variance of $3,104 U:
(a)   Increase in purchase prices
(b)   Purchasing frames of higher quality
(c)   Standards were set incorrectly

Possible explanations for the efficiency variance of $2,134 U:
(a)   Frames damaged in manufacturing
(b)   Frames lost or stolen
(c)   Standards were set incorrectly

Lenses:
Possible explanations for price variance of $4,753 F:
(a)   Astute negotiations in purchasing
(b)   Lower quality lenses purchased at lower price
(c)   Standards were set incorrectly

Possible explanations for efficiency variance of $15,035 U:
(a)   Higher materials usage due to lower quality lenses purchased at lower price
(b)   Lesser trained workers hired at lower rates result in higher materials
(c)   Standards were set incorrectly

Labour:
Possible explanations for the price variance of $1,309.50 F:
(a)   Less overtime wages paid
(b)   Lower skilled employees hired
(c)   Standards were set incorrectly

Possible explanations for the efficiency variance of $10,912.50 U:
(a)   Too much down time in the production schedule
(b)   Workers and equipment operating slower
(c)   Standards were not set correctly

7-40 (cont'd)

2. Possible explanations for price variance of $4,753 F:
   (a) Astute negotiations in purchasing.
   (b) Lower quality lenses purchased at lower price.
   (c) Standards were set incorrectly.

   Possible explanations for efficiency variance of $15,035 U:
   (a) Higher materials usage because of lower quality lenses purchased at lower price.
   (b) Lesser trained workers hired at lower rates result in higher materials usage.
   (c) Standards were set incorrectly.

7-42 (30 min.)   **Variance analysis, solve for unknowns.**

1. Budgeted selling price $= \dfrac{\$4,800,000}{600,000} = \$8.00$ per cap

   Actual selling price $= \dfrac{\$5,000,000}{500,000} = \$10.00$ per cap

2. Budgeted variable cost per unit $= \dfrac{\$1,800,000}{600,000} = \$3.00$ per unit

   Actual variable cost per unit $= \dfrac{\$1,400,000}{500,000} = \$2.80$ per unit

3, 4, 5, and 6.

	Actual Results (1)	Flexible-Budget Variances (2)=(1)−(3)	Flexible Budget (3)	Sales-Volume Variance (4)=(3)−(5)	Static Budget (5)
Units sold	500,000	0	500,000	100,000 U	600,000
Revenues (sales)	$5,000,000	$1,000,000 F	$4,000,000	$800,000 U	$4,800,000
Variable costs	1,400,000	100,000 F	1,500,000	300,000 F	1,800,000
Contribution margin	3,600,000	1,100,000 F	2,500,000	500,000 U	3,000,000
Fixed costs	1,150,000	150,000 U	1,000,000	0	1,000,000
Operating income	$2,450,000	$950,000 F	$1,500,000	$500,000 U	$2,000,000

$950,000 F
Total flexible-budget variance

$500,000 U
Total sales-volume variance

$450,000 F
Total static-budget variance

Total flexible-budget variance = $950,000 F

Total sales-volume variance = $500,000 U

Total static-budget variance = $450,000 F

7-44 (60 min.) Comprehensive variance analysis review.

1. **Actual Results:**

Units sold	1,200,000
Selling price per unit	$3.70
Revenues	$4,440,000
Direct materials purchased and used:	
Total direct materials cost	$960,000
Direct materials per unit	$0.80
Direct manufacturing labour:	
Total direct manufacturing labour costs	$72,000
Manufacturing labour-hours of input	4,800
Labour productivity per hour	250
Actual manufacturing rate per hour	$15
Direct marketing labour:	
Total direct marketing costs	$360,000
Direct marketing cost per unit	$0.30
Fixed costs	$870,000

Static Budgeted Amounts

Units sold	1,500,000
Selling price per unit	$4.00
Revenues	$6,000,000
Direct materials purchased and used:	
Direct materials per unit	$0.85
Total direct materials costs	$1,275,000
Direct manufacturing labour:	
Direct manufacturing rate per hour	$15.00
Labour productivity per hour	300
Manufacturing labour-hours of input	5,000
Total direct manufacturing labour cost	$75,000
Direct marketing labour	
Direct marketing cost per unit	$0.30
Total direct marketing cost	$450,000
Fixed costs	$900,000

7-44 (cont'd)

2.

	Actual Results	Static-Budgeted Amount
Revenues	$4,440,000	$6,000,000
Variable costs		
Direct materials	960,000	1,275,000
Direct manufacturing labour	72,000	75,000
Direct marketing labour	360,000	450,000
Total variable costs	1,392,000	1,800,000
Contribution margin	3,048,000	4,200,000
Fixed costs	870,000	900,000
Operating income	$2,178,000	$3,300,000

Actual operating income	$2,178,000
Static-budget operating income	3,300,000
Total static-budget variance	$1,122,000 U

7-44 (cont'd)

3, 4, and 5.

	Actual Results	Flexible-Budget Variances	Flexible Budget	Sales-Volume Variances	Static Budget
Units sold	1,200,000	—	1,200,000	—	1,500,000
Revenues	$4,440,000	$360,000 U	$4,800,000	$1,200,000 U	$6,000,000
Variable costs					
Direct materials	960,000	60,000 F	1,020,000	255,000 F	1,275,000
Direct manuf. labour	72,000	12,000 U	60,000	15,000 F	75,000
Direct marketing labour	360,000	0	360,000	90,000 F	450,000
Total variable costs	1,392,000	48,000 F	1,440,000	360,000 F	1,800,000
Contribution margin	3,048,000	312,000 U	3,360,000	840,000 U	4,200,000
Fixed costs	870,000	30,000 F	900,000	0	900,000
Operating income	$2,178,000	$282,000 U	$2,460,000	$840,000 U	$3,300,000

$282,000 U
Total flexible-budget variance

$840,000 U
Total sales-volume variance

$1,122,000 U
Total static-budget variance

6, 7, and 8.

Material Variances:

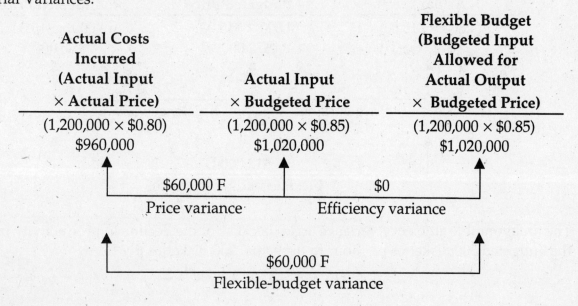

Actual Costs Incurred (Actual Input × Actual Price)		Actual Input × Budgeted Price		Flexible Budget (Budgeted Input Allowed for Actual Output × Budgeted Price)
(1,200,000 × $0.80) $960,000		(1,200,000 × $0.85) $1,020,000		(1,200,000 × $0.85) $1,020,000

$60,000 F
Price variance

$0
Efficiency variance

$60,000 F
Flexible-budget variance

7-44 (cont'd)

Marketing Labour Variances:

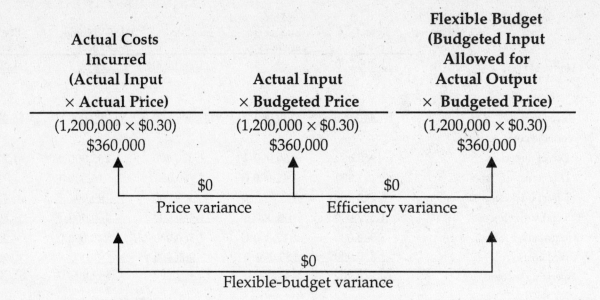

Total price variances = $60,000 F
Total efficiency variances = $12,000 U

Manufacturing Labour Variances:

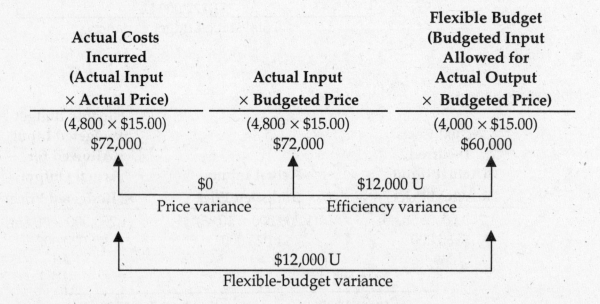

The unfavourable efficiency variance arises because of the decline in productivity from the budgeted 300 diskettes per hour to the actual 250 diskettes per hour.

CHAPTER 8
FLEXIBLE BUDGETS, VARIANCES,
AND MANAGEMENT CONTROL: II

8-2 At the start of an accounting period, a larger percentage of fixed overhead costs are locked-in than is the case with variable overhead costs.

8-4 Steps in developing a budgeted variable-overhead cost rate are:
1. Identify the costs to include in the variable-overhead cost pool(s),
2. Select the cost allocation base(s), and
3. Estimate the budgeted variable-overhead rates(s).

8-6 Reasons for a $25,000 favourable variable-overhead efficiency variance are:
- workers more skillful in using machines than budgeted
- production scheduler was able to schedule jobs better than budgeted, resulting in lower-than-budgeted machine-hours
- machines operated with fewer slowdowns than budgeted
- machine time standards set with padding built in by machine-workers.

8-8 Steps in developing a budgeted fixed-overhead rate are:
Step 1: Choose the time period used to compute the budget,
Step 2: Identify the costs in the fixed-overhead cost pool(s),
Step 3: Estimate the budgeted quantity of the allocation base(s), and
Step 4: Compute the budgeted fixed-overhead rate(s).

8-10 A 4-variance analysis relies on
(a) a breakdown of overhead into its variable and fixed components, and
(b) a breakdown into three components—spending, efficiency, and production volume.

A 3-variance analysis relies only on the breakdown of variances into the three components in (b).

A 2-variance analysis breaks down variances into only two components (flexible-budget and production-volume).

A 1-variance analysis reports only one variance where there is no breakdown of the (a) or (b) categories noted above.

8-12 Variable overhead—efficiency variances
Fixed overhead—production volume variance

8-14 For planning and control purposes, fixed overhead costs are a lump sum amount that is not controlled on a per-unit basis. In contrast, for inventory costing purposes fixed overhead costs are allocated to products on a per-unit basis. See Exhibit 8-4 (page 270) in the text.

8-16 (20 min.) **Variable manufacturing overhead, variance analysis.**

1.

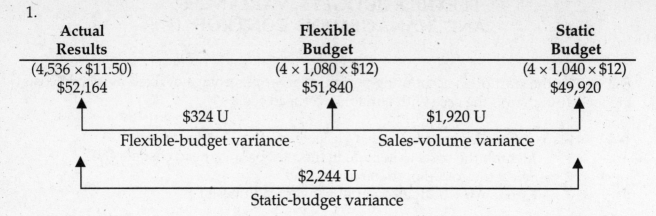

Actual Results	Flexible Budget	Static Budget
(4,536 × $11.50)	(4 × 1,080 × $12)	(4 × 1,040 × $12)
$52,164	$51,840	$49,920

$324 U
Flexible-budget variance

$1,920 U
Sales-volume variance

$2,244 U
Static-budget variance

2.   Esquire manufactured 40 suits more than the 1,040 budgeted. This accounts for the unfavourable sales-volume variance of $1,920 for variable manufacturing overhead.

The actual variable manufacturing overhead of $52,164 exceeds the flexible budget amount of $51,840 for 1,080 suits by $324—hence the flexible budget variance is $324 U.

NOT REQUIRED

Further insight into the flexible-budget variance of $324 U for variable MOH is provided by the spending and efficiency variances:

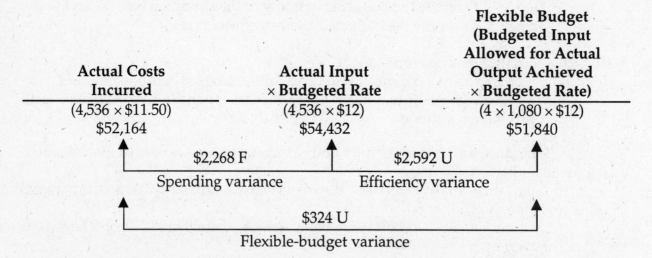

Actual Costs Incurred	Actual Input × Budgeted Rate	Flexible Budget (Budgeted Input Allowed for Actual Output Achieved × Budgeted Rate)
(4,536 × $11.50)	(4,536 × $12)	(4 × 1,080 × $12)
$52,164	$54,432	$51,840

$2,268 F
Spending variance

$2,592 U
Efficiency variance

$324 U
Flexible-budget variance

Esquire had a favourable spending variance of $2,268, (the actual variable overhead rate was $11.50 per direct manufacturing labour-hour versus the $12 budgeted). It had an unfavourable efficiency variance of $2,592 U (each suit average 4.2 labour-hours versus 4.00 budgeted).

8-18 (30 min.) **Variable manufacturing overhead variance analysis.**

1. Denominator level =
   (3,200,000 × 0.02 hours) = 64,000 hours

2.

	Actual Results	Flexible Budget Amount
1. Output units (baguettes)	2,800,000	2,800,000
2. Direct labour-hours	50,400	56,000[a]
3. Labour-hours per output unit (2 ÷ 1)	0.018	0.020
4. Variable MOH costs	$680,400	$560,000
5. Variable MOH per labour-hour (4 ÷ 2)	$13.50	$10
6. Variable MOH per output unit (4 ÷ 1)	$0.243	$0.200

[a]2,800,000 × 0.020= 56,000 hours

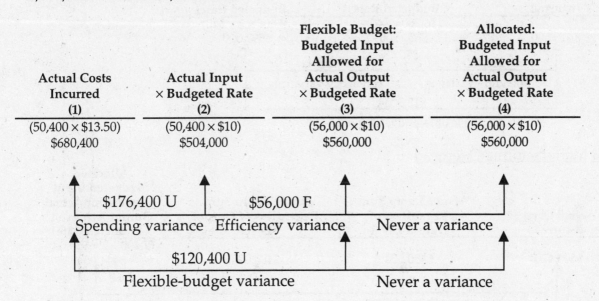

Actual Costs Incurred (1)	Actual Input × Budgeted Rate (2)	Flexible Budget: Budgeted Input Allowed for Actual Output × Budgeted Rate (3)	Allocated: Budgeted Input Allowed for Actual Output × Budgeted Rate (4)
(50,400 × $13.50)	(50,400 × $10)	(56,000 × $10)	(56,000 × $10)
$680,400	$504,000	$560,000	$560,000

$176,400 U $56,000 F

Spending variance   Efficiency variance   Never a variance

$120,400 U

Flexible-budget variance   Never a variance

3. Spending variance of $176,400 U. It is unfavourable because variable manufacturing overhead was 35% higher than planned. A possible explanation could be an increase in energy rates relative to the rate per standard labour-hour assumed in the flexible budget.

Efficiency variance of $56,000 F. It is favourable because the actual number of direct manufacturing labour-hours required was lower than the number of hours budgeted. Labour was more efficient in producing the baguettes than management had anticipated in the budget. This could occur because of improved morale in the company, which could result from an increase in wages or an improvement in the compensation scheme.

Flexible-budget variance of $120,400 U. It is unfavourable because the favourable efficiency variance was not large enough to compensate for the large unfavourable spending variance.

8-20 (30-40 min.) **Manufacturing overhead, variance analysis.**

1. The summary analysis is:

	Spending Variance	Efficiency Variance	Production-Volume Variance
Variable Manufacturing Overhead	$40,700 F	$59,200 U	Never a variance
Fixed-Manufacturing Overhead	$23,420 U	Never a variance	$36,000 U

Variable Manufacturing Overhead

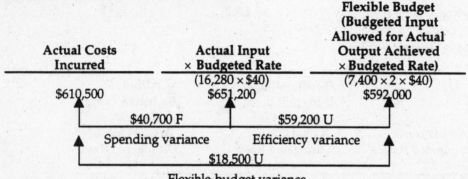

Fixed Manufacturing Overhead

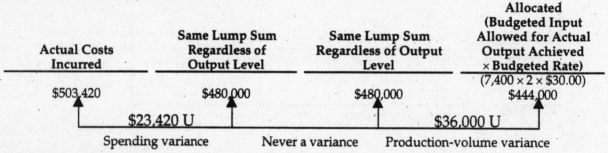

Summary information is:

	Actual	Flexible Budget	Static Budget
Output units	7,400	7,400	8,000
Allocation base (hours)	16,280	14,800[a]	16,000[b]
Allocation base per output unit	2.20	2.00	2.00
Variable MOH	$610,500	$592,000[c]	–
Variable MOH per hour	$37.50[d]	$40.00	–
Fixed MOH	$503,420	$480,000	$480,000
Fixed MOH per hour	$30.92[e]		$30.00[f]

[a] $7,400 \times 2.00 = 14,800$
[b] $8,000 \times 2.00 = 16,000$
[c] $7,400 \times 2 \times \$40 = \$592,000$
[d] $610,500 \div 16,280$ hours $= \$37.50$ per hour
[e] $\$503,420 \div 16,280$ hours $\approx \$30.92$ per hour
[f] $\$480,000 \div 16,000$ hours $= \$30$ per hour

8-20 (cont'd)

2.   Zyton produces 600 fewer CardioX units than were budgeted. The variable manufacturing-overhead-cost-efficiency variance of $59,200 U arises because more assembly time hours per output unit (16,280 ÷ 7,400 = 2.2 hours) were used than the budgeted 2.0 hours per unit. The variable manufacturing overhead cost spending variance of $40,700 F indicates one or more of the following probably occurred—(i) actual prices of individual items included in variable overhead differ from their budgeted prices, or (ii) actual usage of individual items included in variable overhead differs from their budgeted usage.

The fixed manufacturing overhead cost spending variance of $23,420 U means fixed overhead was above that budgeted. For example, it could be due to an unexpected increase in plant leasing costs. The unfavourable production-volume variance of $36,000 arises because actual output of 7,400 units is below the 8,000 units used in determining the $30.00 per assembly-hour budgeted rate.

3.   Planning and control of *variable* manufacturing overhead costs has both a long-run and a short-run focus. It involves Zyton planning to undertake only value-added overhead activities (a long-run view) and then managing the cost drivers of those activities in the most efficient way (a short-run view). Planning and control of *fixed* manufacturing overhead costs at Zyton has primarily a long-run focus. It involves undertaking only value-added fixed-overhead activities for a budgeted level of output. Zyton makes most of the key decisions that determine the level of fixed-overhead costs at the start of the accounting period.

8-22 (20-25 min.) **Spending and efficiency overhead variances, distribution.**

1.   Budgeted variable overhead rate   = $2 per hour of delivery time

$$\text{Budgeted fixed overhead rate} \ = \ \frac{\$120{,}000}{100{,}000 \times 0.25} = \frac{\$120{,}000}{25{,}000}$$
$$= \$4.80 \text{ per hour of delivery time}$$

A detailed comparison of actual and flexible budgeted amounts is:

	Actual	Flexible Budget	Static Budget
Output units (deliveries)	96,000	96,000	100,000
Allocation base (hours)	28,800	24,000[a]	25,000[b]
Allocation base per output unit	0.30[c]	0.25	0.25
Variable MOH	$60,000	$48,000[d]	–
Variable MOH per hour	$2.08[e]	$2.00	$2.00
Fixed MOH	$128,400	$120,000	$120,000
Fixed MOH per hour	$4.46[f]	—	$4.80[g]

[a] $96{,}000 \times 0.25 = 24{,}000$

[b] $100{,}000 \times 0.25 = 25{,}000$

[c] $28{,}800 \div 96{,}000 = 0.30$

[d] $96{,}000 \times 0.25 \times \$2.00 = \$48{,}000$

[e] $\$60{,}000 \div 28{,}800 = \$2.08$

[f] $\$128{,}400 \div 28{,}800 = \$4.46$

[g] $\$120{,}000 \div 25{,}000 = \$4.80$

The required variances are:

	Spending Variance	Efficiency Variance
Variable overhead	$2,400 U	$ 9,600 U
Fixed overhead	$8,400 U	—

8-22 (cont'd)

These variances are computed as follows:

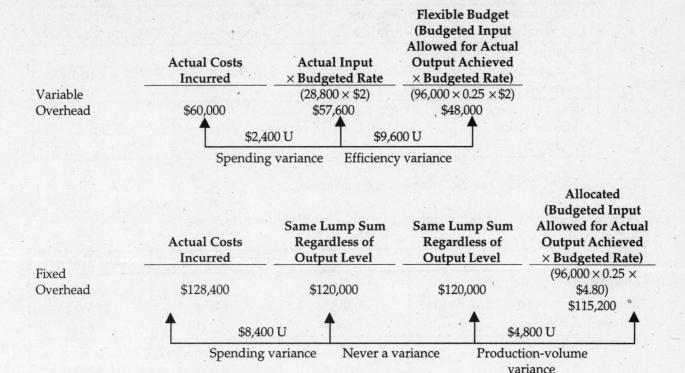

	Actual Costs Incurred	Actual Input × Budgeted Rate	Flexible Budget (Budgeted Input Allowed for Actual Output Achieved × Budgeted Rate)
		(28,800 × $2)	(96,000 × 0.25 × $2)
Variable Overhead	$60,000	$57,600	$48,000

$2,400 U — Spending variance $9,600 U — Efficiency variance

	Actual Costs Incurred	Same Lump Sum Regardless of Output Level	Same Lump Sum Regardless of Output Level	Allocated (Budgeted Input Allowed for Actual Output Achieved × Budgeted Rate)
				(96,000 × 0.25 × $4.80)
Fixed Overhead	$128,400	$120,000	$120,000	$115,200

$8,400 U — Spending variance   Never a variance $4,800 U — Production-volume variance

The spending variances for variable and fixed overhead are both unfavourable. This means that PPS had increases in either or both the cost of individual items (such as gasoline and truck maintenance) or higher-than-budgeted usage of these individual items per unit of the allocation base (delivery time). The unfavourable efficiency variance for variable overhead results from less efficient use of the cost allocation base—each delivery takes 0.30 hours versus a budgeted 0.25 hours.

2.   The single direct cost category is delivery driver payments. The major problem in managing these costs is to restrain the rate of increase in the rate paid to drivers per delivery. PPS faces the challenge of having a low-cost delivery infrastructure. For example, purchasing delivery trucks with low fuel consumption will help reduce variable overhead costs. Purchasing vehicles with low annual maintenance will help reduce fixed overhead costs. Variable overhead costs are controlled by both cost planning, well prior to their incurrence, and day-to-day decisions. In contrast, most fixed overhead cost items are controlled by planning decisions made prior to the start of the year.

8-24 (20-30 min.) **Straightforward four-variance overhead analysis.**

1. The budget for fixed manufacturing overhead is $4,000 \times 6 \times \$15 = \$360,000$.

4-Variance Analysis	Spending Variance	Efficiency Variance	Production-Volume Variance
Variable Manufacturing Overhead	$17,800 U	$16,000 U	Never a Variance
Fixed Manufacturing Overhead	$13,000 U	Never a Variance	$36,000 F

Solution Exhibit 8-24 has details of these variances.

A detailed comparison of actual and flexible budgeted amounts is:

	Actual	Flexible Budget	Static Budget
Output units (auto parts)	4,400	4,400	4,000
Allocation base (machine hours)	28,400	26,400[a]	24,000[b]
Allocation base per output unit	6.45[c]	6.00	6.00
Variable MOH	$245,000	$211,200[d]	–
Variable MOH per hour	$8.63[e]	$8.00	$8.00
Fixed MOH	$373,000	$360,000[f]	$360,000[f]
Fixed MOH per hour	$13.13[g]	–	$15.00[h]

[a] $4,400 \times 6.00 = 26,400$

[b] $4,000 \times 6.00 = 24,000$ hours

[c] $28,400 \div 4,400 = 6.45$

[d] $4,400 \times 6.00 \times \$8.00 = \$211,200$

[e] $\$245,000 \div 28,400 = \$8.63$

[f] $4,000 \times 6.00 \times \$15 = \$360,000$

[g] $\$373,000 \div 28,400 = \$13.13$

[h] $\$360,000 \div 24,000 = \$15.00$

8-24 (cont'd)

2.	Variable Manufacturing Overhead Control	$245,000	
	Accounts Payable Control and other accounts		$245,000
	Work in Process Control	$211,200	
	Variable Manufacturing Overhead Allocated		$211,200
	Fixed Manufacturing Overhead Control	$373,000	
	Wages Payable Control, Accumulated Depreciation Control, etc.		$373,000
	Work in Process Control	$396,000	
	Fixed Manufacturing Overhead Allocated		$396,000

3. The control of variable manufacturing overhead requires the identification of the cost drivers for such items as energy, supplies, and repairs. Control often entails monitoring nonfinancial measures that affect each cost item, one by one. Examples are kilowatts used, quantities of lubricants used, and repair parts and hours used. The most convincing way to discover why overhead performance did not agree with a budget is to investigate possible causes, line item by line item.

Individual fixed manufacturing overhead items are not usually affected very much by day-to-day control. Instead, they are controlled periodically through planning decisions and budgeting procedures that may sometimes have horizons covering six months or a year (for example, management salaries) and sometimes covering many years (for example, long-term leases and depreciation on plant and equipment).

SOLUTION EXHIBIT 8-24

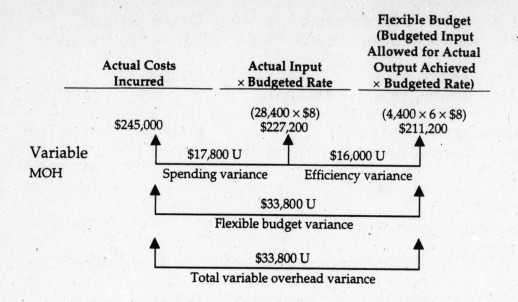

	Actual Costs Incurred	Actual Input × Budgeted Rate	Flexible Budget (Budgeted Input Allowed for Actual Output Achieved × Budgeted Rate)
		(28,400 × $8)	(4,400 × 6 × $8)
Variable MOH	$245,000	$227,200	$211,200

$17,800 U ← Spending variance → $16,000 U ← Efficiency variance

$33,800 U
Flexible budget variance

$33,800 U
Total variable overhead variance

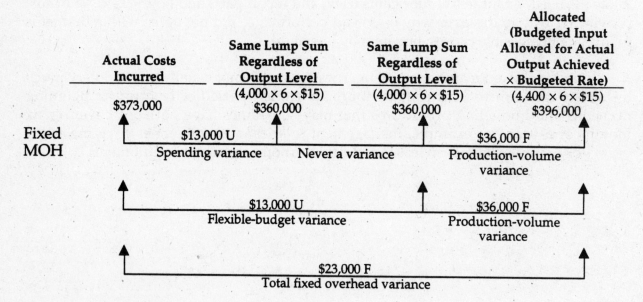

	Actual Costs Incurred	Same Lump Sum Regardless of Output Level	Same Lump Sum Regardless of Output Level	Allocated (Budgeted Input Allowed for Actual Output Achieved × Budgeted Rate)
		(4,000 × 6 × $15)	(4,000 × 6 × $15)	(4,400 × 6 × $15)
Fixed MOH	$373,000	$360,000	$360,000	$396,000

$13,000 U
Spending variance

Never a variance

$36,000 F
Production-volume variance

$13,000 U
Flexible-budget variance

$36,000 F
Production-volume variance

$23,000 F
Total fixed overhead variance

8-26 (35-50 min.) **Total overhead, three-variance analysis.**

1.   This problem has two major purposes: (a) to give experience with data allocated on a total overhead basis instead of on separate variable and fixed bases, and (b) to reinforce distinctions between actual hours of input, budgeted (standard) hours allowed for actual output, and denominator level.

An analysis of direct manufacturing labour will provide the data for actual hours of input and standard hours allowed. One approach is to plug the known figures (designated by asterisks) into the analytical framework and solve for the unknowns. The direct manufacturing labour efficiency variance can be computed by subtracting $9,640 from $14,440. The complete picture is:

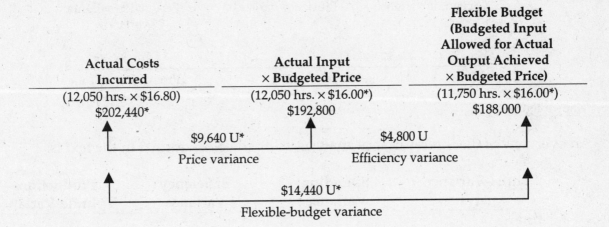

Actual Costs Incurred	Actual Input × Budgeted Price	Flexible Budget (Budgeted Input Allowed for Actual Output Achieved × Budgeted Price)
(12,050 hrs. × $16.80) $202,440*	(12,050 hrs. × $16.00*) $192,800	(11,750 hrs. × $16.00*) $188,000

$9,640 U*
Price variance

$4,800 U
Efficiency variance

$14,440 U*
Flexible-budget variance

Manufacturing Overhead

Variable overhead rate = $64,000* ÷ 8,000* hrs. = $8.00 per standard labour-hour
Budgeted fixed
overhead costs = $197,600* – 10,000*($8.00) = $117,600

If total manufacturing overhead is allocated at 120% of direct standard manufacturing labour-hours, the single overhead rate must be 120% of $16.00, or $19.20 per hour. Therefore, the fixed overhead component of the rate must be $19.20 – $8.00, or $11.20 per direct standard manufacturing labour-hour.

Let D = denominator level in input units

$$\text{Budgeted fixed overhead rate per input unit} = \frac{\text{Budgeted fixed overhead costs}}{\text{Denominator level in input units}}$$

$$\$11.20 = \frac{\$117,600}{D}$$

$$D = 10,500 \text{ standard direct manufacturing labour-hours}$$

8-11

A summary three-variance analysis for October follows:

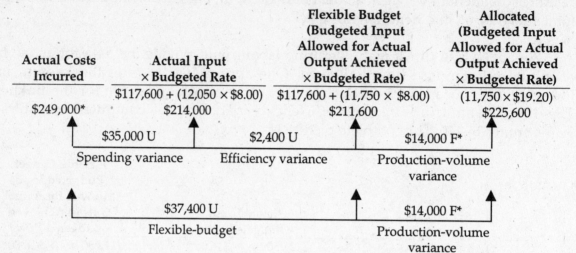

	Actual Costs Incurred	Actual Input × Budgeted Rate	Flexible Budget (Budgeted Input Allowed for Actual Output Achieved × Budgeted Rate)	Allocated (Budgeted Input Allowed for Actual Output Achieved × Budgeted Rate)
	$249,000*	$117,600 + (12,050 × $8.00) $214,000	$117,600 + (11,750 × $8.00) $211,600	(11,750 × $19.20) $225,600

$35,000 U — Spending variance
$2,400 U — Efficiency variance
$14,000 F* — Production-volume variance

$37,400 U — Flexible-budget
$14,000 F* — Production-volume variance

*Known figure

An overview of the three-variance analysis using the block format in the text is:

Three-Variance Analysis	Spending Variance	Efficiency Variance	Production-Volume Variance
Total Manufacturing Overhead	$35,000 U	$2,400 U	$14,000 F

2. The control of variable manufacturing overhead requires the identification of the cost drivers for such items as energy, supplies, equipment, and maintenance. Control often entails monitoring nonfinancial measures that affect each cost item, one by one. Examples are kilowatts used, quantities of lubricants used, and equipment parts and hours used. The most convincing way to discover why overhead performance did not agree with a budget is to investigate possible causes, line item by line item.

Individual fixed manufacturing overhead items are not usually affected very much by day-to-day control. Instead, they are controlled periodically through planning decisions and budgeting that may sometimes have horizons covering six months or a year (for example, management salaries) and sometimes covering many years (for example, long-term leases and depreciation on plant and equipment).

Comprehensive review of Chapters 7 and 8, static budget.

1.

	Actual Results (1)	Static-Budget Amounts (2)	Variances (3)
Revenues			
Circulation	$154,000	$140,000	$14,000 F
Advertising	394,600	360,000	34,600 F
	548,600	500,000	48,600 F
Costs			
Direct materials	224,640	180,000	44,640 U
Direct labour costs	50,112	45,000	5,112 U
Variable indirect costs	63,936	60,000	3,936 U
Fixed indirect costs	97,000	90,000	7,000 U
	435,688	375,000	60,688 U
Operating income	$112,912	$125,000	$12,088 U

2. The *Monthly Herald* had an increase in total revenues of $48,600 above that budgeted. This arose from both a favourable circulation variance ($14,000 increase or 28,000 extra copies sold at $0.50 per copy) and a favourable advertising revenue variance of $34,600.

The actual costs are $60,688 above budget. The largest source of this increase is direct materials. The sources of this increase include (a) 20,000 extra copies printed, and (b) quality problems leading to many pages being unusable. The budgeted print pages for 320,000 copies of 50 pages each was 16,000,000 pages; an extra 1,280,000 pages were used above this budgeted amount.

8-30 (30 min.) Comprehensive variance analysis.

1) Budgeted number of machine-hours planned can be calculated by multiplying the number of units planned (budgeted) by the number of machine-hours allocated per unit:

   2.00 × 17,760 = 35,520 machine-hours.

2) Budgeted fixed MOH costs per machine-hour can be computed by dividing the flexible budget amount for fixed MOH (which is the same as the static budget) by the number of machine-hours planned (calculated in (1.)):

   $6,961,920/35,520 = $196.00 per machine-hour

3) Budgeted variable MOH costs per machine-hour are calculated as budgeted variable MOH costs divided by the budgeted number of machine-hours planned:

   $1,420,800/35,520 = $40.00 per machine-hour.

4) Budgeted number of machine-hours allowed for actual output achieved can be calculated by dividing the flexible-budget amount for variable MOH by budgeted variable MOH costs per machine-hour:

   $1,536,000/$40.00 = 38,400 machine-hours allowed

5) The actual number of output units is the budgeted number of machine-hours allowed for actual output achieved divided by the planned allocation rate of machine-hours per unit:

   38,400/2.00 = 19,200 output units.

8-30 (cont'd)

6) The actual number of machine-hours used per panel is the actual number of machine hours used (given) divided by the actual number of units manufactured:

36,480/19,200 = 1.9 machine-hours used per panel.

7) The allocated amount for fixed MOH is the budgeted input allowed for actual output achieved (4.) multiplied by the budgeted fixed MOH costs per machine-hour (2.):

38,400 × $196.00 = $7,526,400

8-32 (30-40 min.) Graphs and overhead variances.

Variable Manufacturing Overhead

1.

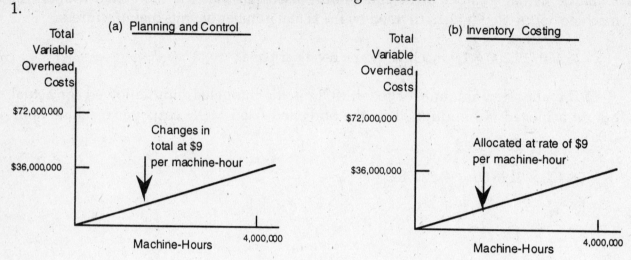

Fixed Manufacturing Overhead

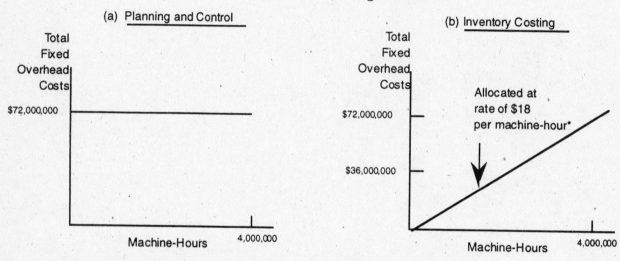

$$*\text{Budgeted fixed - manufacturing -} \atop \text{overhead rate per hour} = \frac{\text{Budgeted fixed - manufacturing overhead}}{\text{Denominator level}}$$

$$= \frac{\$72,000,000}{4,000,000 \text{ hours}} = \$18 \text{ per machine - hour}$$

8-32 (cont'd)

2.

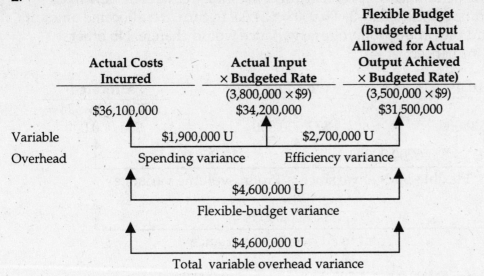

Actual Costs Incurred	Actual Input × Budgeted Rate	Flexible Budget (Budgeted Input Allowed for Actual Output Achieved × Budgeted Rate)
	(3,800,000 × $9)	(3,500,000 × $9)
$36,100,000	$34,200,000	$31,500,000

Variable Overhead

$1,900,000 U — Spending variance

$2,700,000 U — Efficiency variance

$4,600,000 U — Flexible-budget variance

$4,600,000 U — Total variable overhead variance

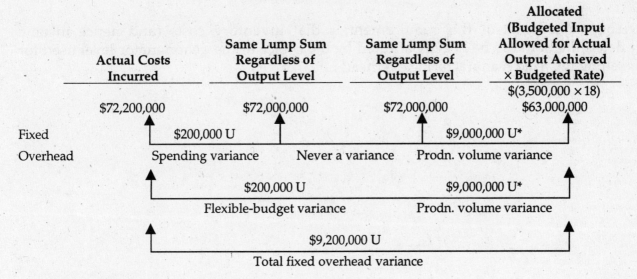

Actual Costs Incurred	Same Lump Sum Regardless of Output Level	Same Lump Sum Regardless of Output Level	Allocated (Budgeted Input Allowed for Actual Output Achieved × Budgeted Rate)
			$(3,500,000 × 18)
$72,200,000	$72,000,000	$72,000,000	$63,000,000

Fixed Overhead

$200,000 U — Spending variance

Never a variance

$9,000,000 U* — Prodn. volume variance

$200,000 U — Flexible-budget variance

$9,000,000 U* — Prodn. volume variance

$9,200,000 U — Total fixed overhead variance

*Alternative computation:
4,000,000 denominator hours − 3,500,000 budgeted hours allowed = 500,000 hours
500,000 × $18 = $9,000,000 U

3. The underallocated manufacturing overheads were: variable, $4,600,000, and fixed, $9,200,000. The flexible-budget variance and underallocated overhead are always the same amount for variable overhead because the flexible-budget amount and the allocated amounts coincide. In contrast, the only time the budget and allocated amounts coincide for fixed overhead is when the budgeted input of the allocation base for the actual output level achieved exactly equals the denominator level.

4.   The choice of the denominator level will affect inventory costs. The new fixed overhead rate would be $72,000,000 ÷ 3,000,000 = $24.00. In turn, the allocated amount of fixed overhead and the production-volume variance would change. No other variances would be influenced:

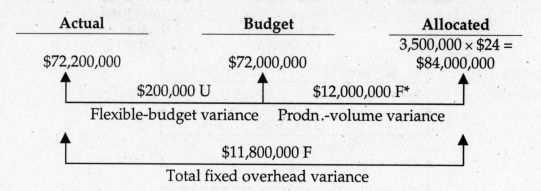

Actual	Budget	Allocated
		3,500,000 × $24 =
$72,200,000	$72,000,000	$84,000,000

$200,000 U — Flexible-budget variance

$12,000,000 F* — Prodn.-volume variance

$11,800,000 F

Total fixed overhead variance

*Alternate computation: (3,000,000 – 3,500,000) × $24 = $12,000,000 F

The major point of this requirement is that inventory costs (and hence income determination) can be heavily affected by the choice of the denominator level used for setting the fixed manufacturing overhead rate.

8-34 (60 min.) **Variance analysis for an activity area.**

The flexible budget is flexed on the number of technical-service hours, which has the budgeted relationship with output units of one hour of technical support for every 5,000 minutes of airtime sold (or every minute of airtime sold has a budgeted 0.0002 minutes of technical service). Key data items for August 31, 2000, are:

	Actual Results	Flexible Budget Amount	Static Budget Amount
1. Output units (minutes)	7,350,000	7,350,000	6,850,000
2. Technical service hours	1,500	1,470	1,370
3. Technical service hours per minute	0.000204	0.0002	0.0002
4. Variable technical service activity area costs	$31,500	$35,280	$32,880
5. Variable technical service activity area costs per technical service hour (4/2)	$21.00	$24.00	$24.00
6. Variable technical service activity area costs per minute (4/1)	$0.004286	$0.004800	$0.004800
7. Fixed technical service activity area costs	$67,500	$69,870	$69,870
8. Fixed technical service activity area costs per technical service hour (7/2)	$45.00	$47.53	$51.00
9. Fixed technical service activity area costs per minute (7/1)	$0.0092	$0.0095	$0.0102

1. Variable technical service activity area costs per technical service hour is calculated by dividing the total variable technical service activity area costs by the number of technical service hours:

Actual: $31,500/1,500 = $21.00
Budgeted: $32,880/1,370 = $24.00

The budgeted denominator of 1,370 is calculated as budgeted airtime sold (6,850,000) divided by 5,000.

8-34 (cont'd)

2. Allocated fixed technical service activity area overhead is calculated by multiplying the budgeted input allowed for actual output achieved (given as 1,470 technical service hours) by the budgeted rate for fixed overhead. The budgeted rate for fixed overhead is calculated by dividing the budgeted amount for fixed technical service activity area costs (given as $69,870) by the budgeted number of technical service hours (1,370):

$$\$69,870/1,370 = \$51.00$$

Allocated fixed technical service activity area overhead is therefore:

$$1,470 \times \$51.00 = \$74,970$$

3. Variable overhead analysis:

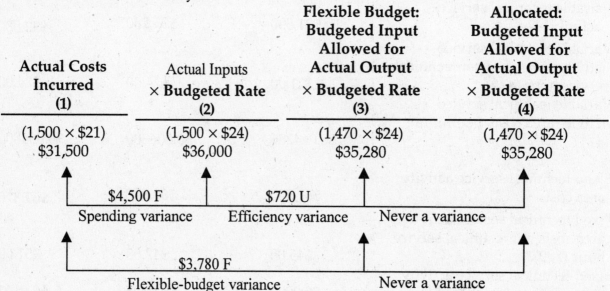

Actual Costs Incurred (1)	Actual Inputs × Budgeted Rate (2)	Flexible Budget: Budgeted Input Allowed for Actual Output × Budgeted Rate (3)	Allocated: Budgeted Input Allowed for Actual Output × Budgeted Rate (4)
(1,500 × $21) $31,500	(1,500 × $24) $36,000	(1,470 × $24) $35,280	(1,470 × $24) $35,280

$4,500 F Spending variance $720 U Efficiency variance   Never a variance

$3,780 F Flexible-budget variance   Never a variance

The favourable spending variance of $4,500 can be attributed to the lower variable costs incurred in the technical service activity area ($21 versus $24). The unfavourable efficiency variance ($720) is due to the larger number of technical service hours utilized compared with the number of hours that would have been allowed per plan for the actual number of minutes sold. Since the favourable spending variance is greater than the unfavourable efficiency variance, the flexible-budget variance, in the amount of $3,780, is favourable.

8-34 (cont'd)

4. Fixed overhead analysis:

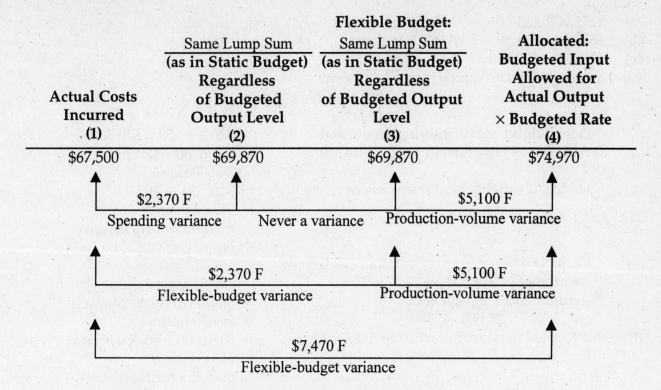

Actual Costs Incurred (1)	Same Lump Sum (as in Static Budget) Regardless of Budgeted Output Level (2)	Flexible Budget: Same Lump Sum (as in Static Budget) Regardless of Budgeted Output Level (3)	Allocated: Budgeted Input Allowed for Actual Output × Budgeted Rate (4)
$67,500	$69,870	$69,870	$74,970

$2,370 F
Spending variance

Never a variance

$5,100 F
Production-volume variance

$2,370 F
Flexible-budget variance

$5,100 F
Production-volume variance

$7,470 F
Flexible-budget variance

CellOne management overallocated fixed overhead by $7,470.

8-36 (30-40 min.) **Working backward from given variances.**

1. Solution Exhibit 8-36 outlines the Chapter 7 and 8 framework underlying this solution.
    (a) $176,000 ÷ $1.10 =   160,000 kilograms
    (b) $69,000 ÷ $11.50 =   6,000 kilograms
    (c) $10,350 – $18,000   = $7,650 F
    (d) Standard direct manufacturing labour rate

    = $800,000 ÷ 40,000 hours
    = $20 per hour

    Actual direct manufacturing labour rate   = $20 + $0.50 = $20.50
    Actual direct manufacturing labour-hours   = $552,750 ÷ $20.50
              = 25,500 hours
    (e)   Standard variable manufacturing overhead rate = $480,000 ÷ 40,000
              = $12 per direct manufacturing labour-hour

    Variable manufacturing overhead efficiency
       variance of $18,000 ÷ $12   = 1,500 excess hours
    Actual hours – Excess hours   = Standard hours allowed
          25,500 – 1,500   = 24,000 hours
    (f)   Budgeted fixed manufacturing overhead rate   = $640,000 ÷ 40,000 hours
              = $16 per direct manufacturing labour-hour

    Fixed manufacturing overhead allocated   = $16 × 24,000 hours
              = $384,000
    Production-volume variance   = $640,000 – $384,000
              = $256,000 U

2. The control of variable manufacturing overhead requires the identification of the cost drivers for such items as energy, supplies, and repairs. Control often entails monitoring nonfinancial measures that affect each cost item, one by one. Examples are kilowatts used, quantities of lubricants used, and repair parts and hours used. The most convincing way to discover why overhead performance did not agree with a budget is to investigate possible causes, line item by line item.

Individual fixed overhead items are not usually affected very much by day-to-day control. Instead, they are controlled periodically through planning decisions and budgeting procedures that may sometimes have planning horizons covering six months or a year (for example, management salaries) and sometimes covering many years (for example, long-term leases and depreciation on plant and equipment).

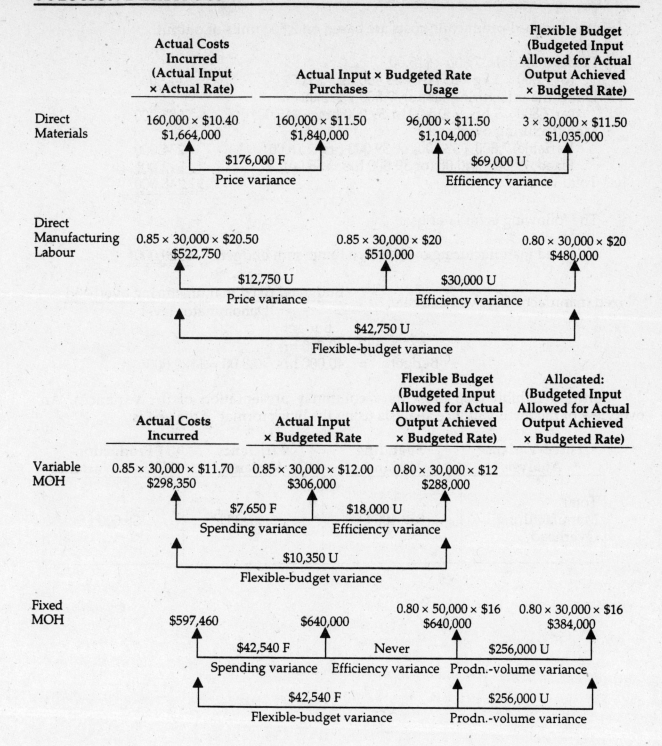

8-38 (30-50 min.) Review of Chapters 7 and 8, three-variance analysis.

1. Total standard production costs are based on 7,800 units of output.

Direct materials, 7,800 × $15.00
   (or 7,800 × 3 kg × $5.00 or 23,400 kg × $5.00)   117,000
Direct manufacturing labour, 7,800 × $75.00
   (or 7,800 × 5 hrs. × $15.00 or 39,000 hrs. × $15.00)   585,000
Manufacturing overhead:
   Variable, 7,800 × $30.00 (or 39,000 hrs. × $6.00)   234,000
   Fixed, 7,800 × $40.00 (or 39,000 hrs. × $8.00)   312,000
Total $1,248,000

The following is for later use:

Fixed manufacturing overhead, a lump-sum budget $320,000*

*Fixed manufacturing overhead rate $= \dfrac{\text{Budgeted fixed manufacturing overhead}}{\text{Denominator level}}$

$$\$8.00 = \dfrac{\text{Budget}}{40{,}000 \text{ hrs.}}$$

$$\text{Budget} = 40{,}000 \text{ hrs.} \times \$8.00 = \$320{,}000$$

2. Solution Exhibit 8-38 presents a columnar presentation of the variances. An overview of the three-variance analysis using the block format of the text is:

Three-Variance Analysis	Spending Variance	Efficiency Variance	Production-Volume Variance
Total Manufacturing Overhead	$39,400 U	$6,600 U	$8,000 U

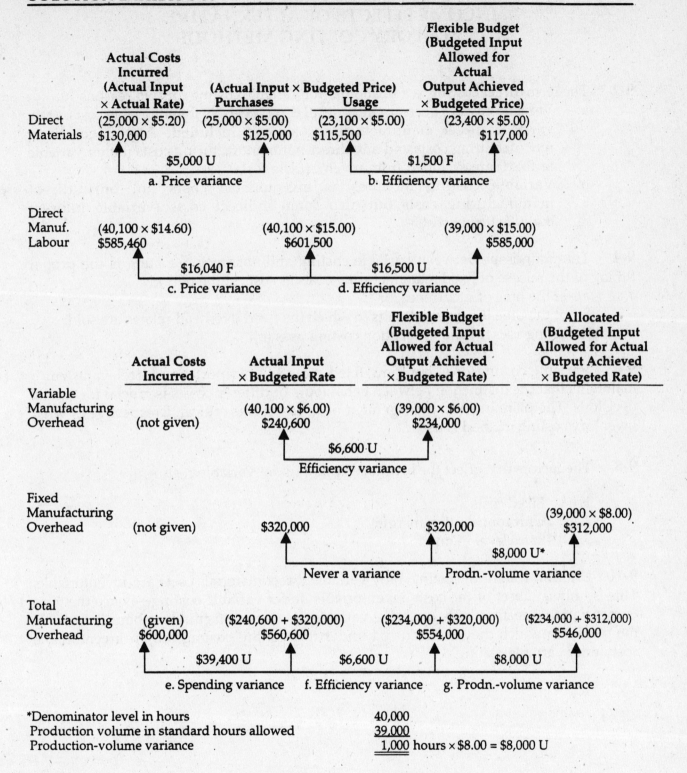

	Actual Costs Incurred (Actual Input × Actual Rate)	(Actual Input × Budgeted Price) Purchases	(Actual Input × Budgeted Price) Usage	Flexible Budget (Budgeted Input Allowed for Actual Output Achieved × Budgeted Price)
Direct Materials	(25,000 × $5.20) $130,000	(25,000 × $5.00) $125,000	(23,100 × $5.00) $115,500	(23,400 × $5.00) $117,000

$5,000 U — a. Price variance $1,500 F — b. Efficiency variance

Direct Manuf. Labour	(40,100 × $14.60) $585,460	(40,100 × $15.00) $601,500		(39,000 × $15.00) $585,000

$16,040 F — c. Price variance $16,500 U — d. Efficiency variance

	Actual Costs Incurred	Actual Input × Budgeted Rate	Flexible Budget (Budgeted Input Allowed for Actual Output Achieved × Budgeted Rate)	Allocated (Budgeted Input Allowed for Actual Output Achieved × Budgeted Rate)
Variable Manufacturing Overhead	(not given)	(40,100 × $6.00) $240,600	(39,000 × $6.00) $234,000	

$6,600 U — Efficiency variance

Fixed Manufacturing Overhead	(not given)	$320,000	$320,000	(39,000 × $8.00) $312,000

Never a variance $8,000 U* — Prodn.-volume variance

Total Manufacturing Overhead	(given) $600,000	($240,600 + $320,000) $560,600	($234,000 + $320,000) $554,000	($234,000 + $312,000) $546,000

$39,400 U — e. Spending variance $6,600 U — f. Efficiency variance $8,000 U — g. Prodn.-volume variance

*Denominator level in hours   40,000
Production volume in standard hours allowed   39,000
Production-volume variance   1,000 hours × $8.00 = $8,000 U

CHAPTER 9
INCOME EFFECTS OF ALTERNATIVE
INVENTORY COSTING METHODS

9-2 The term **direct costing** is a misnomer for variable costing for two reasons:
   a. Variable costing does not include all direct costs as inventoriable costs. Only variable direct manufacturing costs are included. Any fixed direct manufacturing costs and any direct nonmanufacturing costs (either variable or fixed) are excluded from inventoriable costs.
   b. Variable costing includes as inventoriable costs not only direct manufacturing costs but also some indirect costs (variable indirect manufacturing costs).

9-4 The main issue between variable costing and absorption costing is the proper timing of the release of fixed manufacturing costs as costs of the period:
   a. at the time of incurrence, or
   b. at the time the finished units to which the fixed overhead relates are sold.
Variable costing uses (a) and absorption costing uses (b).

9-6 Variable costing does not view fixed costs as unimportant or irrelevant, but it maintains that the distinction between behaviours of different costs is crucial for certain decisions. The planning and management of fixed costs is critical, irrespective of what inventory costing method is used.

9-8 The factors that affect the breakeven point under variable costing are:

   1. Fixed costs
   2. Unit contribution margin
   3. Sales level in units

9-10 Under throughput costing, only variable direct materials costs are inventoriable. This is only a subset of the costs inventoriable under variable costing—hence the term "super-variable costing." For example, variable direct manufacturing labour is a cost of the period in which they are incurred under throughput costing but an inventoriable cost under variable costing.

9-12 Approaches used to reduce the negative aspects associated with using absorption costing include:

    a.   Change the accounting system
- Adopt either variable or throughput costing, both of which reduce the incentives of managers to build for inventory.
- Adopt an inventory holding charge for managers who tie up funds in inventory.

    b.   Extend the time period used to evaluate performance. By evaluating performance over a longer time period (say, three to five years), the incentive to take short-run actions that reduce long-term income is lessened.

    c.   Include nonfinancial as well as financial variables in the measures used to evaluate performance.

9-14 The *theoretical capacity* and *practical capacity* denominator-level concepts emphasize what a plant can supply. The *normal utilization* and *master-budget utilization* concepts emphasize what customers demand in products produced by a plant.

9-16 (30 min.) Variable and absorption costing, explaining operating income differences.

1.   Key inputs for income statement computations are:

	April	May
Beginning inventory	0	150
Production	500	400
Goods available for sale	500	550
Units sold	350	520
Ending inventory	150	30

The unit fixed and total manufacturing costs per unit under absorption costing are:

		April	May
(a)	Fixed manufacturing costs	$2,000,000	$2,000,000
(b)	Units produced	500	400
(c)=(a)÷(b)	Unit fixed manufacturing costs	$4,000	$5,000
(d)	Unit variable manufacturing costs	$10,000	$10,000
(e)=(c)+(d)	Unit total manufacturing costs	$14,000	$15,000

9-16 (cont'd)

(a) Variable costing

	April 2000		May 2000	
Revenues[a]		$8,400,000		$12,480,000
Variable costs				
Beginning inventory	$ 0		$1,500,000	
Variable cost of goods manufactured[b]	5,000,000		4,000,000	
Cost of goods available for sale	5,000,000		5,500,000	
Ending inventory[c]	1,500,000		300,000	
Variable manufacturing cost of goods sold	3,500,000		5,200,000	
Variable marketing costs	1,050,000		1,560,000	
Total variable costs[d]		4,550,000		6,760,000
Contribution margin		3,850,000		5,720,000
Fixed costs				
Fixed manufacturing costs	2,000,000		2,000,000	
Fixed marketing costs	600,000		600,000	
Total fixed costs		2,600,000		2,600,000
Operating income		$1,250,000		$3,120,000

a $24,000 × 350; 520
b $10,000 × 500; 400
c $10,000 × 150; 30
d $3,000 × 350; 520

9-16 (cont'd)

(b) Absorption costing

	April 2000		May 2000	
Revenues[a]		$8,400,000		$12,480,000
Cost of goods sold				
Beginning inventory	0		$2,100,000	
Variable manufacturing costs[b]	$5,000,000		4,000,000	
Fixed manufacturing costs[c]	2,000,000		2,000,000	
Cost of goods available for sale	7,000,000		8,100,000	
Ending inventory[d]	2,100,000		450,000	
Cost of goods sold		4,900,000		7,650,000
Gross margin		3,500,000		4,830,000
Marketing costs				
Variable marketing costs[e]	1,050,000		1,560,000	
Fixed marketing costs	600,000		600,000	
Total marketing costs		1,650,000		2,160,000
Operating income		$1,850,000		$ 2,670,000

[a] $24,000 × 350; 520
[b] $10,000 × 500; 400
[c] ($4,000 × 500); ($5,000 × 400)
[d] ($14,000 × 150; $15,000 × 30)
[e] ($3,000 × 350; $3,000 × 520)

9-4

9-16 (cont'd)

2. $$\begin{pmatrix} \text{Absorption-costing} \\ \text{operating income} \end{pmatrix} - \begin{pmatrix} \text{Variable-costing} \\ \text{operating income} \end{pmatrix} = \begin{pmatrix} \text{Fixed manufacturing} \\ \text{costs in} \\ \text{ending inventory} \end{pmatrix} - \begin{pmatrix} \text{Fixed manufacturing} \\ \text{costs in} \\ \text{beginning inventory} \end{pmatrix}$$

April:

$$\$1,850,000 - \$1,250,000 \quad = \quad (\$4,000 \times 150) - (\$0)$$
$$\$600,000 \quad = \quad \$600,000$$

May:

$$\$2,670,000 - \$3,120,000 \quad = \quad (\$5,000 \times 30) - (\$4,000 \times 150)$$
$$-\$450,000 \quad = \quad \$150,000 - \$600,000$$
$$-\$450,000 \quad = \quad -\$450,000$$

The difference between absorption and variable costing is due solely to moving fixed manufacturing costs into inventories as inventories increase (as in April) and out of inventories as they decrease (as in May).

9-18 (40 min.) Variable and absorption costing, explaining operating income differences.

1. Key inputs for income statement computations are:

	January	February	March
Beginning inventory	0	300	300
Production	1,000	800	1,250
Goods available for sale	1,000	1,100	1,550
Units sold	700	800	1,500
Ending inventory	300	300	50

The unit fixed and total manufacturing costs per unit under absorption costing are:

		January	February	March
(a)	Fixed manufacturing costs	$400,000	$400,000	$400,000
(b)	Units produced	1,000	800	1,250
(c)=(a)÷(b)	Unit fixed manufacturing costs	$ 400	$ 500	$ 320
(d)	Unit variable manufacturing costs	$ 900	$ 900	$ 900
(e)=(c)+(d)	Unit total manufacturing costs	$ 1,300	$ 1,400	$ 1,220

9-18 (cont'd)

(a) Variable Costing

	January 2000	February 2000	March 2000
Revenues[a]	$1,750,000	$2,000,000	$3,750,000
Variable costs			
Beginning inventory[b]	$ 0	$270,000	$ 270,000
Variable cost of goods manufactured[c]	900,000	720,000	1,125,000
Cost of goods available for sale	900,000	990,000	1,395,000
Ending inventory[d]	270,000	270,000	45,000
Variable manufacturing cost of goods sold	630,000	720,000	1,350,000
Variable marketing costs[e]	420,000	480,000	900,000
Total variable costs	1,050,000	1,200,000	2,250,000
Contribution margin	700,000	800,000	1,500,000
Fixed costs			
Fixed manufacturing costs	400,000	400,000	400,000
Fixed marketing costs	140,000	140,000	140,000
Total fixed costs	540,000	540,000	540,000
Operating income	$ 160,000	$ 260,000	$ 960,000

a $2,500 × 700; 800; 1,500

b 0; $900 × 300; 300

c $900 × 1,000; 800; 1,250

d $900 × 300; 300; 50

e $600 × 700; 800; 1,500

9-18 (cont'd)

(b) Absorption Costing

	January 2000		February 2000		March 2000	
Revenues[a]		$1,750,000		$2,000,000		$3,750,000
Cost of goods sold						
Beginning inventory[b]	$ 0		$390,000		420,000	
Variable manufacturing costs[c]	900,000		720,000		1,125,000	
Fixed manufacturing costs[d]	400,000		400,000		400,000	
Cost of goods available for sale	1,300,000		1,510,000		1,945,000	
Ending inventory[e]	390,000		420,000		61,000	
Cost of goods sold		910,000		1,090,000		1,884,000
Gross margin		840,000		910,000		1,866,000
Marketing costs						
Variable marketing costs[f]	420,000		480,000		900,000	
Fixed marketing costs	140,000		140,000		140,000	
Total marketing costs		560,000		620,000		1,040,000
Operating income		$280,000		$ 290,000		$ 826,000

a $2,500 × 700; 800; 1,500
b (0; $1,300 × 300; $1,400 × 300)
c $900 × 1,000, 800, 1,250
d ($400 × 1,000); ($500 × 800); ($320 × 1,250)
e ($1,300 × 300); ($1,400 × 300); ($1,220 × 50)
f $600 × 700; 800; 1,500

9-18 (cont'd)

2. $$\begin{pmatrix} \text{Absorption-costing} \\ \text{operating income} \end{pmatrix} - \begin{pmatrix} \text{Variable-costing} \\ \text{operating income} \end{pmatrix} = \begin{pmatrix} \text{Fixed manufacturing} \\ \text{costs in} \\ \text{ending inventory} \end{pmatrix} - \begin{pmatrix} \text{Fixed manufacturing} \\ \text{costs in} \\ \text{beginning inventory} \end{pmatrix}$$

January: $\$280,000 - \$160,000 = \$120,000 - \$0$

                          $\$120,000 = \$120,000$

February: $\$290,000 - \$260,000 = \$150,000 - \$120,000$

                          $\$30,000 = \$30,000$

March: $\$826,000 - \$960,000 = \$16,000 - \$150,000$

                          $-\$134,000 = -\$134,000$

The difference between absorption and variable costing is due solely to moving fixed manufacturing costs into inventories as inventories increase (as in January) and out of inventories as they decrease (as in March).

9-20 (10 min.)   **Absorption and variable costing.**

The answers are 1(a), $440,000, and 2(c), $200,000. Computations follow:

1.   **Absorption Costing:**

Revenues[a]		$4,800,000
Cost of goods sold:		
Variable manufacturing costs[b]	$2,400,000	
Fixed manufacturing costs[c]	360,000	2,760,000
Gross margin		2,040,000
Marketing and administrative costs:		
Variable marketing and administrative[d]	1,200,000	
Fixed marketing and administrative	400,000	1,600,000
Operating income		$ 440,000

[a]$40 × 120,000
[b]$20 × 120,000
[c]Fixed manufacturing rate   = $600,000 ÷ 200,000
                         = $3 per output unit
$3 × 120,000
[d]$10 × 120,000

2.   **Variable Costing:**

Revenues[a]		$4,800,000
Variable costs:		
Variable manufacturing costs of goods sold[b]	$2,400,000	
Variable marketing and administrative costs[c]	1,200,000	3,600,000
Contribution margin		1,200,000
Fixed costs:		
Fixed manufacturing costs	600,000	
Fixed marketing and administrative costs	400,000	1,000,000
Operating income		$ 200,000

[a]$40 × 120,000
[b]$20 × 120,000
[c]$10 × 120,000

9-22 (30-40 min.) **Income statements.**

1.

The Mass Company
Income Statements for the Year 2001
(in thousands)

(a) **Variable Costing:**

Revenues (25,000 × $40)		$1,000
Variable costs:		
Beginning inventory (1,000 × $24)	$ 24	
Variable cost of goods manufactured (29,000 × $24)	696	
Cost of goods available for sale	720	
Ending inventory (5,000 × $24)	120	
Variable manufacturing cost of goods sold	600	
Variable marketing and administrative costs		
(25,000 × $1.20)	30	
Variable costs		630
Contribution margin		370
Fixed costs:		
Fixed manufacturing overhead costs	120	
Fixed marketing and admin. costs	190	
Fixed costs		310
Operating income	$ 60	

(b) **Absorption Costing:**

Revenues (25,000 × $40)		$1,000
Cost of goods sold:		
Beginning inventory (1,000 × $28)	$ 28	
Variable manufacturing costs (29,000 × $24)	696	
Fixed manufacturing costs (given)	120	
Cost of goods available for sale	844	
Ending inventory (5,000 × $28)	140	
Cost of goods sold		704
Gross margin		296
Marketing and administrative costs:		
Variable marketing and admin. costs (25,000 × $1.20)	30	
Fixed marketing and admin. costs	190	
Marketing and admin. costs		220
Operating income		$ 76

2.
$$\left(\begin{array}{c}\text{Absorption}\\\text{costing}\\\text{operating}\\\text{income}\end{array} - \begin{array}{c}\text{Variable}\\\text{costing}\\\text{operating}\\\text{income}\end{array}\right) = \left(\begin{array}{c}\text{Fixed}\\\text{manuf. costs}\\\text{in ending}\\\text{inventory}\end{array} - \begin{array}{c}\text{Fixed}\\\text{manuf. costs}\\\text{in beginning}\\\text{inventory}\end{array}\right)$$

$$
\begin{aligned}
\$76{,}000 - \$60{,}000 &= [(5{,}000 \times \$4) - (1{,}000 \times \$4)] \\
&= \$20{,}000 - \$4{,}000 \\
&= \$16{,}000
\end{aligned}
$$

9-22 (cont'd)

The operating income figures differ because the amount of fixed manufacturing costs in the ending inventory differs from that in beginning inventory.

3. Advantages:

    (a) The fixed costs are reported as period costs (and not allocated to inventory), thus increasing the likelihood of better control of these costs.
    (b) Operating income is directly influenced by changes in unit sales (and not influenced by build-up of inventory).
    (c) The impact of fixed costs on operating income is emphasized.
    (d) The income statements are in the same form as used for cost-volume-profit analysis.
    (e) Product line, territory, etc., contribution margins are emphasized and more readily ascertainable.

    Disadvantages:
    (a) Total costs may be overlooked when considering operating problems.
    (b) Distinction between fixed and variable costs is arbitrary for many costs.
    (c) Emphasis on variable costs may cause some managers to ignore fixed costs.
    (d) A new variable-costing system may be too costly to install unless top managers think that operating decisions will be improved collectively.

9-24 (10-20 min.)   **Breakeven under absorption costing
(continuation of 9-23).**

1.   The unit contribution margin is $5 – $3 – $1 = $1. Total fixed costs ($540,000) divided by the unit contribution margin ($1.00) equals 540,000 units. Therefore, under variable costing, 540,000 units must be <u>sold</u> to break even.

2.   If there are no changes in inventory levels, the breakeven point can be the same, 540,000 units, under both variable costing and absorption costing. However, as the preceding problem demonstrates, under absorption costing the breakeven point is not unique; operating income is a function of both sales and production. Some fixed overhead is "held back" when inventories rise (10,000 units × $0.70 = $7,000), so operating income is positive even though sales are at the breakeven level as commonly conceived.

$$\text{Breakeven sales in units} = \frac{\left(\begin{array}{c}\text{Total fixed}\\\text{costs}\end{array}\right) + \left[\left(\begin{array}{c}\text{Fixed manuf.}\\\text{overhead}\\\text{rate}\end{array}\right) \times \left(\begin{array}{c}\text{Breakeven}\\\text{sales in}\\\text{units}\end{array} - \begin{array}{c}\text{Units}\\\text{produced}\end{array}\right)\right]}{\text{Unit contribution margin}}$$

Let N = Breakeven sales in units

$$N = \frac{\$540,000 + \$0.70(N - 550,000)}{\$1.00}$$

$$N = \frac{\$540,000 + \$0.70N - \$385,000}{\$1.00}$$

$0.30N$ = $155,000

N =   516,667 units (rounded)

Therefore, under absorption costing when 550,000 units are produced, 516,667 units must be sold for the income statement to report zero operating income.

Proof of 2000 breakeven point:

Gross margin, 516,667 units × ($5.00 – $3.70)		$671,667
Output level MOH variance, as before	$ 35,000	
Marketing and administrative costs:		
Variable, 516,667 units × $1.00	516,667	
Fixed	120,000	671,667
Operating income		$ 0

9-24 (cont'd)

3.   If no units are sold, variable costing will show an operating loss equal to the fixed manufacturing costs, $420,000 in this instance. In contrast, the company would break even under absorption costing, although nothing was sold to customers. This is an extreme example of what has been called "selling fixed manufacturing overhead to inventory."

A final note: We find it helpful to place the following comparisons on the board, keyed to the three parts of this problem:

   1. Breakeven = f (sales)
   2. Breakeven = f (sales and production)
   3. Breakeven = f (0 units sold and 540,000 units produced), an extreme case

9-26 (30 min.)   **Operating income effects of alternative denominator-level concepts (continuation of 9-25).**

1.   Solution Exhibit 9-26 reports the operating income for each denominator-level concept. Computations include:

Denominator- Level Concept	Variable Manufacturing Cost*	Budgeted Fixed Manufacturing Overhead Cost Rate	Total Manufacturing Costs
Theoretical capacity	$46.30	$ 7.99	$54.29
Practical capacity	46.30	12.00	58.30
Normal capacity	46.30	15.00	61.30

* $120,380,000 ÷ 2,600,000 = $46.30 per barrel

The output-level overhead variance for each denominator-level concept is:

(a)   Theoretical capacity: $40,632,000   –   ($7.99 × 2,600,000)
       $40,632,000   – $20,774,000 = $19,858,000 U
(b)   Practical capacity: $40,632,000   –   ($12.00 × 2,600,000)
       $40,632,000   – $31,200,000 = $ 9,432,000 U
(c)   Normal utilization: $40,632,000   –   ($15.00 × 2,600,000)
       $40,632,000   – $39,000,000 = $ 1,632,000 U

Illustration of operating income differences:

Practical – Theoretical: $13,848,000   – $13,046,000   = $ 802,000
Normal – Practical: $14,448,000   – $13,848,000   = $ 600,000
Normal – Theoretical: $14,448,000   – $13,046,000   = $1,402,000

The difference in operating income across the three denominator-level concepts is due solely to differences in fixed manufacturing overhead included in the ending 200,000 barrels of inventory:

Theoretical capacity: 200,000 × $ 7.99 = $1,598,000

}$802,000 difference

Practical capacity: 200,000 × $12.00 = $2,400,000

}$600,000 difference

Normal capacity: 200,000 × $15.00 = $3,000,000

9-26 (cont'd)

SOLUTION EXHIBIT 9-26

	Theoretical Capacity	Practical Capacity	Normal Utilization
Revenues ($68 × 2,400,000)	$163,200,000	$163,200,000	$163,200,000
Cost of goods sold:			
Beginning inventory	0	0	0
Variable manufacturing costs,			
$46.30 × 2,600,000	120,380,000	120,380,000	120,380,000
Fixed manufacturing overhead costs,			
$7.99, $12, $15 × 2,600,000	20,774,000	31,200,000	39,000,000
Cost of goods available for sale	141,154,000	151,580,000	159,380,000
Ending inventory,			
$54.29, $58.30, $61.30 × 200,000	10,858,000	11,660,000	12,260,000
Total cost of goods sold (at budgeted costs)	130,296,000	139,920,000	147,120,000
Adjustment for variances	19,858,000[a]	9,432,000[a]	1,632,000[a]
Cost of goods sold	150,154,000	149,352,000	148,752,000
Gross margin	13,046,000	13,848,000	14,448,000
Other costs	0	0	0
Operating income	$ 13,046,000	$ 13,848,000	$ 14,448,000

[a]See the answer to requirement 1 for computation.

2. Given the data in this question, the theoretical-capacity concept reports the lowest operating income and thus (other things being equal) the lowest tax bill for 2000. Lucky Lager benefits by having deductions as early as possible. The theoretical-capacity denominator-level concept maximizes the deductions for manufacturing costs.

3. Revenue Canada may restrict the flexibility of a company in several ways.
   a. Restrict the denominator-level concept choice.
   b. Restrict the cost line items that can be expensed rather than inventoried.
   c. Restrict the ability of a company to use shorter write-off periods or more accelerated write-off periods for inventoriable costs.

9-28 (40 min.) The All-Fixed Company in 2000.

This problem always generates active classroom discussion.

1. The treatment of fixed manufacturing overhead in absorption costing is affected primarily by what denominator level is selected as a base for allocating fixed manufacturing costs to units produced. In this case, is 10,000 tonnes per year, 20,000 tonnes, or some other denominator level the most appropriate base?

We usually place the following possibilities on the board or overhead projector and then ask the students to indicate by vote how many used one denominator level versus another. Incidentally, discussion tends to move more clearly if variable-costing income statements are discussed first, because there is little disagreement as to computations under variable costing.

(a) Variable-Costing Income Statements:

		1999	2000	Together
Revenues (and contribution margin)		$300,000	$300,000	$600,000
Fixed costs:				
Manufacturing costs	$280,000			
Marketing and administrative cost	40,000	320,000	320,000	640,000
Operating income		$(20,000)	$(20,000)	$(40,000)

(b) Absorption-Costing Income Statements:

The ambiguity about the 10,000- or 20,000-unit denominator level is intentional. If you wish, the ambiguity may be avoided by giving the students a specific denominator level in advance.

Alternative 1. Use 20,000 units as a denominator; fixed manufacturing overhead per unit is $280,000 × 20,000 = $14.

	1999	2000	Together
Revenues	$300,000	$300,000	$ 600,000
Manufacturing costs @ $14	280,000	—	280,000
Deduct ending inventory	140,000	—	—
Cost of goods sold	140,000	140,000*	280,000
Underallocated manuf. overhead—			
output level variance	—	280,000	280,000
Marketing and administrative costs	40,000	40,000	80,000
Total costs	180,000	460,000	640,000
Operating income	$120,000	$(160,000)	$ (40,000)

* Inventory carried forward from 1999 and sold in 2000.

9-28 (cont'd)

<u>Alternative 2</u>.   Use 10,000 units as a denominator; fixed manufacturing overhead per unit is $280,000 ÷ 10,000 = $28.

	1999	2000	Together
Revenues	$300,000	$300,000	$600,000
Manufacturing costs @ $28	560,000	—	560,000
Deduct ending inventory	280,000	—	—
Cost of goods sold*	280,000	280,000	560,000
Underallocated manuf. overhead— output level variance	—	280,000	—
Overallocated manuf. overhead— output level variance	(280,000)	—	—
Marketing and administrative costs	40,000	40,000	80,000
Total costs	40,000	600,000	640,000
Operating income	$260,000	$(300,000)	$ (40,000)

*Inventory carried forward from 1999 and sold in 2000.

Note that operating income under variable costing follows sales and is not affected by inventory changes.

Note also that students will understand the variable-costing presentation much more easily than the alternatives presented under absorption costing.

2.   Breakeven point $= \dfrac{\text{Fixed costs}}{\text{Contribution margin per tonne}} = \dfrac{\$320,000}{\$30}$

$= $ 10,667 tonnes per year or 21,333 for two years.

If the company could sell 667 more tonnes per year at $30 each, it could get the extra $20,000 contribution margin needed to break even.

Most students will say that the breakeven point is 10,667 tonnes per year under both absorption costing and variable costing. The logical question to ask a student who answers 10,667 tonnes for variable costing is: "What operating income do you show for 1999 under absorption costing?" If a student answers $120,000 (alternative 1 above), or $260,000 (alternative 2 above), ask: "But you say your breakeven point is 10,667 tonnes. How can you show an operating income on only 10,000 tonnes sold during 1999?"

The answer to the above dilemma lies in the fact that operating income is affected by both sales and production under absorption costing.

9-28 (cont'd)

<u>Optional</u>: Given that sales would be 10,000 tonnes in 1999, solve for the production level that will provide a breakeven level of zero operating income. Using the formula in the chapter, sales of 10,000 units, and a fixed manufacturing overhead rate of $14 (based on $280,000 ÷ 20,000 units denominator level = $14):

Let P = Production level

$$\text{Breakeven sales in units} = \frac{\left(\begin{array}{c}\text{Total fixed}\\\text{costs}\end{array}\right) + \left[\left(\begin{array}{c}\text{Fixed manuf.}\\\text{overhead}\\\text{rate}\end{array}\right) \times \left(\begin{array}{c}\text{Breakeven}\\\text{sales in}\\\text{units}\end{array} - \begin{array}{c}\text{Units}\\\text{produced}\end{array}\right)\right]}{\text{Unit contribution margin}}$$

10,000 tonnes	=	$\dfrac{\$320,000 + \$14(10,000 - P)}{\$30}$
$300,000	=	$320,000 + $140,000 − $14P
$14P	=	$160,000
P	=	11,429 units (rounded)

Proof:

Gross margin, 10,000 × ($30 − $14)		$160,000
Output level variance, (20,000 − 11,429) × $14	$120,000	
Marketing and administrative costs	40,000	160,000
Operating income		$ 0

Given that production would be 20,000 tonnes in 1999, solve for the breakeven unit sales level. Using the formula in the chapter and a fixed manufacturing overhead rate of $14 (based on a denominator level of 20,000 units):

Let N = Breakeven sales in units

$$N = \frac{\left(\begin{array}{c}\text{Total fixed}\\\text{costs}\end{array}\right) + \left[\left(\begin{array}{c}\text{Fixed manuf.}\\\text{overhead rate}\end{array}\right) \times \left(N - \begin{array}{c}\text{Units}\\\text{produced}\end{array}\right)\right]}{\text{Unit contribution margin}}$$

N	=	$\dfrac{\$320,000 + \$14(N - 20,000)}{\$30}$
$30N	=	$320,000 + $14N − $280,000
$16N	=	$40,000
N	=	2,500 units

Proof:

Gross margin, 2,500 × ($30 – $14)		$40,000
Output level MOH variance	$ 0	
Marketing and administrative costs	40,000	40,000
Operating income		$ 0

We find it helpful to put the following comparisons on the board:

$$\text{Variable costing breakeven} = f(\text{sales})$$
$$= 10,000 \text{ tonnes}$$

$$\text{Absorption-costing breakeven} = f(\text{sales and production})$$
$$= f(10,000 \text{ and } 11,429)$$
$$= f(2,500 \text{ and } 20,000)$$

3.   Absorption costing inventory cost: Either $140,000 or $280,000 at the end of 1999 and zero at the end of 2000.

Variable costing: Zero at all times. This is a major criticism of variable costing and focuses on the issue of the definition of an asset.

4.   Operating income is affected by both production and sales under absorption costing. Hence, most managers would prefer absorption costing because their performance in any given reporting period, at least in the short run, is influenced by how much production is scheduled near the end of a period.

9-30 (25-35 min.) **Comparison of variable costing and absorption costing.**

1. Operating income is a function of both sales and production under absorption costing, whereas it is a function only of sales under variable costing. Therefore, inventory changes can have dramatic effects on operating income under absorption costing. In this case, the severe decline in inventory has resulted in enormous fixed costs from beginning inventory being charged against 2000 operations.

2. The income statement deliberately contains an ambiguity about whether the fixed manufacturing overhead of $1,000,000 is the budgeted or actual amount. Of course, it must be the budgeted amount, because the spending variance and the output level variance are shown separately. Therefore:

$$\begin{array}{ll} \text{Output level} \\ \text{Manuf. costs variance} \end{array} = \begin{array}{l} \text{Budgeted fixed} \\ \text{manufacturing overhead} \end{array} - \begin{array}{l} \text{Fixed manufacturing} \\ \text{overhead allocated} \end{array}$$

$$\$400,000 = \$1,000,000 - \text{Allocated}$$

$$\text{Allocated} = \$600,000, \text{ which is } 60\% \text{ of denominator level}$$

3. Note that the answer to (3) is independent of (2). The difference in operating income of $315,000 ($600,000 – $285,000) is explained by the release of $315,000 of fixed manufacturing costs when the inventories were decreased during 2000:

	Absorption Costing	Variable Costing	Fixed Manuf. Overhead in Inventory
Inventories:			
December 31, 1999	$1,650,000	$1,320,000	$330,000
December 31, 2000	75,000	60,000	15,000
Release of fixed manuf. costs			$315,000

The above schedule in this requirement is a formal presentation of the equation:

$$\begin{array}{l} \text{Absorption} \\ \text{costing} \\ \text{operating} \\ \text{income} \end{array}_L - \begin{array}{l} \text{Variable} \\ \text{costing} \\ \text{operating} \\ \text{income} \end{array}_L = \begin{array}{l} \text{Fixed} \\ \text{manuf. costs} \\ \text{in ending} \\ \text{inventory} \end{array}_L - \begin{array}{l} \text{Fixed} \\ \text{manuf. costs} \\ \text{in beginning} \\ \text{inventory} \end{array}_L$$

$$(\$285,000 - \$600,000) = (\$15,000 - \$330,000)$$
$$= -\$315,000$$

9-30 (cont'd)

Alternatively, the presence of fixed manufacturing overhead costs in each income statement can be analyzed:

Absorption costing,
Fixed manuf. costs in cost of goods sold
($4,575,000 – $3,660,000) $ 915,000
Output level MOH variance   400,000
                                                    1,315,000

Variable costing, fixed manufacturing costs
charged to expense   1,000,000
Difference in operating income explained $ 315,000

Although it is not required, the following supplementary analysis may clarify the relationships:

	Absorption Costing	Variable Costing
Inventory, December 31, 1999	$1,650,000	$1,320,000
Cost of goods manufactured*	3,000,000	2,400,000
Available for sale	4,650,000	3,720,000
Inventory, December 31, 2000	75,000	60,000
Cost of goods sold	$4,575,000	$3,660,000

*Computed from the other data, which are given.

4. a. Absorption costing is more likely than variable costing to lead to inventory buildups. Under absorption costing, operating income in a given accounting period is increased because some fixed manufacturing overhead is accounted for as an asset (inventory) instead of an expense (fixed cost written off during the current period).

    b. Although variable costing will counteract undesirable inventory buildups, other measures can be used without abandoning absorption costing. Examples include budget targets and nonfinancial measures of performance such as maintaining specific inventory levels, inventory turnovers, delivery schedules, and equipment maintenance schedules.

9-32 (30-40 min.)   **Some additional requirements for Problem 9-31; absorption costing and output-level variances.**

1.   Revenues (1,070 × $1,000) $1,070,000
     Cost of goods sold:
       Beginning inventory (50 × $800) $ 40,000
       Variable manufacturing costs (1,180 × $200)   236,000
       Fixed manufacturing costs (1,180 × $600)   708,000
       Cost of goods available for sale   984,000
       Ending inventory (160 × $800)   128,000
         Cost of goods sold (at std. costs)   856,000
     Gross margin (at standard costs)   214,000
     Adjustment for variances[a]   12,000
     Gross margin   202,000
     Marketing and administrative costs:
       Variable marketing and admin. costs   53,500
       Fixed marketing and admin. costs   120,000
       Adjustment for variances   0
         Marketing and admin. costs   173,500
     Operating income $ 28,500

   [a] Unfavourable output level (production volume)
       variance = 20 × $600 = $12,000

The decrease in operating income from $40,000 for Jan.-Nov. 2000 to $28,500 for Jan. - Dec. 2000 arises because:

   Operating income through November 30, 2000 $40,000
   Additional revenues $70,000
   Additional cost of goods sold $56,000
   Additional other variable costs   3,500   59,500   10,500
                                                                                            50,500
   Production-volume variance   12,000
   Additional other fixed costs   10,000   22,000
   Operating income for 2000 $28,500

2.   Fixed manufacturing overhead rate:
       Total fixed manufacturing overhead (1,200 units × $600) $720,000
       Divide by practical capacity (125 units × 12 months)   1,500
       Equals fixed manufacturing overhead rate $480 per unit
       Units produced during 2000   1,180
       Production-volume variance:
           (1,500 − 1,180 units) × $480 = 320 units × $480   = $153,600 U

9-34 (30 min.) **Variable and absorption costing and breakeven points.**

1. Production = Sales + Ending Inventory − Beginning Inventory
   = 242,400 + 24,800 − 32,600
   = 234,600

2. Breakeven point in cases:

   a. Variable Costing:

   $$QT = \frac{\text{Total Fixed Costs } + \text{ Target Operating Income}}{\text{Contribution Margin per Unit}}$$

   $$QT = \frac{(\$3,753,600 + \$6,568,800) + \$0}{\$94 - (\$16 + \$10 + \$6 + \$14 + \$2)}$$

   $$QT = \frac{\$10,322,400}{\$46}$$

   $$QT = 224,400 \text{ cases}$$

   b. Absorption costing:

   $$QT = \frac{\text{Total Fixed Cost} + \text{Target IO} + \left[\text{Fixed Manuf. Cost Rate} \times \left(\text{Breakeven Sales in Units} - \text{Units Produced}\right)\right]}{\text{Contribution Margin per Unit}}$$

   $$QT = \frac{\$10,322,400 + [\$16\,(QT - 234,600)]}{\$46}$$

   $$QT = \frac{\$10,322,400 + 16\,QT - 3,753,600}{\$46}$$

   $$QT = \frac{\$6,568,800 + 16\,QT}{\$46}$$

   $$46\,QT - 16\,QT = \$6,568,800$$

   $$30\,QT = \$6,568,800$$

   $$QT = 218,960 \text{ cases}$$

9-34 (cont'd)

3. If grape prices increase by 25%, the cost of grapes per case will increase from $16 in 2000 to $20 in 2001. This will decrease the unit contribution margin from $46 in 2000 to $42 in 2001.

   a. Variable Costing:

$$QT = \frac{\$10,322,400}{\$42}$$

$$= \ 245,772 \text{ cases}$$

   b. Absorption Costing:

$$QT = \frac{\$6,568,800 + \$16\ QT}{\$42}$$

$$\$42\ QT = \$6,568,800 + \$16\ QT$$

$$\$26\ QT = \$6,568,800$$

$$QT = \ 252,647 \text{ cases}$$

9-36 (20 min.) **Absorption costing, management ethics (continuation of 9-35).**

1. Behaviours that might suggest problems for IEC with the existing bonus plan and accounting system include:

   a. Plant managers switching production orders at year-end to those orders that absorb the highest amount of manufacturing overhead, irrespective of the demand by customers of IEC.

   b. Plant managers at one division of IEC accepting orders that they know another plant of IEC is better suited to handle.

   c. Plant managers deferring maintenance beyond the normal maintenance period.

2. Possible changes include:

   a. Change the incentive scheme so that there are not the major discontinuities at 15% and 10%.

   b. Change the operating income measure to variable costing rather than absorption costing.

   c. Add other performance measures (such as inventory turnover) that explicitly penalize "building for inventory."

   d. Emphasize the importance of managers considering IEC total benefits and costs of their decisions. This could be done via persuasion or by an incentive system based on IEC operating income rather than 100% of each division's operating income.

CHAPTER 10
DETERMINING HOW COSTS BEHAVE

10-2   Three alternative linear cost functions are:
1.   Variable cost function—a cost function in which total costs change in proportion to the cost driver in the relevant range.
2.   Fixed cost function—a cost function in which total costs do not change with changes in the cost driver in the relevant range.
3.   Mixed cost function—a cost function that has both variable and fixed elements. Total costs change but not in proportion to the changes in the cost driver in the relevant range.

10-4   No. High correlation merely indicates that the two variables move together in the data examined. It is essential to consider also economic plausibility before making inferences about cause and effect. Without any economic plausibility for a relationship, it is less likely that a high level of correlation observed in one set of data will be similarly found in other sets of data.

10-6   The conference method develops cost estimates on the basis of analysis and opinions gathered from various departments of an organization (purchasing, process engineering, manufacturing, employee relations, etc.). Advantages of the conference method include:
1.   The speed with which cost estimates can be developed.
2.   The pooling of knowledge from experts across functional areas.
3.   The improved credibility of the cost function to all personnel.

10-8   The six steps are:
1.   Choose the dependent variable (the variable to be predicted, which is some type of cost).
2.   Identify the cost driver(s) (independent variables).
3.   Collect data on the dependent variable and the cost driver(s).
4.   Plot the data.
5.   Estimate the cost function.
6.   Evaluate the estimated cost function.

Step 3 typically is the most difficult for a cost analyst.

10-10   Criteria important when choosing among alternative cost functions are:
1.   Economic plausibility.
2.   Goodness of fit.
3.   Slope of the regression line.

10-12 Frequently encountered problems when collecting cost data on variables included in a cost function are:
1. The time period used to measure the dependent variable is not properly matched with the period used to measure the cost driver(s).
2. Fixed costs are allocated as if they are variable.
3. Data either are not available for all observations or are not uniformly reliable.
4. Extreme values of observations occur.
5. A homogeneous relationship between the individual cost items in the dependent variable and the cost driver(s) does not exist.
6. The relationship between cost and the cost driver is not stationary.
7. Inflation has occurred in a dependent variable, a cost driver, or both.

10-14 No. A cost driver is any factor whose change causes a change in the total cost of a related cost object. A cause-and-effect relationship underlies selection of a cost driver. Some users of regression analysis include numerous independent variables in a regression model in an attempt to maximize goodness of fit, irrespective of the economic plausibility of the independent variables included. Some of the independent variables included may not be cost drivers.

10-16 (10 min.) **Estimating a cost function.**

1. Slope coefficient $= \dfrac{\text{Difference in costs}}{\text{Difference in machine-hours}}$

$$= \dfrac{\$3,900 - \$3,000}{7,000 - 4,000}$$

$$= \dfrac{\$900}{3,000} = \$0.30 \text{ per machine-hour}$$

Constant $=$ Total cost $-$ (Slope coefficient $\times$ Quantity of cost driver)
$= \$3,900 - (\$0.30 \times 7,000) = \$1,800$
$= \$3,000 - (\$0.30 \times 4,000) = \$1,800$

The cost function based on the two observations is:

Maintenance costs $= \$1,800 + \$0.30$ (machine-hours)

2. The cost function in requirement 1 is an estimate of how costs behave within the relevant range, not at cost levels outside the relevant range. If there are no months with zero machine-hours represented in the maintenance account, data in that account cannot be used to estimate the fixed costs at the zero machine-hours level. Rather, the constant component of the cost function provides the best available starting point for a straight line that approximates how a cost behaves within the relevant range.

10-18 (20 min.) **Various cost-behaviour patterns.**

1.   K
2.   B
3.   G
4.   J   Note that A is incorrect because, although the cost per kilogram eventually equals a constant at $9.20, the total dollars of cost increases linearly from that point onward.
5.   I   The total costs will be the same regardless of the volume level.
6.   L
7.   F   This is a classic step-function cost.
8.   K
9.   C

10-20 (20 min.) **Account analysis method.**

1.

	Variable costs:	
	Car wash labour	$240,000
	Soap, cloth, and supplies	32,000
	Water	28,000
	Power to move conveyor belt	72,000
	Total variable costs	$372,000

	Fixed costs:	
	Depreciation	$ 64,000
	Supervision	30,000
	Cashier	16,000
	Total fixed costs	$110,000

2.   Variable costs per car = $\dfrac{\$372,000}{80,000}$ = $4.65 per car

Total costs estimated for 90,000 cars = $110,000 + ($4.65 × 90,000) = $528,500

3.   Average cost in 2000 = $\dfrac{\$372,000 + \$110,000}{80,000} = \dfrac{\$482,000}{80,000}$ = $6.025

   Average cost in 2001 = $\dfrac{\$528,500}{90,000}$ = $5.87

Some students may assume that power costs of running the continuously moving conveyor belt is a fixed cost. In this case the variable costs in 2000 will be $300,000 and the fixed costs $182,000.

The variable costs per car in 2000 = $300,000 ÷ 80,000 cars = $3.75 per car

Total costs for 90,000 cars in 2001 = $182,000 + ($3.75 × 90,000) = $519,500

The average cost of washing a car in 2001 = $519,500 ÷ 90,000 = $5.77.

10-22 (20 min.) **Estimating a cost function, high-low method.**

1. See Solution Exhibit 10-22. There is a positive relationship between the number of service reports (a cost driver) and the customer service department costs. This relationship is economically plausible.

2.

	Number Of Service Reports	Customer Service Department Costs
Highest observation of cost driver	436	$21,890
Lowest observation of cost driver	122	12,941
Difference	314	$ 8,949

Customer service department costs = $a + b$ (number of service reports)

$$\text{Slope coefficient } (b) = \frac{\$8,949}{314} = \$28.50 \text{ per service report}$$

Constant (a) = $21,890 − $28.50 (436) = $9,464
= $12,941 − $28.50 (122) = $9,464

Customer service
department costs = $9,464 + $28.50 (number of service reports)

3. Other possible cost drivers of customer service department costs are:
   (a) Number of products replaced with a new product (and the dollar value of the new products charged to the customer service department).
   (b) Number of products repaired and the time and cost of repairs.

10-22 (cont'd)

SOLUTION EXHIBIT 10-22
Plot of Number of Service Reports Versus
Customer Service Costs for Capitol Products

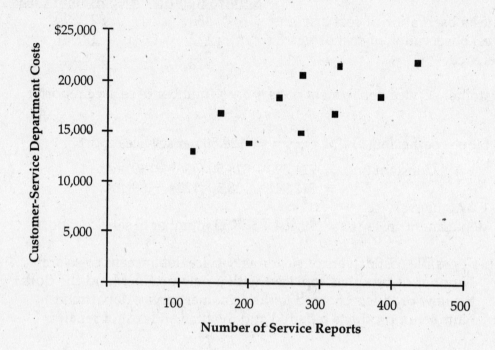

10-24 (20 min.) **Cost-volume-profit and regression analysis**.

1a. Average cost of manufacturing = $\dfrac{\text{Total manufacturing costs}}{\text{Number of bicycle frames}}$

$\qquad\qquad\qquad = \dfrac{\$900,000}{30,000} = \$30$ per frame

This cost is greater than the $28.50 per frame that Ryan has quoted.

1b. Garvin cannot take the average manufacturing cost in 2000 of $30 per frame and multiply it by 36,000 bicycle frames to determine the total cost of manufacturing 36,000 bicycle frames. The reason is that some of the $900,000 (or equivalently the $30 cost per frame) are fixed costs and some are variable costs. Without distinguishing fixed from variable costs, Garvin cannot determine the cost of manufacturing 36,000 frames. For example, if all costs are fixed, the manufacturing costs of 36,000 frames will continue to be $900,000. If, however, all costs are variable, the cost of manufacturing 36,000 frames would be $30 × 36,000 = $1,080,000. If some costs are fixed and some are variable, the cost of manufacturing 36,000 frames will be somewhere between $900,000 and $1,080,000.

Some students could argue that another reason for not being able to determine the cost of manufacturing 36,000 bicycle frames is that not all costs are output unit-level costs. If some costs are, for example, batch-level costs, more information would be needed on the number of batches in which the 36,000 bicycle frames would be produced, in order to determine the cost of manufacturing 36,000 bicycle frames.

2. Expected cost to make 36,000 bicycle frames $= \$432,000 + (\$15 \times 36,000)$

$\qquad\qquad\qquad\qquad\qquad\quad = \$432,000 + \$540,000 = \$972,000$

Purchasing bicycle frames from Ryan will cost $28.50 × 36,000 = $1,026,000. Hence it will cost Garvin $1,026,000 − $972,000 = $54,000 more to purchase the frames from Garvin rather than manufacture them in-house.

3. Garvin would need to consider several factors before being confident that the equation in requirement 2 accurately predicts the cost of manufacturing bicycle frames.
   a. Is the relationship between total manufacturing costs and quantity of bicycle frames economically plausible? For example, is the quantity of bicycles made the only cost driver or are there other cost-drivers (for example, batch-level costs of setups, production-orders, or material handling) that affect manufacturing costs?
   b. How good is the goodness of fit? That is, how well does the estimated line fit the data?
   c. Is the relationship between the number of bicycle frames produced and total manufacturing costs linear?
   d. Does the slope of the regression line indicate that a strong relationship exists between manufacturing costs and the number of bicycle frames produced?

10-24 (cont'd)

e. Are there any data problems such as, for example, errors in measuring costs, trends in prices of materials, labour or overheads that might affect variable or fixed costs over time, extreme values of observations, or a nonstationary relationship over time between total manufacturing costs and the quantity of bicycles produced?

10-26 (30–40 min.) **Regression analysis, activity-based costing, choosing cost drivers.**

1a. Solution Exhibit 10-26A presents the plots and regression line of number of packaged units moved on distribution costs.

SOLUTION EXHIBIT 10-26A
Plots and Regression Line of Number of Packaged Units Moved on Distribution Costs

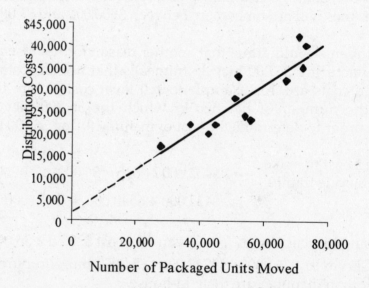

1b. Solution Exhibit 10-26B presents the plots and regression line of number of shipments made on distribution costs.

10-26 (cont'd)

Plots and Regression Line of Number of Shipments Made on Distribution Costs

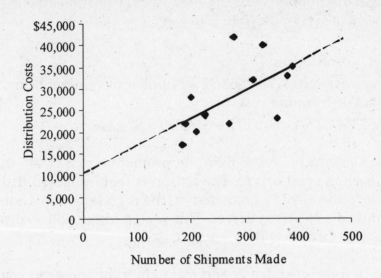

Number of packaged units moved appears to be a better cost driver of distribution costs for the following reasons:

(i) *Economic plausibility.* Both number of packaged units moved and number of shipments are economically plausible cost drivers. Because the product is heavy, however, costs of freight are likely to be a sizable component of distribution costs. Thus, number of packaged units moved will affect distribution costs significantly because freight costs are largely a function of the number of units transported.

(ii) *Goodness of fit.* Compare Solution Exhibits 10-26A and 10-26B. Number of packaged units moved has a better goodness of fit with distribution costs than do number of shipments made. That is, the vertical differences between actual and predicted number of shipments made are smaller for the number of packaged units moved regression than for the number of shipments made regression.

(iii) *Slope of regression line.* Again, compare Solution Exhibits 10-26A and 10-26B. The number of packaged units moved regression line has a relatively steep slope indicating a strong relationship between number of packaged units moved and distribution costs. On average, distribution costs increase with the number of packaged units moved. The number of shipments made regression line is flatter and has a wider scatter of observations about the line, indicating a weak relationship between number of shipments made and distribution costs. On average, the number of shipments made has a smaller effect on distribution costs.

10-26 (cont'd)

2. Using the preferred cost function,

    Distribution costs = $1,349 + ($0.496 × Number of packaged units moved),
Flaherty would budget distribution costs of

    $1,349 + ($0.496 × 40,000) = $1,349 + 19,840 = $21,189

3. Using the "other" cost function

    Distribution costs = $10,417 + ($63.77 × Number of shipments made),
Flaherty would budget distribution costs of

    $10,417 + ($63.77 × 220) = $10,417 + $14,029 = $24,446

The actual costs are likely to be lower than the prediction of $24,446 made using the number of shipments as the cost driver. The reason is that budgeted distribution costs are likely to be closer to the $21,189 predicted by the regression equation with number of packaged units moved as the cost driver. This regression equation provides a better explanation of the factors that affect distribution costs.

Choosing the "wrong" cost driver and estimating the incorrect cost function can have repercussions for pricing, cost management, and cost control. To the extent that Flaherty uses predicted costs of $24,446 for making pricing decisions, she may overprice the 40,000 packages she expects to move and could potentially lose business.

To see the problems in cost management, suppose Waterloo Corporation moves 40,000 units in 220 shipments in the next month while incurring actual costs of $23,500. Compared with the budget of $24,446, management would consider this a good performance and seek ways to replicate it. In fact, on the basis of the preferred cost driver, the number of packaged units moved, actual distribution costs of $23,500 are higher than what they should be ($21,189)—a performance that management should seek to correct and improve rather than replicate.

10-28 (20 min.) **Learning curve, incremental unit-time learning curve**

1. The direct manufacturing labour-hours (DMLH) required to produce the first 2, 3, and 4 units given the assumption of an incremental unit-time learning curve of 90% is as follows:

Cumulative Number of Units (1)	Individual Unit Time for Xth Unit (2)	Cumulative Total Time (3)
1	3,000	3,000
2	2,700 (3,000 × 0.90)	5,700
3	2,539	8,239
4	2,430 (2,700 × 0.90)	10,669

Values in column 2 are calculated using the formula $y = pX^q$

where p = 3,000, X = 2, 3, or 4 and q = –0.1520, which gives

when X = 2, $y = 3,000 \times 2^{-0.1520} = 2,700$
when X = 3, $y = 3,000 \times 3^{-0.1520} = 2,539$
when X = 4, $y = 3,000 \times 4^{-0.1520} = 2,430$

	Variable costs of producing		
	2 units	3 units	4 units
Direct materials $80,000 × 2; 3; 4	$160,000	$240,000	$ 320,000
Direct manufacturing labour $25 × 5,700; 8,239; 10,669	142,500	205,975	266,725
Variable manufacturing overhead $15 × 5,700; 8,239; 10,669	85,500	123,585	160,035
Total variable costs	$388,000	$569,560	$746,760

2.

	Variable costs of producing	
	2 units	4 units
Incremental unit-time learning curve (from requirement 1)	$388,000	$746,760
Cumulative average-time learning curve (from Exercise 10-27)	376,000	708,800
Difference	$ 12,000	$ 37,960

10-28 (cont'd)

Total variable costs for manufacturing 2 and 4 units are lower under the cumulative average-time learning curve relative to the incremental unit-time learning curve. Direct manufacturing labour-hours required to make additional units declines more slowly in the incremental unit-time learning curve relative to the cumulative average-time learning curve assuming the same 90% factor is used for both curves. The reason is that, in the incremental unit-time learning curve, as the number of units doubles, only the last unit produced has a cost of 90% of the initial cost. In the cumulative average-time model, doubling the number of units causes the average cost of *all* the additional units produced (not just the last unit) to be 90% of the initial cost.

10-30 (30–40 min.) **High-low versus regression method.**

1.   Solution Exhibit 10-30 presents the plots of advertising costs on revenues.

SOLUTION EXHIBIT 10-30
Plot and Regression Line of Advertising Costs on Revenues

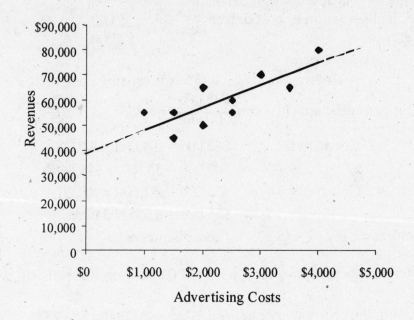

2.   Solution Exhibit 10-30 also shows the regression line of advertising costs on revenues. We evaluate the estimated regression equation using the criteria of economic plausibility, goodness of fit, and slope of the regression line.

Economic plausibility. Advertising costs appears to be a plausible cost driver of revenues. Restaurants frequently use newspaper advertising to promote their restaurants and increase their patronage.

Goodness of fit. The vertical differences between actual and predicted revenues appears to be reasonably small. This indicates that advertising costs are related to restaurant revenues.

Slope of regression line. The slope of the regression line appears to be relatively steep. This indicates that, on average, restaurant revenues increase with newspaper advertising.

10-30 (cont'd)

3. The high-low method would estimate the cost function as follows:

	Advertising Costs	Revenues
Highest observation of cost driver	$4,000	$80,000
Lowest observation of cost driver	1,000	55,000
Difference	$3,000	$25,000

$$\text{Revenues} = a + (b \times \text{advertising costs})$$

$$\text{Slope coefficient } (b) = \frac{\$25,000}{\$3,000} = 8.333$$

$$\text{Constant } (a) = \$80,000 - (\$4,000 \times 8.333)$$
$$= \$80,000 - 33,332 = \$46,668$$
$$or \quad \text{Constant } (a) = \$55,000 - (\$1,000 \times 8.333)$$
$$= \$55,000 - 8,333 = \$46,667$$

$$\text{Revenues} = \$46,667 + (8.333 \times \text{Advertising costs})$$

4. The increase in revenues for each $1,000 spent on advertising within the relevant range is

   a. Using the regression equation, 8.723 × $1,000 = $8,723
   b. Using the high-low equation, 8.333 × $1,000 = $8,333

5. The high-low equation does fairly well in estimating the relationship between advertising costs and revenues. However, Martinez and Brown should use the regression equation. The reason is that the regression equation uses information from all observations, whereas the high-low method relies only on the observations that have the highest and lowest values of the cost driver. These observations are generally not representative of all the data.

10-32 (30-40 min.) **Cost estimation, cumulative average-time learning curve.**

1.   Cost to Produce the Second through the Eighth Troop Deployment Boats:

Direct materials, 7 × $100,000	$ 700,000
Direct manufacturing labour, 39,130* × $30	1,173,900
Variable manufacturing overhead, 39,130 × $20	782,600
Other manufacturing overhead, 25% of $1,173,900	293,475
Total costs	$2,949,975

*The direct manufacturing labour-hours to produce the second to eighth boats can be calculated in several ways, given the assumption of a cumulative average-time learning curve of 85%:

(a)   Use of Table Format:

Cumulative Number of Units	Cumulative Average-Time per Unit	Cumulative Total Time
1	10,000.00	10,000
2	8,500.00 (10,000 × 0.85)	17,000
4	7,225.00 (8,500 × 0.85)	28,900
8	6,141.25 (7,225 × 0.85)	49,130

The direct labour-hours required to produce the second through the eight boats is 49,130 − 10,000 = 39,130 hours.

10-32 (cont'd)

(b)   Use of Formula:

$$y = pX^q$$

where $p = 10,000$, $X = 8$, and $q = -.2345$.

$$y = 10,000 \times 8^{-.2345} = 6,141 \text{ hours (rounded)}$$

The total direct labour-hours for 8 units is $6,141 \times 8 = 49,128$ hours

The direct labour-hours required to produce the second through the eighth boats is $49,128 - 10,000 = 39,128$ hours. (By taking the q factor to 6 decimal digits, an estimate of 49,130 hours would result.)

Note: Some students will debate the exclusion of the tooling cost. The question specifies that the tooling cost was assigned to the first boat. Although Nautilus may well seek to ensure that its total revenue covers the $725,000 cost of the first boat, the concern in this question is only with the cost of producing seven more PT109s.

2.   Cost to Produce the Second through the Eighth Boats Assuming Linear Function for Direct Labour-Hours and Units Produced:

Direct materials, 7 × $100,000	$ 700,000
Direct manufacturing labour, 7 × 10,000 hours × $30	2,100,000
Variable manufacturing overhead, 7 × 10,000 hours × $20	1,400,000
Other manufacturing overhead, 25% of $2,100,000	525,000
Total costs	$4,725,000

The difference in predicted costs is:

• Predicted cost in requirement 2 (based on linear cost function)	$4,725,000
• Predicted cost in requirement 1 (based on an 85% learning curve)	2,949,975
Difference	$1,775,025

10-34 (30 min.)   **Appendix: Promotion of a new product, simple and multiple regression analysis.**

1.   The t-values (value of the coefficient ÷ standard error of the coefficient) of the coefficients in each of the regressions follow. A t-value greater than 2 indicates that the coefficient is significantly different from zero.

Regression 1: t-value of coefficient of X_1 = \$3.98 ÷ \$1.73 = 2.30, indicating that there is a relation between dollars incurred on discount coupons and estimated sales.

Regression 2: t-value of coefficient of X_2 = \$4.23 ÷ \$1.86 = 2.27, indicating that there is a relation between dollars spent on TV advertising and estimated sales.

Regression 3: t-value of coefficient of X_1 = \$0.87 ÷ \$0.79 = 1.11, indicating that there is no relation between dollars incurred on discount coupons and estimated sales given direct materials costs; t-value of coefficient of X_2 = \$0.91 ÷ \$0.99 = 0.92, indicating that there is no relation between dollars spent on TV advertising and estimated sales given dollars incurred on discount coupons.

2.   The t-value indicates that the coefficients in the simple regressions are statistically significant, but that the coefficients of the same variables are insignificant in a multiple regression. The likely reason is multicollinearity. Because the two independent variables are correlated, the standard errors of the coefficients increase and make the variables appear insignificant and difficult to interpret.

3.   Omitting a correlated variable (as the first two regressions do) causes the estimated coefficient of the independent variable to be biased away from its true value. Including both variables induces multicollinearity, which makes interpreting the significance of the coefficients difficult. To make predictions about estimated sales, it is probably best to use both dollars incurred on discount coupons and dollars spent on TV advertising despite the multicollinearity problems.

   To understand the separate effects of dollars incurred on discount coupons and dollars spent on TV advertising on estimated sales, Rivk would need to find months of data where either dollars incurred on discount coupons and dollars spent on TV advertising were high, but not both. Such new data will not suffer from the problems of multicollinearity and will allow Rivk to estimate the relationship between each cost driver and estimated sales.

10-36 (30 min.)   **Appendix: Evaluating multiple regression models, not for profit (continuation of 10-35).**

1.   It is economically plausible that the correct form of the model of overhead costs includes both number of academic programs and number of enrolled students as cost drivers. The findings in Problem 10-35 indicate that each of the independent variables affects overhead costs. (Each regression has a significant r^2 and t-value on the independent variable.) Hanks could choose to divide overhead costs into two cost pools, (i) those overhead costs that are more closely related to number of academic programs and (ii) those overhead costs more closely related to number of enrolled students, and rerun the simple regression analysis on each overhead cost pool. Alternatively, Hanks could run a multiple regression analysis with total overhead costs as the dependent variable and the number of academic programs and number of enrolled students as the two independent variables.

2.   Solution Exhibit 10-36A evaluates the multiple regression model using the format of Exhibit 10-21. Hanks should use the multiple regression model rather than the two simple regression models of Problem 10-35. The multiple regression model appears economically plausible and the regression model performs very well when estimating overhead costs. It has an excellent goodness of fit, significant t-values on both independent variables, and meets all the specification assumptions for ordinary least squares regression.

There is some correlation between the two independent variables, but multi-collinearity does not appear to be a problem here. The significance of both independent variables (despite some correlation between them) suggests that each variable is a 'river of overhead cost. Of course, as the chapter describes, even if the independent variables exhibited multicollinearity, Hanks should still prefer to use the multiple regression model over the simple regression models of Problem 10-35. Omitting any one of the variables will cause the estimated coefficient of the independent variable included in the model to be biased away from its true value.

3.   Possible uses for the multiple regression results include:

a.   Planning and budgeting at Eastern University. The regression analysis indicates the variables (number of academic programs and number of enrolled students) that help predict changes in overhead costs.

b.   Cost control and performance evaluation. Hanks could compare actual performance with budgeted or expected numbers and seek ways to improve the efficiency of the university operations, and evaluate the performance of managers responsible for controlling overhead costs.

c.   Cost management. If cost pressures increase, the University could save costs by closing down academic programs that have few students enrolled.

10-36 (cont'd)

SOLUTION EXHIBIT 10-36A
Evaluation of Cost Function for Overhead Costs Estimated with Multiple Regression for Eastern University

Criterion	Number of Academic Programs and Number of Enrolled Students as Independent Variables
1. Economic Plausibility	A positive relationship between overhead costs and number of academic programs and number of enrolled students is economically plausible at Eastern University.
2. Goodness of Fit	$r^2 = 0.81$ Excellent goodness of fit
3. Significance of Independent Variable(s)	t-values of 3.46 on number of academic programs and 2.03 on number of enrolled students are both significant.
4. Specification Analysis of Estimation Assumptions	The assumptions of linearity, constant variance, and normality of residuals hold, but inferences drawn from only 12 observations are not reliable; the Durbin Watson statistic = 1.84 indicates that independence of residuals holds.

10-38 (30-40 min.) **Appendix: Purchasing department cost drivers, multiple regression analysis (continuation of 10-37).**

The problem reports the exact t-values from the computer runs of the data. Because the coefficients and standard errors given in the problem are rounded to three decimal places, dividing the coefficient by the standard error may yield slightly different t-values.

(a)   Regression 4 is a well-specified regression model:

Economic plausibility: Both independent variables are plausible and are supported by the findings of the Couture Fabrics study.

Goodness of fit: The r^2 of 0.63 indicates an excellent goodness of fit.

Significance of independent variables: The t-value on # of POs is 2.14, while the t-value on # of Ss is 2.00. These t-values are either significant or border on significance.

Specification analysis: Results are available to examine the independence of residuals assumption. The Durbin-Watson statistic of 1.90 indicates that the assumption of independence is not rejected.

Regression 4 is consistent with the findings in Problem 10-37 that both the number of purchase orders and the number of suppliers are drivers of purchasing department costs. Regressions 2, 3, and 4 all satisfy the four criteria outlined in the text. Regression 4 has the best goodness of fit (0.63 for Regression 4 compared with 0.42 and 0.39 for Regressions 2 and 3, respectively). Most importantly, it is economically plausible that both the number of purchase orders and the number of suppliers drive purchasing department costs. We would recommend that Lee use Regression 4 over Regressions 2 and 3.

2.   Regression 5 adds an additional independent variable (MP$) to the two independent variables in Regression 4. This additional variable (MP$) has a t-value of –0.07, implying that its slope coefficient is insignificantly different from zero. The r^2 in Regression 5 (0.63) is the same as that in Regression 4 (0.63), implying that the addition of this third independent variable adds close to zero explanatory power. In summary, Regression 5 adds very little to Regression 4. We would recommend that Lee use Regression 4 over Regression 5.

3.   Budgeted purchasing department costs for the Saskatoon store next year are:

$485,384 + ($123.22 × 3,900) + ($2,952 × 110) = $1,290,662

4. Multicollinearity is a frequently encountered problem in cost accounting; it does not arise in simple regression because there is only one independent variable in a simple regression. One consequence of multicollinearity is an increase in the standard errors of the coefficients of the individual variables. This frequently shows up in reduced t-values in the multiple regression relative to the t-values in the simple regression:

Variables	t-value in Multiple Regression	t-value from Simple Regressions in Problem 10-37
Regression 4:		
# of POs	2.14	2.43
# of Ss	2.00	2.28
Regression 5:		
# of POs	1.95	2.43
# of Ss	1.84	2.28
MP$	–0.07	0.84

The declines in the t-values in the multiple regressions are consistent with some (but not very high) collinearity among the independent variables. Pairwise correlations between the independent variables are:

	Correlation
# of POs / # of Ss	0.29
# of POs / MP $	0.27
# of Ss / MP$	0.34

5. Decisions in which the regression results in Problems 10-37 and 10-38 could be used are:

Cost management decisions: Fashion Flair could restructure relationships with the suppliers so that fewer separate purchase orders are made. Alternatively, it may aggressively reduce the number of existing suppliers.

Purchasing policy decisions: Fashion Flair could set up an internal charge system for individual retail departments within each store. Separate charges to each department could be made for each purchase order and each new supplier added to the existing ones. These internal changes would signal to each department ways in which their own decisions affect the total costs of Fashion Flair.

Accounting system design decisions: Fashion Flair may want to discontinue allocating purchasing department costs on the basis of the dollar value of merchandise purchased. Allocation bases better capturing cause-and-effect relations at Fashion Flair are the number of purchase orders and the number of suppliers.

10-40   (20 min.)   **Data analysis and ethics.**

1(a)	Average annual labour costs over the last ten years	$1,200,000
	Expected annual labour costs if robots introduced	550,000
	Expected annual savings	$ 650,000
1(b)	Average annual labour costs over the last three years	$ 800,000
	Expected annual labour costs if robots introduced	550,000
	Expected annual savings	$ 250,000

Yes, it makes a difference in terms of justifying the robot investment. Using a 10-year average, the expected annual savings exceed the desired amount of $400,000 per year. Using average annual labour costs over the last three years, expected annual savings in labour costs falls short of the $400,000 target needed to justify the robot investment.

2.   One explanation for average labour costs over the most recent three-year period being less than the average labour costs over the past ten years is learning curve effects. Learning-by-doing has caused workers to become more efficient. Alternatively, Comdex may have changed the VCR design to simplify manufacturing and reduce costs. Comdex may also have introduced new equipment that reduced labour costs.

3.   The behaviour of both Helen Gibbs and Joan Hansen to overestimate deliberately the savings in labour costs to justify investments in robots is unethical. In assessing the situation, and considering the "Code of Professional Ethics" described in Exhibit 1-5, the issues that Joan Hansen, the management accountant, should consider are listed below.

(a)   Clear reports using relevant and reliable information should be prepared. Reports prepared on the basis of overestimating savings in direct and indirect manufacturing labour (by considering older costs that are much higher than current costs) violate the management accountant's responsibility for competence. It is unethical for Gibbs to suggest that Hansen overestimate the cost savings that were computed for the robot investment and for Hansen to change the numbers to justify the investment in robots.

(b)   Management accountants should communicate favourable as well as unfavourable information. In this regard, both Gibbs's and Hansen's behaviour of inflating manufacturing labour cost savings to justify the investment in robots could be viewed as unethical.

10-40 (cont'd)

(c) Management accountants should communicate information fairly and objectively and all relevant information should be disclosed. From a management accountant's standpoint, overestimating manufacturing labour cost savings to justify the robot investment violates objectivity. For the various reasons cited above, we should take the position that the behaviour of Gibbs and Hansen is unethical.

4. Hansen should indicate to Gibbs that the savings in manufacturing labour costs alone are not large enough to justify the robot investment. She should also indicate to Gibbs her concern about inflating cost savings to justify the robot investment, quite independent of how important she thinks it is for the company to invest in the robots. She may wish to point out that part of the problem is the excessive focus on cost savings alone to justify the robot investment. An important benefit of the robot investment is the ability to generate higher revenues by producing superior products. If Gibbs still insists on inflating costs to justify the investment, Hansen should raise the matter with Gibbs's superior. If, after taking all these steps, there is continued pressure to overstate cost savings, Hansen should consider resigning from the company, rather than engage in unethical behaviour.

CHAPTER 11
DECISION MAKING AND
RELEVANT INFORMATION

11-2 *Relevant costs* are those expected future costs that differ among alternative courses of action. Historical costs are irrelevant because they are past costs and therefore cannot differ among alternative future courses of action.

11-4 *Quantitative factors* are outcomes that are measured in numerical terms. Some quantitative factors are financial—that is, they can be easily expressed in financial terms. Direct materials is an example of a quantitative financial factor. *Qualitative factors* are factors that are not measured in numerical terms. An example is employee morale.

11-6 No. Some variable costs may not differ among the alternatives under consideration and hence will be irrelevant. Some fixed costs may differ among the alternatives and hence will be relevant.

11-8 *Opportunity cost* is the contribution to income that is forgone (rejected) by not using a limited resource in its next-best alternative use.

11-10 No. Managers should aim to get the highest contribution margin per unit of the constraining (that is, scarce, limiting, or critical) factor. The constraining factor is what restricts or limits the production or sale of a given product (for example, availability of machine-hours).

11-12 Cost written off as amortization is irrelevant when it pertains to a past cost. But the purchase cost of new equipment to be acquired in the future that will then be written off as depreciation is often relevant.

11-14 The three steps in solving a linear programming problem are:
(a) Determine the objective.
(b) Specify the constraints.
(c) Compute the optimal solution.

11-16 (20 min.) Disposal of assets.

1.   This is an unfortunate situation, yet the $80,000 costs are irrelevant regarding the decision to remachine or scrap. The only relevant factors are the future revenues and future costs. By ignoring the accumulated costs and deciding on the basis of expected future costs, operating income will be maximized (or losses minimized). The difference in favour of remachining is $3,000:

	(a) Remachine	(b) Scrap
Future revenues	$35,000	$2,000
Deduct future costs	30,000	—
Operating income	$ 5,000	$2,000

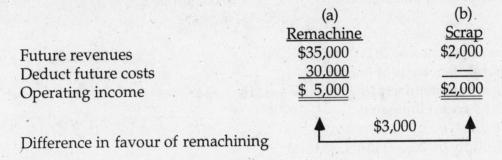

Difference in favour of remachining $3,000

2.   This too is an unfortunate situation. But the $100,000 original cost is irrelevant to this decision. The difference in favour of rebuilding is $7,000:

	(a) Replace	(b) Rebuild
New truck	$102,000	–
Deduct current disposal price of existing truck	10,000	–
Rebuild existing truck	–	$85,000
	$ 92,000	$85,000

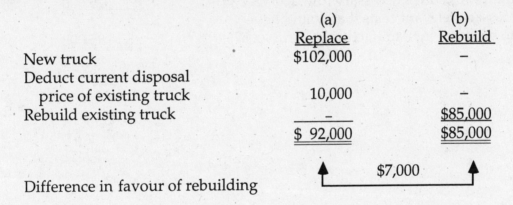

Difference in favour of rebuilding $7,000

Note here that the current disposal price of $10,000 is relevant, but the original cost (or book value, if the truck were not brand new) is irrelevant.

11-18 (15 min.) Multiple choice.

1. (b)

Special order price per unit	$6.00
Variable manufacturing costs per unit	4.50
Contribution margin per unit	$1.50

Effect on operating income = $1.50 × 20,000 units
= $30,000 increase

2. (b)

Costs of purchases, 20,000 units × $60		$1,200,000
Total relevant costs of making:		
Variable manufacturing costs, $64 – $16	$48	
Fixed costs eliminated	9	
Costs saved by not making	$57	
Multiply by 20,000 units, so total		
costs saved are $57 × 20,000		1,140,000
Extra costs of purchasing outside		60,000
Minimum savings necessary for Part No. 575		25,000
Necessary relevant costs that would have		
to be saved in manufacturing Part No. 575		$ 85,000

11-20 (30 min.)   Make versus buy, activity-based costing.

1.   The expected manufacturing cost per unit of CMCBs in 2001 is as follows:

	Total Manufacturing Costs of CMCB (1)	Manufacturing Cost per Unit (2) = (1) ÷ 10,000
Direct materials $170 × 10,000	$1,700,000	$170
Direct manufacturing labour $45 × 10,000	450,000	45
Variable batch manufacturing costs $1,500 × 80	120,000	12
Fixed manufacturing costs		
Avoidable fixed manufacturing costs	320,000	32
Unavoidable fixed manufacturing costs	800,000	80
Total manufacturing costs	$3,390,000	$339

2.   The following table identifies the incremental costs in 2001 if Svenson (a) made CMCBs and (b) purchased CMCBs from Minton.

Incremental Items	Total Incremental Costs Make	Total Incremental Costs Buy	Per-Unit Incremental Costs Make	Per-Unit Incremental Costs Buy
Cost of purchasing CMCBs from Minton		$		$300
Direct materials	$1,700,000	3,000,000	$170	
Direct manufacturing labour	450,000		45	
Variable batch manufacturing costs	120,000		12	
Avoidable fixed manufacturing costs	320,000		32	
Total incremental costs	$2,590,000		$259	$300
		$3,000,000		
Difference in favour of making	↑ $410,000 ↑		↑ $41 ↑	

Note that the opportunity cost of using capacity to make CMCBs is zero since Svenson would keep this capacity idle if it purchases CMCBs from Minton.

Svenson should continue to manufacture the CMCBs internally, since the incremental costs to manufacture are $259 per unit compared with the $300 per unit that Minton has quoted. Note that the unavoidable fixed manufacturing costs of $800,000 ($80 per unit) will continue to be incurred whether Svenson makes or buys CMCBs. These are not incremental costs under either the make or the buy alternative and are hence irrelevant.

3.   Svenson should continue to make CMCBs. The simplest way to solve this problem is to recognize that Svenson would prefer to keep any excess capacity idle rather than use it to make CB3s. Why? Because expected incremental future revenues from CB3s ($2,000,000) are less than expected incremental future costs ($2,150,000). If Svenson keeps its capacity idle, we know from requirement 2 that it should make CMCBs rather than buy them.

11-20 (cont'd)

An important point to note is that, because Svenson forgoes no contribution by not being able to make and sell CB3s, the opportunity cost of using its facilities to make CMCBs is zero. It is therefore not forgoing any profits by using the capacity to manufacture CMCBs. If it does not manufacture CMCBs, rather than lose money on CB3s, Svenson will keep the capacity idle.

A longer and more detailed approach is to use the total alternatives or opportunity cost analyses shown in the chapter.

TOTAL-ALTERNATIVES APPROACH TO MAKE-OR-BUY DECISIONS

	Choices for Svenson		
Relevant Items	Make CMCBs and Do Not Make CB3s	Buy CMCBs and Do Not Make CB3s	Buy CMCBs and Make CB3s
Total incremental costs of making/buying CMCBs (from requirement 2)	$2,590,000	$3,000,000	$3,000,000
Excess of future costs over future revenues from CB3s	0	0	150,000
Total relevant costs	$2,590,000	$3,000,000	$3,150,000

Svenson will minimize manufacturing costs by making CMCBs.

OPPORTUNITY COST APPROACH TO MAKE-OR-BUY DECISIONS

	Choices for Svenson	
Relevant Items	Make CMCB	Buy CMCB
Total incremental costs of making/buying CMCBs (from requirement 2)	$2,590,000	$3,000,000
Opportunity cost: profit contribution forgone because capacity cannot be used to make CB3s	0*	0
Total relevant costs	$2,590,000	$3,000,000

Difference in favour of making CMCBs $410,000

* Opportunity cost is 0 because Svenson does not give up anything by manufacturing CMCBs. Had it not manufactured CMCBs, it would be best off leaving the capacity idle (rather than manufacturing and selling CB3s).

11-22 (10 min.) **Inventory decision, opportunity cost.**

1. Unit cost, orders of 20,000 $8.00
     Unit cost, order of 240,000 (0.95 × $8.00) $7.60

     Alternatives under consideration:
     (a)   Buy 240,000 units at start of year.
     (b)   Buy 20,000 units at start of each month.

     Average investment in inventory:

(a) (240,000 × $7.60) ÷ 2	$912,000
(b) (20,000 × $8.00) ÷ 2	80,000
Difference in average investment	$832,000

Opportunity cost of interest forgone from 240,000-unit purchase at start of year
= $832,000 × 0.08 = $66,560

2. No. The $66,560 is an opportunity cost rather than an incremental or outlay cost. No actual transaction records the $66,560 as an entry in the accounting system.

3.   The following table presents the two alternatives:

	Alternative A: Purchase 240,000 spark plugs at beginning of year (1)	Alternative B: Purchase 20,000 spark plugs at beginning of each month (2)	Difference (3)=(1)–(2)
Annual purchase (incremental) costs (240,000 × $7.60; 240,000 × $8)	$1,824,000	$1,920,000	$(96,000)
Annual interest income that could be earned if investment in inventory were invested (opportunity cost) (8% × $912,000; 8% × $80,000)	72,960	6,400	66,560
Relevant costs	$1,896,960	$1,926,400	$(29,440)

Column (3) indicates that purchasing 240,000 spark plugs at the beginning of the year is preferred relative to purchasing 20,000 spark plugs at the beginning of each month because the lower purchase cost exceeds the opportunity cost of holding larger inventory. If other incremental benefits of holding lower inventory such as lower insurance, materials handling, storage, obsolescence, and breakage costs were considered, the costs under Alternative A would have been higher, and Alternative B might have been preferred.

11-24 (10 min.) **Selection of most profitable product.**

Only Model 14 should be produced. The key to this problem is the relationship of manufacturing overhead to product. Note that it takes twice as long to produce Model 9; machine-hours for Model 9 are twice that for Model 14. Management should choose the product mix that maximizes operating income for a given production capacity (the scarce resource in this situation). In this case, Model 14 will yield a $19.00 contribution to fixed costs per unit of machine time, and Model 9 will yield $18.00:

	Model 9	Model 14
Selling price per unit	$100.00	$70.00
Variable costs per unit	82.00	60.50
Contribution margin per unit	$ 18.00	$ 9.50
Relative use of machine-hours per unit of product	× 1	× 2
Contribution margin per unit of machine time	$ 18.00	$19.00

11-26 (20-25 min.) **Customer profitability, choosing customers.**

1.   Broadway should not drop the Kelly Corporation business as the following analysis shows.

Loss in revenues from dropping Kelly	$(80,000)
Savings in costs:	
Variable costs	48,000
Fixed costs 20% × $100,000	20,000
Total savings in costs	68,000
Effect on operating income	$(12,000)

Broadway Printers would be worse off by $12,000 if it drops the Kelly Corporation business.

2.   If Broadway accepts the additional business from Kelly, it would take an additional 500 hours of machine time. If Broadway accepts all of Kelly's and Taylor's business for February, it would require 2,500 hours of machine time (1,500 hours for Taylor and 1,000 hours for Kelly). Broadway only has 2,000 hours of machine capacity. It must therefore choose how much of the Taylor and Kelly business to accept. If Broadway accepts any additional business from Kelly, it must forgo some of Taylor's business.

To maximize operating income, Broadway should maximize contribution margin per unit of the constrained resource. (Fixed costs will remain unchanged at $100,000, whatever business Broadway chooses to accept in February, and is therefore irrelevant.) The contribution margin per unit of the constrained resource for each customer in January is:

	Taylor Corporation	Kelly Corporation
Revenues	$120,000	$80,000
Variable costs	42,000	48,000
Contribution margin	$ 78,000	$32,000
Contribution margin per machine-hour	$\dfrac{\$78,000}{1,500} = \$52$	$\dfrac{\$32,000}{500} = \$64$

Since the $80,000 of additional Kelly business in February is identical to jobs done in January, it will also have a contribution margin of $64 per machine-hour, which is greater than the contribution margin of $52 per machine-hour from Taylor. To maximize operating income, Broadway should first allocate all the capacity needed to take the Kelly Corporation business (1,000 machine-hours) and then allocate the remaining 1,000 (2,000 − 1,000) machine-hours to Taylor. Broadway's operating income in February would then be $16,000 as shown below, greater than the $10,000 operating income in January.

	Taylor Corporation	Kelly Corporation	Total
Contribution margin per machine-hour	$ 52	$ 64	
Machine hours to be worked	1,000	1,000	
Contribution margin	$52,000	$64,000	$116,000
Fixed costs			100,000
Operating income			$ 16,000

Alternatively, we could present Broadway's operating income by taking 2/3rds (1,000 ÷ 1,500 machine-hours) of Taylor's January revenues and variable costs, and doubling (1,000 ÷ 500 machine-hours) Kelly's January revenues and variable costs.

	Taylor Corporation	Kelly Corporation	Total
Revenues	$80,000	$160,000	$240,000
Variable costs	28,000	96,000	124,000
Contribution margin	52,000	64,000	116,000
Fixed costs			100,000
Operating income			$ 16,000

The problem indicated that Broadway could choose to accept as much of the Taylor and Kelly business for February as it wants. However, some students may raise the question that Broadway should think more strategically before deciding what to do. For example, how would Taylor react to Broadway's inability to satisfy its needs? Will Kelly continue to give Broadway $160,000 of business each month or is the additional $80,000 of business in February a special order? For example, if Kelly's additional work in February is only a special order and Broadway wants to maintain a long-term relationship with Taylor, it may in fact prefer to turn down the additional Kelly business. It may feel that the additional $6,000 in operating income in February is not worth jeopardizing Taylor's long-term relationship. Other students may raise the possibility of Broadway accepting all the Taylor and Kelly business for February if it can subcontract some of it to another reliable, high-quality printer.

11-28 (30 min.) **Equipment upgrade versus replacement.**

1.   Solution Exhibit 11-28 presents a cost comparison of the upgrade and replacement alternatives for the three years taken together. It indicates that Pacifica Corporation should replace the production line because it is better off by $180,000 by replacing rather than upgrading.

2(a)   Suppose the capital expenditure to replace the production line is $X. Using data from Solution Exhibit 11-28, the cost of replacing the production line is equal to $1,620,000 − $90,000 + $X. Using data from Solution Exhibit 11-28, the cost of upgrading the production line is equal to $2,160,000 + $300,000 = $2,460,000. We want to find $X such that

$1,620,000 − $90,000 + $X	=	$2,460,000
that is, $1,530,000 + $X	=	$2,460,000
that is, $X	=	$2,460,000 − $1,530,000
or $X	=	$ 930,000

Pacifica would prefer replacing rather than upgrading the existing line if the replacement cost of the new line does not exceed $930,000.

2(b)   Suppose the units produced and sold each year equals y. Using data from Solution Exhibit 11-28, the cost of replacing the production line is $9y − $90,000 + $750,000, while the cost of upgrading is $12y + $300,000. We solve for the y at which the two costs are the same:

$9y − $90,000 + $750,000	=	$12y + $300,000
$9y + $660,000	=	$12y + $300,000
$3y	=	$360,000
y	=	120,000 units

For expected production and sales of less than 120,000 units over 3 years (40,000 units per year), the upgrade alternative is cheaper. When production and sales are low the higher operating costs of upgrading are more than offset by the significant savings in capital costs when upgrading relative to replacing. For expected production and sales exceeding 120,000 units over 3 years, the replace alternative is cheaper. For high output the benefits of the lower operating costs of replacing relative to upgrading exceed the higher capital costs.

11-28 (cont'd)

SOLUTION EXHIBIT 11-28
Comparing Upgrade and Replace Alternatives

	Three Years Together		
	Upgrade (1)	Replace (2)	Difference (3) = (1) – (2)
Cash-operating costs $12; $9 × 180,000	$2,160,000	$1,620,000	$ 540,000
Current disposal price		(90,000)	90,000
One-time capital costs, written off periodically as depreciation	300,000	750,000	(450,000)
Total relevant costs	$2,460,000	$2,280,000	$ 180,000

Note that sales and book value of the existing machine are the same under both alternatives and hence irrelevant.

3.   Operating income for the first year under the upgrade and replace alternatives are as follows:

	Upgrade	Replace
Sales $25 × 60,000	$1,500,000	$1,500,000
Cash-operating costs $12; $9 × 60,000	720,000	540,000
Depreciation	220,000[a]	250,000[b]
Loss on disposal of old production line	—	270,000[c]
Total costs	940,000	1,060,000
Operating income	$ 560,000	$ 440,000

[a] $360,000 + $300,000 ÷ 3 = $220,000   [b] $750,000 ÷ 3 = $250,000
[c] Book value – current disposal price = $360,000 – $90,000 = $270,000

First-year operating income is higher by $120,000 under the upgrade alternative. If first year's operating income is an important component of Azinger's bonus, he would prefer the upgrade over the replace alternative even though the decision model in requirement 1 prefers the replace to the upgrade alternative. This exercise illustrates the conflict between the decision model and the performance-evaluation model (requirement 3).

11-30 (30-40 min.) Product mix, relevant costs.

	R3	HP6
Selling price	$100	$150
Variable manufacturing costs per unit	60	100
Variable marketing costs per unit	15	35
Total variable costs per unit	75	135
Contribution margin per unit	$ 25	$ 15
Contribution margin per hour of the constrained resource (the regular machine)	$\frac{\$25}{1} = \$25$	$\frac{\$15}{0.5} = \$30$
Total contribution margin from selling		
Only R3 or only HP6		
R3: $25 × 50,000; HP6: $30 × 50,000	$1,250,000	$1,500,000
Less: Lease costs of high-precision machine		
to produce and sell HP6	–	300,000
Net relevant benefit	$1,250,000	$1,200,000

Even though HP6 has the higher contribution margin per unit of the constrained resource, the fact that Pendleton must incur additional costs of $300,000 to achieve this higher contribution margin means that Pendleton is better off using its entire 50,000-hour capacity on the regular machine to produce and sell 50,000 units (50,000 hours ÷ 1 hour per unit) of R3. The additional contribution from selling HP6 rather than R3 is $250,000 ($1,500,000 – $1,250,000), which is not enough to cover the additional costs of leasing the high-precision machine. Note that, because all other overhead costs are fixed and cannot be changed, they are irrelevant for the decision.

2. If capacity of the regular machines is increased by 15,000 machine-hours to 65,000 machine-hours (50,000 originally + 15,000 new), the net relevant benefit from producing R3 and HP6 is as follows:

	R3	HP6
Total contribution margin from selling only		
R3 or only HP6		
R3: $25 × 65,000; HP6: $30 × 65,000	$1,625,000	$1,950,000
Less: Lease costs of high-precision machine		
that would be incurred if HP6 is produced and sold	—	300,000
Less: Cost of increasing capacity by		
15,000 hours on regular machine	150,000	150,000
Net relevant benefit	$1,475,000	$1,500,000

Investing in the additional capacity increases Pendleton's operating income by $250,000 ($1,500,000 calculated in requirement 2 *minus* $1,250,000 calculated in requirement 1), so Pendleton should add 15,000 hours to the regular machine. With the extra capacity available to it, Pendleton should use its entire capacity to produce HP6. Using all 65,000

11-30 (cont'd)

hours of capacity to produce HP6 rather than to produce R3 generates additional contribution margin of $325,000 ($1,950,000 − $1,625,000) which is more than the additional cost of $300,000 to lease the high-precision machine. Pendleton should therefore produce and sell 130,000 units of HP6 (65,000 hours ÷ 0.5 hours per unit of HP6) and zero units of R3.

3.

	R3	HP6	S3
Selling price per unit	$100	$150	$120
Variable manufacturing costs per unit	60	100	70
Variable marketing costs per unit	15	35	15
Total variable costs per unit	75	135	85
Contribution margin per unit	$ 25	$ 15	$ 35
Contribution margin per hour of the constrained resource (the regular machine)	$\dfrac{\$25}{1}=\$25$	$\dfrac{\$15}{0.5}=\$30$	$\dfrac{\$35}{1}=\$35$

The first step is to compare the operating profits that Pendleton could earn if it accepted the Carter Corporation offer for 20,000 units with the operating profits Pendleton is currently earning. S3 has the highest contribution margin per hour on the regular machine and requires no additional investment such as leasing a high-precision machine. To produce the 20,000 units of S3 requested by Carter Corporation, Pendleton would require 20,000 hours on the regular machine, resulting in a contribution margin of $35 × 20,000 = $700,000.

Pendleton now has 45,000 hours available on the regular machine to produce R3 or HP6.

	R3	HP6
Total contribution margin from selling only R3 or only HP6		
R3: $25 × 45,000; HP6: $30 × 45,000	$1,125,000	$1,350,000
Less: Lease costs of high-precision machine		
to produce and sell HP 6	–	300,000
Net relevant benefit	$1,125,000	$1,050,000

Pendleton should use all the 45,000 hours of available capacity to produce 45,000 units of R3. Thus, the product mix that maximizes operating income is 20,000 units of S3, 45,000 units of R3, and zero units of HP6. This optimal mix results in a contribution margin of $1,825,000 ($700,000 from S3 and $1,125,000 from R3). Relative to requirement 2, operating income increases by $325,000 ($1,825,000 minus $1,500,000 calculated in requirement 2). Hence, Pendleton should accept the Carter Corporation business and supply 20,000 units of S3.

11-13

11-32 (20 min.) **Opportunity cost.**

1.   The opportunity cost to Wolverine of producing the 2,000 units of Orangebo is the contribution margin lost on the 2,000 units of Rosebo that would have to be forgone, as computed below:

Revenue per unit		$20
Variable costs per unit:		
Direct materials	$ 2	
Direct manufacturing labour	3	
Variable manufacturing overhead	2	
Variable nonmanufacturing costs	4	11
Contribution margin per unit		$ 9
Contribution margin for 2,000 units		$ 18,000

The opportunity cost is $18,000. Opportunity cost is the maximum contribution to operating income that is forgone (rejected) by not using a limited resource in its next-best alternative use.

2.   Contribution margin from manufacturing 2,000 units of Orangebo and purchasing 2,000 units of Rosebo from Buckeye is $16,000 as follows:

	Manufacture Orangebo	Purchase Rosebo	Total
Revenue per unit	$15	$20	
Variable costs per unit:			
Purchase costs	–	14	
Direct materials	2		
Direct manufacturing labour	3		
Variable manufacturing overhead	2		
Variable nonmanufacturing overhead	2	4	
Variable costs per unit	9	18	
Contribution margin per unit	$ 6	$ 2	
Contribution margin from selling 2,000 units of Orangebo and 2,000 units of Rosebo	$12,000	$4,000	$16,000

As calculated in requirement 1, Wolverine's contribution margin from continuing to manufacture 2,000 units of Rosebo is $18,000. Accepting the Windsor Company order and the Buckeye offer will cost Wolverine $2,000 ($16,000 – $18,000). Hence Wolverine should refuse the Windsor Company order and Buckeye Corporation's offer.

3.   The minimum price would be $9, the sum of the incremental costs as computed in requirement 2. This follows because if Wolverine has surplus capacity, the opportunity cost = $0. For the short-run decision of whether to accept Orangebo's offer, fixed costs of Wolverine are irrelevant. Only the incremental costs need to be covered for it to be worthwhile for Wolverine to accept the Orangebo offer.

11-34 (30-40 min.) Make or buy, unknown level of volume.

1. Let X = 1 starter assembly. The variable costs required to manufacture 150,000X are:

Direct materials	$200,000
Direct manufacturing labour	150,000
Variable manufacturing overhead	100,000
Total variable costs	$450,000

The total variable costs per unit is $450,000 ÷ 150,000 = $3.00 per unit.

The data can be presented in both "all data" and "relevant data" formats:

	All Data		Relevant Data	
	Alternative 1: Make	Alternative 2: Buy	Alternative 1: Make	Alternative 2: Buy
Variable manufacturing costs	$ 3X	–	$ 3X	–
Fixed general manufacturing overhead	150,000	$150,000	–	–
Fixed overhead—avoidable	100,000	–	100,000	–
Division 2 manager's salary	40,000	50,000	40,000	$50,000
Division 3 manager's salary	50,000	–	50,000	–
Purchase cost—if bought from Tidnish Electronics	–	4X	–	4X
Total	$340,000 + $ 3X	$200,000 + $ 4X	$190,000 + $ 3X	$50,000 + $ 4X

The number of units at which the costs of make and buy are equivalent is:

All data analysis:
$$\$340,000 + \$3X = \$200,000 + \$4X$$
$$X = 140,000$$

or

Relevant data analysis:
$$\$190,000 + \$3X = \$50,000 + \$4X$$
$$X = 140,000$$

Assuming cost minimization is the objective, then:
- If production is expected to be less than 140,000 units, it is preferable to buy units from Tidnish.
- If production is expected to exceed 140,000 units, it is preferable to manufacture internally (make) the units.
- If production is expected to be 140,000 units, this is the indifference point between buying units from Tidnish and internally manufacturing (making) the units.

11-34 (cont'd)

2.   The information on the storage cost, which is avoidable if self-manufacture is discontinued, is relevant; these storage charges represent current outlays that are avoidable if self-manufacture is discontinued. Assume these $50,000 charges are represented as an opportunity cost of the make alternative. The costs of internal manufacture that incorporate this $50,000 opportunity cost is:

All data analysis:	$390,000 + $3X
Relevant data analysis:	$240,000 + $3X

The number of units at which the costs of make and buy are equivalent are:

All data analysis:
$$\$390,000 + \$3X = \$200,000 + \$4X$$
$$X = 190,000$$

Relevant data analysis:
$$\$240,000 + \$3X = \$50,000 + \$4X$$
$$X = 190,000$$

If production is expected to be less than 190,000, it is preferable to buy units from Tidnish. If production is expected to exceed 190,000, it is preferable to manufacture the units internally.

11-36 (30-40 min.)   **Relevant cost of materials.**

1.   Hernandez Corporation has already purchased the 10,000 kilograms of the special cement that it needs, so it will incur no incremental costs. Alternatively stated, the costs of materials are past (sunk) costs.

If Hernandez obtained Contract No. 2 a month from now, it would cost $21,000 in substitute material (10,000 kilograms x $2.10 per kilogram). There is, therefore, a cost (lost benefit) of $21,000 by using the special cement on Contract No. 1 now. Alternatively, Hernandez could sell the special cement immediately for $16,000. The opportunity cost that Hernandez should use is the benefit it would get in the next-best alternative should it not use the cement in Contract No. 1. The greater of these two benefits is using the cement in Contract No. 2. The opportunity cost is $21,000. The relevant cost that Gomez should use when bidding on Contract No. 1 is:

Incremental cost	$ 0
<u>Plus</u> opportunity cost	<u> 21,000</u>
Relevant cost	<u>$21,000</u>

2.   As in Question 1, the incremental costs of acquiring the special cement for use on Contract No. 1 are zero because Hernandez has already purchased the material. If Hernandez does not land Contract No. 2, the opportunity cost of using the special cement for Contract No. 1 is $15,000 (10,000 kilograms × $1.50 per kilogram), the amount Hernandez would get if it sold the special cement one month from now.

Gomez assesses a probability of 0.7 that the special cement will be used on Contract No. 2 and a probability of 0.3 that the special cement will be sold.

The expected benefit of holding the special cement and not using it on Contract No. 1 is

=	(0.7 × $21,000*) + (0.3 × $15,000**)
=	$14,700 + $4,500 = $19,200

* relevant cost if special cement is used in Contract No. 2 (see requirement 1)
** relevant cost if special cement is sold one month from now

Alternatively, the special cement can be sold right away and fetch $16,000. The opportunity cost is the greater of these two benefits and hence equals $19,200. When bidding on the Contract, Gomez should use:

Incremental cost	$ 0
<u>Plus</u> opportunity cost	<u> 19,200</u>
Relevant cost	<u>$19,200</u>

3.   In this case, the benefit of selling the cement now is $23,000, while the benefit of using the cement in Contract No. 2 is $21,000. The opportunity cost of using the cement in Contract No. 1 is the greater of these two numbers, $23,000.

Incremental cost	$ 0
<u>Plus</u> opportunity cost	<u> 23,000</u>
Relevant cost	<u>$23,000</u>

11-38 (30-40 min.) Considering three alternatives.

1. The 5% surcharge is irrelevant.

	Sell to Kaytell as Special Order	Convert to Standard Model	Sell as Special Order as Is
Selling price	$68,400	$62,500	$52,000
Deduct cash discount	–	1,250	–
Net selling price	68,400	61,250	52,000
Additional manufacturing costs:			
Direct materials	6,200	2,850	–
Direct manufacturing labour	4,200	3,300	–
Variable manufacturing overhead	2,100	1,650	–
Total additional manufacturing costs	12,500	7,800	–
Commissions	2,052	1,225	1,560
Total costs	14,552	9,025	1,560
Contribution to operating income	$53,848	$52,225	$50,440

2.

Kaytell contribution	$53,848
Next-best alternative:	
Standard model contribution	52,225
Change in contribution to operating income	$ 1,623

$$\text{Change in net sales price} = \frac{\text{Change in contribution}}{1 - \text{Commission \%}}$$

$$= \frac{\$1,623}{1 - .03} = \frac{\$1,623}{0.97}$$

$$= \$1,673 \text{ (rounded)}$$

Original Kaytell price	$68,400
Reduction in contribution permissible before Auer switches to the next-best alternative	1,673
Minimum price Auer should accept from Kaytell and be indifferent between standard model and Kaytell offer.	$66,727

11-38 (cont'd)

3. Fixed manufacturing overhead should have no influence on the selling price quoted by Auer Company for (one-time-only) special orders:

(a) Auer Company should accept special orders whenever the company is operating substantially below capacity, including below the breakeven point, if incremental revenue from an order exceeds incremental cost. Normally, this approach would mean that the order should be accepted as long as the selling price of the order exceeds the variable manufacturing costs. The special order will result in a positive contribution toward fixed costs. The fixed manufacturing overhead is not considered in the pricing because it will be incurred whether the order is accepted or not.

(b) If Auer Company is operating above its breakeven point and if a special order will allow the company to utilize unused capacity efficiently, the special order should be accepted as long as incremental revenue exceeds incremental cost, or, in most cases, the selling price exceeds the variable manufacturing costs. If the selling price exceeds the variable manufacturing costs, the order will yield a positive contribution toward the company's fixed costs. Fixed manufacturing overhead is not considered because it will be incurred whether the order is accepted or not. The only time the fixed manufacturing overhead would be relevant would be if Auer were near capacity and additional fixed costs would have to be incurred to complete the order. If this situation occurred, Auer's incremental costs would be higher, and they would have to be covered by the selling price.

11-40 (15 min.) **Make or buy (continuation of 11-39).**

The maximum price Class Company should be willing to pay is $3.9417 per unit.

Expected unit production and sales of the new product must be half of the old product (1/2 × 240,000 = 120,000) because the fixed manufacturing overhead rate for the new product is twice that of the fixed manufacturing overhead rate for the old product.

	Present	Proposed Make New Product	Proposed Old Product	Proposed Total
Sales	$1,440,000	$1,080,000	$1,440,000	$2,520,000
Variable (or purchase) costs:				
Manufacturing	720,000	600,000	946,000*	1,546,000
Marketing and other	360,000	240,000	288,000	528,000
Total variable costs	1,080,000	840,000	1,234,000	2,074,000
Contribution margin	360,000	240,000	206,000	446,000
Fixed costs:				
Manufacturing	120,000	120,000	–	120,000
Marketing and other	216,000	60,000	216,000	276,000
Total fixed costs	336,000	180,000	216,000	396,000
Operating Income	$ 24,000	$ 60,000	$ –10,000	$ 50,000

*This is an example of opportunity costs, whereby subcontracting at a price well above the $3.50 current manufacturing (absorption) cost is still desirable because the old product will be displaced in manufacturing by a new product that is more profitable.

Because the new product promises an operating income of $60,000 (ignoring the irrelevant problems of how fixed marketing costs may be newly reallocated between products), the old product can sustain up to a $10,000 loss and still help accomplish management's overall objectives. Maximum costs that can be incurred on the old product are $1,440,000 plus the $10,000 loss, or $1,450,000. Maximum purchase cost: $1,450,000 − ($288,000 + $216,000) = $946,000. Maximum purchase cost per unit: $946,000 ÷ 240,000 units = $3.9417 per unit.

11-40 (cont'd)

Alternative Computation

Operating income is $9.00 − $8.50 = $0.50 per unit
   for 120,000 new units $60,000

Target operating income   50,000

Maximum loss allowed on old product $10,000

Maximum loss per unit allowed on old product,
   $10,000 ÷ 240,000 = $0.0417

Sales price of old product $6.0000

Allowance for loss   0.0417

Total costs allowed per unit   6.0417

Continuing costs for old product other than purchase cost:
  Fixed manufacturing costs—all transferred to
   new product $ —
  Variable marketing costs   1.20
  Fixed marketing costs   0.90   2.1000

Maximum purchase cost per unit $3.9417

11-42 (30-40 min.)   **Appendix: Optimal sales mix for a retailer, sensitivity analysis.**

1.   Let G = floor space of grocery products carried
        D = floor space of dairy products carried

The LP formula for the decision is:

Maximize: $10G + $3D
Subject to: G + D ≤ 40,000
                 G   ≥ 10,000
                      D ≥ 8,000

2.   Always Open may wish to maintain its reputation as a full-service food store carrying both grocery and dairy products. Customers may not be attracted if Always Open carries only the product line with the highest unit contribution margins. (Marketing and economics courses examine this issue under the label of interdependencies in the demand for products.)

3. . Solution Exhibit 11-42 presents the graphic solution. The optimal solution is 32,000 square metres of grocery products and 8,000 square metres of dairy products.

The trial-and-error solution approach is:

Trial	Corner (G; D)	TCM = $10G + $3D
1	(10,000; 8,000)	$10(10,000) + $3(8,000) = $124,000
2	(10,000; 30,000)	10(10,000) + 3(30,000) = 190,000
3	(32,000; 8,000)	10(32,000) + 3(8,000) = 344,000*

* Optimal solution is G = 32,000 and D = 8,000.

4.   The optimal mix determined in requirement 3 will not change if the contribution margins per square metre change to grocery products, $8, and dairy products, $5. To avoid cluttering the graphic solution in Solution Exhibit 11-42, we demonstrate this using the trial-and-error solution approach.

Trial	Corner (G; D)	TCM = $8G + $5D
1	(10,000; 8,000)	$8(10,000) + $5 (8,000) = $120,000
2	(10,000; 30,000)	$8(10,000) + $5 (30,000) = $230,000
3	(32,000; 8,000)	$8(32,000) + $5 (8,000) = $296,000*

* Optimal solution is still G = 32,000 and D = 8,000.

The student can also verify by drawing lines parallel to the line through G = 5,000 and D = 8,000 (the equal contribution line for $40,000) so that the furthest point where the equal contribution line intersects the feasible region is the point G = 32,000 and D = 8,000.

11-42 (cont'd)

SOLUTION EXHIBIT 11-42
Graphic Solution to Find Optimal Mix, Always Open, Inc.

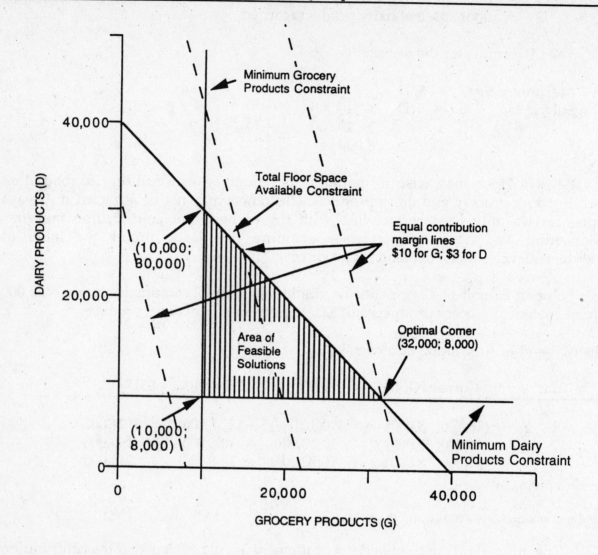

11-44 (20 min.) Ethics and relevant costs.

1.   On the basis of Gray's information, Pastel should buy RG1 from York Corporation rather than make it in-house. The relevant costs and benefits analysis is as follows:

Incremental costs of purchasing 40,000 units of RG1, $21 × 40,000		$(840,000)
Cost savings:		
Direct materials costs	$600,000	
Direct manufacturing labour costs	200,000	
Manufacturing overhead costs	239,500	
Total cost savings		1,039,500
Net benefit of outsourcing		$ 199,500

2.   We need to determine the quantity of purchases from York Corporation at which the cost of purchasing equals the cost savings of $1,039,500. This quantity is $1,039,500 ÷ $21 = 49,500. If Pastel's yield improves to 49,500 or greater (that is, scrap levels fall to 500 units or less), then continuing to manufacture in-house will be preferred to purchasing from York. For example, if yields were 49,750, the cost savings from outsourcing would still be $1,039,500, but the incremental costs of purchasing 49,750 units from York Corporation would be $1,044,750 ($21 × 49,750), which exceeds the cost savings.

3.   In assessing the situation, a management accountant should consider the following:

Clear reports using relevant and reliable information should be prepared. It is unethical for Berry to suggest that Gray change the cost numbers for the make alternative and for Gray to change the numbers in order to favour the make alternative.

The management accountant has a responsibility to avoid actual or apparent conflicts of interest and to advise all appropriate parties of any potential conflict. Berry's motivation for wanting Gray to reduce costs of the make alternative was to help his friends even though this may not be in the best interests of the company. In this regard, both Berry's and Gray's behaviours (if Gray agrees to reduce the cost of the make alternative) could be viewed as unethical.

Gray should indicate to Berry that the costs derived under the make alternative are correct and consistent with the yield and quality experienced at the plant. If Berry still insists on making the changes and reducing the costs of manufacturing RG1 in-house, Gray should raise the matter with Berry's superior, after informing Berry of his plans. If, after taking all these steps, there is continued pressure to understate the costs, Gray should consider resigning from the company, instead of engaging in unethical behaviour.

CHAPTER 12
PRICING DECISIONS, PRODUCT PROFITABILITY DECISIONS, AND COST MANAGEMENT

12-2 Not necessarily. For a one-time-only special order the relevant costs are only those costs that will change as a result of accepting the order. In this case, full product costs will rarely be relevant. It is more likely that full product costs will be relevant costs for long-run pricing decisions.

12-4 Activity-based costing helps managers in pricing decisions in two ways.
(a) It gives managers more accurate product-cost information for making pricing decisions.
(b) It helps managers to manage costs during value engineering by identifying the cost impact of eliminating, reducing or changing various activities.

12-6 A target cost per unit is the estimated long-run cost per unit of a product (or service) that, when sold at the target price, enables the company to achieve the targeted operating income per unit.

12-8 A value-added cost is a cost that customers perceive as adding value, or utility, to a product or service. Examples are costs of materials, direct labour, tools, and machinery. Examples of nonvalue-added costs are costs of rework, scrap, expediting, and breakdown maintenance.

12-10 Cost-plus pricing is a pricing approach in which managers add a markup to cost in order to determine price.

12-12 Two examples where the difference in the incremental or outlay costs of two products or services is much smaller than the differences in their prices follow:
1. The difference in prices charged for a telephone call, hotel room, or car rental during busy versus slack periods is often much greater than the difference in costs to provide these services.
2. The difference in incremental or outlay costs for an airplane seat sold to a passenger travelling on business or a passenger travelling for pleasure is roughly the same. However, airline companies routinely charge business travellers—those who are likely to start and complete their travel during the same week excluding the weekend—a much higher price than pleasure travellers, who generally stay at their destinations over at least one weekend.

12-14 Three benefits of using a product life-cycle reporting format are:
1. The full set of revenues and costs associated with each product becomes more visible.
2. Differences among products in the percentage of total costs committed at early stages in the life cycle are highlighted.
3. Interrelationships among business function cost categories are highlighted.

12-16 (20-30 min.) **Relevant-cost approach to pricing decisions, special order.**

1.
Relevant revenues, $3.80 × 1,000		$3,800
Relevant costs		
Direct materials, $1.50 × 1,000	$1,500	
Direct manufacturing labour, $0.80 × 1,000	800	
Variable manufacturing overhead, $0.70 × 1,000	700	
Variable selling costs, 0.05 × $3,800	190	
Total		3,190
Increase in operating income		$ 610

This calculation assumes that:
  (a) The monthly fixed manufacturing overhead of $150,000 and $65,000 of monthly fixed marketing costs will be unchanged by acceptance of the 1,000 unit order.
  (b) The price charged and the volumes sold to other customers are not affected by the special order.

Chapter 12 uses the phrase "one-time-only special order" to describe this special case.

2. The president's reasoning is defective on at least two counts:
  (a) The inclusion of irrelevant costs—assuming the monthly fixed manufacturing overhead of $150,000 will be unchanged; it is irrelevant to the decision.
  (b) The exclusion of relevant costs—variable selling costs (5% of the selling price) are excluded.

3. Key issues are:
  (a) Will the existing customer base demand price reductions? If this 1,000-tape order is not independent of other sales, cutting the price from $5.00 to $3.80 can have a large negative effect on total revenues.
  (b) Is the 1,000-tape order a one-time-only order, or is there the possibility of sales in subsequent months? The fact that the customer is not in Dill Company's "normal marketing channels" does not necessarily mean it is a one-time-only order. Indeed, the sale could well open a new marketing channel. Dill Company should be reluctant to consider only short-run variable costs for pricing long-run business.

12-18 (25 min.) Short-run pricing, capacity constraints.

1.   With no constraints on availability of Pyrone or on plant capacity, Boutique would want to charge a minimum price for Seltium that would cover its incremental costs to manufacture Seltium. (Because there is excess capacity, there is no opportunity cost.)   In this case, the incremental costs are the variable costs to manufacture a kilogram of Seltium:

Pyrone (2 kilograms × $4 per kilogram)	$ 8
Direct manufacturing labour	4
Variable manufacturing overhead costs	3
Total variable manufacturing costs	$15

Hence, the minimum price that Boutique should charge to manufacture Seltium is $15 per kilogram. For 3,000 kilograms of Seltium it should charge a minimum of $45,000 ($15 × 3,000).

2.   Now Pyrone is in short supply. Using it to make Seltium reduces the Bolzene that Boutique can make and sell. There is therefore an opportunity cost of manufacturing Seltium, the lost contribution from using the Pyrone to manufacture Bolzene. To make 3,000 kilograms of Seltium requires 6,000 (2 × 3,000) kilograms of Pyrone.

The 6,000 kilograms of Pyrone can be used to manufacture 4,000 (6,000 ÷ 1.5) kilograms of Bolzene, since each kilogram of Bolzene requires 1.5 kilograms of Pyrone.

The contribution margin from 4,000 kilograms of Bolzene is $24,000 ($6 per kilogram × 4,000 kilograms). This is the opportunity cost of using Pyrone to manufacture Seltium. The minimum price that Boutique should charge to manufacture Seltium should cover not only the incremental (variable) costs of manufacturing Seltium but also the opportunity cost:

	Costs of Manufacturing Seltium	
Relevant costs	Total for 3,000 Kilograms (1)	Per Kilogram (2) = (1) ÷ 3,000
Incremental (variable) costs of manufacturing Seltium	$45,000	$15
Opportunity cost of forgoing manufacture and sale of Bolzene	24,000	8
Minimum cost of order	$69,000	$23

The minimum price per kilogram that Boutique should charge for Seltium is $23 per kilogram. For 3,000 kilograms of Seltium, Boutique should charge a minimal of $69,000 ($23 × 3,000 kgs).

12-20 (25–30 min.) **Target operating income, value-added costs, service company.**

1. The classification of total costs in 2000 into value-added, non-value added, or in the gray area in between follows.

	Value Added (1)	Gray Area (2)	Non-value added (3)	Total (4)= (1)+(2)+(3)
Doing calculations and preparing drawings				
75% × $400,000	$300,000			$300,000
Checking calculations and drawings				
4% × $400,000		$16,000		16,000
Correcting errors found in drawings				
7% × $400,000			$28,000	28,000
Making changes in response to client requests				
6% × $400,000	24,000			24,000
Correcting errors to meet government building code, 8% × $400,000			32,000	32,000
Total professional labour costs	324,000	16,000	60,000	400,000
Administration and support costs at 40% ($160,000 ÷ $400,000) of professional labour costs	129,600	6,400	24,000	160,000
Travel	18,000		–	18,000
Total	$471,600	$22,400	$84,000	$578,000

Doing calculations and responding to client requests for changes are value-added costs because customers perceive these costs as necessary for the service of preparing architectural drawings. Costs incurred in correcting errors in drawings and making changes because they were inconsistent with building codes are non-value-added costs. Customers do not perceive these costs as necessary and would be unwilling to pay for them. Carasco should seek to eliminate these costs. Checking calculations and drawings is in the gray area (some, but not all, checking may be needed). There is room for disagreement on these classifications. For example, checking calculations may be regarded as value added, and making changes to conform to the building code might be regarded as in the gray area.

Carasco's staff can reduce non-value-added costs by checking government building code requirements before drawing up the plans and taking more care when doing the actual work. To reduce value-added costs, Carasco's staff must work faster and more efficiently while at the same time maintaining quality. To achieve these goals, Carasco may want to consider investing in computer-aided drawing programs and training its professional staff to work with these tools.

12-20 (cont'd)

2. Reduction in professional labour-hours by

(a) Correcting errors in drawings (7% × 8,000)	560 hours
(b) Correcting errors to conform to building code (8% × 8,000)	640 hours
Total	1,200 hours
Cost savings in professional labour costs (1,200 hours × $50)	$ 60,000
Cost savings in variable administration and support costs (40% × $60,000)	24,000
Total cost savings	$ 84,000

Current operating income in 2001	$102,000
Add: Cost savings from eliminating errors	84,000
Operating income in 2001 if errors are eliminated	$186,000

3. Currently 85% × 8,000 hours = 6,800 hours are billed to clients generating revenues of $680,000. The remaining 15% of professional labour-hours (15% × 8,000 = 1,200 hours) is lost in making corrections. Carasco bills clients at the rate of $\frac{\$680,000}{6,800} = \$100$ per professional labour-hour. If the 1,200 professional labour-hours currently not being billed to clients were billed to clients, Carasco's revenues would increase by 1,200 hours × $100 = $120,000 from $680,000 to $800,000.

Costs remaining unchanged	
Professional labour costs	$400,000
Administration and support (40% × $400,000)	160,000
Travel	18,000
Total costs	$578,000

Carasco's operating income would be	
Revenues	$800,000
Total costs	578,000
Operating income	$222,000

12-22 (20 min.) **Cost-plus target return on investment pricing.**

1. Target operating income = target return on investment × invested capital

Target operating income , 25% of $960,000	$240,000
Total fixed costs	352,000
Target contribution margin	$592,000

Target contribution per room, ($592,000 ÷ 16,000)	$37
Add variable costs per room	3
Price to be charged per room	$40

Proof

Total room revenues ($40 × 16,000 rooms)		$640,000
Total costs:		
Variable costs ($3 × 16,000)	$ 48,000	
Fixed costs	352,000	
Total costs		400,000
Operating income		$240,000

The full cost of a room = variable cost per room + fixed cost per room
The full cost of a room = $3 + ($352,000 ÷ 16,000) = $3 + $22 = $25

Markup per room   =   Rental price per room – Full cost of a room
          = $40 – $25 = $15
Markup percentage as a fraction of full cost = $15 ÷ $25 = 60%

2. If price is reduced by 10%, the number of rooms Beck could rent would increase by 10%.

The new price per room would be 90% of $40	= $36
The number of rooms Beck expects to rent is 110% of 16,000	= 17,600
The contribution margin per room would be $36 – $3	= $33
Contribution margin = $33 × 17,600	= $580,800

Since the contribution margin at the reduced price of $36 is less than the contribution margin at a price of $40, Beck should not reduce the price of the rooms. Note that the fixed costs of $352,000 will be the same under the $40 and the $36 price alternatives and are hence irrelevant to the analysis.

12-24 (25 min.) **Target costs, effect of product-design changes on product costs.**

1. & 2. Indirect cost-allocation rates for 2000 and 2001 are as follows:

	2000			2001		
Indirect cost category	Total Costs (1)	Quantity of Cost-Allocation Base (2)	Cost Allocation Rate (3)= (1) ÷ (2)	Total Costs (4)	Quantity of Cost-Allocation Base (5)	Cost-Allocation Rate (6)= (4) ÷ (5)
Batch-level costs	$ 7,200,000	900	$ 8,000	$ 7,500,000	1,000	$ 7,500
Manuf. operations costs	12,100,000	220,000	55	12,500,000	250,000	50
Engineering change costs	2,640,000	220	12,000	2,000,000	200	10,000

Manufacturing costs of HJ6 in 2000 and 2001 are as follows:

	2000		2001	
	Total (1)	Per Unit (2)= (1) ÷ 3,500	Total (3)	Per Unit (4)= (3) ÷ 4,000
Direct materials, $1,200 × 3,500; $1,100 × 4,000	$4,200,000	$1,200	$4,400,000	$1,100
Batch-level costs, $8,000 × 70; $7,500 × 80	560,000	160	600,000	150
Manuf. operations costs, $55 × 21,000; $50 × 22,000	1,155,000	330	1,100,000	275
Engineering change costs, $12,000 × 15; $10,000 × 10	180,000	51	100,000	25
Total	$6,095,000	$1,741	$6,200,000	$1,550

3. $\dfrac{\text{Target manufacturing cost}}{\text{per unit of HJ6 in 2001}} = \dfrac{\text{Manufacturing cost}}{\text{per unit in 2000}} \times 88\%$

$= 1,741 \times 0.88 = \$1,532.08$

Actual manufacturing cost per unit of HJ6 in 2001 was $1,550. Hence, Medical Instruments did not achieve its target manufacturing cost per unit of $1,532.08.

4. To reduce the manufacturing cost per unit in 2001, Medical Instruments reduced the cost per unit in each of the four cost categories—direct materials costs, batch-level costs, manufacturing operations costs, and engineering change costs. It achieved this by reducing setup, production order, and materials handling costs per batch, the cost per machine hour, and cost per engineering change, perhaps by becoming more efficient in performing these activities. Efficiency improvements also helped Medical Instruments reduce the quantities of the cost allocation bases used to manufacture HJ6. For example, although production of HJ6 increased by 14.3% [(4,000 − 3,500) ÷ 3,500] between 2000 and 2001, machine-hours worked increased by only 4.8% [(22,000 ÷ 21,000) ÷ 21,000]. Medical Instruments achieved these gains through value engineering activities that retained only those product features that customers wanted while eliminating non-value-added activities and costs.

12-26 (30-40 min.) Life-cycle product costing, product emphasis.

1. A life-cycle income statement traces revenue and costs of each individual software package from its initial research and development to its final customer servicing and support in the marketplace. The two main differences from a calendar-based income statement are:
    (a) Costs incurred in different calendar periods are included in the same statement.
    (b) Costs and revenue of each package are reported separately rather than aggregated into company-wide categories.

    The benefits of using a product life-cycle report are:
    (a) The full set of revenues and costs associated with each product becomes visible.
    (b) Differences among products in the percentage of total costs committed at early stages in the life cycle are highlighted.
    (c) Interrelationships among business function cost categories are highlighted. What is the effect, for example, of cutting back on R&D and product-design cost categories on customer-service costs in subsequent years?

2.

	EE-46		ME-83		IE-17	
Revenue ($000s)		$2,500		$1,500		$1,600
Costs ($000s)						
Research and development	$700		$450		$240	
Design	200		120		96	
Production	300		210		208	
Marketing	500		270		448	
Distribution	75		60		96	
Customer service	375	2,150	150	1,260	608	1,696
Operating income ($000s)		$ 350		$ 240		$ (96)

As emphasized in this chapter, the time value of money is not taken into account when summing life-cycle revenue or life-cycle costs. Chapters 21 and 22 discuss this topic in detail.

Rankings of the three packages on profitability (and relative profitability) are:

Operating income		$\dfrac{\text{Operating income}}{\text{Revenues}}$	
1. EE-46:	$350,000	1. ME-83:	16.0%
2. ME-83:	$240,000	2. EE-46:	14.0%
3. IE-17:	$ (96,000)	3. IE-17:	(6.0%)

The EE-46 and ME-83 packages should be emphasized, and the IE-17 package should be de-emphasized. It is interesting that IE-17 had the lowest R&D costs but was the least profitable.

3.   The cost structures of the three software packages are:

	EE-46	ME-83	IE-17
Research and development	32.5%	35.7%	14.1%
Design	9.3	9.5	5.7
Production	14.0	16.7	12.3
Marketing	23.3	21.4	26.4
Distribution	3.5	4.8	5.7
Customer service	17.4	11.9	35.8
	100.0%	100.0%	100.0%

The major differences are:
   (a)   EE-46 and ME-83 have over 40% of their costs in the R&D/product design categories compared to less than 20% (19.8%) for IE-17.
   (b)   IE-17 has 35.8% of its costs in the customer-service category compared to 17.4% for EE-46 and 11.9% for ME-83.

There are several explanations for these differences:
   (a)   EE-46 and ME-83 differ sizably from IE-17 in their R&D/product design intensity. For example, EE-46 and ME-83 may require considerably (a) more interaction with users, and (b) more experimentation with software algorithms than does IE-17.
   (b)   The software division should have invested more in the R&D/product design categories for IE-17. The high percentage for customer service could reflect the correcting of problems that should have been corrected prior to manufacture. Life-cycle reports highlight possible causal relationships among cost categories.

12-28 (30 min.) **Relevant-cost approach to pricing decisions.**

1. Revenues (1,000 crates at $100 per crate) $100,000
    Variable costs:
        Manufacturing $40,000
        Marketing   14,000
            Total variable costs   54,000
    Contribution margin   46,000
    Fixed costs:
        Manufacturing $20,000
        Marketing   16,000
            Total fixed costs   36,000
    Operating income $ 10,000

Normal markup percentage: $46,000 ÷ $54,000 = 85.19% of total variable costs.

2. Only the manufacturing-cost category is relevant to considering this special order; no additional marketing costs will be incurred. The relevant manufacturing costs for the 200-crate special order are:

        Variable manufacturing cost per unit
            $40 × 200 crates $ 8,000
        Special packaging   2,000
                                                        $10,000

Any price above $50 per crate ($10,000 ÷ 200) will make a positive contribution to operating income.

The reasoning based on a comparison of $55 per-crate price with the $60 per-crate absorption cost ignores monthly cost-volume-profit relationships. The $60 per-crate absorption cost includes a $20 per-crate cost component that is irrelevant to the special order. The relevant range for the fixed manufacturing costs is from 500 to 1,500 crates per month; the special order will increase production from 1,000 to 1,200 crates per month. Furthermore, the special order requires no incremental marketing costs.

3. If the new customer is likely to remain in business, Stardom should consider whether a strictly short-run focus is appropriate. For example, what is the likelihood of demand from other customers increasing over time? If Stardom accepts the 200-crate special order for more than one month, it may preclude accepting other customers at prices exceeding $55 per crate. Moreover, the existing customers may learn about Stardom's willingness to set a price based on variable cost plus a small contribution margin. The longer time frame over which Stardom keeps selling 200 crates of canned peaches at $55 a crate, the more likely that the existing customers will approach Stardom for their own special price reductions.

12-30 (25 min.) **Cost-plus and market-based pricing.**

1. Construction Temps' full cost per hour of supplying contract labour is:

Variable costs	$12
Fixed costs ($240,000 ÷ 80,000 hours)	3
Full cost per hour	$15

Price per hour at full cost plus 20% = $15 × 1.20 = $18 per hour.

2. Contribution margins for different prices and demand realizations are as follows:

Price per Hour (1)	Variable Cost per Hour (2)	Contribution Margin per Hour (3)=(1)–(2)	Demand in Hours (4)	Total Contribution (5)=(3)×(4)
$16	$12	$4	120,000	$480,000
17	12	5	100,000	500,000
18	12	6	80,000	480,000
19	12	7	70,000	490,000
20	12	8	60,000	480,000

Fixed costs will remain the same regardless of the demand realizations. Fixed costs are therefore irrelevant since they do not differ among the alternatives.

The table above indicates that Construction Temps can maximize contribution margin and hence operating income by charging a price of $17 per hour.

3. The cost-plus approach to pricing in requirement 1 does not explicitly consider the effect of prices on demand. The approach in requirement 2 models the interaction between price and demand and determines the optimal level of profitability using concepts of relevant costs. The two different approaches lead to two different prices in requirements 1 and 2. As the chapter describes, pricing decisions should consider both demand or market considerations and supply or cost factors. The approach in requirement 2 is the more balanced approach. In most cases, of course, managers use the cost-plus method of requirement 1 as only a starting point. They then modify the cost-plus price on the basis of market considerations—anticipated customer reaction to alternative price levels and the prices charged by competitors for similar products.

12-32 (40-45 min.)   **Target prices, target costs, value engineering, cost incurrence, locked-in cost, activity-based costing.**

1.

	Old CE100	Cost Change	New CE100
Direct materials costs	$182,000	$2.20 × 7,000 = $15,400 less	$166,600
Direct manufacturing labour costs	28,000	$0.50 × 7,000 = $3,500 less	24,500
Machining costs	31,500	Fixed cost, so unchanged	31,500
Testing costs	35,000	(20% × 2.5 × 7,000) × $2 =$7,000 less	28,000
Rework costs	14,000	(See Note 1.)	5,600
Ordering costs	3,360	(See Note 2.)	2,100
Engineering costs	21,140	Fixed cost, so unchanged	21,140
Total manufacturing costs	$315,000		$279,440

Note 1:
10% of old CE100s are reworked. That is, 700 (10% of 7,000) CE100's made are reworked. Rework costs = $20 per unit reworked × 700 = $14,000. If rework falls to 4% of New CE100's manufactured, 280 (4% of 7,000) New CE100's manufactured will require rework. Rework costs = $20 per unit × 280 = $5,600.

Note 2 :
Ordering costs for New CE100 = 2 orders/month × 50 components × $21/order
$$= \$2,100$$

Unit manufacturing costs of New CE100 = $279,440 ÷ 7,000 = $39.92

2.   Total manufacturing cost reductions based on new design = $315,000 − $279,440
= $35,560

Reduction in unit manufacturing costs based on new design   = $35,560 ÷ 7,000
= $5.08 per unit.

The reduction in unit manufacturing costs based on the new design can also be calculated as :
  Unit cost of old design, $45 ($315,000 ÷ 7,000 units) − Unit cost of new design, $39.92 = $5.08

Hence the target cost reduction of $6 per unit is not achieved by the redesign.

3.   Changes in design have a considerably bigger impact on costs per unit compared with improvements in manufacturing efficiency ($5.08 versus $1.50). One explanation is that many costs are locked-in once the design of the radio-cassette is completed. Improvements in manufacturing efficiency cannot reduce many of these costs. Design choices can influence many direct and overhead cost categories, for example, by reducing direct materials requirements, by reducing defects requiring rework, and by designing in fewer components which translates into fewer orders being placed and lower ordering costs.

12-34 (50-60 min.) **Target cost, activity-based costing systems (continuation of 12-33).**

1. A target cost per unit is the estimated long-run cost per unit of a product (or service) that, when sold at the target price, enables the company to achieve the target operating income per unit. A target cost per unit is the estimated unit long-run cost of a product that will enable a company to enter or to remain in the market and compete profitably against its competitors.

2. The following table presents the manufacturing cost per unit for different cost categories for P-41REV and P-63 REV.

Cost Categories	P-41 REV	P-63 REV
Direct manufacturing product costs:		
Direct materials	$381.20	$263.10
Indirect manufacturing product costs:		
Materials handling		
(71 × $1.20; 39 × $1.20)	85.20	46.80
Assembly management		
(2.1 × $40; 1.6 × $40)	84.00	64.00
Machine-insertion of parts		
(59 × $0.70; 29 × $0.70)	41.30	20.30
Manual-insertion of parts		
(12 × $2.10; 10 × $2.10)	25.20	21.00
Quality testing		
(1.2 × $25; 0.9 × $25)	30.00	22.50
Total indirect manufacturing costs	265.70	174.60
Total manufacturing costs	$646.90	$437.70
Target cost	$680.00	$390.00

P-41 REV is $33.10 below its target cost. However, P-63 REV is $47.70 above its target cost. It appears that Executive Power will have major problems competing with the foreign printer costing $390.

12-34 (cont'd)

3.
P-41	=	$782.40	P-63	=	$504.00
P-41 REV	=	646.90	P-63 REV	=	437.70
Difference	=	$135.50	Difference	=	$ 66.30

The sources of the cost reductions in the redesigned products are:

	P-41	P-63
(a) Reduction in direct materials costs	$ 26.30	$29.00
(b) Changes in design:		
Reduced materials handling costs because of fewer parts $(85 - 71); (46 - 39) \times \$1.20$	16.80	8.40
Reduced assembly time $(3.2 - 2.1); (1.9 - 1.6) \times \$40$	44.00	12.00
Reduced insertion of parts[1] $(49 - 59) \times \$0.70 + (36 - 12) \times \$2.10$	43.40	
$(31 - 29) \times \$0.70 + (15 - 10) \times \$2.10$		11.90
Reduced quality testing $(1.4 - 1.2); (1.1 - 0.9) \times \$25$	5.00	5.00
	$135.50	$66.30

[1] Note that the reduced costs for insertion of parts comes from two sources: (a) a reduction in total number of parts to be inserted, and (b) an increase in the percentage of parts inserted by the lower-cost machine method.

4. The $12 reduction in cost per hour of assembly time (from $40 to $28) reduces product costs as follows:

P-41 REV: 12×2.1 hours = $25.20. The new total manufacturing product cost is $621.70 ($646.90 − $25.20)

P-63 REV: 12×1.6 hours = $19.20. The new total manufacturing product cost is $418.50 ($437.70 − $19.20)

The reduction in the assembly management activity rate further reduces the cost of P-41 REV below the target cost. It also makes it more likely that P-63 REV will achieve its target cost.

12-36 (25 min.) Ethics and pricing.

1. Full product costs for the new ball-bearings order are as follows:

Direct materials		$40,000
Direct manufacturing labour		10,000
Overhead costs		
Design and parts administration overhead	$4,000	
Production-order overhead	5,000	
Setup overhead	5,500	
Materials handling overhead	6,500	
General and administration overhead	9,000	
Total overhead costs		30,000
Full product costs		$80,000

Baker prices at full product costs plus a markup of 10% = $80,000 + 10% of $80,000 = $80,000 + $8,000 = $88,000.

2. The incremental costs of the order are as follows:

Direct materials	$40,000
Direct manufacturing labour	10,000
30% of overhead costs 30% × $30,000	9,000
Incremental costs	$59,000

Any bid above $59,000 will generate positive contribution margin for Baker. Baker may prefer to use full product costs because it regards the new ball-bearings order as a long-term business relationship rather than a special order. For long-run pricing decisions, managers prefer to use full product costs because it indicates the bare minimum costs they need to recover to continue in business rather than shut down. For a business to be profitable in the long run, it needs to recover *both* its variable and its fixed product costs. Using only variable costs may tempt the manager to engage in excessive long-run price cutting as long as prices give a positive contribution margin. Using full product costs for pricing thereby prompts price stability.

If Baker had regarded the ball-bearings order as a one-time-only special order and if Baker had excess capacity, it might have bid on the basis of its incremental costs with the goal of earning some contribution margin. On the other hand, if this were a special order and Baker were already operating at capacity, it would need to consider *both* the incremental costs and the opportunity costs of using limited capacity to satisfy the ball-bearings order, once again driving the price up toward its full product costs.

3. Not using full product costs (including an allocation of fixed overhead) to price the order, particularly if it is in direct contradiction of company policy, may be unethical.

12-36 (cont'd)

Clear reports using relevant and reliable information should be prepared. Reports prepared on the basis of excluding certain fixed costs that should be included would violate the management accountant's responsibility for competence. It is unethical for Lazarus to suggest that Decker change the cost numbers that were prepared for the bearings order and for Decker to change the numbers in order to make Lazarus's performance look good.

The management accountant has a responsibility to avoid actual or apparent conflicts of interest and advise all appropriate parties of any potential conflict. Lazarus's motivation for wanting Decker to reduce costs was precisely to earn a larger bonus. In this regard both Lazarus's and Decker's behaviour (if Decker agrees to reduce the cost of the order) could be viewed as unethical.

From a management accountant's standpoint, reducing fixed overhead costs in deciding on the price to bid are clearly violating both of these precepts. For the various reasons cited above, we should take the position that the behaviour described by Lazarus and Decker (if he goes along with Lazarus's wishes) is unethical.

Decker should indicate to Lazarus that the costs were correctly computed given the long-term nature of the ball-bearings contract, and that determining prices on the basis of full product costs plus a markup of 10% are also required by company policy. If Lazarus still insists on making the changes and reducing the costs of the order, Decker should raise the matter with Lazarus's superior. If, after taking all these steps, there is continued pressure to understate the costs, Decker should consider resigning from the company, rather than engaging in unethical behaviour.

CHAPTER 13
STRATEGY, BALANCED SCORECARD, AND STRATEGIC PROFITABILITY ANALYSIS

13-2 The five key forces to consider in industry analysis are: (a) competitors, (b) potential entrants into the market, (c) equivalent products, (d) bargaining power of customers, and (e) bargaining power of input suppliers.

13-4 The four key perspectives in the balanced scorecard are: (1) Financial perspective—this perspective evaluates the profitability of the strategy, (2) Customer perspective—this perspective identifies the targeted market segments and measures the company's success in these segments, (3) Internal business process perspective—this perspective focuses on internal operations that further both the customer perspective by creating value for customers and the financial perspective by increasing shareholder wealth, and (4) Learning and growth perspective—this perspective identifies the capabilities in which the organization must excel in order to achieve superior internal processes that create value for customers and shareholders.

13-6 A good balanced scorecard design has several features:
1. It tells the story of a company's strategy by articulating a sequence of cause-and-effect relationships.
2. It helps to communicate the strategy to all members of the organization by translating the strategy into a coherent and linked set of understandable and measurable operational targets.
3. It places strong emphasis on financial objectives and measures in for-profit companies. Nonfinancial measures are regarded as part of a program to achieve future financial performance.
4. It limits the number of measures to only those that are critical to the implementation of strategy.
5. It highlights suboptimal tradeoffs that managers may make when they fail to consider operational and financial measures together.

13-8 Three key components in doing a strategic analysis of operating income are:
1. The growth component which measures the change in operating income attributable solely to an increase in the quantity of output sold from one year to the next.
2. The price-recovery component which measures the change in operating income attributable solely to changes in the prices of inputs and outputs from one year to the next.
3. The productivity component which measures the change in costs attributable to a change in the quantity of inputs used in the current year relative to the quantity of inputs that would have been used in the previous year to produce current year output.

13-10   Engineered costs result from a cause-and-effect relationship between the cost driver, output, and the (direct or indirect) resources used to produce that output. Discretionary costs arise from periodic (usually) annual decisions regarding the maximum amount to be incurred. There is no measurable cause-and-effect relationship between output and resources used.

13-12   Downsizing (also called rightsizing) is an integrated approach configuring processes, products, and people in order to match costs to the activities that need to be performed for operating effectively and efficiently in the present and future.

13-14   Total factor productivity is the quantity of output produced divided by the costs of all inputs used, where the inputs are costed on the basis of current period prices.

13-16 (15 min.)   **Balanced scorecard.**

1.   La Quinta's 2001 strategy is a cost leadership strategy. La Quinta plans to grow by producing high-quality boxes at a low cost delivered to customers in a timely manner. La Quinta's boxes are not differentiated, and there are many other manufacturers who produce similar boxes. To succeed, La Quinta must achieve lower costs relative to competitors through productivity and efficiency improvements.

2.   Measures that we would expect to see on La Quinta's balanced scorecard for 2001 are

Financial Perspective
(1) Operating income from productivity gain, (2) operating income from growth, (3) cost reductions in key areas.
      These measures evaluate whether La Quinta has successfully reduced costs and generated growth through cost leadership.

Customer Perspective
(1) Market share, (2) new customers, (3) customer satisfaction index, (4) customer retention, (5) time taken to fulfill customer orders.
      The logic is that improvements in these customer measures are leading indicators of superior financial performance.

Internal Business Process Perspective
(1) Yield, (2) productivity, (3) order delivery time, (4) on-time delivery.
      Improvements in these measures are expected to lead to more satisfied customers and in turn to superior financial performance.

Learning and Growth Perspective
(1) Percentage of employees trained in process and quality management, (2) employee satisfaction, (3) number of major process improvements.
      Improvements in these measures have a cause-and-effect relationship with improvements in internal business processes, which in turn lead to customer satisfaction and financial performance.

13-18 (15 min.) **Strategy, balanced scorecard.**

1.   Meredith Corporation follows a product differentiation strategy in 2000. Meredith's D4H machine is distinct from its competitors and generally regarded as superior to competitors' products. To succeed, Meredith must continue to differentiate its product and charge a premium price.

2.   Balanced Scorecard measures for 2000 follow:

Financial Perspective
(1) Increase in operating income from charging higher margins, (2) Price premium earned on products.

These measures indicate whether Meredith has been able to charge premium prices and achieve operating income increases through product differentiation.

Customer Perspective
(1) Market share in high-end special-purpose textile machines, (2) customer satisfaction, (3) new customers.

Improvements in these customer measures are leading indicators of superior financial performance.

Internal Business Process Perspective
(1) Manufacturing quality, (2) new product features added, (3) order delivery time.

Improvements in these measures are expected to result in more satisfied customers and in turn superior financial performance.

Learning and Growth Perspective
(1) Development time for designing new machines, (2) improvements in manufacturing processes, (3) employee education and skill levels, (4) employee satisfaction.

Improvements in these measures have a cause-and-effect relationship with improvements in internal business processes, which in turn lead to customer satisfaction and financial performance.

13-20 (20 min.)   **Analysis of growth, price-recovery, and productivity components.** (Continuation of 13-19)

Effect of the industry-market-size factor

    If the 10-unit increase in sales from 200 to 210 units, 3% or 6 (3% × 200) units is due to growth in market size, and 4 (10 – 6) units is due to an increase in market share. The change in Meredith's operating income from the industry-market-size factor rather than from specific strategic actions is:

$$\$280{,}000 \text{ (the growth component in Exercise 13-19)} \times \frac{6}{10} \qquad \$168{,}000 \text{ F}$$

Effect of product differentiation
The change in operating income due to:
Increase in the selling price of D4H (revenue effect of price recovery)	$420,000 F
Increase in price of inputs (cost effect of price recovery)	184,500 U
Growth in market share due to product differentiation	

$$\$280{,}000 \text{ (the growth component in Exercise 13-19)} \times \frac{4}{10} \qquad \underline{112{,}000 \text{ F}}$$

Change in operating income due to product differentiation	$\underline{\$347{,}500}$ F

Effect of cost leadership
The change in operating income from cost leadership is:

Productivity component	$92,000 F

The change in operating income between 1999 and 2000 can be summarized as follows:

Change due to industry-market-size	$168,000 F
Change due to product differentiation	347,500 F
Change due to cost leadership	$\underline{92{,}000}$ F
Change in operating income	$\underline{\$607{,}500}$ F

    Meredith has been successful in implementing its product differentiation strategy. Nearly 57% ($347,500 ÷ $607,500) of the increase in operating income during 2000 was due to product differentiation. Meredith's operating income increase in 2000 was also helped by a growth in the overall market and some productivity improvements.

13-22 (15 min.)   **Strategy, balanced scorecard, service company.**

1.   Snyder Corporation's strategy in 2000 is cost leadership. Snyder's consulting services for implementing sales management software is not distinct from its competitors. The market for these services is very competitive. To succeed, Snyder must deliver quality service at low cost. Improving productivity while maintaining quality is key.

2.   Balanced Scorecard measures for 2000 follow:

Financial Perspective
(1) Increase operating income from productivity gains and growth, (2) revenues per employee, (3) cost reductions in key areas, for example, software implementation and overhead costs.
     These measures indicate whether Snyder has been able to reduce costs and achieve operating income increases through cost leadership.

Customer Perspective
(1) Market share, (2) new customers, (3) customer responsiveness, (4) customer satisfaction.
     Improvements in these customer measures are regarded as leading indicators of superior financial performance.

Internal Business Process Perspective
(1) Time to complete customer jobs, (2) time lost due to errors, (3) quality of job (Is system running smoothly after job is completed?).
     Improvements in these measures are expected to lead to more satisfied customers, lower costs, and superior financial performance.

Learning and Growth Perspective
(1) Time required to analyze and design implementation steps, (2) time taken to perform key steps implementing the software, (3) skill levels of employees, (4) hours of employee training, (5) employee satisfaction and motivation.
     Improvements in these measures have a cause-and-effect relationship with improvements in internal business processes, customer satisfaction, and financial performance.

13-24 (25 min.) **Analysis of growth, price-recovery and productivity components.** (Continuation of 13-23)

Effect of industry-market-size factors
Of the 10-unit increase in sales from 60 to 70 units, 5% or 3 units (5% × 60) is due to growth in market size, and 7 (10 − 3) units is due to an increase in market share. The change in Snyder's operating income from the industry market-size factor rather than from specific strategic actions is:

$200,000 (the growth component in Exercise 13-23) × $\frac{3}{10}$ $60,000 F

Effect of product differentiation
Of the $2,000 decrease in selling price, 1% or $500 (1% × $50,000) is due to a general decline in prices, and the remaining decrease of $1,500 ($2,000 − $500) is due to a strategic decision by Snyder's management to implement its cost leadership strategy of lowering prices to stimulate demand.

The change in operating income due to a decline in selling price (other than the strategic reduction in price included in the cost leadership component) $500 × 70 units	$ 35,000 U
Increase in prices of inputs (cost effect of price recovery)	129,000 U
Change in operating income due to product differentiation	$164,000 U

Effect of cost leadership

Productivity component	$189,000 F
Effect of strategic decision to reduce selling price, $1,500 × 70	105,000 U

Growth in market share due to productivity improvement and strategic decision to reduce selling price

$200,000 (the growth component in Exercise 13-23) × $\frac{7}{10}$	140,000 F
Change in operating income due to cost leadership	$224,000 F

The change in operating income between 1999 and 2000 can then be summarized as

Change due to industry-market-size	$ 60,000 F
Change due to product differentiation	164,000 U
Change due to cost leadership	224,000 F
Change in operating income	$120,000 F

Snyder has been very successful in implementing its cost leadership strategy. Due to a lack of product differentiation, Snyder was unable to pass along increases in labour costs by increasing the selling price—in fact selling price declined by $2,000 per work unit. However, Snyder was able to take advantage of its productivity gains to reduce price, gain market share, and increase operating income.

13-26 (20 min.)   **Balanced scorecard.**

1.   Caltex's strategy is to focus on "service-oriented customers" who are willing to pay a higher price for services. Even though its product is largely a commodity product, gasoline, Caltex wants to differentiate itself through the service it provides at its retailing stations.

Does the scorecard represent Caltex's strategy? By and large it does. The focus of the scorecard is on measures of process improvement, quality, market share, and financial success from product differentiation. There are some deficiencies that the subsequent assignment questions raise but, abstracting from these concerns for the moment, the scorecard does focus on implementing a product differentiation strategy.

Having concluded that the scorecard has been reasonably well designed, how has Caltex performed relative to its strategy in 2001? It appears from the scorecard that Caltex was successful in implementing its strategy in 2001. It achieved all targets in the financial, internal business, and learning and growth perspectives. The only target it missed was the market share target in the customer perspective. At this stage, students may raise some questions about whether this is a good scorecard measure. Requirement 3 gets at this issue in more detail. The bottom line is that measuring "market share in the overall gasoline market" rather than in the "service-oriented customer market segment" is not a good scorecard measure, so not achieving this target may not be as big an issue as it may seem at first.

2.   Yes, Caltex should include some measure of employee satisfaction and employee training in the learning and growth perspective. Caltex's differentiation strategy and ability to charge a premium price is based on customer service. The key to good, fast, and friendly customer service is well-trained and satisfied employees. Untrained and dissatisfied employees will have poor interactions with customers and cause the strategy to fail. Hence, training and employee satisfaction are very important to Caltex for implementing its strategy. These measures are leading indicators of whether Caltex will be able to successfully implement its strategy and, hence, should be measured on the balanced scorecard.

3.   Caltex's strategy is to focus on the 60% of gasoline consumers who are service-oriented not on the 40% price-shopper segment. To evaluate if it has been successful in implementing its strategy, Caltex needs to measure its market share in its targeted market segment, "service-oriented customer," not its market share in the overall market. Given Caltex's strategy, it should not be concerned if its market share in the price-shopper segment declines. In fact, charging premium prices will probably cause its market share in this segment to decline. Caltex should replace "market share in overall gasoline market" with "market share in the service-oriented customer segment" in its balanced scorecard customer measure. Caltex may also want to consider putting a customer satisfaction measure on the scorecard. This measure should capture an overall evaluation of customer reactions to the facility, the convenience store, employee interactions, and quick turnaround. The customer satisfaction measure would serve as a leading indicator of market share in the service-oriented customer segment.

13-26 (cont'd)

4.   Although there is a cause-and-effect link between internal business process measures and customer measures on the current scorecard, Caltex should add more measures to tighten this linkage. In particular, the current scorecard measures focus exclusively on refinery operations and not on gas station operations. Caltex should add measures of gas station performance such as cleanliness of the facility, turnaround time at the gas pumps, the shopping experience at the convenience store, and the service provided by employees. Many companies do random audits of their facilities to evaluate how well their branches and retail outlets are performing. These measures would serve as leading indicators of customer satisfaction and market share in Caltex's targeted segments.

5.   Caltex is correct in not measuring changes in operating income from productivity improvements on its scorecard under the financial perspective. Caltex's strategy is to grow by charging premium prices for customer service. The scorecard measures focus on Caltex's success in implementing this strategy. Productivity gains per se are not critical to Caltex's strategy and, hence, should not be measured on the scorecard.

13-28 (35 min.) **Analysis of growth, price-recovery, and productivity improvements.**

1. Halsey is following a product differentiation strategy. Halsey offers a wide selection of clothes and excellent customer service. Halsey's strategy is to distinguish itself from its competitors and to charge a premium price.

2. Operating income for each year is as follows:

	2001	2002
Revenues ($60 × 40,000; $59 × 40,000)	$2,400,000	$2,360,000
Costs		
Materials costs ($40 × 40,000; $41 × 40,000)	1,600,000	1,640,000
Selling & customer service costs ($7 × 51,000); $6.90 × 43,000)	357,000	296,700
Purchasing & admin. costs ($250 × 980; $240 × 850)	245,000	204,000
Total costs	2,202,000	2,140,700
Operating income	$ 198,000	$ 219,300
Change in operating income		▲ $21,300 F ▲

3. **The Growth Component**

$$\begin{matrix} \text{Revenue effect} \\ \text{of growth} \\ \text{component} \end{matrix} = \left(\begin{matrix} \text{Actual units of} \\ \text{output sold} \\ \text{in 2002} \end{matrix} - \begin{matrix} \text{Actual units of} \\ \text{output sold} \\ \text{in 2001} \end{matrix} \right) \times \begin{matrix} \text{Output} \\ \text{price} \\ \text{in 2001} \end{matrix}$$

$$= (40{,}000 - 40{,}000) \times \$60 = \$0$$

$$\begin{matrix} \text{Cost effect of} \\ \text{price - recovery} \\ \text{component} \end{matrix} = \left(\begin{matrix} \text{Actual units of input or} \\ \text{capacity that would} \\ \text{have been used to produce} \\ \text{year 2002 output assuming} \\ \text{the same input - output} \\ \text{relationship that existed in 2001} \end{matrix} - \begin{matrix} \text{Actual units of} \\ \text{inputs or capacity} \\ \text{used to produce} \\ \text{2001 output} \end{matrix} \right) \times \begin{matrix} \text{Input} \\ \text{prices} \\ \text{in 2001} \end{matrix}$$

Materials costs that would be required in 2002 would be the same as that required in 2001 because output is the same between 2001 and 2002. Manufacturing conversion costs and selling and customer-service costs will not change since adequate capacity exists in 2001 to support year 2002 output and customers.

The cost effects of growth component are:

Materials costs	(40,000 − 40,000) ×	$60	=	$0
Selling & cust.-serv. costs	(51,000 − 51,000) ×	$7	=	0
Purch. & admin. costs	(980 − 980) ×	$250	=	0
Cost effect of growth component				$0

13-28 (cont'd)

In summary, the net effect on operating income as a result of the growth component equals:

Revenue effect of growth component	$0
Cost effect of growth component	0
Change in operating income due to growth component	$0

The Price-Recovery Component

$$\begin{array}{c} \text{Revenue effect} \\ \text{of price-recovery} \\ \text{component} \end{array} = \left(\begin{array}{c} \text{Output price} \\ \text{in 2002} \end{array} - \begin{array}{c} \text{Output price} \\ \text{in 2001} \end{array} \right) \times \begin{array}{c} \text{Actual units} \\ \text{of output} \\ \text{sold in 2002} \end{array}$$

$$= \ (\$59 - \$60) \times 40{,}000 \ = \$40{,}000 \text{ U}$$

$$\begin{array}{c} \text{Cost effect of} \\ \text{price-recovery} \\ \text{component} \end{array} = \left(\begin{array}{c} \text{Input} \\ \text{prices} \\ \text{in 2002} \end{array} - \begin{array}{c} \text{Input} \\ \text{prices} \\ \text{in 2001} \end{array} \right) \times \begin{array}{c} \text{Actual units of inputs or} \\ \text{capacity that would} \\ \text{have been used to produce} \\ \text{year 2002 output assuming} \\ \text{the same input-output} \\ \text{relationship that existed in 2001} \end{array}$$

Materials costs	($41 – $40)	×	40,000	=	$40,000 U
Selling & cust.-serv. costs	($6.90 – $7)	×	51,000	=	5,100 F
Purchas. & admin. costs	($240 – $250)	×	980	=	9,800 F
Total cost effect of price-recovery component					$25,100 U

In summary, the net decrease in operating income as a result of the price-recovery component equals:

Revenue effect of price-recovery component	$40,000 U
Cost effect of price-recovery component	25,100 U
Change in operating income due to price-recovery component	$65,100 U

The Productivity Component

$$\begin{array}{c} \text{Productivity} \\ \text{component} \end{array} = \left(\begin{array}{c} \text{Actual units of} \\ \text{inputs or capacity} \\ \text{used to produce} \\ \text{year 2002 output} \end{array} - \begin{array}{c} \text{Actual units of inputs or} \\ \text{capacity that would} \\ \text{have been used to produce} \\ \text{year 2002 output assuming} \\ \text{the same input-output} \\ \text{relationship that existed in 2001} \end{array} \right) \times \begin{array}{c} \text{Input} \\ \text{prices} \\ \text{in 2002} \end{array}$$

The productivity component of cost changes are:

Materials costs	$(40{,}000 - 40{,}000)$	$\times$ $41	=	0
Selling & cust.-serv. costs	$(43{,}000 - 51{,}000)$	$\times$ $6.90	=	$55,200 F
Purchasing & admin. costs	$(850 - 980)$	$\times$ $240	=	31,200 F
Change in operating income due to productivity component				$86,400 F

The change in operating income between 2001 and 2002 can be analyzed as follows:

	Income Statement Amounts in 1999 (1)	Revenue and Cost Effects of Growth Component in 2000 (2)	Revenue and Cost Effects of Price-Recovery Component in 2000 (3)	Cost Effect of Productivity Component in 2000 (4)	Income Statement Amounts in 2000 (5) = (1) + (2) + (3) + (4)
Revenues	$2,400,000	$0	$40,000 U	—	$2,360,000
Costs	2,202,000	0	25,100 U	$ 86,400 F	2,140,700
Operating income	$ 198,000	$0	$65,100 U	$ 86,400 F	$ 219,300

$21,300 F

Change in operating income

4.   The analysis of operating income indicates that a significant amount of the increase in operating income resulted from productivity gains rather than product differentiation. The company was unable to charge a premium price for its clothes. Thus, the strategic analysis of operating income indicates that Halsey has not been successful at implementing its premium price, product differentiation strategy, despite the fact that operating income increased by more than 10% between 2001 and 2002. Halsey could not pass on increases in purchase costs to its customers via higher prices. Halsey must either reconsider its strategy or focus managers on increasing margins and growing market share by offering better product variety and superb customer service.

13-30 (20 min.) **Engineered and discretionary overhead costs, unused capacity, repairs and maintenance.**

1. Rowland's repair and maintenance costs are indirect, engineered costs. The amount of repair and maintenance costs each year may not correlate directly to the quantity of gears produced. Over time, however, there is a clear cause-and-effect relationship between the output (quantity of gears produced) and repair and maintenance costs—the more gears that are produced, the greater the number of hours the machines will be run, and the greater the repairs and maintenance the machines will need.

2.   (1)   Available repair and maintenance capacity
          8 hours per day × 250 days × 4 workers   8,000 hours
     (2)   Repair and maintenance work actually done   6,000 hours
     (3) = (1) − (2) Hours of unused repair and maintenance capacity   2,000 hours
     (4)   Repair and maintenance cost per hour, $40,000 ÷ 2,000 $20 per hour
     (5) = (3) × (4) Cost of unused repair and maintenance capacity $40,000

Reasons why Rowland might want to downsize its repair and maintenance capacity are:
    a.   to reduce costs of carrying unused capacity
    b.   to create a culture of streamlining processes and operating efficiently

Reasons why Rowland might not want to downsize its repair and maintenance capacity are:
    a.   it projects greater demand for repairs and maintenance activity in the near future
    b.   it would negatively affect employee morale
    c.   it may want to use the expertise of the repairs and maintenance staff in other areas such as process improvements
    d.   it does not regard the unused capacity as particularly excessive

3. If repair and maintenance costs are discretionary costs, calculating unused capacity is much more difficult. Repair and maintenance costs would be discretionary if repair and maintenance are mostly of a preventive type that management can choose when to do. In this case, the lack of a cause-and-effect relationship between output and repair and maintenance activity means that Rowland cannot determine the repair and maintenance resources used and, hence, the amount of unused capacity.

13-32 (20 min.) Partial productivity measurement.

1. Berkshire Corporation's partial productivity ratios in 2002 are as follows:

$$\text{Direct materials partial productivity} = \frac{\text{Quantity of output produced in 2002}}{\text{Kilograms of direct materials used in 2002}} = \frac{525{,}000}{610{,}000} = 0.86 \text{ units per kg}$$

$$\text{Direct manuf. labour partial productivity} = \frac{\text{Quantity of output produced in 2002}}{\text{Direct manuf. labour-hours used in 2002}} = \frac{525{,}000}{9{,}500} = 55.26 \text{ units per labour-hour}$$

$$\text{Manufacturing overhead partial productivity} = \frac{\text{Quantity of output produced in 2002}}{\text{Units of manuf. capacity in 2002}} = \frac{525{,}000}{582{,}000} = 0.90 \text{ units per unit of capacity}$$

To compare partial productivities in 2002 with partial productivities in 2001, we first calculate the inputs that would have been used in 2001 to produce year 2002's 525,000 units of output assuming the year 2001 relationship between inputs and outputs.

$$\text{Direct materials} = 450{,}000 \text{ kg (2001)} \times \frac{525{,}000 \text{ output units in 2002}}{375{,}000 \text{ output units in 2001}}$$

$$= 450{,}000 \times 1.4 = 630{,}000 \text{ kg}$$

$$\text{Direct manuf. labour} = 7{,}500 \text{ hours (2001)} \times \frac{525{,}000 \text{ output units in 2002}}{375{,}000 \text{ output units in 2001}}$$

$$= 7{,}500 \times 1.4 = 10{,}500 \text{ labour-hours}$$

Manufacturing capacity = 600,000 units of capacity, because manufacturing capacity is fixed, and adequate capacity existed in 2001 to produce year 2002 output.

13-32 (cont'd)

Partial productivity calculations for 2001 based on year 2002 output (to make the partial productivities comparable across the two years)

$$\text{Direct materials partial productivity} = \frac{\text{Quantity of output produced in 2002}}{\text{Kilograms of direct materials that would have been used in 2001 to produce year 2002 output}} = \frac{525{,}000}{630{,}000} = 0.83 \text{ units per kg}$$

$$\text{Direct manuf. labour partial productivity} = \frac{\text{Quantity of output produced in 2002}}{\text{Direct manuf. labour-hours that would have been used in 2001 to produce year 2002 output}} = \frac{525{,}000}{10{,}500} = 50 \text{ units per labour-hour}$$

$$\text{Manufacturing overhead partial productivity} = \frac{\text{Quantity of output produced in 2002}}{\text{Units of manuf. capacity that would have been used in 2001 to produce year 2002 output}} = \frac{525{,}000}{600{,}000} = 0.875 \text{ units per unit of capacity}$$

The calculations indicate that Berkshire improved the partial productivity of all its inputs between 2001 and 2002 via improvements in efficiency of direct materials and direct manufacturing labour and by reducing unused manufacturing capacity.

2.   All partial productivity ratios increase from 2001 to 2002. We can therefore conclude that total factor productivity definitely increased from 2001 to 2002. Partial productivities cannot, however, tell us how much total factor productivity changed, because partial productivity measures cannot be aggregated over different inputs.

3.   Berkshire Corporation management can use the partial productivity measures to set targets for the next year. Partial productivity measures can easily be compared over multiple periods. For example, they may specify bonus payments if partial productivity of direct manufacturing labour increases to 60 units of output per direct manufacturing labour-hour and if partial productivity of direct materials improves to 0.90 units of output per kilogram of direct materials. A major advantage of partial productivity measures is that they focus on a single input; hence, they are simple to calculate and easy to understand at the operations level. Managers and operators can also examine these numbers to understand the reasons underlying productivity changes from one period to the next—better training of workers, lower absenteeism, lower labour turnover, better incentives, or improved methods. Management can then implement and sustain these factors in the future.

13-34 (25 min.) **Balanced scorecard, ethics.**

1. Yes, the Household Products Division (HPD) should include measures of employee satisfaction and customer satisfaction even if these measures are subjective. For a maker of kitchen dishwashers, employee and customer satisfaction are leading indicators of future financial performance. There is a cause-and-effect linkage between these measures and future financial performance. If HPD's strategy is correct and if the scorecard has been properly designed, employee and customer satisfaction information is very important in evaluating the implementation of HPD's strategy.

HPD should use employee and customer satisfaction measures even though these measures are subjective. One of the pitfalls to avoid when implementing a balanced scorecard is not to use only objective measures in the scorecard. Of course, HPD should guard against imprecision and potential for manipulation. Patricia Conley appears to be aware of this. She has tried to understand the reasons for the poor scores and has been able to relate these scores to other objective evidence such as employee dissatisfaction with the new work rules and customer unhappiness with missed delivery dates.

2. Incorrect reporting of employee and customer satisfaction ratings to make divisions performance look good is unethical. In assessing the situation, a management accountant should consider the following:

Clear reports using relevant and reliable information should be prepared. Preparing reports on the basis of incorrect employee and customer satisfaction ratings in order to make the division's performance look better than it is is unethical.

The management accountant has a responsibility to avoid actual or apparent conflicts of interest and advise all appropriate parties of any potential conflict. Conley may be tempted to report better employee and customer satisfaction ratings to please Emburey. The management accountant should communicate favourable as well as unfavourable information.

A management accountant should require that information be fairly and objectively communicated and that all relevant information should be disclosed.

Conley should indicate to Emburey that the employee and customer satisfaction ratings are, indeed, appropriate. If Emburey still insists on reporting better employee and customer satisfaction numbers, Conley should raise the matter with one of Emburey's superiors. If, after taking all these steps, there is continued pressure to overstate employee and customer satisfaction ratings, Conley should consider resigning from the company and not engage in unethical behaviour.

CHAPTER 14
COST ALLOCATION

14-2 The salary of a plant security guard would be a direct cost when the cost object is the security department or the plant. It would be an indirect cost when the cost object is a product.

14-4 Exhibit 14-2 lists four criteria used to guide cost allocation decisions:
1. Cause and effect.
2. Benefits received.
3. Fairness or equity.
4. Ability to bear.

Either the cause-and-effect criterion or the benefits received criterion is the dominant one when the purpose of the allocation is related to the economic decision purpose or the motivation purpose.

14-6 Cost-benefit considerations can affect costing choices in several ways:

(a) Classifying some immaterial costs as indirect when they could, at high cost, be traced to products, services or customers as direct costs.

(b) Using a small number of indirect cost pools when, at high cost, an increased number of indirect cost pools would provide more homogeneous cost pools.

(c) Using allocation bases that are readily available (or can be collected at low cost) when, at high cost, more appropriate cost allocation bases could be developed.

14-8 Examples of bases used to allocate corporate cost pools to operating divisions are:

Corporate Cost Pools	Possible Allocation Bases
Corporate executive dept.	Sales; assets employed; operating income
Treasury department	Sales; assets employed; estimated time or usage
Legal department	Estimated time or usage; sales; assets employed
Marketing department	Sales; number of sales personnel
Payroll department	Number of employees; payroll dollars
Personnel department	Number of employees; payroll dollars; number of new hires

14-10 Disagree. Allocating costs on "the basis of estimated long-run use by user department managers" means department managers can lower their cost allocations by deliberately underestimating their long-run use.

14-12 The *reciprocal method* is theoretically the most defensible method because it explicitly recognizes the mutual services rendered among all departments, irrespective of whether those departments are operating or support departments.

14-14 The basis for the cost allocation should be defined within the government contract.

14-16 (15-20 min.)   **Single-rate versus dual-rate cost allocation methods.**

1.   The total costs in the single-cost pool are fixed ($1,000,000) and variable ($2,000,000) = $3,000,000. Ontario Power could use one of two allocation bases (budgeted usage or actual usage) given the information provided.

- Allocation to Ontario based on budgeted usage: $(60/200) \times \$3,000,000 = \$900,000$
- Allocation to Ontario based on actual usage: $(120/240) \times \$3,000,000 = \$1,500,000$

2.   Using the dual-rate method (with separate fixed and variable cost pools), several combinations of the budgeted and actual usage allocation bases are possible:

Fixed Cost Pool: Total costs of $1,000,000:
- Allocation to Ontario based on budgeted usage: $(60/200) \times \$1,000,000 = \$300,000$
- Allocation to Ontario based on actual usage: $(120/240) \times \$1,000,000 = \$500,000$

Variable Cost Pool: Total costs of $2,000,000:
- Allocation to Ontario based on budgeted usage: $(60/200) \times \$2,000,000 = \$600,000$
- Allocation to Ontario based on actual usage: $(120/240) \times \$2,000,000 = \$1,000,000$

The combinations possible are:

Combination	Fixed Cost Pool	Variable Cost Pool	Allocation Function
I	Budgeted Usage	Budgeted Usage	= $300,000 + $600,000 = $900,000
II	Budgeted Usage	Actual Usage	= $300,000 + $1,000,000 = $1,300,000
III	Actual Usage	Budgeted Usage	= $500,000 + $600,000 = $1,100,000
IV	Actual Usage	Actual Usage	= $500,000 + $1,000,000 = $1,500,000

Combinations I and IV give the same cost allocations as in requirement 1. Combination II is a frequently used dual-rate method. The fixed costs are allocated using budgeted usage on the rationale that it better captures the cost of providing capacity. The variable costs are allocated using actual usage on a cause-and-effect rationale. Combination III is rarely encountered in practice.

14-18 (30 min.) **Cost allocation to divisions.**

1.

	Hotel	Restaurant	Casino	Rembrandt
Revenue	$16,425,000	$5,256,000	$12,340,000	$34,021,000
Direct costs	9,819,260	3,749,172	4,284,768	17,853,200
Segment margin	$ 6,605,740	$1,506,828	$ 8,055,232	16,167,800
Indirect costs				14,550,000
Income before taxes				$ 1,617,800
Segment margin %	40.22%	28.67%	65.28%	

2.

	Hotel	Restaurant	Casino	Rembrandt
Direct costs	$9,819,260	$3,749,172	$4,284,768	$17,853,200
Direct cost %	55.00%	21.00%	24.00%	100.00%
Square metres	80,000	16,000	64,000	160,000
Square metres %	50.00%	10.00%	40.00%	100.00%
# of employees	200	50	250	500
# of employees %	40.00%	10.00%	50.00%	100.00%

A: Cost allocation based on direct costs:

	Hotel	Restaurant	Casino	Rembrandt
Revenue	$16,425,000	$5,256,000	$12,340,000	$34,021,000
Direct costs	9,819,260	3,749,172	4,284,768	17,853,200
Segment margin	6,605,740	1,506,828	8,055,232	16,167,800
Allocated indirect costs	8,002,500	3,055,500	3,492,000	14,550,000
Segment pre-tax income	($1,396,760)	($1,548,672)	$ 4,563,232	$ 1,617,800
Segment pre-tax income %	−8.50%	−29.46%	36.98%	4.76%

B: Cost allocation based on floor space:

	Hotel	Restaurant	Casino	Rembrandt
Allocated indirect costs	$7,275,000	$1,455,000	$5,820,000	$14,550,000
Segment pre-tax income	($669,260)	$51,828	$2,235,232	$1,617,800
Segment pre-tax income %	−4.07%	0.99%	18.11%	4.76%

14-18 (cont'd)

C: Cost allocation based on # of employees

	Hotel	Restaurant	Casino	Rembrandt
Allocated indirect costs	$5,820,000	$1,455,000	$7,275,000	$14,550,000
Segment pre-tax income	$785,740	$51,828	$780,232	$1,617,800
Segment pre-tax income %	4.78%	0.99%	6.32%	4.76%

3. The segment fine-tax income percentages show the dramatic effect of choice of the cost allocation base on reported numbers:

Denominator	Hotel	Restaurant	Casino
Direct costs	−8.50%	−29.46%	36.98%
Floor space	−4.07	0.99	18.11
# of employees	4.78	0.99	6.32

The decision context should guide a. whether costs should be allocated, and b. the preferred cost allocation base. Decisions about, say, performance measurement may be made on a combination of financial and nonfinancial measures. It may well be that Rembrandt may prefer to exclude allocated costs from the financial measures to reduce areas of dispute.

Where cost allocation is required, the cause-and-effect and benefits-received criteria are recommended in Chapter 14. The $14,550,000 is a fixed overhead cost. This means that on a short-run basis, the cause-and-effect criterion is not appropriate. Rembrandt should look at how the $14,550,000 cost benefits the three divisions. This will help guide the choice of an allocation base.

4. The analysis in requirement 2 should not guide the decision on whether to shut down any of the divisions. Each division is not independent of the other two. A decision to shut down, say, the restaurant likely would negatively affect the attendance at the casino and possibly the hotel. Rembrandt should examine the future revenue and future cost implications of different resource investments in the three divisions. This is a future-oriented exercise, whereas the analysis in requirement 2 is an analysis of past costs.

14-20 (20 min.) **Dual-rate cost allocation method, budgeted versus actual costs and quantities** (continuation of 14-19).

1.   Charges with Dual-Rate Method

Variable indirect cost rate   = $1,500 per trip

Fixed indirect cost rate $= \dfrac{\$200{,}000 \text{ budgeted costs}}{250 \text{ budgeted trips}}$

    = $800 per budgeted trip

Orange Juice Division
    Variable indirect costs, $1,500 × 200 $300,000
    Fixed indirect costs, $800 × 150   <u>120,000</u>
    <u>$420,000</u>

Grapefruit Division
    Variable indirect costs, $1,500 × 100 $150,000
    Fixed indirect costs, $800 × 100   <u>80,000</u>
    <u>$230,000</u>

2.

	Orange Juice Division	Grapefruit Juice Division
Single Rate I (budgeted rate × actual use)	$460,000	$230,000
Single Rate II (Actual rate × actual use)	430,000	215,000
Dual rate	420,000	230,000

If the dual-rate method used actual trips made as the allocation base, it would give the same answer as Single Rate I. The dual rate changes how the fixed indirect cost component is treated. By using budgeted trips made, the Orange Juice Division is unaffected by changes from its own budgeted usage or that of other divisions.

14-22 (20-30 min.) **Allocation of common costs.**

1.   The available criteria to guide cost allocations include:

(a)   Cause and effect. It is not possible to trace individual causes (either basic news <u>or</u> premium movies <u>or</u> premium sports) to individual effects (viewing by Sam or Sarah or Tony). The $70 total package is a bundled product.

(b)   Benefits received. There are various ways of operationalizing the benefits received:

(i)   Monthly service charge for their prime interest—basic news for Sam ($32), premium movies for Sarah ($25), and premium sports for Tony ($30). This measure captures the services available to be used by each person.

(ii)   Actual usage by each person. This would involve having a record of viewing by each person and then allocating the $70 on a % viewing time basis. This measure captures the services actually used by each person.

(c)   Ability to pay. This criteria requires the three people to agree upon their relative ability to pay. One measure here would be their respective salaries with the Toronto Fire Department.

(d)   Fairness or equity. This criteria is relatively nebulous. A straightforward approach would be to split the $70 equally among the three parties.

14-22 (cont'd)

2.   Three methods of allocating the $70 are:

	Sam	Sarah	Tony
Stand-alone	$25.76	$20.09	$24.15
Incremental	13.00	25.00	32.00
Equal	23.33	23.33	23.33

(a)   Stand-alone cost allocation method.

$$\text{Sam:} \quad \frac{\$32}{\$32 + \$25 + \$30} \times \$70 \quad = 36.8\% \times \$70$$
$$= \$25.76$$

$$\text{Sarah:} \quad \frac{\$25}{\$32 + \$25 + \$30} \times \$70 \quad = 28.7\% \times \$70$$
$$= \$20.09$$

$$\text{Tony:} \quad \frac{\$30}{\$32 + \$25 + \$30} \times \$70 \quad = 34.5\% \times \$70$$
$$= \$24.15$$

(b)   Incremental cost allocation method:

Assume Tony (the owner) is the primary person, Sarah is first incremental party, and Sam the second incremental party.

Party	Cost Allocated	Cost Remaining to Be Allocated to Other Parties
Tony	$32	$38 ($70 – $32)
Sarah	25	13 ($70 – $32 – $25)
Sam	13	0
Total	$70	

This method is sure to generate disputes over the ranking of the three parties. Notice that Sam pays only $13 despite his prime interest in the most expensive basic news package.

(c)   Equal sharing of the $70 amount. Sam, Sarah and Tony each pay $23.33.

Note: One student suggested the owner of the apartment (Tony) should pay the $70 and include the cable television service in the rental charge.

14-24 (30 min.) **Support department cost allocation, direct and step-down methods.**

			A/HR	IS	GOVT	CORP
1.	(a)	Direct Method				
		Costs	$600,000	$2,400,000		
		Alloc. of A/HR				
		(40/75, 35/75)	(600,000)		$ 320,000	$ 280,000
		Alloc. of I.S.				
		(30/90, 60/90)		(2,400,000)	800,000	1,600,000
			$ 0	$ 0	$1,120,000	$1,880,000
	(b)	Step-Down (A/HR first)				
		Costs	$600,000	2,400,000		
		Alloc. of A/HR				
		(0.25, 0.40, 0.35)	(600,000)	150,000	240,000	210,000
		Alloc. of I.S.				
		(30/90, 60/90)		(2,550,000)	850,000	1,700,000
			$ 0	$ 0	$1,090,000	$1,910,000
	(c)	Step-Down (I.S. first)				
		Costs	$600,000	2,400,000		
		Alloc. of I.S.				
		(0.10, 0.30, 0.60)	240,000	(2,400,000)	720,000	$1,440,000
		Alloc. of A/HR				
		(40/75, 35/75)	(840,000)		448,000	392,000
			$ 0	$ 0	$1,168,000	$1,832,000

		GOVT	CORP
2.	Direct method	$1,120,000	$1,880,000
	Step-Down (A/HR first)	1,090,000	1,910,000
	Step-Down (I.S. first)	1,168,000	1,832,000

The direct method ignores any services to other support departments. The step-down method partially recognizes support to other service departments. The information systems support group (with total budget of $2,400,000) provides 10% of its services to the A/HR group. The A/HR support group (with total budget of $600,000) provides 25% of its services to the information systems support group.

14-24 (cont'd)

3. Three criteria that could determine the sequence in the step-down method are:

    (a) Allocate service departments on a ranking of the % of their total services provided to other service departments.
1.	Administrative/HR	25%
2.	Information Systems	10%

    (b) Allocate service departments on a ranking of the total dollar amount in the service departments.
1.	Information Systems	$2,400,000
2.	Administrative/HR	$ 600,000

    (c) Allocate service departments on a ranking of the dollar amounts of service provided to other service departments

        1. Information Systems
            $(0.10 \times \$2,400,000)$ = $240,000
        2. Administrative/HR
            $(0.25 \times \$600,000)$ = $150,000

14-26 (30 min.) Support department cost allocation.

1.   Using computer usage time as the allocation base for the Information Systems Department and square metres of floor space for the Facilities Department, the allocation of overhead from the support departments under the Direct and Step Methods, are presented below.

Direct Method

	Support Departments		Operating Departments		
	IS	Facilities	Programming	Consulting	Training
Budgeted overhead	$50,000	$25,000	$ 75,000	$110,000	$ 85,000
Proportion of service furnished:					
By IS:(1)			12/27	6/27	9/27
Allocation	(50,000)		$ 22,222	$ 11,111	$ 16,667
By Facilities:(2)			4/18	6/18	8/18
Allocation		(25,000)	$ 5,556	$ 8,333	$ 11,111
Totals	$ 0	$ 0	$102,778	$129,444	$112,778

(1) Allocated on the basis of 2,700 hours of computer usage.

(2) Allocated on the basis of 1,800 thousand square metres of floor space.

Step Method

	Support Departments		Operating Departments		
	IS	Facilities	Programming	Consulting	Training
Budgeted overhead	$50,000	$25,000	$ 75,000	$110,000	$ 85,000
Proportion of service furnished:					
By IS:(1)		3/30	12/30	6/30	9/30
Allocation	(50,000)	$ 5,000	$ 20,000	$ 10,000	$ 15,000
By Facilities:(2)			4/18	6/18	8/18
Allocation		($30,000)	$ 6,667	$ 10,000	$ 13,333
Totals	$ 0	$ 0	$101,667	$130,000	$113,333

(1) Allocated on the basis of 3,000 hours of computer usage.

(2) Allocated on the basis of 1,800 thousand square metres of floor space.

2.   The step method recognizes the services that Information Systems provides to the other support department (Facilities). In contrast, the direct method only recognizes services that support departments provide to operating departments.

The step-down method is conceptually preferable to the direct method. Birch might consider using the reciprocal method. This method fully recognizes the reciprocal services provided between the Information System and Facilities departments.

14-28 (30 min.)   **Reciprocal cost allocation.**

1.   The reciprocal allocation method explicitly includes the mutual services provided among all support departments. Interdepartmental relationships are fully incorporated into the support department cost allocations.

2. $AD = \$72,700 + .0833IS$

$IS = \$234,400 + .2308AD$

$AD = \$72,700 + [.0833(\$234,400 + .2308AD)]$

$\quad\quad = \$72,700 + [\$19,525.52 + 0.019226AD]$

$0.980774AD = \$92,225.52$

$\quad\quad AD = \$92,225.52 \div 0.980774$

$\quad\quad\quad = \$94,033$

$\quad IS = \$234,400 + (0.2308 \times \$94,033)$

$\quad\quad\quad = \$256,103$

	Support Depts		Operating Depts		
	Admin.	Info. Systems	Corporate	Consumer	Total
Costs Incurred	$72,700	$234,400	$ 998,270	$489,860	$1,795,230
Alloc. of Admin. (21/91, 42/91, 28/91)	(94,033)	21,700	43,400	28,933	
Alloc. of Info. Syst. (320/3,840, 1,920/3,840, 1,600/3,840)	21,342	(256,103)	128,051	106,710	
	$ 9*	$ (3)*	$1,169,721	$625,503	$1,795,230

*Rounding causes not to be exactly $0.

3. The reciprocal method is more accurate than the direct and step-down methods when there is reciprocal relationships among support departments.

14-28 (cont'd)

A summary of the alternatives is:

	Corporate Sales	Consumer Sales
Direct method	$1,169,745	$625,485
Step-down method		
(Admin. first)	1,168,830	626,400
Reciprocal method	1,169,721	625,503

The reciprocal method is the preferred method, although for September 2001 the numbers do not appear materially different across the alternatives.

14-30 (20 min.)   **Division managers' reactions to the allocation of central corporate costs to divisions (continuation of 14-29).**

The effect of the changes proposed by Dusty Rhodes for divisional income is:

	Oil & Gas Upstream	Oil & Gas Downstream	Chemical Products	Copper Mining
Divisional income—single-cost pool allocation scheme	$3,300	$(600)	$(200)	$(500)
Divisional income—four-cost pool allocation scheme	$2,522.4	$ 83.2	$(166.4)	$(439.2)

Given these changes, the reactions of the division managers are predictable. Rhodes should consider several general points when drafting his response:

- A controller is a staff function, while the division managers are line managers running multi-billion dollar enterprises.
- Cost allocation problems are ongoing issues in any organization, and ongoing refinements will likely occur continually in the future.
- Keep a clear distinction between evaluating the performance of a division and evaluating the performance of a division manager.

Oil & Gas Upstream: Observe that the proposed cost allocation scheme better captures cause-and-effect relationships than does the existing scheme. Note that the upstream division is highly capital intensive and that much of the debt was raised to acquire or develop those assets. Rhodes should also describe how Richfield Oil takes into account the Upstream's generation of a substantial positive cash flow in its performance evaluation of activities and managers.

Oil & Gas Downstream: Comment that you are glad that the proposed scheme was well received. However, stress that the changes are designed to capture cause-and-effect relationships. (You will be responding to the same manager in subsequent years and it is important that the motivations for the changes be understood. In subsequent years the same manager likely will argue the proposed changes are "unfair and inequitable.")

Chemical Products: Note that the manager's complaints are against cost allocation schemes in general and not against Rhodes' proposed changes. The appropriate response is to stress that the top management of Richfield Oil has decided to allocate central corporate costs (for reasons noted in requirement 1 of Problem 14-26). The manager should consider developing ways to improve the existing or proposed cost allocation schemes. Stress to the manager that top management distinguishes between the performance of a division and the performance of its manager. In evaluating the chemical products division, a better appreciation of the returns on Richfield Oil's investment can be obtained by considering the central corporate costs associated with the division. However, in evaluating managers, the

14-30 (cont'd)

ability to outperform competitors facing the same environment and to implement company-wide economy drives is highly valued (and hopefully rewarded by Richfield Oil).

Copper Mining: Agree with the manager that both the existing and the proposed schemes have imperfections. Specifically, admit that sometime in the future refinements in allocations of R&D may be made. One possible approach would be identification of R&D costs with projects done for each division; if no R&D is done for Copper Mining, no allocation of R&D cost would be made to Copper Mining. However, note that changes are being made gradually at Richfield Oil and that the current major issue is to get the proposed changes accepted. One point to stress is that the proposal recognizes the special problems of divisions with negative operating income (such as faced by the Copper Mining division). Rhodes proposes to allocate public affairs costs only to divisions with positive operating income.

Note: Richfield Oil may want to consider changes in its division compensation scheme if it makes changes in its cost allocation scheme. Major changes in one component of a management control system should not be made without considering changes in other components of the management control system.

14-32 (20-30 min.) **Cost allocation downward demand spiral.**

1.
Total costs, six months ended June 30, 2000	$64,800,000
Fixed costs	16,200,000
Variable costs	$48,600,000

Fixed costs per month per square metre

$$= \frac{\$16,200,000 \div 6}{2,250,000} = \$7.20/6 = \$1.20$$

Variable costs per month per square metre

$$= \frac{\$48,600,000 \div 6}{2,250,000} = \$21.60/6 = \$3.60$$

2.   Variable costs per month per square metre   = $3.60

Fixed costs per month per square metre

$$= \frac{\$36,000,000 \div 12}{2,500,000} \qquad\qquad = \qquad \underline{1.20}$$

Total costs per month per square metre	=	$4.80
Total costs per day per square metre (assuming 30 days)	=	$0.16

The cost per square metre of $0.16 per day is above the competitive rate of $0.14. Thus it is not surprising that many of his internal clients are seeking external bids.

3.   Bubba should base his prices upon his total capacity of 5,000,000 square metres. This would result in costs as follows:

Variable costs per month per metre	=	$3.60
Fixed costs per month per metre		
($36,000,000 ÷ 12 ÷ 5,000,000 metres)	=	0.60
Total costs per month per metre	=	$4.20
Total costs per day per metre (assuming 30 days)	=	$0.14

Thus to generate a profit, Bubba needs to operate closer to capacity and seek ways to reduce costs.

14-34 (40-60 min.) **Support department cost allocations; single-department cost pools; direct, step-down, and reciprocal methods.**

All the following computations are in dollars.
1.

Direct method:

		To X			**To Y**	
A	$250/400 \times \$100,000 =$	$62,500	$150/400 \times \$100,000 =$	$37,500
B	$100/500 \times \$40,000 =$	8,000	$400/500 \times \$40,000 =$	32,000
Total		$70,500		$69,500

2. Step-down method, allocating B first:

	A	**B**	**X**	**Y**
Costs to be allocated	$100,000	$40,000	—	—
Allocate B: (0.5, 0.1, 0.4)	20,000	(40,000)	$ 4,000	$16,000
Allocate A: (250/400, 150/400)	(120,000)	—	75,000	45,000
Total	$ 0	$ 0	$79,000	$61,000

Step-down method, allocating A first:

	A	**B**	**X**	**Y**
Costs to be allocated	$100,000	$40,000	—	—
Allocate A: (0.2, 0.5, 0.3)	(100,000)	20,000	$50,000	$30,000
Allocate B: (0.2, 0.8)	—	(60,000)	12,000	48,000
Total	$ 0	$ 0	$62,000	$78,000

Note that these methods produce significantly different results, so the choice of method may frequently make a difference in the budgeted department overhead rates.

3. Reciprocal method:

Stage 1: Let   A =   total costs of materials-handling department
           B =   total costs of power-generating department
     (1)   A = $\$100,000 + 0.5B$
     (2)   B = $\$40,000 + 0.2A$

Stage 2: Substituting in (1):
$$A = \$100,000 + 0.5(\$40,000 + 0.2A)$$
$$A = \$100,000 + \$20,000 \quad + 0.1A$$
$$0.9A = \$120,000$$
$$A = \$133,333$$

Substituting in (2):
$$B = \$40,000 + 0.2(\$133,333)$$
$$B = \$66,666$$

14-34 (cont'd)

Stage 3:

	A	B	X	Y
Original amounts	100,000	40,000	—	—
Allocation of A	(133,333)	26,666(20%)	66,667(50%)	40,000(30%)
Allocation of B	33,333(50%)	(66,666)	6,666(10%)	26,667(40%)
Totals accounted for	—	—	73,333	66,667

Comparison of methods:

Method of Allocation	X	Y
Direct method	$70,500	$69,500
Step-down: B first	79,000	61,000
Step-down: A first	62,000	78,000
Reciprocal method	73,333	66,667

Note that in this case the direct method produces answers that are the closest to the "correct" answers (that is, those from the reciprocal method), step-down allocating B first is next, and step-down allocating A first is least accurate.

2. At first glance, it appears that the cost of power is $40 per unit plus the material handling costs. If so, Manes would be better off by purchasing from the power company. However, the decision should be influenced by the effects of the interdependencies and the fixed costs. Note that the power needs would be less (students miss this) if they were purchased from the outside:

	Outside Power Units Needed
X	100
Y	400
A (500 units minus 20% of 500 units, because there is no need to service the nonexistent power department)	400
Total units	900

Total costs, 900 × $40 = $36,000

14-34 (cont'd)

In contrast, the total costs that would be saved by not producing the power inside would depend on the effects of the decision on various costs:

	Avoidable Costs of 100 Units of Power Produced Inside
Variable indirect labour and indirect material costs	$10,000
Supervision in power department	10,000
Materials handling, 20% of $70,000*	14,000
Probable minimum cost savings	$34,000
Possible additional savings:	
a. Can any supervision in materials handling be saved because of overseeing less volume? Minimum savings is probably zero; the maximum is probably 20% of $10,000 or $2,000.	?
b. Is any depreciation a truly variable, wear-and-tear type of cost?	?
Total savings by not producing 100 units of power	$34,000 + ?

*Materials-handling costs are higher because the power department uses 20% of materials handling. Therefore, materials-handling costs will decrease by 20%.

In the short-run (at least until a capital investment in equipment is necessary) the data suggest continuing to produce internally because the costs eliminated would probably be less than the comparable purchase costs.

14-36 (20 min.) **Division cost allocation, R&D, ethics.**

1. The overhead cost charged to each division for use of the Waterloo facility is:

$$\begin{bmatrix} \text{Budgeted \% use} \\ \text{by division of} \\ \text{Waterloo facility} \end{bmatrix} \times \begin{bmatrix} \text{Budgeted overhead costs} \\ \text{at Waterloo facility} \end{bmatrix}$$

If the ASD division understates its budgeted use of the Waterloo facility and all other divisions provide unbiased estimates of their budgeted use, the ASD division will have a lower budgeted % use factor for the Waterloo facility, and thus a lower overhead cost charge. If all divisions understate their budgeted use, those division(s) providing the greatest understatements will be those benefiting by their understatement.

2. Alternative approaches Waterloo might take include:
    a. Charging a division a penalty rate when it uses a higher number of hours than it submitted as its budgeted amount.
    b. Change the charge structure so that each hour of research scientist time used has a budgeted overhead charge component. (This approach only partially reduces the problem because the fixed overhead rate per hour must be determined.)
    c. Use actual costs per hour rather than budgeted costs per hour as the charge to each using division.

3. Goodwin's first response should be to develop a well-constructed argument to present to Roy Masters for using the 30,000 number. Masters should be given at least one more chance to respond to Goodwin's concerns. Ideally, Goodwin should give Masters a short time period (say one week) to think about her concerns. This is especially the case if there is already documentation at ASD for the 30,000 number. Goodwin might note that if internal control people at WS are called in to consider any allegations by other divisions that ASD is deliberately understating budgeted usage, the 30,000 figure likely will be observable.

    If Masters continues with his threats about dropping Goodwin from "the ASD team," she should contact the corporate controller at WS to seek guidance on how to handle the situation.

CHAPTER 15
COST ALLOCATION: JOINT PRODUCTS AND BYPRODUCTS

15-2 A *joint cost* is a cost of a single process that yields multiple products simultaneously.

15-4 A *product* is any output that has a positive sales value (or an output that enables an organization to avoid incurring costs). In some joint-cost settings, outputs can occur that do not have a positive sales value. The offshore processing of hydrocarbons yields water that is recycled back into the ocean as well as yielding oil and gas. The processing of mineral ore to yield gold and silver also yields dirt as an output, which is recycled back into the ground.

15-6 The joint production process yields individual products that are either sold this period or held as inventory to be sold in subsequent periods. Hence the joint costs need to be allocated between total production rather than just those sold this period.

15-8 Both methods use market selling-price data in allocating joint costs, but they differ in which sales-price data they use. The *sales value at splitoff method* allocates joint costs on the basis of each product's relative sales value at the splitoff point. The *estimated net realizable value method* allocates joint costs on the basis of the relative estimated net realizable value (expected final sales value in the ordinary course of business minus the expected separable costs of production and marketing).

15-10 The estimated NRV method can be simplified by assuming (a) a standard set of post-splitoff point processing steps and (b) a standard set of selling prices. The use of (a) and (b) achieves the same benefits that the use of standard costs does in costing systems.

15-12 No. Any method used to allocate joint costs to individual products that is applicable to the problem of joint product-cost allocation should not be used for management decisions regarding whether a product should be sold or processed further. When a product is an inherent result of a joint process, the decision to process further should not be influenced by either the size of the total joint costs or the portion of the joint costs assigned to particular products. Joint costs are irrelevant for these decisions. The only relevant items for these decisions are the incremental revenue and the incremental costs beyond the splitoff point.

15-14 Two methods to account for byproducts are:
a.   Production method—recognizes byproducts in the financial statements at the time production is completed.
b.   Sales method—delays recognition of byproducts until the time of sale.

15-16 (20-30 min.) **Joint-cost allocation, insurance settlement.**

1. (a) Sales value at splitoff point method.

	Kilograms of Product	Wholesale Selling Price per Kilogram	Sales Value at Splitoff	Weighting: Sales Value at Splitoff	Joint Costs Allocated	Allocated Costs per Kilogram
Breasts	100	$1.10	$110	0.675	$ 67.50	0.6750
Wings	20	0.40	8	0.049	4.90	0.2450
Thighs	40	0.70	28	0.172	17.20	0.4300
Bones	80	0.20	16	0.098	9.80	0.1225
Feathers	10	0.10	1	0.006	0.60	0.0600
	250		$163	1.000	$100.00	

Costs of Destroyed Product

Breasts: $0.6750 × 20 = $13.50
Wings: $0.2450 × 10 = 2.45
$15.95

(b) Physical measures method

	Kilograms of Product	Weighting: Physical Measures	Joint Costs Allocated	Allocated Costs per Kilogram
Breasts	100	0.400	$ 40.00	$0.400
Wings	20	0.080	8.00	0.400
Thighs	40	0.160	16.00	0.400
Bones	80	0.320	32.00	0.400
Feathers	10	0.040	4.00	0.400
	250	1.000	$100.00	

Costs of Destroyed Product

Breast: $0.40 × 20 = $ 8
Wings: $0.40 × 10 = 4
$12

15-16 (cont'd)

Note: Although not required, it is useful to highlight the individual product profitability figures:

Product	Sales Value	Sales Value at Splitoff Method		Physical Measures Method	
		Joint Costs Allocated	Gross Income	Joint Costs Allocated	Gross Income
Breasts	$110	$67.50	$42.50	$40.00	$70.00
Wings	8	4.90	3.10	8.00	0.00
Thighs	28	17.20	10.80	16.00	12.00
Bones	16	9.80	6.20	32.00	(16.00)
Feathers	1	0.60	0.40	4.00	(3.00)

2.   The sales-value at splitoff method captures the benefits-received criterion of cost allocation. The costs of processing a chicken are allocated to products in proportion to the ability to contribute revenue. Chicken Little's decision to process chicken is heavily influenced by the revenues from breasts and thighs. The bones provide relatively few benefits to Chicken Little despite their high physical volume.

The physical measures method shows profits on breasts and thighs and losses on bones and feathers. Given that Chicken Little has to jointly process all the chicken products, it is non-intuitive to single out individual products that are being processed simultaneously as making losses while the overall operations make a profit.

15-18 (10 min.) **Estimated net realizable value method.**

A diagram of the situation is in Solution Exhibit 15-18 (all numbers are in thousands).

	Cooking Oil	Soap Oil	Total
Expected final sales value of production, CO, 1,000 × $50; SO, 500 × $25	$50,000	$12,500	$62,500
Deduct expected separable costs to complete and sell	30,000	7,500	37,500
Estimated net realizable value at splitoff point	$20,000	$ 5,000	$25,000
Weighting	$\frac{$20,000}{$25,000} = 0.8$	$\frac{$5,000}{$25,000} = 0.2$	
Joint costs allocated, CO, 0.8 × $24,000; SO, 0.2 × $24,000	$19,200	$ 4,800	$24,000

SOLUTION EXHIBIT 15-18

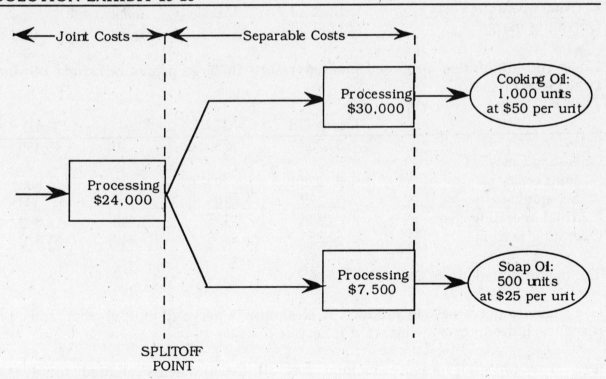

15-20 (20 min.) **Joint-cost allocation, physical measures method (continuation of 15-19).**

1.

	Crude Oil	NGL	Total
Expected final sales value of production	$2,700	$ 750	$ 3,450
Deduct expected separable costs			
Estimated NRV at splitoff	175	105	280
Weighting	$2,525	$ 645	$3,170
Joint costs allocated	0.7965	0.2035	1.000
(Weights × $1,800)			
	$1,433.70	$366.30	$1,800

	Crude Oil	NGL	Total
Sales	$2,700.00	$750.00	$3,450
Operating Costs			
Joint costs	1,433.70	366.30	1,800
Separable costs	175.00	105.00	280
Total operating costs	1,608.70	471.30	2,080
Operating margin	$1,091.30	$278.70	$1,370

2.   The authorities' proposed method results in large profits on crude oil and large losses on gas:

	Crude Oil	NGL	Gas	Total
Sales	$2,700	$750	$0	$3,450
Operating Costs				
Joint costs	270	90	1,440	1,800
Separable costs	175	105	0	280
Total operating costs	445	195	1,440	2,080
Operating margin	$2,255	$555	$(1,440)	$1,370

The main points to note are:

(a)   Gas is not a salable product. It is simply a recycled output that adds no revenues. Indeed, costs are incurred to recycle the gas.

(b)   The physical measure method has all the problems alluded to in the literature—e.g., it ignores the revenue-earning potential of products and it may not have a consistent denominator.

15-22 (20-30 min.) **Net realizable value cost-allocation method, further process decision.**

A diagram of the situation is in Solution Exhibit 15-22.

1.

	Quantity in Kilograms	Sales Price per Kilogram	Final Sales Value	Separable Processing Costs	Estimated Net Realizable Value at Splitoff	Weighting
Alco	20,000	$20	$400,000	$100,000	$300,000	30/56
Devo	60,000	6	360,000	200,000	160,000	16/56
Holo	100,000	1	100,000	0	100,000	10/56
Totals			$860,000	$300,000	$560,000	

Allocation of $420,000 joint costs:

Alco	30/56 × $420,000	= $225,000
Devo	16/56 × 420,000	= 120,000
Holo	10/56 × 420,000	= 75,000
		$420,000

	Joint Costs Allocated	Separable Processing Costs	Total Costs	Units	Unit Cost
Alco	$225,000	$100,000	$325,000	20,000	$16.25
Devo	120,000	200,000	320,000	60,000	5.33
Holo	75,000	0	75,000	100,000	0.75
Totals	$420,000	$300,000	$720,000	180,000	

The ending inventory is:

Alco	1,000 × $16.25	= $16,250
Devo	1,000 × $ 5.33	= 5,330
Holo	1,000 × $ 0.75	= 750
		$22,330

2.

	Unit Sales Price	Unit Cost	Gross Margin	Gross-Margin Percentage
Alco	$20	$16.25	$3.75	18.75%
Devo	6	5.33	0.67	11.17
Holo	1	0.75	0.25	25.00

3. Further processing of Devo yields incremental income of $40,000:

Incremental revenue of further processing Devo, ($6 – $2) • 60,000	$240,000
Incremental processing costs	200,000
Incremental operating income from further processing	$ 40,000

Tuscania should process Devo further. Note that joint costs are irrelevant to this decision; they remain the same, whichever alternative (sell at splitoff or process further) is selected.

SOLUTION EXHIBIT 15-22

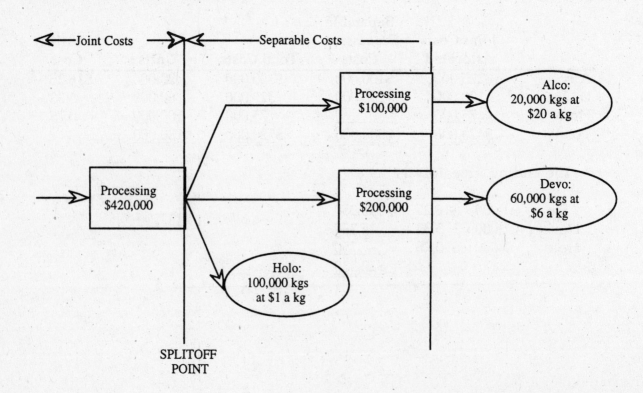

15-24 (40 min.) Process further or sell, byproduct.

1. The analysis shown below indicates that it would be more profitable for Newcastle Mining Company to continue to sell raw bulk coal without further processing. (This analysis ignores any value related to coal fines.)

Incremental sales revenues:

Sales revenue after further processing (9,500,000 tonnes × $36)	$342,000,000
Sales revenue from bulk raw coal (10,000,000 tonnes × $27)	270,000,000
Incremental sales revenue	72,000,000

Incremental costs:

Direct labour	600,000
Supervisory personnel	100,000
Heavy equipment costs ($25,000 × 12 months)	300,000
Sizing and cleaning (10,000,000 tonnes × $3.50)	35,000,000
Outbound rail freight (9,500,000 tonnes ÷ 60 tons) × $240 per car	38,000,000
Incremental costs	74,000,000
Incremental gain (loss)	$(2,000,000)

2. The analysis shown below indicates that the potential revenue from the coal fines byproduct would result in additional revenue, ranging between $5,250,000 and $9,000,000, depending on the market price of the fines.

a. Coal fines = 75% of 5% of raw bulk tonnage
= $0.75 \times (10,000,000 \times 0.05)$
= 375,000 tonnes

Potential additional revenue:

	Market price	
	Minimum	Maximum
	$14 per tonne	$24 per tonne
Additional revenue	$5,250,000	$9,000,000

Since the incremental loss is $2 million, as calculated in requirement 1, including the coal fines in the analysis indicates that further processing provides a positive result and is, therefore, favourable.

15-24 (cont'd)

b. Other factors that should be considered in evaluating a sell-or-process-further decision include:

- Stability of the current customer market and how it compares to the market for sized and cleaned coal.
- Storage space needed for the coal fines until they are sold and the handling costs of coal fines.
- Reliability of cost (e.g., rail freight rates) and revenue estimates, and the risk of depending on these estimates.
- Timing of the revenue stream from coal fines and impact on the need for liquidity.
- Possible environmental problems, i.e., dumping of waste and smoke from unprocessed coal.

15-26 (35-45 min.) Joint costs and byproducts.

A diagram of the situation is in Solution Exhibit 15-26.

1.   Computing byproduct deduction to joint costs:

Marketing price of X, 100,000 × $3	$300,000
Deduct: Gross margin, 10% of sales	30,000
Marketing costs, 25% of sales	75,000
Department 3 separable costs	50,000
Estimated net realizable value of X	$145,000
Joint costs	$800,000
Deduct byproduct contribution	145,000
Net joint costs to be allocated	$655,000

	Quantity	Unit Sales Price	Final Sales Value	Deduct Separable Processing Cost	Est. Net Realizable Value at Splitoff	Weighting	Allocation of $655,000 Joint Costs
L	50,000	$10	$ 500,000	$100,000	$ 400,000	40%	$262,000
W	300,000	2	600,000	-	600,000	60%	393,000
Totals			$1,100,000	$100,000	$1,000,000		$655,000

	Joint Costs Allocation	Add Separable Processing Costs	Total Costs	Units	Unit Cost
L	$262,000	$100,000	$362,000	50,000	$7.24
W	393,000	-	393,000	300,000	1.31
Totals	$655,000	$100,000	$755,000	350,000	

Unit cost for X: $1.45 + $0.50   = $1.95,
or $3.00 − $0.30 − $0.75 = $1.95.

15-26 (cont'd)

2. If all three products are treated as joint products:

	Quantity	Unit Sales Price	Final Sales Value	Deduct Separable Processing Cost	Est. Net Realizable Value at Splitoff	Weighting	Allocation of $800,000 Joint Costs
L	50,000	$10	$ 500,000	$100,000	$ 400,000	40/125	$256,000
W	300,000	2	600,000	-	600,000	60/125	384,000
X	100,000	3	300,000	50,000	250,000	25/125	160,000
Totals			$1,400,000	$150,000	$1,250,000		$800,000

	Joint Costs Allocation	Add Separable Processing Costs	Total Costs	Units	Unit Cost
L	$256,000	$100,000	$356,000	50,000	$7.12
W	384,000	-	384,000	300,000	1.28
X	160,000	50,000	210,000	100,000	2.10
Totals	$800,000	$150,000	$950,000	450,000	

Call the attention of students to the differing unit "costs" between the two assumptions regarding the relative importance of Product X. The point is that costs of individual products depend heavily on which assumptions are made and which accounting methods and techniques are used.

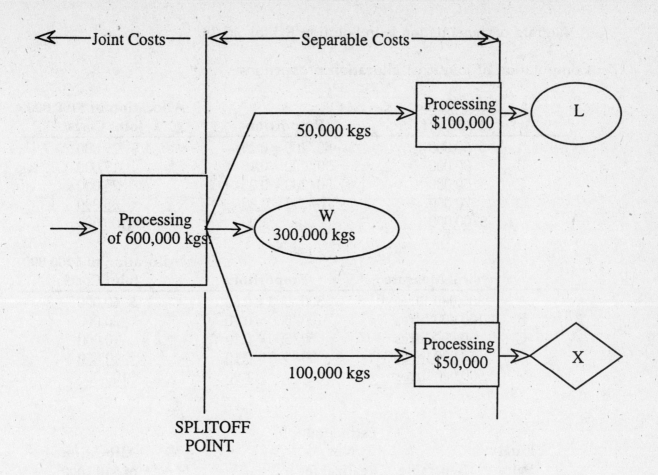

15-28 (40 min.) Alternative methods of joint-cost allocation, product-mix decisions.

A diagram of the situation is in Solution Exhibit 15-28.

1. Computation of joint-cost allocation proportions:

a.

	Sales Value at Splitoff	Proportions	Allocation of $100,000 Joint Costs
A	$ 50,000	50/200 = 0.25	$ 25,000
B	30,000	30/200 = 0.15	15,000
C	50,000	50/200 = 0.25	25,000
D	70,000	70/200 = 0.35	35,000
	$200,000	1.00	$100,000

b.

	Physical Measure	Proportions	Allocation of $100,000 Joint Costs
A	300,000 litres	300/500 = 0.60	$ 60,000
B	100,000 litres	100/500 = 0.20	20,000
C	50,000 litres	50/500 = 0.10	10,000
D	50,000 litres	50/500 = 0.10	10,000
	500,000 litres	1.00	$100,000

c.

	Final Sales Value	Separable Costs	Estimated Net Realizable Value	Proportions	Allocation of $100,000 Joint Costs
A	$300,000	$200,000	$100,000	100/200 =0.50	$ 50,000
B	100,000	80,000	20,000	20/200 = 0.10	10,000
C	50,000	–	50,000	50/200 = 0.25	25,000
D	120,000	90,000	30,000	30/200 = 0.15	15,000
			$200,000	1.00	$100,000

Computation of gross-margin percentages:

a. Sales value at splitoff method:

	Super A	Super B	C	Super D	Total
Sales	$300,000	$100,000	$50,000	$120,000	$570,000
Joint costs	25,000	15,000	25,000	35,000	100,000
Separable costs	200,000	80,000	0	90,000	370,000
Total costs	225,000	95,000	25,000	125,000	470,000
Gross margin	$ 75,000	$ 5,000	$25,000	$ (5,000)	$100,000
Gross-margin percentage	25%	5%	50%	(4.17%)	17.54%

15-28 (cont'd)

b.   Physical-measure method:

	Super A	Super B	C	Super D	Total
Sales	$300,000	$100,000	$50,000	$120,000	$570,000
Joint costs	60,000	20,000	10,000	10,000	100,000
Separable costs	200,000	80,000	0	90,000	370,000
Total costs	260,000	100,000	10,000	100,000	470,000
Gross margin	$ 40,000	$ 0	$40,000	$ 20,000	$100,000
Gross-margin percentage	13.33%	0%	80%	16.67%	17.54%

c.   Estimated net realizable value method:

	Super A	Super B	C	Super D	Total
Sales	$300,000	$100,000	$50,000	$120,000	$570,000
Joint costs	50,000	10,000	25,000	15,000	100,000
Separable costs	200,000	80,000	0	90,000	370,000
Total costs	250,000	90,000	25,000	105,000	470,000
Gross margin	$ 50,000	$ 10,000	$25,000	$ 15,000	$100,000
Gross-margin percentage	16.67%	10%	50%	12.5%	17.54%

Summary of gross-margin percentages:

Joint-Cost Allocation Method	Super A	Super B	C	Super D
Sales value at splitoff	25.00%	5%	50%	(4.17%)
Physical measure	13.33%	0%	80%	16.67%
Estimated net realizable value	16.67%	10%	50%	12.50%

15-28 (cont'd.)

2. Further Processing of A into Super A:

Incremental revenue, $300,000 – $50,000	$250,000
Incremental costs	200,000
Incremental operating income from further processing	$ 50,000

Further processing of B into Super B:

Incremental revenue, $100,000 – $30,000	$ 70,000
Incremental costs	80,000
Incremental operating income from further processing	($ 10,000)

Further Processing of D into Super D:

Incremental revenue, $120,000 – $70,000	$ 50,000
Incremental costs	90,000
Incremental operating income from further processing	$ (40,000)

Operating income can be increased by $50,000 if both B and D are sold at their splitoff point.

SOLUTION EXHIBIT 15-28

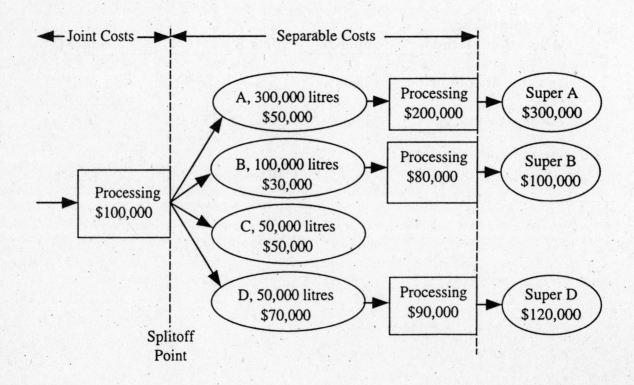

15-30 (30 min.) Joint-cost allocation, process further or sell.

1.
a. Relative sales value method at splitoff.

	Monthly Unit Output	Selling Price per Unit	Relative Sales Value at Splitoff	% of Sales	Allocated Joint Costs
Studs (Building)	75,000	$ 8	$ 600,000	46.15%	$ 461,539
Decorative Pieces	5,000	60	300,000	23.08	230,769
Posts	20,000	20		30.77	307,692
			400,000		
Totals			$1,300,000	100.00%	$1,000,000

b. Physical output (volume) method at splitoff.

	Physical Unit Volume	% of Total Unit Volume	Allocated Joint Costs
Studs (Building)	75,000	75.00%	$ 750,000
Decorative Pieces	5,000	5.00	50,000
Posts	20,000	20.00	200,000
Totals	100,000	100.00%	$1,000,000

c. Estimated net realizable value method.

	Monthly Unit Output	Fully Processed Selling Price per Unit	Estimated Net Realizable Value	% of Sales	Allocated Joint Costs
Studs (Building)	75,000	$8	$ 600,000	44.44%	$ 444,445
Decorative Pieces	4,500[a]	100	350,000[b]	25.93	259,259
Posts	20,000	20	400,000	29.63	296,296
Totals			$1,350,000	100.00%	$1,000,000

Notes:
a. 5,000 monthly units of output – 10% normal spoilage = 4,500 good units.
b. 4,500 good units × $100 = $450,000 – Further processing costs of $100,000 = $350,000

2.   Presented below is an analysis for Sonimad Sawmill Inc. comparing the processing of decorative pieces further versus selling the rough-cut product immediately at splitoff.

	Units	Dollars
Monthly unit output	5,000	
Less: Normal further processing shrinkage	500	
Units available for sale	4,500	
Final sales value (4,500 units @ $100 per unit)		$450,000
Less: Sales value at splitoff		300,000
Differential revenue		150,000
Less: Further processing costs		100,000
Additional contribution from further processing		$ 50,000

15-16

15–30 (cont'd.)

3. Assuming Sonimad Sawmill Inc. announces that in six months it will sell the rough-cut product at split-off, due to increasing competitive pressure, at least three types of likely behavior that will be demonstrated by the skilled labor in the planing and sizing process include the following.

- Poorer quality.
- Reduced motivation and morale.
- Job insecurity, leading to nonproductive employee time looking for jobs elsewhere.

Management actions that could improve this behavior include the following.

- Improve communication by giving the workers a more comprehensive explanation as to the reason for the change in order to better understand the situation and bring out a plan for future operation of the rest of the plant.
- The company can offer incentive bonuses to maintain quality and production and align rewards with goals.
- The company could provide job relocation and internal job transfers.

SOLUTION EXHIBIT 15-30

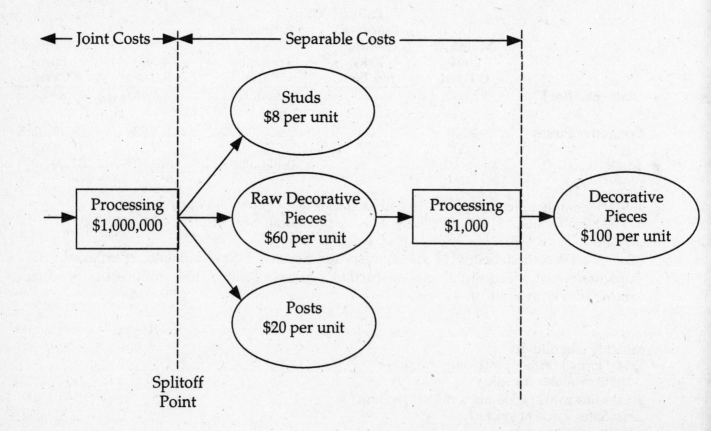

15-32 (30 min.) **Estimated net realizable value method, byproducts.**

1.

a. For the month of November 2000, Princess Corporation's output was:
- apple slices   89,100
- applesauce   81,000
- apple juice   67,500
- animal feed   27,000

These amounts were calculated as follows:

Product	Input	Proportion	Total Kilograms	Kilograms Lost	Net Kilograms
Slices	270,000 kg	0.33	89,100	–	89,100
Sauce	270,000	0.30	81,000	–	81,000
Juice	270,000	0.27	72,900	5,400	67,500*
Feed	270,000	0.10	27,000	–	27,000
		1.00	270,000	5,400	264,600

*Net kilograms: =   72,900 – (0.08 × net kilograms)
1.08 net kilograms   =   72,900
Net kilograms   =   67,500

b. The estimated net realizable value for each of the three main products is calculated below:

Product	Net Kilograms	Price	Revenue	Separable Costs	Estimated Net Realizable Value
Slices	89,100	$0.80	$ 71,280	$11,280	$ 60,000
Sauce	81,000	0.55	44,550	8,550	36,000
Juice	67,500	0.40	27,000	3,000	24,000
			$142,830	$22,830	$120,000

c. and d.

The estimated net realizable value of the byproduct is deducted from the production costs prior to allocation to the joint products, as presented below:

Allocation of Cutting Department Costs
to Joint Products and Byproducts

Net realizable value
(NRV) of byproduct

$$= \text{By-product revenue} - \text{Separable costs}$$
$$= \$0.10 \ (270,000 \times 10\%) - \$700$$
$$= \$2,700 - \$700$$
$$= \$2,000$$

Costs to be allocated

$$= \text{Joint costs} - \text{NRV of byproduct}$$
$$= \$60,000 - \$2,000$$
$$= \$58,000$$

Product	Revenue	Separable Costs	Joint Costs	Gross Margin
Slices	$ 71,280	$11,280	$29,000	$31,000
Sauce	44,550	8,550	17,400	18,600
Juice	27,000	3,000	11,600	12,400
	$142,830	$22,830	$58,000	$62,000

2. The gross-margin dollar information by main product is determined by the arbitrary allocation of joint production costs. As a result, these cost figures and the resulting gross-margin information are of little significance for planning and control purposes. The allocation is made only for purposes of inventory costing and income determination.

CHAPTER 16
REVENUES, REVENUE VARIANCES, AND
CUSTOMER-PROFITABILITY ANALYSIS

16-2 The *stand-alone revenue-allocation method* uses information about individual products in their separate markets when allocating bundled revenues to individual products. The *incremental revenue-allocation method* ranks the individual products in a bundle and then uses this ranking to allocate the bundled revenues to these individual products.

16-4 A dispute over allocation of revenues of a bundled product could be resolved by (a) having an agreement that outlines the preferred method in the case of a dispute or (b) having a third party (such as the company president or an independent arbitrator) make a decision.

16-6 The total sales-mix variance for revenues arises from shifts in the revenues of individual products. The composite product unit concept enables the effect of individual product changes to be summarized in a single intuitive number.

16-8 The sales-quantity variance can be decomposed into (a) a market-size variance (the actual total market-size change from that budgeted) and (b) a market-share variance (the actual market-share change from that budgeted). Both variances use the budgeted average selling price per unit, when the focus is on revenues.

16-10 Customer profitability analysis highlights to managers how individual customers differentially contribute to total profitability. It helps managers to see whether customers who contribute sizably to total profitability are receiving a comparable level of attention from the organization.

16-12 No. A customer profitability profile highlights differences in current period's profitability across customers. Dropping customers should be the last resort. An unprofitable customer in one period may be highly profitable in subsequent future periods. Moreover, costs assigned to individual customers need not be purely variable with respect to short-run elimination of sales to those customers. Thus, when customers are dropped, costs assigned to those customers may not disappear in the short run.

16-14 A process where the inputs are nonsubstitutable leaves workers no discretion as to the components to use. A process where the inputs are substitutable means there is discretion about the exact number and type of inputs or about the weighting of inputs where the number and type is mandated.

16-16 (30 min.) **Revenue allocation, speaking fees.**

1. The total revenues from the seminar are:

$500 \times \$200 = \$100,000.$

Revenues to be shared by speakers

$0.30 \times \$100,000 = \$30,000.$

The stand-alone revenue allocation method could guide the allocations. Possible weights are individual speaking fees, number of speeches, and speaking fee revenues:

	Individual Speaking Fee (1)	Relative Speaking Fee % (2)=(1)÷16,000	# of Speeches (3)	Relative Number of Speeches (4)=(3)÷96	Speaking Fee Revenues (5)=(1)×(3)	Relative Speaking Fee Revenues (6)=(5)÷34,000
Linda Young	$10,000	0.625	6	0.0625	$ 60,000	0.1765
Vince Rock	4,000	0.250	50	0.5208	200,000	0.5882
Juan Malvido	2,000	0.125	40	0.4167	80,000	0.2353
	$16,000	1.000	96	1.0000	$340,000	1.0000

These three weightings give the following allocation of $30,000:

	Relative Speaking Fee Weights (1)	Allocation of $30,000 (2)	Relative Number of Speeches Weights (3)	Allocation of $30,000 (4)	Relative Speaking Fee Revenues (5)	Allocation of $30,000 (6)
Linda Young	0.625	$18,750	0.0625	$ 1,875	0.1765	$ 5,295
Vince Rock	0.250	7,500	0.5208	15,624	0.5882	17,646
Juan Malvido	0.125	3,750	0.4167	12,501	0.2353	7,059
	1.000	$30,000	1.0000	$30,000	1.0000	$30,000

The incremental revenue-allocation method is not straightforward, as the sum of the individual speaking fees ($10,000 + $4,000 + $2,000 = $16,000) is less than the total $30,000 to be allocated.

2. Young could argue that she has the highest individual speaking fee and is high in demand. In contrast, the other two speakers have given numerous talks and likely will attract fewer people to the seminar. She could argue that Malvido should pay to be on the program, as he is marketing for the television network. The net of these arguments is that Young wants more than $10,000.

Rock could argue that he is in huge demand as a speaker, as is evidenced by his 50 speeches at $4,000. People pay this amount because he is both entertaining and dynamic. He could also claim his Olympic gold medal brings an aura of accomplishment to the seminar. The net of these arguments is that Rock wants more than $10,000.

Malvido could argue that he is the "television personality" everyone wants to meet and hear. He could also argue he could give the seminar invaluable publicity by promoting it on his television show. The net of these arguments is that Malvido wants more than $10,000.

16-18 (10-15 min.) **Revenue allocation, bundled products,
                additional complexities (continuation of 16-17).**

Alternatives include:

(a)   Use information about how each individual package is used to make the revenue allocations. Thus if one party uses only lodging and food, the $700 is allocated among those two groups. This would be the most accurate approach as it captures actual usage and non-usage of the facilities.

(b)   Use the average non-usage information to compute an "adjusted unit selling price:"

Lodging: $640 × 1.00   = $ 640

Food: $160 × 0.95   =   152

Recreation: $300 × 0.90   =   270
                                  $1,062

These adjusted revenues can be used in either the stand-alone or incremental methods. For example, the stand-alone allocations are:

Lodging: $\frac{640}{\$1,062}$ × $700   = $422

Food: $\frac{152}{\$1,062}$ × $700   = $100

Recreation: $\frac{270}{\$1,062}$ × $700   = $178
                                               $700

16-20 (20 min.)   **7-Up using variances to read the market.**

1. 7-Up should have conducted a Level 1 to 4 variance analysis that is focused on the U.S. soft-drink market. If information is available, individual 7-Up products (7-Up and Diet 7-Up) could be included to compute a sales mix-variance. The sales-quantity variance could be divided into a market-share variance and a market-size variance. 7-Up's market share has steadily declined from 3.2% to 2.4% over a 10-year period. This is a large decline.

7-Up could also conduct more detailed analyses, including:
1) Changes in the market share and the market size of the citrus-flavoured category.
2) Changes in its market share and market size share by demographic segment (0-11 years, 12-24 years, and so on).

2. The brand objectives are critical to consider when evaluating 7-Up's strategy. The *Fortune* article has a negative tone. Much depends on whether 7-Up's management has attempted to make the brand investments required to compete in the soft drink market. If 7-Up's management has invested heavily in marketing, sales promotions, product extension, and so on, its decline in market share is a negative indicator. Suppose, however, 7-Up management has decided that they do not have the resources to compete with Coca-Cola or Pepsi-Cola. Their strategy is to budget for market declines, but extract higher profitability from the brand in the short run. This is a classic "milk-the-brand" strategy. Here, the issue is what is the optimal "milk-the-brand" strategy, which would consider the time period over which a market-share decline is predicted and the rate of decrease with alternative cutbacks in marketing outlays.

16-22 (30-40 min.) **Variance analysis of revenues, multiple countries.**

1.   All amounts are in thousands.

Budget for 2000

	Selling Price per Carton (1)	Units Sold (Cartons in 000s) (2)	Sales Mix (3)	Revenues (4) = (1) × (2)
Canada	$6.00	400,000	16%	$ 2,400,000
Mexico	4.00	600,000	24	2,400,000
U.S.	7.00	1,500,000	60	10,500,000
		2,500,000	100%	$15,300,000

Actual for 2000

	Selling Price per Carton (1)	Units Sold (Cartons in 000s) (2)	Sales Mix (3)	Revenues (4) = (1) × (2)
Canada	$6.20	480,000	16%	$ 2,976,000
Mexico	4.25	900,000	30	3,825,000
U.S.	6.80	1,620,000	54	11,016,000
		3,000,000	100%	$17,817,000

Solution Exhibit 16-22 summarizes the Level 1 to Level 3 variance analysis. Details of the underlying computations are presented below.

$$\text{Static-budget variance of revenue} = \text{Actual results} - \text{Static-budget amount}$$

Canada	=	$ 2,976,000	− $ 2,400,000	=	$ 576,000 F
Mexico	=	3,825,000	− 2,400,000	=	1,425,000 F
United States	=	11,016,000	− 10,500,000	=	516,000 F
Total					$2,517,000 F

$$\text{Flexible-budget variance of revenue} = \text{Actual results} - \text{Flexible-budget amount}$$

Canada	=	$ 2,976,000	− ($6.00 × 480,000)	=	$ 96,000 F
Mexico	=	3,825,000	− (4.00 × 900,000)	=	225,000 F
United States	=	11,016,000	− (7.00 × 1,620,000)	=	324,000 U
Total					$ 3,000 U

$$\text{Sales-volume variance of revenue} = \left(\begin{array}{c} \text{Actual sales} \\ \text{quantity} \\ \text{in units} \end{array} - \begin{array}{c} \text{Budgeted sales} \\ \text{quantity} \\ \text{in units} \end{array} \right) \times \begin{array}{c} \text{Budgeted} \\ \text{revenue} \\ \text{per unit} \end{array}$$

Canada	= (480,000 –	400,000) × $6.00	=	$ 480,000 F
Mexico	= (900,000 –	600,000) × $4.00	=	$1,200,000 F
United States	= (1,620,000 –	1,500,000) × $7.00	=	$ 840,000 F
Total				$2,520,000 F

$$\text{Sales-quantity variance of revenue} = \left(\begin{array}{c} \text{Actual units} \\ \text{of all products} \\ \text{sold} \end{array} - \begin{array}{c} \text{Budgeted units} \\ \text{of all products} \\ \text{sold} \end{array} \right) \times \begin{array}{c} \text{Budgeted} \\ \text{sales-mix} \\ \text{percentage} \end{array} \times \begin{array}{c} \text{Budgeted} \\ \text{revenue} \\ \text{per unit} \end{array}$$

Canada	=	(3,000,000 – 2,500,000) × 0.16 × $6.00	=	$ 480,000 F
Mexico	=	(3,000,000 – 2,500,000) × 0.24 × $4.00	=	$ 480,000 F
United States	=	(3,000,000 – 2,500,000) × 0.60 × $7.00	=	$2,100,000 F
Total				$3,060,000 F

$$\text{Sales-mix variance of revenue} = \begin{array}{c} \text{Actual units} \\ \text{of all} \\ \text{products sold} \end{array} \times \left(\begin{array}{c} \text{Actual} \\ \text{sales-mix} \\ \text{percentage} \end{array} - \begin{array}{c} \text{Budgeted} \\ \text{sales-mix} \\ \text{percentage} \end{array} \right) \times \begin{array}{c} \text{Budgeted} \\ \text{revenue} \\ \text{per unit} \end{array}$$

Canada	=	3,000,000 × (0.16 – 0.16) × $6.00	=	$ 0
Mexico	=	3,000,000 × (0.30 – 0.24) × $4.00	=	$ 720,000 F
United States	=	3,000,000 × (0.54 – 0.60) × $7.00	=	$1,260,000 U
Total				$ 540,000 U

2. There is a sizable favourable static-budget variance (Level 1) of revenue of $2,517,000. The flexible-budget variance (Level 2) of $3,000 U shows that the net effect of the selling price changes is minimal (Canada increases $0.20 per carton, Mexico increases $0.25 per carton, and U.S. decreases $0.20 per carton).

The Level 3 breakdown of the favourable sales-volume variance of $2,520,000 for revenues shows that the biggest contributor is the 500,000 unit increase in sales. There is a partially offsetting unfavourable sales-mix variance.

SOLUTION EXHIBIT 16-22
Revenue Analysis for Cola-King

Static-Budget Variance of Revenues
Canada	$ 576,000 F
Mexico	1,425,000 F
United States	516,000 F
Total	$2,517,000 F

Flexible-Budget Variance of Revenues		Sales-Volume Variance of Revenues	
Canada	$ 96,000 F	Canada	$ 480,000 F
Mexico	225,000 F	Mexico	1,200,000 F
United States	324,000 U	United States	840,000 F
Total	$ 3,000 U		$2,520,000 F

Sales-Mix Variance of Revenues		Sales-Quantity Variance of Revenues	
Canada	$ 0	Canada	$ 480,000 F
Mexico	720,000 F	Mexico	480,000 F
United States	1,260,000 U	United States	2,100,000 F
Total	$ 540,000 U		$3,060,000 F

16-24 (20-25 min.) **Customer profitability, distribution.**

1. The activity-based costing for each customer is:

	Maple Pharmacy	Oak Pharmacy
1. Order processing,		
$40 × 12; 10	$ 480	$ 400
2. Line-item ordering,		
$3 × (12 × 10;10 × 18)	360	540
3. Store deliveries,		
$50 × 6; 10	300	500
4. Carton deliveries,		
$1 × (6 × 24; 10 × 20)	144	200
5. Shelf-stocking,		
$16 × (6 × 0; 10 × 0.5)	0	80
Operating costs	$1,284	$1,720

The operating income of each customer is:

	Maple Pharmacy	Oak Pharmacy
Revenues,		
$2,400 × 6; 1,800 × 10	$14,400	$18,000
Cost of goods sold,		
$2,100 × 6; $1,650 × 10	12,600	16,500
Gross margin	1,800	1,500
Operating costs	1,284	1,720
Operating income	$ 516	$ (220)

2. Ways Figure Four could use this information include:

(a) Pay increased attention to the top 20% of the customers. This could entail asking them for ways you can improve service. Alternatively, you may want to highlight to your own personnel the importance of these customers, e.g., it could entail stressing to delivery people the importance of never missing delivery dates for these customers.

(b) Work out ways internally at Figure Four to reduce the rate per cost driver, e.g., reduce the cost per order by having better order placement linkages with customers. This cost reduction by Figure Four will improve the profitability of all customers.

(c) Work with customers so that their behaviour reduces the total "system-wide" costs. At a minimum, this approach could entail having customers make fewer orders and fewer line items. This latter point is controversial with students; the rationale is that a reduction in the number of line items (diversity of products) carried by Ma and Pa stores may reduce the diversity of products Figure Four carries.

16-26 (35 min.)   **Direct materials price, efficiency, mix, and yield variances.**

1.   Solution Exhibit 16-26A presents the total price variance ($3,100F), the total efficiency variance ($2,560U) and the total flexible-budget variance ($540F).

Total direct materials price variance can also be computed as:

$$\text{Direct materials price variance for each input} = \left(\begin{array}{cc}\text{Actual} & \text{Budgeted} \\ \text{Price} & \text{Price}\end{array}\right) \times \begin{array}{c}\text{Actual} \\ \text{Inputs}\end{array}$$

Tolman	= ($0.28 – $0.30) × 62,000 =	$1,240 F
Golden Delicious	= ($0.26 – $0.26) × 155,000 =	0
Ribston	= ($0.20 – $0.22) × 93,000 =	1,860 F
Total direct materials price variance		$3,100 F

Total direct materials efficiency variance can also be computed as:

$$\text{Direct materials efficiency variance for each input} = \left(\begin{array}{cc}\text{Actual} & \text{Budgeted inputs allowed} \\ \text{inputs} & \text{for actual outputs achieved}\end{array}\right) \times \begin{array}{c}\text{Budgeted} \\ \text{prices}\end{array}$$

Tolman	= (62,000 – 45,000) × $0.30 =	$5,100 U
Golden Delicious	= (155,000 – 180,000) × $0.26 =	6,500 F
Ribston	= (93,000 – 75,000) × $0.22 =	3,960 U
Total direct materials efficiency variance		$2,560 U

SOLUTION EXHIBIT 16-26A
Columnar Presentation of Direct Materials Price and Efficiency Variances for Greenwood Inc. for November 2000

	Actual Costs Incurred (Actual Inputs × Actual Prices) (1)		Actual Input × Budgeted Prices (2)		Flexible Budget (Budgeted Inputs Allowed for Actual Outputs Achieved × Budgeted Prices) (3)	
Tolman	62,000 × $0.28 =	$17,360	62,000 × $0.30 =	$18,600	45,000 × $0.30 =	$13,500
Golden Delicious	155,000 × $0.26 =	40,300	155,000 × $0.26 =	40,300	180,000 × $0.26 =	46,800
Ribston	93,000 × $0.20 =	18,600	93,000 × $0.22 =	20,460	75,000 × $0.22 =	16,500
		$76,260		$79,360		$76,800

$3,100 F ← Total price variance

$2,560 U ← Total efficiency variance

$540 F ← Total flexible-budget variance

F = favourable effect on operating income; U = unfavourable effect on operating income

16-26 (cont'd)

2. Solution Exhibit 16-26B presents the total direct materials yield and mix variances for Greenwood Inc. for November 2000.

The total direct materials yield variance can also be computed as the sum of the direct materials yield variances for each input:

$$
\begin{pmatrix} \text{Direct} \\ \text{materials} \\ \text{yield variance} \\ \text{for each input} \end{pmatrix} = \begin{pmatrix} \text{Actual total} \\ \text{quantity of all} \\ \text{direct materials} \\ \text{inputs used} \end{pmatrix} - \begin{pmatrix} \text{Budgeted total quantity} \\ \text{of all direct materials} \\ \text{inputs allowed for} \\ \text{actual output achieved} \end{pmatrix} \times \begin{pmatrix} \text{Budgeted} \\ \text{direct materials} \\ \text{input mix} \\ \text{percentage} \end{pmatrix} \times \begin{pmatrix} \text{Budgeted} \\ \text{price of} \\ \text{direct materials} \\ \text{inputs} \end{pmatrix}
$$

Tolman	= $(310,000 - 300,000) \times 0.15 \times \$0.30 = 10,000 \times 0.15 \times \$0.30 =$	\$ 450 U
Golden Delicious	= $(310,000 - 300,000) \times 0.60 \times \$0.26 = 10,000 \times 0.60 \times \$0.26 =$	1,560 U
Ribston	= $(310,000 - 300,000) \times 0.25 \times \$0.22 = 10,000 \times 0.25 \times \$0.22 =$	550 U
Total direct materials yield variance		\$2,560 U

The total direct materials mix variance can also be computed as the sum of the direct materials mix variances for each input:

$$
\begin{pmatrix} \text{Direct} \\ \text{materials} \\ \text{mix variance} \\ \text{for each input} \end{pmatrix} = \begin{pmatrix} \text{Actual} \\ \text{direct materials} \\ \text{input mix} \\ \text{percentage} \end{pmatrix} - \begin{pmatrix} \text{Budgeted} \\ \text{direct materials} \\ \text{input mix} \\ \text{percentage} \end{pmatrix} \times \begin{pmatrix} \text{Actual total} \\ \text{quantity of all} \\ \text{direct materials} \\ \text{inputs used} \end{pmatrix} \times \begin{pmatrix} \text{Budgeted} \\ \text{price of} \\ \text{direct materials} \\ \text{inputs} \end{pmatrix}
$$

Tolman	= $(0.20 - 0.15) \times 310,000 \times \$0.30 =$	$0.05 \times 310,000 \times \$0.30 =$	\$4,650 U
Golden Delicious	= $(0.50 - 0.60) \times 310,000 \times \$0.26 =$	$-0.10 \times 310,000 \times \$0.26 =$	8,060 F
Ribston	= $(0.30 - 0.25) \times 310,000 \times \$0.22 =$	$0.05 \times 310,000 \times \$0.22 =$	3,410 U
Total direct materials mix variance			\$ 0 U

3. Greenwood paid less for Tolman and Ribston apples and, so, had a favourable direct materials price variance of \$3,100. It also had an unfavourable efficiency variance of \$2,560. Greenwood would need to evaluate if these were unrelated events or if the lower price resulted from the purchase of apples of poorer quality that affected efficiency. The net effect in this case from a cost standpoint was favourable—the savings in price being greater than the loss in efficiency. Of course, if the applesauce is of poorer quality, Greenwood must also evaluate the potential effects on current and future revenues that have not been considered in the variances described in requirements 1 and 2.

16-26 (cont'd)

The unfavourable efficiency variance is entirely attributable to an unfavourable yield. The actual mix does deviate from the budgeted mix but at the budgeted prices, the greater quantity of Tolman and Ribston apples used in the actual mix exactly offsets the fewer Golden Delicious apples used. Again, management should evaluate the reasons for the unfavourable yield variance. Is it due to poor quality Tolman and Ribston apples (recall from requirement 1 that these apples were acquired at a price lower than the standard price)? Is it due to the change in mix (recall that the mix used is different from the budgeted mix, even though the mix variance is $0)? Isolating the reasons can lead management to take the necessary corrective actions.

SOLUTION EXHIBIT 16-26B
Columnar Presentation of Direct Materials, Yield, and Mix Variances for Greenwood Inc. for November 2000

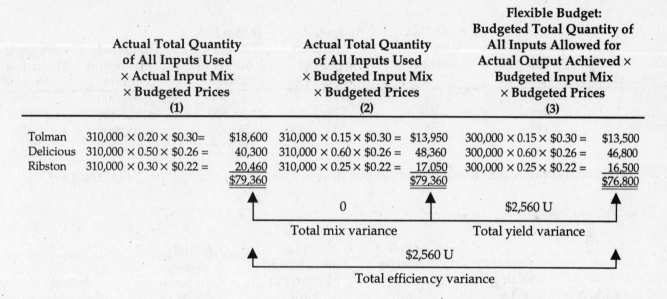

F = favourable effect on operating income; U = unfavourable effect on operating income

16-28 (60 min.) **Variance analysis, sales-mix, and sales-quantity variances.**

1. Actual Contribution Margins

Product	Actual Selling Price	Actual Variable Costs per Unit	Actual Contribution Margin per Unit	Actual Sales Volume in Units	Actual Contribution Dollars	Actual Contribution Percent
PalmPro	$349	$178	$171	11,000	$ 1,881,000	16%
PalmCE	285	92	193	44,000	8,492,000	71%
PalmKid	102	73	29	55,000	1,595,000	13%
				110,000	$11,968,000	100%

The actual average contribution margin per unit is $108.80 ($11,968,000 ÷ 110,000 units).

Budgeted Contribution Margins

Product	Budgeted Selling Price	Budgeted Variable Costs per Unit	Budgeted Contribution Margin per Unit	Budgeted Sales Volume in Units	Budgeted Contribution Dollars	Budgeted Contribution Percent
PalmPro	$379	$182	$197	12,500	$ 2,462,500	19%
PalmCE	269	98	171	37,500	6,412,500	49%
PalmKid	149	65	84	50,000	4,200,000	32%
				100,000	$13,075,000	100%

The budgeted average contribution margin per unit is $130.75 ($13,075,000 ÷ 100,000 units).

2. Actual Sales Mix

Product	Actual Selling Price	Actual Variable Costs per Unit	Actual Contribution Margin per Unit	Actual Sales Volume in Units	Actual Sales Mix
PalmPro	$349	$178	$171	11,000	10.0%
PalmCE	285	92	193	44,000	40.0%
PalmKid	102	73	29	55,000	50.0%
				110,000	100%

Budgeted Sales Mix

Product	Budgeted Selling Price	Budgeted Variable Costs per Unit	Budgeted Contribution Margin per Unit	Budgeted Sales Volume in Units	Budgeted Sales Mix
PalmPro	$379	$182	$197	12,500	12.5%
PalmCE	269	98	171	37,500	37.5%
PalmKid	149	65	84	50,000	50.0%
				100,000	100%

3. Flexible-budget variance of contribution margin:

$$= \frac{\text{Actual}}{\text{Results}} - \frac{\text{Flexible-budget}}{\text{amount}}$$

PalmPro = ($171 × 11,000) − ($197 × 11,000)

= $1,881,000 − $2,167,000   = $ 286,000 U

PalmCE = (193 × 44,000) − ($171 × 44,000)

= $8,492,000 − $7,524,000   = 968,000 F

PalmKid = ($29 × 55,000) − ($84 × 55,000)

= $1,595,000 − $4,620,000   = <u>3,025,000</u> U

Total flexible-budget variance   = <u>$2,343,000</u> U

Sales-volume variance of contribution margin:

$$= \left(\begin{array}{c} \text{Actual sales} \\ \text{quantity} \\ \text{in units} \end{array} - \begin{array}{c} \text{Budgeted sales} \\ \text{quantity} \\ \text{in units} \end{array} \right) \times \begin{array}{c} \text{Budgeted} \\ \text{contrib. margin} \\ \text{per unit} \end{array}$$

PalmPro = (11,000 − 12,500) × $197

= −1,500 × $197   = $ 295,500 U

PalmCE = (44,000 − 37,500) × $171

= 6,500 × $171   = 1,111,500 F

PalmKid = (55,000 − 50,000) × $84

= 5,000 × $84   = <u>420,000</u> F

Total sales-volume variance   = <u>$1,236,000</u> F

16-28 (cont'd)

Sales-mix variance of contribution-margin:

$$= \begin{pmatrix} \text{Actual units} \\ \text{of all} \\ \text{products sold} \end{pmatrix} \times \begin{pmatrix} \text{Actual} \\ \text{sales mix} \\ \text{percentage} \end{pmatrix} - \begin{pmatrix} \text{Budgeted} \\ \text{sales mix} \\ \text{percentage} \end{pmatrix} \times \begin{pmatrix} \text{Budgeted} \\ \text{contrib. margin} \\ \text{per unit} \end{pmatrix}$$

PalmPro $= 110,000 \times (0.10 - 0.125) \times \$197$

$= 110,00 \times -0.025 \times \$197$ $= \$541,750$ U

PalmCE $= 110,000 \times (0.40 - 0.375) \times \$171$

$= 110,000 \times 0.025 \times \$171$ $= 470,250$ F

PalmKid $= 110,000 \times (0.50 - 0.50) \times \$84$

$= 110,000 \times 0.00 \times \$84$ $= 0$ F

Total sales-mix variance $= \underline{\$\ 71,500}$ U

Sales-quantity variance of contribution margin:

$$= \begin{pmatrix} \text{Actual units} \\ \text{of all} \\ \text{products sold} \end{pmatrix} - \begin{pmatrix} \text{Budgeted units} \\ \text{of all} \\ \text{products sold} \end{pmatrix} \times \begin{pmatrix} \text{Budgeted} \\ \text{sales mix} \\ \text{percentage} \end{pmatrix} \times \begin{pmatrix} \text{Budgeted} \\ \text{contrib. margin} \\ \text{per unit} \end{pmatrix}$$

PalmPro $= (110,000 - 100,000) \times 0.125 \times \$197$

$= 10,000 \times 0.125 \times \$197$ $= \$\ 246,250$ F

PalmCE $= (110,000 - 100,000) \times 0.375 \times \$171$

$= 10,000 \times 0.375 \times \$171$ $= 641,250$ F

PalmKid $= (110,000 - 100,000) \times 0.50 \times \$84$

$= 10,000 \times 0.50 \times \$84$ $= 420,000$ F

Total sales-quantity variance $= \underline{\$1,307,500}$ F

4.

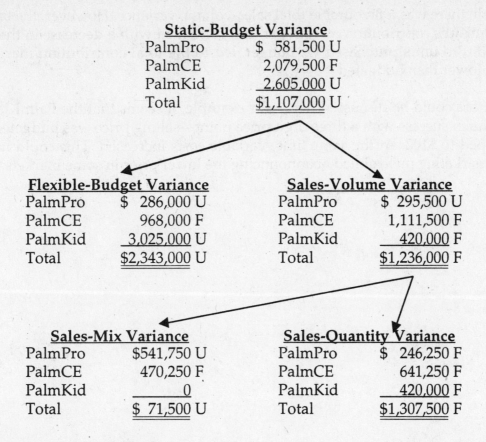

Static-Budget Variance

PalmPro	$ 581,500 U
PalmCE	2,079,500 F
PalmKid	2,605,000 U
Total	$1,107,000 U

Flexible-Budget Variance

PalmPro	$ 286,000 U
PalmCE	968,000 F
PalmKid	3,025,000 U
Total	$2,343,000 U

Sales-Volume Variance

PalmPro	$ 295,500 U
PalmCE	1,111,500 F
PalmKid	420,000 F
Total	$1,236,000 F

Sales-Mix Variance

PalmPro	$541,750 U
PalmCE	470,250 F
PalmKid	0
Total	$ 71,500 U

Sales-Quantity Variance

PalmPro	$ 246,250 F
PalmCE	641,250 F
PalmKid	420,000 F
Total	$1,307,500 F

5. Some factors to consider are:
  - The difference in actual vs. budgeted contribution was $1,107,000. However, the contribution from the PalmCE exceeded budget by $2,079,500 while the contributions from the PalmPro and the PalmKid were lower than expected to an offsetting degree.
  - In percentage terms, the PalmCE accounted for 71% of total contribution vs. a planned 49% contribution. However, the PalmPro accounted for 16% vs. planned 19% and the PalmKid accounted for only 13% vs. a planned 32%.
  - In unit terms (rather than in contribution terms), the PalmKid accounted for 50% of the sales mix as planned. However, the PalmPro accounted for only 10% vs. a budgeted 12.5% and the PalmCE accounted for 40% vs. a planned 37.5%.
  - Variance analysis for the PalmPro shows an unfavourable sales-mix variance outweighing a favourable sales-quantity variance and producing an unfavourable sales-volume variance of $295,500. The drop in sales-mix share was far larger than the gain from an overall greater quantity sold.
  - The PalmCE gained both from an increase in share of the sales mix as well as from the increase in the overall number of units sold. These factors combined to a $1,111,500 favourable sales-volume variance.
  - The PalmKid maintained sales-mix share—as a result, the sales-mix variance is zero. However, PalmKid sales did gain from the overall increase in units sold.

16-28 (cont'd)

- Overall, there was a favourable total sales-volume variance. However, the large drop in PalmKid's contribution margin per unit combined with a decrease in the number of PalmPro units purchased vs. budget, led to the total contribution margin being much lower than budgeted.

Other factors could be discussed here—for example, it seems that the PalmKid did not achieve much success with a three digit price point—selling price was budgeted at $149 but dropped to $102. At the same time, variable costs increased. This could have been due to a marketing push aimed at announcing the lower price in some markets.

16-30 (40 min.) **Variance analysis of contribution margin, multiple products.**

1, 2, and 3. Solution Exhibit 16-30 presents the sales-volume, sales-quantity, and sales-mix variances for each type of cookie and in total for Debbie's Delight Inc. in August 2000.

The sales-volume variances can also be computed as:

$$\begin{pmatrix} \text{Sales-volume} \\ \text{variance of} \\ \text{contribution margin} \end{pmatrix} = \begin{pmatrix} \text{Actual sales} \\ \text{quantity in kilograms} - \frac{\text{Budgeted sales}}{\text{quantity in kilograms}} \end{pmatrix} \times \begin{matrix} \text{Budgeted contribution} \\ \text{margin per kilogram} \end{matrix}$$

The sales-volume variances are:

Chocolate chip	= (57,600 – 45,000) × $2.00	=	$25,200 F
Oatmeal raisin	= (18,000 – 25,000) × $2.30	=	16,100 U
Coconut	= (9,600 – 10,000) × $2.60	=	1,040 U
White chocolate	= (13,200 – 5,000) × $3.00	=	24,600 F
Macadamia nut	= (21,600 – 15,000) × $3.10	=	20,460 F
All cookies			$53,120 F

The sales-quantity variance can also be computed as :

$$\begin{pmatrix} \text{Sales-quantity} \\ \text{variance of} \\ \text{contribution margin} \end{pmatrix} = \begin{pmatrix} \text{Actual kilograms} \\ \text{of all cookies} - \frac{\text{Budgeted kilograms}}{\text{of all cookies}} \\ \text{sold} \qquad \text{sold} \end{pmatrix} \times \begin{matrix}\text{Budgeted} \\ \text{sales-mix} \\ \text{percentage}\end{matrix} \times \begin{matrix}\text{Budgeted} \\ \text{contribution} \\ \text{margin per kilogram}\end{matrix}$$

The sales-quantity variances are:

Chocolate chip	= (120,000 – 100,000) × 0.45 × $2.00 =		$18,000 F
Oatmeal raisin	= (120,000 – 100,000) × 0.25 × $2.30 =		11,500 F
Coconut	= (120,000 – 100,000) × 0.10 × $2.60 =		5,200 F
White chocolate	= (120,000 – 100,000) × 0.05 × $3.00 =		3,000 F
Macadamia nut	= (120,000 – 100,000) × 0.15 × $3.10 =		9,300 F
All cookies			$47,000 F

The sales-mix variance can also be computed as:

$$\begin{pmatrix} \text{Sales-mix} \\ \text{variance of} \\ \text{contribution margin} \end{pmatrix} = \begin{pmatrix} \text{Actual sales-} \\ \text{mix percentage} - \frac{\text{Budgeted sales-}}{\text{mix percentage}} \end{pmatrix} \times \begin{matrix}\text{Actual kilograms} \\ \text{of all cookies} \\ \text{sold}\end{matrix} \times \begin{matrix}\text{Budgeted} \\ \text{contribution} \\ \text{margin per kilogram}\end{matrix}$$

The sales-mix variances are:

Chocolate chip	= (0.48 – 0.45) × 120,000 × $2.00	=	$ 7,200 F
Oatmeal raisin	= (0.15 – 0.25) × 120,000 × $2.30	=	27,600 U
Coconut	= (0.08 – 0.10) × 120,000 × $2.60	=	6,240 U
White chocolate	= (0.11 – 0.05) × 120,000 × $3.00	=	21,600 F
Macadamia nut	= (0.18 – 0.15) × 120,000 × $3.10	=	11,160 F
All cookies			$ 6,120 F

16-30 (cont'd)

A summary of the variances is:

Sales-Volume Variance of C.M.

Chocolate chip	$25,200 F
Oatmeal raisin	16,100 U
Coconut	1,040 U
White chocolate	24,600 F
Macadamia nut	20,460 F
All cookies	$53,120 F

Sales-Mix Variance of C.M.		Sales-Quantity Variance of C.M.	
Chocolate chip	$ 7,200 F	Chocolate chip	$18,000 F
Oatmeal raisin	27,600 U	Oatmeal raisin	11,500 F
Coconut	6,240 U	Coconut	5,200 F
White chocolate	21,600 F	White chocolate	3,000 F
Macadamia nut	11,160 F	Macadamia nut	9,300 F
All cookies	$ 6,120 F	All cookies	$47,000 F

4.   Debbie's Delight shows a favourable sales-quantity variance because it sold more cookies in total than was budgeted. Together with the higher quantities, Debbie's also sold more of the high-contribution margin white chocolate and macadamia nut cookies relative to the budgeted mix—hence Debbie's also showed a favourable total sales-mix variance.

SOLUTION EXHIBIT 16-30
Columnar Presentation of Sales-Volume, Sales-Quantity and Sales-Mix Variances for Debbie's Delight Inc.

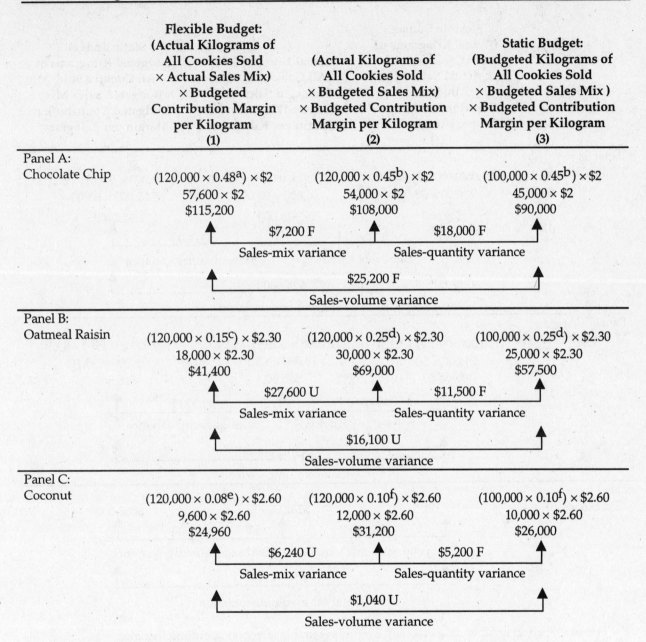

	Flexible Budget: (Actual Kilograms of All Cookies Sold × Actual Sales Mix) × Budgeted Contribution Margin per Kilogram (1)	(Actual Kilograms of All Cookies Sold × Budgeted Sales Mix) × Budgeted Contribution Margin per Kilogram (2)	Static Budget: (Budgeted Kilograms of All Cookies Sold × Budgeted Sales Mix) × Budgeted Contribution Margin per Kilogram (3)
Panel A: Chocolate Chip	$(120,000 \times 0.48^a) \times \$2$ $57,600 \times \$2$ $\$115,200$	$(120,000 \times 0.45^b) \times \$2$ $54,000 \times \$2$ $\$108,000$	$(100,000 \times 0.45^b) \times \$2$ $45,000 \times \$2$ $\$90,000$

$\$7,200$ F ← Sales-mix variance → $\$18,000$ F ← Sales-quantity variance

$\$25,200$ F ← Sales-volume variance

Panel B: Oatmeal Raisin	$(120,000 \times 0.15^c) \times \$2.30$ $18,000 \times \$2.30$ $\$41,400$	$(120,000 \times 0.25^d) \times \$2.30$ $30,000 \times \$2.30$ $\$69,000$	$(100,000 \times 0.25^d) \times \$2.30$ $25,000 \times \$2.30$ $\$57,500$

$\$27,600$ U ← Sales-mix variance → $\$11,500$ F ← Sales-quantity variance

$\$16,100$ U ← Sales-volume variance

Panel C: Coconut	$(120,000 \times 0.08^e) \times \$2.60$ $9,600 \times \$2.60$ $\$24,960$	$(120,000 \times 0.10^f) \times \$2.60$ $12,000 \times \$2.60$ $\$31,200$	$(100,000 \times 0.10^f) \times \$2.60$ $10,000 \times \$2.60$ $\$26,000$

$\$6,240$ U ← Sales-mix variance → $\$5,200$ F ← Sales-quantity variance

$\$1,040$ U ← Sales-volume variance

F = favourable effect on operating income; U = unfavourable effect on operating income.

Actual Sales Mix:
[a]Chocolate Chip = 57,600 ÷ 120,000 = 48%
[c]Oatmeal Raisin = 18,000 ÷ 120,000 = 15%
[e]Coconut = 9,600 ÷ 120,000 = 8%

Budgeted Sales Mix:
[b]Chocolate Chip = 45,000 ÷ 100,000 = 45%
[d]Oatmeal Raisin = 25,000 ÷ 100,000 = 25%
[f]Coconut = 10,000 ÷ 100,000 = 10%

SOLUTION EXHIBIT 16-30 (Cont'd.)
Columnar Presentation of Sales-Volume, Sales-Quantity, and Sales-Mix Variances for Debbie's Delight Inc.

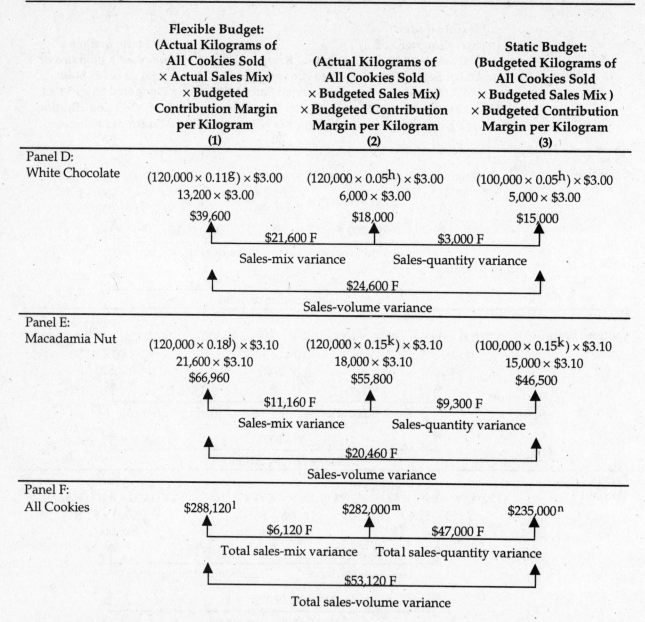

F = favourable effect on operating income; U = unfavourable effect on operating income.

Actual Sales Mix:

[g]White Chocolate = 13,200 ÷ 120,000 = 11%

[j]Macadamia Nut = 21,600 ÷ 120,000 = 18%

[l]$115,200 + $41,400 + $24,960
        + $39,600 + $66,960 = $288,120

Budgeted Sales Mix:

[h]White Chocolate = 5,000 ÷ 100,000 = 5%

[k]Macadamia Nut = 15,000 ÷ 100,000 = 15%

[m]$108,000 + $69,000 + $31,200
        + $18,000 + $55,800 = $282,000

[n]$90,000 + $57,500 + $26,000
        + $15,000 + $46,500 = $235,000

16-32 (60 min.) **Customer-profitability analysis**

1. Solution Exhibit 16-32 shows the customer-profitability analysis. Alternative rankings are:
   a. Customer-level operating income
      1. Brothers $507,440
      2. April   459,390
      3. Suitors   123,140

   b. Gross margin/Net revenues
      1. Suitors, $304,800 ÷ $863,600   35.29%
      2. Brothers, $572,000 ÷ $1,830,400   31.25
      3. April, $501,600 ÷ $2,340,800   21.43

   c. Customer-level operating income/Net revenues
      1. Brothers, $507, 440 ÷ $1,830,400   27.72%
      2. April, $459,390 ÷ $2,340,800   19.63
      3. Suitors, $123,140 ÷ $863,600   14.26

A breakdown of the revenues at list prices is:

	April	Brothers	Suitors
Revenues at list prices	100.00%	100.00%	100.00%
Discount	30.00	20.00	15.00
Sales returns	3.50	6.20	17.11
Cost of goods sold	52.25	50.74	43.93
Gross margin	14.25	23.06	23.96
Customer-level costs	1.20	2.60	14.28
Customer-level operating Income	13.05%	20.46%	9.68%

The following conclusions relate to these percentages:

April – has high price discounting as its major differential to Brothers
Brothers – has lower price discounting than April and lower sales returns than Suitors
Suitors – has highest sales returns and highest customer-level costs

2. Key challenges facing Sims are:
   a. Reduce level of price discounting, especially by April,
   b. Reduce level of sales returns, especially by Suitors, and
   c. Reduce level of customer-level costs, especially by Suitors.

The ABC cost system highlights areas where the Suitors account is troublesome—it has a high number of orders, a high number of customer visits, a high number of rushed deliveries, and a high number of sales returns. Sims needs to consider whether this high level of activity can be reduced without reducing customer revenues.

16-32 (cont'd)

SOLUTION EXHIBIT 16-32
Customer-Profitability Analysis for Zoot's Suits

	April	Brothers	Suitors
Revenues at list prices			
44 × 400 × $200; 62 × 200 × $200; 212 × 30 × $200	$3,520,000	$2,480,000	$1,272,000
Discount			
44 × 400 × $60[a]; 62 × 200 × $40[b]; 212 × 30 × $30[c]	1,056,000	496,000	190,800
Net revenues before returns	2,464,000	1,984,000	1,081,200
Sales returns			
880 × $140; 960 × $160; 1,280 × $170	123,200	153,600	217,600
Net revenues	2,340,800	1,830,400	863,600
Cost of goods sold			
16,720[d] × 110; 11,440[e] × 110; 5,080[f] × 110	1,839,200	1,258,400	558,800
Gross margin	501,600	572,000	304,800
Customer-level costs			
Order processing			
44, 62, 212 × $245	10,780	15,190	51,940
Customer visits			
8, 12, 22 × $1,430	11,440	17,160	31,460
Delivery—regular			
41, 48, 166 × $300	12,300	14,400	49,800
Delivery—rushed			
3, 14, 46 × $850	2,550	11,900	39,100
Returns processing			
4, 6, 16 × $185	740	1,110	2,960
Return stocking fee			
880, 960, 1,280 × $5	4,400	4,800	6,400
Total customer-level costs	42,210	64,560	181,660
Customer-level operating income	$ 459,390	$ 507,440	$ 123,140

[a] $200 − $140 = $60
[b] $200 − $160 = $40
[c] $200 − $170 = $30
[d] (44 × 400) − 880 = 16,720
[e] (62 × 200) − 960 = 11,440
[f] (212 × 30) − 1,280 = 5,080

16-34 (40 min.)   **Customer loyalty clubs and profitability analysis.**

1.

Gold Program

Revenues

2,430 × 20 × ($200 × 0.90)	$ 8,748,000
2,430 × 30 × ($200 × 0.80)	11,664,000
2,430 × 10 × ($200 × 0.70)	3,402,000
Total revenues	23,814,000

Variable Costs

Hotel variable costs, 2,430 × 60 × $65	9,477,000
Wine Costs	
2,430 × 50 × $5	607,500
2,430 × 10 × $20	486,000
Restaurant costs	
2,430 × 20 × $10	486,000
2,430 × 30 × $15	1,093,500
2,430 × 10 × $20	486,000
Total variable costs	12,636,000
Contribution margin	$11,178,000

Silver Program

Revenues

8,340 × 20 × ($200 × 0.90)	$30,024,000
8,340 × 15 × ($200 × 0.80)	20,016,000
Total revenues	50,040,000

Variable Costs

Hotel variable costs, 8,340 × 35 × $65	18,973,500
Wine costs, 8,340 × 35 × $5	1,459,500
Restaurant Costs	
8,340 × 20 × $10	1,668,000
8,340 × 15 × $15	1,876,500
Total variable costs	23,977,500
Contribution margin	$26,062,500

Bronze Program

Revenues, 80,300 × 10 × ($200 × 0.90)	$144,540,000
Variable costs	
Hotel variable costs, 80,300 × 10 × $65	52,195,000
Wine costs 80,300 × 10 × $5	4,015,000
Restaurant costs 80,300 × 10 × $10	8,030,000
Total variable costs	64,240,000
Contribution margin	$ 80,300,000

16-34 (cont'd)

No Program

Revenues, 219,000 × 1 × $200	$43,800,000
Variable costs, 219,000 × 1 × $65	14,235,000
Contribution margin	$29,565,000

Loyalty Program	Total Revenues	Variable Costs	Contribution Margin	Contrib. Margin Total Revenues
Gold	$ 23,814,000	$ 12,636,000	$ 11,178,000	46.94%
Silver	50,040,000	23,977,500	26,062,500	52.08
Bronze	144,540,000	64,240,000	80,300,000	55.56
No program	43,800,000	14,235,000	29,565,000	67.50
Total	$262,194,000	$115,088,500	$147,105,500	

The no-program group of customers has the highest contribution margin per revenue dollar. However, it comprises only 16.71% ($43,800,000 ÷ $262,194,000) of total revenues. The gold program has the lowest contribution margin per revenue dollar. However, it is misleading to evaluate each program in isolation. A key aim of loyalty programs is to promote a high frequency of return business. The contribution margin to total revenue ratio of each program in isolation does not address this issue.

2.

Revenues	$262,194,000
Variable costs	115,088,500
Contribution margin	147,105,500
Fixed costs	140,580,000
Operating income	$ 6,525,500

3. Number of room nights

Gold, 2,430 × 60	145,800
Silver, 8,340 × 35	291,900
Bronze, 80,300 × 10	803,000
No program, 219,000 × 1	219,000
	1,459,700

Average room rate per night: $\dfrac{\$262,194,000}{1,459,700} = \$179.62$

Average variable cost per night: $\dfrac{\$115,088,500}{1,459,700} = \$78.84$

4. Sherriton Hotels has fixed costs of $140,580,000. A key challenge is to attract a high number of repeat business customers. Loyalty programs aim to have customers return to Sherriton multiple times. Their aim is increasing the revenues beyond what they would be without the program. It is to be expected that the higher the level of nights stayed, the greater the inducements necessary to keep attracting the customer to return. However, given the low level of variable costs to room rates, there is considerable cushion available for Sherriton to offer high inducements for frequent stayers.

Sherriton could adopt a net present value analysis of customers who are in the different loyalty clubs. It would be informative for Sherriton to have information on how much of each customer's total lodging industry expenditures it captures. It may well want to give higher levels of inducements to frequent stayers if the current program attracts only, say, 30% of each of its frequent customer's total business in cities where it has lodging properties available.

16-36 (15-20 min.) **Customer profitability, responsibility for environmental clean-up, ethics.**

1. Customer-profitability analysis examines how individual customers differ in their profitability. The revenues and costs of each customer can be estimated with varying degrees of accuracy. Revenues of IF typically would be known at the time of sale. Many costs also would be known, e.g., the cost of materials used to manufacture the fluids sold to each customer. A major area of uncertainty is future costs associated with obligations arising from the sale. There are several issues here:

(a) Uncertainty as to the existence and extent of legal liability. Each customer has primary responsibility to dispose of their own toxic waste. Papandopolis needs to determine the extent of IF's liability. It would be necessary to seek legal guidance on this issue.

(b) Uncertainty as to when the liability will occur. The further in the future, the lower the amount of the liability (assuming discounting for the time value of money occurs.)

(c) Uncertainty as to the amount of the liability given that the liability exists and the date of the liability can be identified. Papandopolis faces major difficulties here—see the answer to requirement 2.

Many companies argue that uncertainties related to (a), (b), and (c) make the inclusion of "hard-dollar estimates meaningless." However, at a minimum, a contingent liability should be recognized and included in the internal customer-profitability reports.

2. Papandopolis' controller may believe that if estimates of future possible legal exposure are sufficiently uncertain they should not be recorded. His concern about "smoking guns" may have a very genuine basis—that is, if litigation arises, third parties may misrepresent Papandopolis' concerns to the detriment of IF. Any written comments that she makes may surface 5 or 10 years later and be interpreted as "widespread knowledge" within IF that they have responsibility for large amounts of environmental clean-up.

Given this background, Papandopolis still has the responsibility to prepare a report in an objective and competent way. Moreover, she has visited 10 customer sites and has details as to their toxic-waste-handling procedures. If Acme goes bankrupt and has no liability insurance, one of the "deep pockets" available to meet toxic-waste-handling costs is likely to be IF. At a minimum, she should report the likely bankruptcy and the existence of IF's contingent liability for toxic-waste clean-up in her report. Whether she quantifies this contingent liability is a more difficult question. Papandopolis has limited information available to make a meaningful quantification. She is not an employee of Acme Metal and has no information about Acme's liability insurance. Moreover, she does not know what other parties (such as other suppliers) are also jointly liable to pay Acme's clean-up costs.

The appropriate course appears to be to highlight the contingent liability but not to attempt to quantify it.

CHAPTER 17
PROCESS COSTING SYSTEMS

17-2 Process-costing systems separate costs into cost categories according to the timing of when costs are introduced into the process. Often, only two cost classifications, direct materials and conversion costs, are necessary. Direct materials are frequently added at one point in time, often the start or the end of the process and all conversion costs are added at about the same time, but in a pattern different from direct materials costs.

17-4 The five key steps in process costing follow:
Step 1: Summarize the flow of physical units of output.
Step 2: Compute output in terms of equivalent units.
Step 3: Compute equivalent unit costs.
Step 4: Summarize total costs to account for.
Step 5: Assign these costs to units completed and to units in ending Work in Process.

17-6 Three inventory methods associated with process costing are:
* Weighted average.
* First-in, first-out.
* Standard costing.

17-8 FIFO computations are distinctive because they assign the cost of the earliest equivalent units available (starting with equivalent units in beginning work in process inventory) to units completed and transferred out, and the cost of the most recent equivalent units worked on during the period to ending work in process inventory. In contrast, the weighted-average method costs units completed and transferred out and in ending work in process at the same average cost.

17-10 A major advantage of FIFO is that managers can judge the performance in the current period independently from the performance in the preceding period.

17-12 Standard-cost procedures are particularly appropriate to process-costing systems where there are various combinations of materials and operations. Standard-cost procedures avoid the intricacies involved in detailed tracking with weighted-average or FIFO methods when there are frequent price variations over time.

17-14 No. Transferred-in costs or previous department costs are costs incurred in a previous department that have been charged to a subsequent department. These costs may be costs incurred in that previous department during this accounting period or a preceding accounting period.

17-16 (25 min.)   **Equivalent units: no beginning inventory.**

1.   Direct materials cost per unit ($720,000 ÷ 10,000) $ 72
     Conversion cost per unit ($760,000 ÷ 10,000)   76
     Assembly Department cost per unit $148

2.   Solution Exhibit 17-16A calculates the equivalent units of direct materials and conversion costs in the Assembly Department of International Electronics in February 2000.

Solution Exhibit 17-16B computes equivalent units costs

Direct materials cost per unit $ 72
Conversion cost per unit   80
Assembly Department cost per unit $152

3.   The difference in the Assembly Department cost per unit calculated in requirements 1 and 2 arises because the costs incurred in January and February are the same but fewer equivalent units of work are done in February relative to January. In January, all 10,000 units introduced are fully completed resulting in 10,000 equivalent units of work done with respect to direct materials and conversion costs. In February, of the 10,000 units introduced, 10,000 equivalent units of work is done with respect to direct materials but only 9,500 equivalent units of work is done with respect to conversion costs. The Assembly Department cost per unit is therefore higher.

17-16 (cont'd)

SOLUTION EXHIBIT 17-16A
Steps 1 and 2: Summarize Output in Physical Units and Compute Equivalent Units
Assembly Department of International Electronics for February 2000

Flow of Production	(Step 1) Physical Units	(Step 2) Equivalent Units Direct Materials	Conversion Costs
Completed and transferred out during current period	9,000	9,000	9,000
Add work in process, ending* 1,000 × 100%; 1,000 × 50%	1,000	1,000	500
Total accounted for	10,000	10,000	9,500
Deduct work in process, beginning	0	0	0
Started during current period	10,000		
Work done in current period only		10,000	9,500

*Degree of completion in this department: direct materials, 100%; conversion costs, 50%.

SOLUTION EXHIBIT 17-16B
Step 3 : Compute Equivalent Unit Costs
Assembly Department of International Electronics for February 2000

	Direct Materials	Conversion Costs
Costs added during February (given)	$720,000	$760,000
Divide by equivalent units of work done in February 2000 (from Soln Exh 17-16A)	÷ 10,000	÷ 9,500
Cost per equivalent unit of work done in February 2000	$ 72	$ 80

17-18 (25 min.) **No beginning inventory, materials introduced in middle of process.**

1.   Solution Exhibit 17-18A shows equivalent units of work done in the current period of Chemical P, 50,000; Chemical Q, 35,000; Conversion costs, 45,000.

2(a)   Solution Exhibit 17-18B calculates cost per equivalent unit of work done in the current period for chemical P, Chemical Q, and conversion costs.

2(b)   Solution Exhibit 17-18C summarizes the total Mixing Department costs for July 2000, and assigns these costs to units completed (and transferred out) and to units in ending work in process.

SOLUTION EXHIBIT 17-18A
Steps 1 and 2: Summarize Output in Physical Units and Compute Equivalent Units
Mixing Department of Vaasa Chemicals for July 2000

| | (Step 1) | (Step 2) Equivalent Units | | |
Flow of Production	Physical Units	Chemical P	Chemical Q	Conversion Costs
Completed and transferred out during current period	35,000	35,000	35,000	35,000
Add work in process, ending*	15,000†			
15,000 × 100%; 15,000 × 0%;				
15,000 × 66 2/3%		15,000	0	10,000
Total accounted for	50,000	50,000	35,000	45,000
Deduct work in process, beginning	0	0	0	0
Started during current period	50,000			
Work done in current period only		50,000	35,000	45,000

*Degree of completion in this department: chemical P, 100%; chemical Q, 0%; conversion costs, 66 2/3%. Note that chemical Q has not been included in the ending work in process, since the ending WIP is 66 2/3% complete and chemical Q is only added when the units are 75% or three-fourths complete.

†Ending work in process   = Beginning work in process + Units started – Units completed
         = 0 + 50,000 – 35,000 = 15,000 units

SOLUTION EXHIBIT 17-18B
Step 3 : Compute Equivalent Unit Costs
Mixing Department of Vaasa Chemicals for July 2000

	Chemical P	Chemical Q	Conversion Costs
Costs added during July (given)	$250,000	$70,000	$135,000
Divide by equivalent units of work done in July 2000 (from Solution Exhibit 17-18A)	÷ 50,000	÷35,000	÷45,000
Cost per equivalent unit of work done in July 2000	$ 5	$ 2	$ 3

17-18 (cont'd)

SOLUTION EXHIBIT 17-18C
Step 4: Summarize Total Costs to Account For and Assign These Costs to
Units Completed, and Units in Ending Work in Process
Mixing Department of Vaasa Chemicals for July 2000

	Chemical P			Chemical Q			Conversion Costs			Total Production Costs
	Equivalent Unit	Cost per Equivalent Unit	Total Costs	Equivalent Unit	Cost per Equivalent Unit	Total Costs	Equivalent Unit	Cost per Equivalent Unit	Total Costs	
	(1)	(2)	(3)=(1)×(2)	(4)	(5)	(6)=(4)×(5)	(7)	(8)	(9)=(7)×(8)	(10)= (3)+(6)+(9)
Panel A: Total Costs to Account For										
Work done in July (from Solution Exhibit 17-18B)	50,000	$5	$250,000	35,000	$2	$70,000	45,000	$3	$135,000	$455,000
Panel B: Assignment of Costs										
Completed and transferred out: (35,000 physical units)	35,000[1]	$5	$175,000	35,000[1]	$2	$70,000	35,000[1]	$3	$105,000	$350,000
Work in process, ending (15,000 physical units)	15,000[1]	$5	75,000	0[1]	$2	0	10,000[1]	$3	30,000	105,000
Accounted for (50,000 physical units)	50,000		$250,000	35,000		$70,000	45,000		$135,000	$455,000

[1] From Solution Exhibit 17-18A.

17-20 (25 min.) FIFO method. See Solution Exhibit 17-20 below.

SOLUTION EXHIBIT 17-20
Step 4: Summarize Total Costs to Account For and Assign These Costs to Units Completed, and Units in Ending Work in Process Using the FIFO Method
Chatham Company for July 2000

	Direct Materials			Conversion Costs			Total Production Costs
	Equivalent Units (1)	Cost per Equivalent Unit (2)	Total Costs (3)=(1)×(2)	Equivalent Units (4)	Cost per Equivalent Unit (5)	Total Costs (6)=(4)×(5)	(7)=(3)+(6)
Panel A: Total Costs to Account For							
Work in process, beginning	20,000	$6.00	$120,000	14,000	$10.00	$140,000	$260,000
Work done in current period only	30,000	$7.00	210,000	28,000	$10.75	301,000	511,000
To account for	50,000		$330,000	42,000		$441,000	$771,000
Panel B: Assignment of Costs							
Completed and transferred out:							
Work in process, beginning	20,000	$6.00	$120,000	14,000	$10.00	$140,000	$260,000
Work done in current period to complete beginning work in process	0*	$7.00	0	6,000†	$10.75	64,500	64,500
Total from beginning inventory	20,000		120,000	20,000		204,500	324,500
Started and completed	14,000‡	$7.00	98,000	14,000‡	$10.75	150,500	248,500
Total completed and transferred out	34,000		218,000	34,000		355,000	573,000
Work in process, ending	16,000	$7.00	112,000	8,000	$10.75	86,000	198,000
Accounted for	50,000		$330,000	42,000		$441,000	$771,000

*Beginning work in process is 100% complete as to direct materials so zero equivalent units of direct materials need to be added to complete beginning work in process.
†Beginning work in process is 70% complete, which equals 14,000 equivalent units of conversion costs. To complete the 20,000 physical units of beginning work in process, 6,000 (20,000 – 14,000) equivalent units of conversion costs need to be added.
‡34,000 total equivalent units completed and transferred out minus 20,000 equivalent units completed and transferred from beginning inventory equals 14,000 equivalent units.

17-22 (15 min.) **Weighted-average method, equivalent units.**

Under the weighted-average method, equivalent units are calculated as the equivalent units of work done to date. Solution Exhibit 17-22 shows equivalent units of work done to date for the Satellite Assembly Division of Aerospatiale for direct materials and conversion costs.

SOLUTION EXHIBIT 17-22
Steps 1 and 2: Summarize Output in Physical Units and Compute Equivalent Units Weighted-Average Method of Process Costing, Satellite Assembly Division of Aerospatiale for May 2001

Flow of Production	(Step 1) Physical Units (given)	(Step 2) Equivalent Units Direct Materials	Conversion Costs
Work in process beginning	8		
Started during current period	50		
To account for	58		
Completed and transferred out during current period	46	46.0	46.0
Work in process, ending* (12 × 60%; 12 × 30%)	12	7.2	3.6
Accounted for	58		
Work done to date		53.2	49.6

*Degree of completion in this department: direct materials, 60%; conversion costs, 30%.

17-24 (15 min.) FIFO method, equivalent units.

1.   Under the FIFO method, equivalent units are calculated as the equivalent units of work done in the current period only. Solution Exhibit 17-24 shows equivalent units of work done in May 2001 in the Assembly Department of Aerospatiale for direct materials and conversion costs.

SOLUTION EXHIBIT 17-24
Steps 1 and 2: Summarize Output in Physical Units and Compute Equivalent Units
FIFO Method of Process Costing, Satellite Assembly Division of Aerospatiale for May 2000

Flow of Production	(Step 1) Physical Units	(Step 2) Equivalent Units	
		Direct Materials	Conversion Costs
Work in process, beginning (given)	8	(work done before current period)	
Started during current period (given)	50		
To account for	58		
Completed and transferred out during current period:			
From beginning work in process[§]	8		
8 × (100% − 90%); 8 × (100% − 40%)		0.8	4.8
Started and completed	38[†]		
38 × 100%, 38 × 100%		38.0	38.0
Work in process, ending* (given)	12		
12 × 60%; 12 × 30%	—	7.2	3.6
Accounted for	58		
Work done in current period only		46.0	46.4

[§]Degree of completion in this department: direct materials, 90%; conversion costs, 40%.

[†]46 physical units completed and transferred out minus 8 physical units completed and transferred out from beginning work-in-process inventory.

*Degree of completion in this department: direct materials, 60%; conversion costs, 30%.

2.		
Direct material costs	$32,200,000	
Equivalent units	46	
Cost per equivalent unit	$700,000	
Conversion costs	$13,920,000	
Equivalent units	46.4	
Cost per equivalent units	$300,000	

17-26 (25-30 min.) **Standard-costing method, assigning costs.**

1.   The calculations of equivalent units for direct materials and conversion costs are identical to the calculations of equivalent units under the FIFO method. Solution Exhibit 17-24 shows the equivalent unit calculations under standard costing given by the equivalent units of work done in May 2000 in the Assembly Department.

2.   Solution Exhibit 17-26 summarizes the total costs to account for, and assigns these costs to, units completed and transferred out, and to units in ending work in process.

3.   Solution Exhibit 17-26 shows the direct materials and conversion cost variances for

Direct materials $230,000 U
Conversion costs $232,000 U

17-26 (cont'd)

SOLUTION EXHIBIT 17-26
Steps 3, 4, and 5: Compute Equivalent Unit Costs, Summarize Total Costs to Account For, and Assign Costs to Units Completed and to Units in Ending Work in Process
Use of Standard Costs in Process Costing, Satellite Assembly Division of Aerospatiale for May 2000.

	Total Production Costs	Direct Materials	Conversion Costs
(Step 3) Standard cost per equivalent unit (given)		$ 695,000	$ 295,000
Work in process, beginning (given)			
Direct materials, 7.2 × $695,000; Conversion costs, 3.2 × $295,000	$ 5,948,000		
Costs added in current period at standard costs			
Direct materials, 46.0 × $695,000; Conversion costs, 46.4 × $295,000	45,658,000	$31,970,000	$13,688,000
(Step 4) Costs to account for	$51,606,000		
(Step 5) Assignment of costs at standard costs:			
Completed and transferred out (46 units):			
Work in process, beginning (8 units)	$ 5,948,000		
Direct materials added in current period	556,000	0.8* × $695,000	
Conversion costs added in current period	1,416,000		4.8* × $295,000
Total from beginning inventory	7,920,000		
Started and completed (38 units)	37,620,000	38† × $695,000	+ 38† × $295,000
Total costs of units transferred out	45,540,000		
Work in process, ending (12 units)			
Direct materials	5,004,000	7.2# × $695,000	
Conversion costs	1,062,000		3.6# × $295,000
Total work in process, ending	6,066,000		
Total costs accounted for	$51,606,000		
Summary of variances for current performance:			
Costs added in current period at standard prices (see above)		$31,970,000	$13,688,000
Actual costs incurred (given)		32,200,000	13,920,000
Variance		$ 230,000 U	$ 232,000 U

*Equivalent units to complete beginning work in process from Solution Exhibit 17-24, Step 2.
†Equivalent units started and completed from Solution Exhibit 17-24, Step 2.
#Equivalent units in work in process, ending from Solution Exhibit 17-24, Step 2.

17-28 (35-40 min.) Transferred-in costs, FIFO method.

1. The calculations for equivalent tonnes of solvent completed and ending work in process for each cost element are exactly as in requirement 1 of Exercise 17-27 shown in Solution Exhibit 17-27A.

2. Solution Exhibit 17-28A presents computations of equivalent unit costs under the FIFO method.

3. Solution Exhibit 17-28B presents a summary of total costs to account for and assigns these costs to tonnes completed and to tonnes in ending work in process using the FIFO method.

SOLUTION EXHIBIT 17-28A
Step 3: Compute Equivalent Unit Costs Under the FIFO Method
Cooking Department of Hideo Chemicals for June 2000

	Transferred-in Costs	Direct Materials	Conversion Costs
Equivalent unit costs of beginning work in process			
Work in process, beginning (given)	$39,200	—	$18,000
Divide by equivalent units of beginning work in process (from Solution Exhibit 17-27A)	÷ 40	—	÷ 30
Cost per equivalent unit of beginning work in process	$ 980	—	$ 600
Equivalent unit costs of work done in current period only			
Costs added in current period (given)	$85,600	$36,000	$49,725
Divide by equivalent units of work done in current period (from Solution Exhibit 17-27A)	÷ $80	÷ 90	÷ 75
Cost per equivalent unit of work done in current period only	$ 1,070	$ 400	$ 663

17-28 (cont'd)

SOLUTION EXHIBIT 17-28B

Step 4: Summarize Total Costs to Account For and Assign These Costs to Units Completed, and Units in Ending Work in Process Using the FIFO Method Cooking Department of Hideo Chemicals June

	Transferred-in Costs			Direct Materials			Conversion Costs			Total Production Costs
	Equivalent Units (1)	Cost per Equivalent Unit (2)	Total Costs (3)=(1)×(2)	Equivalent Units (4)	Cost per Equivalent Unit (5)	Total Costs (6)=(4)×(5)	Equivalent Units (7)	Cost per Equivalent Unit (8)	Total Costs (9)=(7)×(8)	(10)=(3)+(9)... (10)=(3)+(6)+(9)
Panel A: Total Costs to Account For										
Work in process, beginning (from Solution Exhibit 17-28A)	40	$980	$ 39,200	0	—	$ 0	30	$600	$18,000	$ 57,200
Work done in current period only (from Solution Exhibit 17-28A)	80	$1,070	85,600	90	$400	36,000	75	$663	49,725	171,325
To account for	120		$124,800	90		$36,000	105		$67,725	$228,525
Panel B: Assignment of Costs										
Completed and transferred out: (90 physical tons)										
Work in process, beginning (40 physical tons)	40	$980	$ 39,200	0		$ 0	30	$600	$18,000	$ 57,200
Work done in current period to complete beginning work in process	0*		0	40†	$400	16,000	10‡	$663	6,630	22,630
Total from beginning inventory	40		39,200	40		16,000	40		24,630	79,830
Started and completed (50 physical tons)	50‖	$1,070	53,500	50‖	$400	20,000	50‖	$663	33,150	106,650
Total completed and transferred out (90 physical tons)	90§		92,700	90§		36,000	90§		57,780	186,480
Work in process, ending (30 physical tons)	30§	$1,070	32,100	0§		0	15§	$663	9,945	42,045
Accounted for	120		$124,800	90		$36,000	105		$67,725	$228,525

*Beginning work in process is 100% complete as to transferred-in costs so zero equivalent tons of transferred-in costs need to be added to complete beginning work in process.

†Beginning work in process is 0% complete as to direct materials, which equals 0 equivalent tons of direct materials. To complete the 40 physical tons of beginning work in process, 40 equivalent tons of direct materials need to be added.

‡Beginning work in process is 75% complete as to conversion costs, which equals 30 equivalent tons of conversion costs. To complete the 40 physical tons of beginning work in process, 10 (40 – 30) equivalent tons of conversion costs need to be added.

‖90 total equivalent tons completed and transferred out (Solution Exhibit 17-28A) minus 40 equivalent tons from beginning inventory equals 50 equivalent tons.

§From Solution Exhibit 17-28A.

17-30 (25 min.) Weighted-average method.

1.   Solution Exhibit 17-30A shows equivalent units of work done in the current period of

Direct materials   80 equivalent units
Conversion costs   85 equivalent units

2.   Solution Exhibit 17-30B calculates cost per equivalent unit of beginning work in process and of work done in the current period for direct materials and conversion costs.

3.   Solution Exhibit 17-30C summarizes the total Assembly Department costs for October 2000, and assigns these costs to units completed (and transferred out) and to units in ending work in process using the weighted-average method.

SOLUTION EXHIBIT 17-30A
Steps 1 and 2: Summarize Output in Physical Units and Compute Equivalent Units
Assembly Department of Global Defence Inc. for October 2000

Flow of Production	(Step 1) Physical Units	(Step 2) Equivalent Units	
		Direct Materials	Conversion Costs
Completed and transferred out during current period		9090	90
Add work in process, ending*	10		
10 × 100[†]%; 10 × 70%		10	7
Total accounted for	100	100	97
Deduct work in process, beginning[§]	20		
20 × 100[†]%; 20 × 60%		20	12
Started during current period	80	—	—
Work done in current period only		80	85

[†]Direct materials are 100% complete in work in process inventories since all direct materials are introduced at the beginning of the Assembly Process.

*Degree of completion in this department: direct materials, 100%; conversion costs, 50%.

[§]Degree of completion in this department: direct materials, 100%; conversion costs, 60%.

17-30 (cont'd)

SOLUTION EXHIBIT 17-30B
Step 3: Compute Equivalent Unit Costs:
Assembly Department of Global Defence Inc. for October 2000

	Direct Materials	Conversion Costs
Equivalent unit costs of beginning work in process		
Work in process, beginning (given)	$ 460,000	$120,000
Divide by equivalent units of beginning work in process (from Solution Exhibit 17-27A)	÷ 20	÷ 12
Cost per equivalent unit of beginning work in process		
	$ 23,000	$ 10,000
Equivalent unit costs of work done in current period only		
Costs added in current period (given)	$2,000,000	$935,000
Divide by equivalent units of work done in current period (from Solution Exhibit 17-30A)	÷ 80	÷ 85
Cost per equivalent unit of work done in current period only	$ 25,000	$ 11,000

17-30 (cont'd)

SOLUTION EXHIBIT 17-30C

Step 4: Summarize Total Costs to Account For and Assign These Costs to Units Completed, and Units in Ending Work in Process Using the Weighted-Average Method Assembly Department of Global Defence Inc. for October 2000

	Direct Materials			Conversion Costs			Total Production Costs
	Equivalent Units (1)	Cost per Equivalent Unit (2)	Total Costs (3)=(1)×(2)	Equivalent Units (4)	Cost per Equivalent Unit (5)	Total Costs (6)=(4)×(5)	(7)=(3)+(6)
Panel A: Total costs to account for							
Work in process, beginning from Solution Exhibit 17-28B)	20	$23,000	$ 460,000	12	$10,000	$ 120,000	$ 580,000
Work done in current period only (from Solution Exhibit 17-28B)	80	$25,000	2,000,000	85	$11,000	935,000	2,935,000
To account for	100	$24,600*	2,460,000	97	$10,876.29†	1,055,000	$3,515,000
Panel B: Assignment of costs							
Complete and transferred out: (90 physical units)	90‡	$24,600	$2,214,000	90‡	$10,876.29	$ 978,866	$3,192,866
Work in process, ending (10 physical units)	10‡	$24,600	246,000	7‡	$10,876.29	76,134	322,134
Accounted for	100		$2,460,000	97		$1,055,000	$3,515,000

*Weighted-average cost per equivalent unit of direct materials = Total direct materials costs divided by total equivalent units of direct materials
$2,460,000 ÷ 100 = $24,600

†Weighted-average cost per equivalent unit of conversion costs = Total conversion costs divided by total equivalent units of conversion costs
$1,055,000 ÷ 97 = $10,876.29

‡From Solution Exhibit 17-30A.

17-32 (20 min.) **FIFO method.**

1.   The equivalent units of work done in the Assembly Department in October 2000 for direct materials and conversion costs are the same as in Problem 17-30 and are shown in Solution Exhibit 17-30A.

2.   The cost per equivalent unit of work done in the Assembly Department in October 2000 for direct materials and conversion costs are calculated in Problem 17-30 in Solution Exhibit 17-30B.

3.   Solution Exhibit 17-32 summarizes the total Assembly Department costs for October 2000, and assigns these costs to units completed (and transferred out) and units in ending work in process under the FIFO method.

The cost per equivalent unit of beginning inventory and of work done in the current period differ:

	Beginning Inventory	Work Done in Current Period
Direct materials	$23,000	$25,000
Conversion costs	$10,000	$11,000

The following table summarizes the costs assigned to units completed and those still in process under the weighted-average and FIFO process-costing methods for our example.

	Weighted Average (Solution Exhibit 17-30C)	FIFO (Solution Exhibit 17-32)	Difference
Cost of units completed and transferred out	$3,192,866	$3,188,000	−$4,866
Work in process, ending	322,134	327,000	+$4,866
Total costs accounted for	$3,515,000	$3,515,000	

The FIFO ending inventory is higher than the weighted-average ending inventory by $4,866. This is because, FIFO assumes that all the lower-cost prior-period units in work in process are the first to be completed and transferred out while ending work in process consists of only the higher-cost current-period units. The weighted-average method, however, smoothes out cost per equivalent unit by assuming that more of the higher-cost units are completed and transferred out, while some of the lower-cost units in beginning work in process are placed in ending work in process. Hence, in this case, the weighted-average method results in a higher cost of units completed and transferred out and a lower ending work-in-process inventory relative to FIFO.

17-32 (cont'd)

SOLUTION EXHIBIT 17-32

Step 4: Summarize Total Costs to Account For and Assign These Costs to Units Completed, and Units in Ending Work in Process Using the FIFO Method Testing Department of Global Defence Inc. for October 2000

	Direct Materials			Conversion Costs			Total Production Costs
	Equivalent Units (1)	Cost per Equivalent Unit (2)	Total Costs (3)=(1)×(2)	Equivalent Units (4)	Cost per Equivalent Unit (5)	Total Costs (6)=(4)×(5)	(7)=(3)+(6)
Panel A: Total costs to account for							
Work in process, beginning from Solution Exhibit 17-30B)	20	$23,000	$ 460,000	12	$10,000	$ 120,000	$ 580,000
Work done in current period only (from Solution Exhibit 17-30B)	80	$25,000	2,000,000	85	$11,000	935,000	2,935,000
To account for	100		2,460,000	97		$1,055,000	$3,515,000
Panel B: Assignment of costs							
Completed and transferred out: (90 physical units)							
Work in process, beginning (20 physical units)	20	$23,000	$460,000	12	$10,000	$ 120,000	$ 580,000
Work done in current period to complete beginning work in process	0*	$25,000	0	8†	$11,000	88,000	88,000
Total from beginning inventory	20		460,000	20		208,000	668,000
Started and completed (70 physical units)	70‡	$25,000	1,750,000	70‡	$11,000	770,000	2,520,000
Total completed and transferred out (90 physical units)	90		2,210,000	90		978,000	3,188,000
Work in process, ending (10 physical units)	10§	$25,000	250,000	7§	$11,000	77,000	327,000
Accounted for	100		$2,460,000	97		$1,055,000	$3,515,000

*Beginning work in process is 100% complete as to direct materials so zero equivalent units of direct materials need to be added to complete beginning work in process.
†Beginning work in process is 60% complete as to conversion costs, which equals 12 equivalent units of conversion costs. To complete the 20 physical units of beginning work in process, 8 (20 – 12) equivalent units of conversion costs need to be added.
‡90 total equivalent units completed and transferred out (Solution Exhibit 17-30) minus 20 equivalent units completed and transferred from beginning inventory equals 70 equivalent units.
§From Solution Exhibit 17-30A.

17-34 (30 min.) Transferred-in costs, FIFO costing.

1.   As explained in Problem 17-33, requirement 1, transferred-in costs are 100% complete and direct materials are 0% complete in both beginning and ending work in process inventory.

2.   The equivalent units of work done in October 2000 in the Testing Department for transferred-in costs, direct materials and conversion costs are exactly as in Solution Exhibit 17-33A.

3.   Solution Exhibit 17-34A calculates the cost per equivalent unit of beginning work in process and of work done in October 2000 in the Testing Department for transferred-in costs, direct materials, and conversion costs.

4.   Solution Exhibit 17-34B summarizes total Testing Department costs for October 2000, and assigns these costs to units completed and transferred out and to units in ending work in process using the FIFO method.

5.   Journal entries:
  i.   Work in Process—Testing Department   3,188,000
          Work in Process—Assembly Department   3,188,000
        Cost of goods completed and transferred out
          during October from the Assembly Dept. to
          the Testing Dept.

  ii.   Finished Goods   9,281,527
          Work in Process—Testing Department   9,281,527
        Cost of goods completed and transferred out
          during October from the Testing Department
          to Finished Goods inventory

17-34 (cont'd)

SOLUTION EXHIBIT 17-34A
Step 3: Compute Equivalent Unit Costs Under the FIFO Method
Testing Department of Global Defence Inc. for October 2000

	Transferred-in Costs	Direct Materials	Conversion Costs
Equivalent unit costs of beginning work in process			
Work in process, beginning (given)	$ 980,060	—	$ 331,800
Divide by equivalent units of beginning work in process (from Solution Exhibit 17-33A)	÷ 30	—	÷ 21
Cost per equivalent unit of beginning work in process	$ 32,668.67	—	$ 15,800
Equivalent unit costs of work done in current period only			
Costs added in current period (given)	$3,188,000	$3,885,000	$1,581,000
Divide by equivalent units of work done in current period (from Solution Exhibit 17-33A)	÷ 90	÷ 105	÷ 93
Cost per equivalent unit of work done in current period only	$35,422.22	$ 37,000	$ 17,000

17-34 (cont'd)

SOLUTION EXHIBIT 17-34B
Step 4: Summarize Total Costs to Account For and Assign These Costs to Units Completed, and Units in Ending Work in Process Using the FIFO Method
Testing Department of Global Defence Inc. for October 2000

	Transferred-in Costs			Direct Materials			Conversion Costs			Total Production Costs
	Equivalent Units (1)	Cost per Equivalent Unit (2)	Total Costs (3)=(1)×(2)	Equivalent Units (4)	Cost per Equivalent Unit (5)	Total Costs (6)=(4)×(5)	Equivalent Units (7)	Cost per Equivalent Unit (8)	Total Costs (9)=(7)×(8)	(10)=(3)+(6)+(9)
Panel A: Total Costs to Account for										
Work in process, beginning (from Solution Exhibit 17-34A)	30	$32,668.67	$ 980,050	0	— $	$ 0	21	$15,800	$ 331,800	$1,311,860
Work done in current period only (from Solution Exhibit 17-34A)			3,188,000			3,885,000			1,581,000	8,654,000
To account for	90 / 120	$35,422.22	$4,168,060	105 / 105	$37,000	3,885,000 / $3,885,000	93 / 114	$17,000	1,581,000 / $1,912,800	$9,965,860
Panel B: Assignment of Costs										
Completed and transferred out (105 physical units)										
Work in process, beginning (30 physical units)	30	$32,668.67	$ 980,060	0	— $	$ 0	21	$15,800	$ 331,800	$1,311,860
Work done in current period to complete beginning work in process	0*		0	30†	$37,000	1,110,000	9‡	$17,000	153,000	1,263,000
Total from beginning inventory	30		980,060	30		1,110,000	30		484,800	2,574,860
Started and completed (75 physical units)	75‖	$35,422:22	2,656,667	75‖	$37,000	2,775,000	75‖	$17,000	1,275,000	6,706,667
Total completed and transferred out (105 physical units)	105§		3,636,727	105§		3,885,000	105§		1,759,800	9,281,527
Work in process, ending (15 physical tons)	15§	$35,422.22	531,333	0§	$37,000	0	9§	$17,000	153,000	684,333
Accounted for	120		$4,168,060	105		$3,885,000	114		$1,912,800	$9,965,860

*Beginning work in process is 100% complete as to transferred-in costs so zero equivalent tons of transferred-in costs need to be added to complete beginning work in process.

†Beginning work in process is 0% complete as to direct materials, which equals 0 equivalent tons of direct materials. To complete the 30 physical tons of beginning work in process, 30 equivalent tons of direct materials need to be added.

‡Beginning work in process is 70% complete as to conversion costs, which equals 21 equivalent tons of conversion costs. To complete the 30 physical tons of beginning work in process, 9 (30 − 21) equivalent tons of conversion costs need to be added.

‖105 total equivalent tons completed and transferred out (Solution Exhibit 17-31A) minus 30 equivalent tons completed and transferred from beginning inventory equals 75 equivalent tons.

§From Solution Exhibit 17-33A.

17-36 (5-10 min.) **Journal entries.**

1. Work in Process—Forming Department   70,000
       Accounts Payable   70,000
   To record direct materials purchased and
      used in production during April

2. Work in Process—Forming Department   42,500
       Various Accounts   42,500
   To record Forming Department conversion
      costs for April

3. Work in Process—Finishing Department   104,000
       Work in Process—Forming Department   104,000
   To record cost of goods completed and transferred out
      in April from the Forming Department
      to the Finishing Department

Work in Process—Forming Department		
Beginning inventory, April 1	9,625	3. Transferred out to
1. Direct materials	70,000	Work in Process–finishing 104,000
2. Conversion costs	42,500	
Ending inventory, April 30	18,125	

17-38 (30 min.) **Transferred-in costs, weighted average.**

1.   Solution Exhibit 17-38A computes the equivalent units of work done in April 2000 in the Finishing Department for transferred-in costs, direct materials, and conversion costs.

        Solution Exhibit 17-38B calculates the cost per equivalent unit of beginning work in process and of work done in April 2000 in the Finishing Department for transferred-in costs, direct materials, and conversion costs.

        Solution Exhibit 17-38C summarizes total Finishing Department costs for April 2000, and assigns these costs to units completed and transferred out and to units in ending work in process using the weighted-average method.

2.   Journal entries:
        i.   Work in Process—Finishing Department   104,000
                    Work in Process—Forming Department   104,000
                Cost of goods completed and transferred out
                    during April from the Forming Department
                    to the Finishing Department

        ii.   Finished Goods   168,552
                    Work in Process—Finishing Department   168,552
                Cost of goods completed and transferred out
                    during April from the Finishing Department
                    to Finished Goods inventory

17-38 (cont'd)

SOLUTION EXHIBIT 17-38A
Steps 1 and 2: Summarize Output in Physical Units and Compute Equivalent Units
Finishing Department of Star Toys for April 2000

| | (Step 1) | (Step 2) Equivalent Units | | |
Flow of Production	Physical Units	Transferred-in Costs	Direct Materials	Conversion Costs
Completed and transferred out during current period	2,100	2,100	2,100	2,100
Add work in process, ending*	400			
(400 × 100%; 400 × 0%; 400 × 60%)		400	0	120
Total accounted for	2,500	2,500	2,100	2,220
Deduct work in process, beginning‖	500			
(500 × 100%; 500 × 0%; 500 × 60%)		500	0	300
Transferred in during current period	2,000			
Work done in current period only		2,000	2,100	1,920

*Degree of completion in this department: transferred-in costs, 100%; direct materials, 0%; conversion costs, 30%.

‖Degree of completion in this department: transferred-in costs, 100%; direct materials, 0%; conversion costs, 60%.

SOLUTION EXHIBIT 17-38B
Step 3: Compute Equivalent Unit Costs Under the Weighted-Average Method
Finishing Department of Star Toys for April 2000

	Transferred-in Costs	Direct Materials	Conversion Costs
Equivalent unit costs of beginning work in process			
Work in process, beginning (given)	$ 17,750	—	$ 7,250
Divide by equivalent units of beginning work in process (from Solution Exhibit 17-38A)	÷ 500	—	÷ 300
Cost per equivalent unit of beginning work in process	$ 35.50	—	$24.167
Equivalent unit costs of work done in current period only			
Costs added in current period (given)	$104,000	$23,100	$38,400
Divide by equivalent units of work done in current period (from Solution Exhibit 17-38A)	÷ 2,000	÷ 2,100	÷ 1,920
Cost per equivalent unit of work done in current period only	$ 52	$ 11	$ 20

17-23

17-38 (cont'd)

SOLUTION EXHIBIT 17-38C
Step 4: Summarize Total Costs to Account For and Assign These Costs to Units Completed, and Units in Ending Work in Process Using the Weighted-Average Method
Finishing Department of Star Toys for April 2000

	Transferred-in Costs			Direct Materials			Conversion Costs			Total Production Costs
	Equivalent Unit (1)	Cost per Equivalent Unit (2)	Total Costs (3)=(1)×(2)	Equivalent Unit (4)	Cost per Equivalent Unit (5)	Total Costs (6)=(4)×(5)	Equivalent Unit (7)	Cost per Equivalent Unit (8)	Total Costs (9)=(7)×(8)	(10)= (3)+(6)+(9)
Panel A: Total Costs to Account for:										
Work in process, beginning (from Solution Exhibit 17-38B)	500	$35.50	$ 17,750	0	—	$ 0	300	$24.167	$ 7,250	$ 25,000
Work done in current period only (from Solution Exhibit 17-38B)	2,000	$52.00	104,000	2,100	$11	23,100	1,920	$20	38,400	165,500
To account for	2,500	$48.70*	$121,750	2,100	$11†	$23,100	2,220	$20.563‡	$45,650	$190,500
Panel B: Assignment of Costs										
Completed and transferred out: (2,100 physical units)	2,100**	$48.70	$102,270	2,100**	$11	$23,100	2,100**	$20.563	$43,182	$168,552
Work in process, ending (400 physical units)	400**	$48.70	19,480	0**	—	0	120**	$20.563	2,468	21,948
Accounted for	2,500		$121,750	2,100		$23,100	2,220		$45,650	$190,500

*Weighted-average cost per equivalent unit of transferred-in costs = Total transferred-in costs divided by total equivalent units of transferred-in costs
 = $121,750 ÷ 2,500 = $48.70
†Weighted average costs per equivalent unit of direct materials = Total direct materials costs divided by total equivalent units of direct materials
 = $23,100 ÷ 2,100 = $11.
‡Weighted-average cost per equivalent unit of conversion costs = Total conversion costs divided by total equivalent units of conversion costs
 = $45,650 ÷ 2,220 = $20.563
*From Exhibit 17-38A.

17-40 (45 min.) **Transferred-in costs, weighted average and FIFO.**

1.   Solution Exhibit 17-40A computes the equivalent units of work done in week 37 in the Drying and Packaging Department for transferred-in costs, direct materials, and conversion costs.

2.   Solution Exhibit 17-40B calculates the cost per equivalent unit of beginning work in process and of work done in week 37 in the Drying and Packaging Department for transferred-in costs direct materials, and conversion costs.

     Solution Exhibit 17-40C summarizes total drying and packaging Department costs for week 37, and assigns these costs to units completed and transferred out and to units in ending work in process using the weighted-average method.

3.   Solution Exhibit 17-40D calculates the cost per equivalent unit of beginning work in process and of work done in week 37 in the Drying and Packaging Department for transferred-in costs, direct materials, and conversion costs.

     Solution Exhibit 17-40E summarizes total Drying and Packaging Department costs for week 37, and assigns these costs to units completed and transferred out and to units in ending work in process using the FIFO method.

17-40 (cont'd)

SOLUTION EXHIBIT 17-40A

Steps 1 and 2: Summarize Output in Physical Units and Compute Equivalent Units
Drying and Packaging Department of Frito-Lay Inc. for Week 37

| | (Step 1) | (Step 2) Equivalent Units | | |
Flow of Production	Physical Units	Transferred-in Costs	Direct Materials	Conversion Costs
Completed and transferred out during current period	5,250	5,250	5,250	5,250
Add work in process, ending*	1,000			
(1,000 × 100%; 1,000 × 0%;1,000 × 40%)		1,000	0	400
Total accounted for	6,250	6,250	5,250	5,650
Deduct work in process, beginning ‖	1,250			
(1,250 × 100%; 1,250 × 0%; 1,250 × 80%)		1,250	0	1,000
Transferred in during current period	5,000			
Work done in current period only		5,000	5,250	4,650

*Degree of completion in this department: transferred-in costs, 100%; direct materials, 0%; conversion costs, 40%.

‖Degree of completion in this department: transferred-in costs, 100%; direct materials, 0%; conversion costs, 80%.

SOLUTION EXHIBIT 17-40B

Step 3: Compute Equivalent Unit Costs Under the Weighted-Average Method
Drying and Packaging Department of Frito-Lay Inc. for Week 37

	Transferred-in Costs	Direct Materials	Conversion Costs
Equivalent unit costs of beginning work in process			
Work in process, beginning (given)	$29,000	—	$ 9,060
Divide by equivalent units of beginning work in process (from Solution Exhibit 17-40A)	÷ 1,250	—	÷ 1,000
Cost per equivalent unit of beginning work in process	$ 23.20	—	$ 9.06
Equivalent unit costs of work done in current period only			
Costs added in current period (given)	$96,000	$25,200	$38,400
Divide by equivalent units of work done in current period (from Solution Exhibit 17-40A)	÷ 5,000	÷ 5,250	÷ 4,650
Cost per equivalent unit of work done in current period only	$ 19.20	$ 4.80	$ 8.258

17-26

17-40 (cont'd)

SOLUTION EXHIBIT 17-40C
Step 4: Summarize Total Costs to Account For and Assign These Costs to Units Completed, and Units in Ending Work in Process Using the Weighted-Average Method Drying and Packaging Department of Frito-Lay for Week 37

	Transferred-in Costs			Direct Materials			Conversion Costs			Total Production Costs
	Equivalent Units (1)	Cost per Equivalent Unit (2)	Total Costs (3)=(1)×(2)	Equivalent Units (4)	Cost per Equivalent Unit (5)	Total Costs (6)=(4)×(5)	Equivalent Units (7)	Cost per Equivalent Unit (8)	Total Costs (9)=(7)×(8)	Total Production Costs (10)= (3)+(6)+(9)
Panel A: Total Costs to Account for										
Work in process, beginning (from Solution Exhibit 17-40B)	1,250	$23.20	$ 29,000	0	—	$ 0	1,000	$9.060	$ 9,060	38,060
Work done in current period only (from Solution Exhibit 17-40B)	5,000	$19.20	96,000	5,250	$4.80	25,200	4,650	$8.258	38,400	159,600
To account for	6,250	$20.00*	$125,000	5,250	$4.80†	$25,200	5,650	$8.400‡	$47,460	$197,660
Panel B: Assignment of Costs										
Completed and transferred out: (5,250 physical units)	5,250**	$20.00	$105,000	5,250**	$4.80	$25,200	5,250**	$8.400	$44,100	$174,300
Work in process, ending (1,000 physical units)	1,000**	$20.00	20,000	0**	—	0	400**	$8.400	3,360	23,360
Accounted for	6,250		$125,000	5,250		$25,200	5,650		$47,460	$197,660

*Weighted-average cost per equivalent unit of transferred-in costs = Total transferred-in costs divided by total equivalent units of transferred-in costs = $125,000 ÷ 6,250 = $20.

†Weighted-average costs per equivalent unit of direct materials = Total direct materials costs divided by total equivalent units of direct materials = $25,200 ÷ 5,250 = $4.80.

‡Weighted-average cost per equivalent unit of conversion costs = Total conversion costs divided by total equivalent units of conversion costs = $47,460 ÷ 5,650 = $8.40.
**From Solution Exhibit 17-40A.

17-40 (cont'd)

SOLUTION EXHIBIT 17-40D
Step 3: Compute Equivalent Unit Costs Under the FIFO Method
Drying and Packaging Department of Frito-Lay Inc. for Week 37

	Transferred-in Costs	Direct Materials	Conversion Costs
Equivalent unit costs of beginning work in process			
Work in process, beginning (given)	$28,920	—	$ 9,060
Divide by equivalent units of beginning work in process (from Solution Exhibit 17-40A)	÷ 1,250	—	÷ 1,000
Cost per equivalent unit of beginning work in process	$23.136	—	$ 9.06
Equivalent unit costs of work done in current period only			
Costs added in current period (given)	$94,000	$25,200	$38,400
Divide by equivalent units of work done in current period (from Solution Exhibit 17-40A)	÷ 5,000	÷ 5,250	÷ 4,650
Cost per equivalent unit of work done in current period only	$ 18.80	$ 4.80	$ 8.258

17-40 (cont'd)

SOLUTION EXHIBIT 17-40E
Step 4: Summarize Total Costs to Account For and Assign These Costs to Units Completed, and Units in Ending Work in Process Using the FIFO Method Drying and Packaging Department of Frito-Lay for Week 37

	Transferred-in Costs			Direct Materials			Conversion Costs			Total Production Costs
	Equivalent Units (1)	Cost per Equivalent Unit (2)	Total Costs (3)=(1)×(2)	Equivalent Units (4)	Cost per Equivalent Unit (5)	Total Costs (6)=(4)×(5)	Equivalent Units (7)	Cost per Equivalent Unit (8)	Total Costs (9)=(7)×(8)	(10)= (3)+(6)+(9)
Panel A: Total Costs to Account for										
Work in process, beginning (from Solution Exhibit 17-40D)	1,250	$23.18	$ 28,920	0	—	$ 0	1,000	$9.06	$ 9,060	$37,980
Work done in current period only (from Solution Exhibit 17-40D)	5,000	$18.80	94,000	5,250	$4.80	25,200	4,650	$8.258	38,400	157,600
To account for	6,250		$122,920	5,250		$25,200	5,650		$47,460	$195,580
Panel B: Assignment of Costs										
Completed and transferred out: (5,250 physical units)										
Work in process, beginning (1,250 physical units)	1,250	$23.13	$ 28,920	0	—	$ 0	1,000	$9.06	$ 9,060	$ 37,980
Work done in current period to complete beginning work in process	0*		0	1,250†	$4.80	6,000	250‡	$8.258	2,065	8,065
Total from beginning inventory	1,250		28,920	1,250		6,000	1,250		11,125	46,045
Started and completed (4,000 physical units)	4,000"	$18.80	75,200	4,000"	$4.80	19,200	4,000"	$8.258	33,032	127,432
Total completed and transferred out (5,250 physical units)	5,250§		104,120	5,250§		25,200	5,250§		44,157	173,477
Work in process, ending (1,000 physical units)	1,000§	$18.80	18,800	0§		0	400§	$8.258	3,303	22,103
Accounted for	6,250		$122,920	5,250		$25,200	5,650		$47,460	$195,580

*Beginning work in process is 100% complete as to transferred-in costs so zero equivalent units of transferred-in costs need to be added to complete beginning work in process.

†Beginning work in process is 0% complete as to direct materials, which equals 0 equivalent units of direct materials. To complete the 1,250 physical units of beginning work in process, 1,250 equivalent units of direct materials need to be added.

‡Beginning work in process is 80% complete as to conversion costs, which equals 1,000 equivalent units of conversion costs. To complete the 1,250 physical units of beginning work in process, 250 (1,250 – 1,000) equivalent units of conversion costs need to be added.

"5,250 total equivalent units completed and transferred out (Solution Exhibit 17-40A) minus 1,250 equivalent units completed and transferred from beginning inventory equals 4,000 equivalent units.

§From Solution Exhibit 17-40A.

17-42 (15-30 min.) **Operation costing, equivalent units.**

1.   Materials and conversion costs of each operation, the total units produced, and the material and conversion cost per unit for the month of May are as follows:

	Extrusion	Form	Trim	Finish
Units produced	16,000	11,000	5,000	2,000
Materials costs	$192,000	$ 44,000	$15,000	$12,000
Materials cost per unit	12.00	4.00	3.00	6.00
Conversion costs*	392,000	132,000	69,000	42,000
Conversion cost per unit	24.50	12.00	13.80	21.00

*Direct manufacturing labour and manufacturing overhead.

The unit cost and total costs in May for each product are as follows:

Cost Elements	Plastic Sheets	Standard Model	Deluxe Model	Executive Model
Extrusion materials (EM)	$ 12.00	$ 12.00	$ 12.00	$ 12.00
Form materials (FM)	–	4.00	4.00	4.00
Trim materials (TM)	–	–	3.00	3.00
Finish materials	–	–	–	6.00
Extrusion conversion (EC)	24.50	24.50	24.50	24.50
Form conversion (FC)	–	12.00	12.00	12.00
Trim conversion (TC)	–	–	13.80	13.80
Finish conversion	–	–	–	21.00
Total unit cost	$ 36.50	$ 52.50	$ 69.30	$ 96.30
Multiply by units produced	× 5,000	× 6,000	× 3,000	× 2,000
Total product costs	$182,500	$315,000	$207,900	$192,600

17-42 (cont'd)

2.

	Equivalent Units			
	Materials		Conversion Costs	
Entering trim operation:	Percent Complete	Quantity	Percent Complete	Quantity
2,000 Deluxe units	100	2,000	100	2,000
1,000 Deluxe units	100	1,000	60	600
2,000 Executive units	100	2,000	100	2,000
Total equivalent units		5,000		4,600

Conversion cost per equivalent unit in trim operation:
($30,000 + $39,000) ÷ 4,600 units = $15 per unit

Materials cost per equivalent unit in trim operation (as before)
$15,000 ÷ 5,000 units = $3 per unit

	Unit Cost	Equivalent Units	Total Costs
Deluxe model work-in-process costs at the trim operation			
Extrusion material (100% complete when transferred in)	$12.00	1,000	$12,000
Extrusion conversion (100% complete when transferred in)	24.50	1,000	24,500
Form material (100% complete when transferred in)	4.00	1,000	4,000
Form conversion (100% complete when transferred in)	12.00	1,000	12,000
Trim material (100% complete)	3.00	1,000	3,000
Trim conversion (60% complete)	15.00	600	9,000
Work-in-process costs	$70.50		$64,500

CHAPTER 18
SPOILAGE, REWORK, AND SCRAP

18-2   Spoilage—unacceptable units of production that are discarded or sold for net disposal proceeds.

Reworked units—unacceptable units of production that are subsequently reworked and sold as acceptable finished goods.

Scrap—product that has minimal (frequently zero) sales value compared with the sales value of the main or joint product(s).

18-4   Abnormal spoilage is spoilage that is not expected to arise under efficient operating conditions. Costs of abnormal spoilage are "lost costs," measures of inefficiency that should be written off directly as losses for the accounting period.

18-6   Normal spoilage typically is expressed as a percentage of good units passing the inspection point. Given actual spoiled units, we infer abnormal spoilage as follows:

Abnormal spoilage = Actual spoilage – Normal spoilage

18-8   Yes. Normal spoilage rates should be computed from the good output or from the <u>normal</u> input, not the <u>total</u> input. Normal spoilage is a given percentage of a certain output base. This base should never include abnormal spoilage, which is included in total input. Abnormal spoilage does not vary in direct proportion to units produced, and to include it would cause the normal spoilage count to fluctuate irregularly but not vary in direct proportion to the output base.

18-10   No. If abnormal spoilage is detected at a different point in the production cycle than normal spoilage, then unit costs would differ. If, however normal and abnormal spoilage are detected at the same point in the production cycle, their unit costs would be the same.

18-12   No. Unless there are special reasons for charging rework to jobs that contained the bad units, the costs of extra materials, labour, and so on are usually charged to manufacturing overhead and allocated to all jobs.

18-14   A company is justified in inventorying scrap when its estimated net realizable value is significant and the time between storing it and selling or reusing it may be quite long.

18-16 (5-10 min.) **Normal and abnormal spoilage in units.**

1. Total spoiled units   12,000
    Normal spoilage in units 5% × 132,000   6,600
    Abnormal spoilage in units   5,400

2. Abnormal spoilage, 5,400 × $10 $ 54,000
    Normal spoilage, 6,600 × $10   66,000
    Potential savings, 12,000 × $10 $120,000

Regardless of the targeted normal spoilage, abnormal spoilage is non-recurring and avoidable. The targeted normal spoilage rate is subject to change. Many companies have reduced their spoilage to almost zero, which would realize all potential savings. Of course, zero spoilage usually means higher-quality products, more customer satisfaction, more employee satisfaction, and various effects on nonmanufacturing (for example, purchasing) costs of direct materials.

18-18 (25 min.) **FIFO method.**

1.   The calculation of the cost per equivalent unit of beginning work in process and of work done in the current period for direct materials and conversion costs is the same as in Solution Exhibit 18-17A, since this calculation does not depend on the specific weighted-average or FIFO cost-flow assumption.

2.   Solution Exhibit 18-18 summarizes the total costs to account for, and assigns these costs to units completed, normal spoilage, abnormal spoilage and ending work in process using the FIFO method.

3.   From Solution Exhibit 18-18, under the FIFO method,

$$\text{Cost of a good unit completed (and transferred out)} = \frac{\text{Total production costs of good units transferred out}}{\text{Number of good units completed}}$$

$$= \frac{\$423,950}{20,000} = \$21.1975$$

Note that this cost is higher than the cost per equivalent unit of $18.75 (direct materials, $8.25 and conversion costs, $10.50). Why? Because the cost of good units completed and transferred out also includes the cost of normal spoilage of 15%.

18-18 (cont'd)

SOLUTION EXHIBIT 18-18

Step 4: Summarize Total Costs to Account For, and Assign These Costs to, Units Completed, Units Spoiled and Units in Ending Work in Process Using the FIFO Method
Molding Department of Anderson Plastics for April 2000

	Direct Materials			Conversion Costs			Total Production Costs
	Equivalent Units (1)	Cost per Equivalent Unit (2)	Total Costs (3)=(1)×(2)	Equivalent Units (4)	Cost per Equivalent Unit (5)	Total Costs (6)=(4)×(5)	(7)=(3)+(6)
Panel A: Total Costs to Account For							
Work in process, beginning (from Solution Exhibit 18-17A)	15,000	$8.00	$120,000	14,000	$10.00	$140,000	$260,000
Work done in current period only (from Solution Exhibit 18-17A)	25,000	$8.40	210,000	28,000	$10.75	301,000	511,000
To account for	40,000		$330,000	42,000		$441,000	$771,000
Panel B: Assignment of Costs							
Good units completed and transferred out (20,000 physical units):							
Work in process, beginning	15,000	$8.00	$120,000	14,000	$10.00	$140,000	$260,000
Work done in current period to complete beginning work in process	0*	$8.40	0	1,000†	$10.75	10,750	10,750
Total from beginning inventory before normal spoilage	15,000		120,000	15,000		150,750	270,750
Started and completed before normal spoilage (5,000 units)	5,000‡	$8.40	42,000	5,000‡	$10.75	53,750	95,750
Normal spoilage (15% of good units transferred out = 3,000)	3,000	$8.40	25,200	3,000	$10.75	32,250	57,450
(A) Total costs of good units transferred out			187,200			236,750	423,950
(B) Abnormal spoilage (4,000 – normal spoilage)	1,000	$8.40	8,400	1,000	$10.75	10,750	19,150
(C) Work in process, ending (20,000 units)	16,000	$8.40	134,400	18,000	$10.75	193,500	327,900
(A)+(B)+(C) Accounted for	40,000		$330,000	42,000		$441,000	$771,000

*Beginning work in process is 100% complete as to direct materials so zero equivalent units of direct materials need to be added to complete beginning work in process.

†Beginning work in process is 14/15 complete, as to conversion costs which equals 14,000 equivalent units of conversion costs. To complete the 15,000 physical units of beginning work in process, 1,000 (15,000 – 14,000) equivalent units of conversion costs need to be added.

‡20,000 total equivalent units completed and transferred out (given) minus 15,000 equivalent units completed and transferred out from beginning inventory equal to 5,000 equivalent units.

18-20 (20 min.) Equivalent units, equivalent unit costs, spoilage.

1.   Solution Exhibit 18-20A calculates equivalent units of work done in the current period for direct materials and conversion costs.

2.   Solution Exhibit 18-20B calculates cost per equivalent unit of beginning work in process and of work done in the current period for direct materials and conversion costs.

SOLUTION EXHIBIT 18-20A

Step 1 and Step 2: Summarize Output in Physical Units and Compute Equivalent Units, Gray Manufacturing Company for November 2000

| | (Step 1) | (Step 2) Equivalent Units | |
Flow of Production	Physical Units	Direct Materials	Conversion Costs
Good units completed and transferred out during November 2000	9,000	9,000	9,000
Normal spoilage[†]	100		
100 × 100%; 100 × 100%		100	100
Abnormal spoilage[‡]	50		
50 × 100%; 50 × 100%		50	50
Work in process, ending[§]	2,000		
2,000 × 100%; 2,000 × 30%		2,000	600
Total accounted for	11,150	11,150	9,750
Deduct work in process, beginning[≠]			
1,000 × 100%; 1,000 × 50%	1,000	1,000	500
Started during current period	10,150		
Work done in current period only		10,150	9,250

[†] Degree of completion of normal spoilage: direct materials, 100%; conversion costs, 100%.
[‡] Degree of completion of abnormal spoilage: direct materials, 100%; conversion costs, 100%.
[§] Degree of completion of ending work in process: direct materials, 100%; conversion costs, 30%.
[≠] Degree of completion of beginning work in process: direct materials, 100%; conversion costs, 50%.

18-20 (cont'd)

SOLUTION EXHIBIT 18-20B
Step 3: Compute Equivalent Unit Costs:
Gray Manufacturing Company Inc. for November 2000

	Direct Materials	Conversion Costs
<u>Equivalent unit costs of beginning work in process</u>		
Work in process, beginning (given)	$ 1,300	$ 1,250
Divide by equivalent units in beginning work in process (from Solution Exhibit 18-20A)	÷1,000	÷ 500
Cost per equivalent unit of beginning work in process	$ 1.30	$ 2.50
<u>Equivalent unit costs of work done in current period only</u>		
Costs added in current period (given)	$12,180	$27,750
Divide by equivalent units of work done in current period (from Solution Exhibit 18-20A)	÷10,150	÷ 9,250
Costs per equivalent unit of work done in current period only	$ 1.20	$ 3.00

18-22 (15 min.) **FIFO method, spoilage, equivalent units.**

Solution Exhibit 18-22 calculates equivalent units of work done in the current period for direct materials and conversion costs and the costs per equivalent unit for direct materials and conversion costs.

SOLUTION EXHIBIT 18-22
Summarize Output in Physical Units and Compute Equivalent Units.
First-in, First-out (FIFO) Method of Process Costing with Spoilage
Gray Manufacturing Company for November 2000

Flow of Production	(Step 1) Physical Units	(Step 2) Equivalent Units	
		Direct Materials	Conversion Costs
Work in process, beginning (given)	1,000		
Started during current period (given)	10,150		
To account for	11,150		
Good units completed and transferred out during current period:			
From beginning work in process[¹¹]	1,000		
1,000 × (100% −100%); 1,000 × (100% − 50%)		0	500
Started and completed	8,000[#]		
8,000 × 100%; 8,000 × 100%		8,000	8,000
Normal spoilage*	100		
100 × 100%; 100 × 100%		100	100
Abnormal spoilage[†]	50		
50 × 100%; 50 × 100%		50	50
Work in process, ending[‡]	2,000		
2,000 × 100%; 2,000 × 30%		2,000	600
	11,150	10,150	9,250
Accounted for			
Work done in current period only			

[¹¹]Degree of completion in this department: direct materials, 100%; conversion costs, 50%.
[#]9,000 physical units completed and transferred out minus 1,000 physical units completed and transferred out from beginning work-in-process inventory.
*Degree of completion of normal spoilage in this department: direct materials, 100%; conversion costs, 100%.
[†]Degree of completion of abnormal spoilage in this department: direct materials, 100%; conversion costs, 100%.
[‡]Degree of completion in this department: direct materials, 100%; conversion costs, 30%.

Cost of direct materials	$12,180
Equivalent units	10,150
Cost per equivalent unit	$1.20
Cost of conversion costs	$27,750
Equivalent units	9,250
Cost per equivalent unit	$3.00

18-24 (25 min.) **Weighted-Average Method, spoilage**

1.   Solution Exhibit 18-24A calculates the equivalent units of work done for each cost element in September 2000.

2.   Solution Exhibit 18-24B presents computations of the cost per equivalent unit of beginning inventory and of work done in the current period for each cost element under the weighted-average method.

3.   Solution Exhibit 18-24C presents a summary of total costs to account for and assigns these costs to units completed, normal spoilage, abnormal spoilage, and to units in ending work in process using the weighted-average method.

18-24 (cont'd)

SOLUTION EXHIBIT 18-24A
Steps 1 and 2: Summarize Output in Physical Units and Compute Equivalent Units
Microchip Department of Superchip Company for September 2000

	(Step 1) Physical Units	(Step 2) Equivalent Units	
Flow of Production		Direct Materials	Conversion Costs
Good units completed and transferred out during current period	1,400	1,400	1,400
Normal spoilage[†]	210		
210 × 100%; 210 × 100%		210	210
Abnormal spoilage[‡]	190		
190 × 100%; 190 × 100%		190	190
Work in process, ending[§]	300		
300 ×100%; 300 × 40%		300	120
Total accounted for	2,100	2,100	1,920
Deduct work in process, beginning[≠]	400		
400 × 100%; 400 × 30%		400	120
Started during current period	1,700		
Work done in current period only		1,700	1,800

[†] Normal spoilage is 15% of good units transferred out: 15% × 1,400 = 210 units; Degree of completion of normal spoilage in this department: direct materials, 100%; conversion costs, 100%.

[‡] Abnormal spoilage = Actual spoilage – Normal spoilage = 400 – 210 = 190 units; Degree of completion of abnormal spoilage in this department: direct materials, 100%; conversion costs, 100%.

[§] Degree of completion in this department: direct materials, 100%; conversion costs, 40%.

[≠] Degree of completion in this department: direct materials, 100%; conversion costs, 30%.

18-24 (cont'd)

SOLUTION EXHIBIT 18-24B
Step 3: Compute Equivalent Unit Costs:
Microchip Department of Superchip Company for September 2000

	Direct Materials	Conversion Costs
<u>Equivalent unit costs of beginning work in process</u>		
Work in process, beginning (given)	$ 64,000	$ 10,200
Divide by equivalent units in beginning work in process (from Solution Exhibit 18-24A)	÷ 400	÷ 120
Cost per equivalent unit of beginning work in process	$ 160	$ 85
<u>Equivalent unit costs of work done in current period only</u>		
Costs added in current period (given)	$378,000	$153,600
Divide by equivalent units of work done in current period (from Solution Exhibit 18-24A)	÷ 1,700	÷ 1,800
Costs per equivalent unit of work done in current period only	$ 222.35	$ 85.33

18-24 (cont'd)

SOLUTION EXHIBIT 18-24C
Step 4: Summarize Total Costs to Account For and Assign These Costs to Units Completed, Units Spoiled and Units in Ending Work in Process Using the Weighted-Average Method Microchip Department of Superchip for September 2000

	Direct Materials			Conversion Costs			Total Production Costs
	Equivalent Units (1)	Cost per Equivalent Unit (2)	Total Costs (3)=(1)×(2)	Equivalent Units (4)	Cost per Equivalent Unit (5)	Total Costs (6)=(4)×(5)	(7)=(3)+(6)
Panel A: Total Costs to Account For							
Work in process, beginning (from Solution Exhibit 18-24B)	400	$160	$ 64,000	120	$85	$ 10,200	$ 74,200
Work done in current period only (from Solution Exhibit 18-24B)	1,700	$222.35	378,000	1,800	$85.33	153,600	531,600
To account for	2,100	$210.476*	$442,000	1,920	$85.3125†	$163,800	$605,800
Panel B: Assignment of costs							
Good units completed and transferred out (1,400 units):							
Costs before adding normal spoilage	1,400‡	$210.476	$294,667	1,400‡	$85.3125	$119,437	$414,104
Normal spoilage (15% of good units)	210‡	$210.476	44,200	210‡	$85.3125	17,916	62,116
(A) Total costs of good units transferred out			338,867			137,353	476,220
(B) Abnormal spoilage (4,000 − normal spoilage)	190‡	$210.476	39,990	190‡	$85.3125	16,209	56,199
(C) Work in process, ending	300‡	$210.476	63,143	120‡	$85.3125	10,238	73,381
(A)+(B)+(C) Accounted for	2,100		$442,000	1,920		$163,800	$605,800

*Weighted-average cost per equivalent unit of direct materials = Total costs of direct materials divided by total equivalent units of direct materials
= 442,000 ÷ 2,100 = $210.4762

†Weighted-average cost per equivalent unit of conversion costs = Total conversion costs divided by total equivalent units of conversion costs
= 163,800 ÷ 1,920 = $85.3125

‡From Solution Exhibit 18-24A.

18-26 (30 min.) **Standard costing method, spoilage.**

1.   Solution Exhibit 18-24A shows the computation of the equivalent units of work done in September 2000 for direct materials (1,700 units) and conversion costs (1,800 units).

2.   The direct materials cost per equivalent unit of beginning work in process and of work done in September 2000 is the standard cost of $205 given in the problem.

The conversion cost per equivalent of beginning work in process and of work done in September 2000 is the standard cost of $80 given in the problem.

3.   Solution Exhibit 18-26 summarizes the total costs to account for, and assigns these costs to units completed, normal spoilage, abnormal spoilage and ending work in process using the standard costing method.

18-26 (cont'd)

SOLUTION EXHIBIT 18-26
Step 4: Summarize Total Costs to Account For and Assign These Costs to Units Completed, Units Spoiled and Units in Ending Work in Process Using Standard Costs
Microchip Department of Superchip for September 2000

		Direct Materials			Conversion Costs			Total Production Costs
		Equivalent Units (Solution Exhibit 18-24A) (1)	Cost per Equivalent Unit (2)	Total Costs (3)=(1)×(2)	Equivalent Units (Solution Exhibit 18-24A) (4)	Cost per Equivalent Unit (5)	Total Costs (6)=(4)×(5)	(7)=(3)+(6)
Panel A:	**Total Costs to Account For**							
	Work in process, beginning	400	$205	$ 82,000	120	$80	$ 9,600	$ 91,600
	Work done in current period only	1,700	$205	348,500	1,800	$80	144,000	574,500
	To account for	2,100	$205	$430,500	1,920	$80	$153,600	$584,100
Panel B:	**Assignment of Costs**							
	Good units completed and transferred out (1,400 units):							
	Costs before adding normal spoilage	1,400	$205	$287,000	1,400	$80	$112,000	$399,000
	Normal spoilage (15% of good units)	210	$205	43,050	210	$80	16,800	59,850
(A)	Total costs of good units transferred out			330,050			128,800	458,850
(B)	Abnormal spoilage (400 – normal spoilage)	190	$205	38,950	190	$80	15,200	54,150
(C)	Work in process, ending	300	$205	61,500	120	$80	9,600	71,100
(A)+(B)+(C)	Accounted for	2,100		$430,500	1,920		$153,600	$584,100

18-28 (15 min.) **Reworked units, costs of rework.**

1. The two alternative approaches to accounting for the materials costs of reworked units are:
    (a) To charge the costs of rework to the current period as a separate expense item. This approach would highlight to White Goods the costs of the supplier problem.
    (b) To charge the costs of the rework to manufacturing overhead.

2. The $50 tumbler cost is the cost of the actual tumblers included in the washing machines. The $44 tumbler units from the new supplier units were never used in any washing machine and that supplier is now bankrupt.

3. The total costs of rework due to the defective tumbler units include:
    (a) The labour and other conversion costs spent on substituting the new tumbler units.
    (b) The costs of any extra negotiations to obtain the replacement tumbler units.
    (c) Any higher price the existing supplier may have charged to do a rush order for the replacement tumbler units.

18-30 (30 min.) **Weighted-average method, spoilage.**

Solution Exhibit 18-30A calculates the equivalent units of work done for each cost element; Solution Exhibit 18-30B presents computations of the cost per equivalent unit of beginning inventory and of work done in the current period for each cost element under the weighted-average method; Solution Exhibit 18-30C presents a summary of total costs to account for and assigns these costs to units completed, normal spoilage, abnormal spoilage, and to units in ending work in process using the weighted-average method.

SOLUTION EXHIBIT 18-30A
Steps 1 and 2: Summarize Output in Physical Units and Compute Equivalent Units
Cleaning Department of Alston Company for May

		(Step 2)	
	(Step 1)	Equivalent Units	
Flow of Production	Physical Units	Direct Materials	Conversion Costs
Good units completed and transferred out during current period	7,400	7,400	7,400
Normal spoilage[†]	740		
740 × 100%; 740 × 100%		740	740
Abnormal spoilage[‡]	260		
260 × 100%; 260 × 100%		260	260
Work in process, ending[§]	1,600		
1,600 ×100%; 1,600 × 25%		1,600	400
Total accounted for	10,000	10,000	8,800
Deduct work in process, beginning[≠]	1,000		
1,000 × 100%; 1,000 × 80%		1,000	800
Started during current period	9,000		
Work done in current period only		9,000	8,000

[†] Normal spoilage is 10% of good units transferred out: 10% × 7,400 = 740 units; Degree of completion of normal spoilage in this department: direct materials, 100%; conversion costs, 100%.

[‡] Degree of completion of abnormal spoilage in this department: direct materials, 100%; conversion costs, 100%.

[§] Degree of completion in this department: direct materials, 100%; conversion costs, 25%.

[≠] Degree of completion in this department: direct materials, 100%; conversion costs, 80%.

18-30 (cont'd)

Step 3: Compute Equivalent Unit Costs:
Cleaning Department of Alston Company for May

	Direct Materials	Conversion Costs
Equivalent unit costs of beginning work in process		
Work in process, beginning (given)	$1,000	$ 800
Divide by equivalent units in beginning work in process (from Solution Exhibit 18-30A)	÷1,000	÷ 800
Cost per equivalent unit of beginning work in process	$ 1	$ 1
Equivalent unit costs of work done in current period only		
Costs added in current period (given)	$9,000	$8,000
Divide by equivalent units of work done in current period (from Solution Exhibit 18-30A)	÷9,000	÷8,000
Costs per equivalent unit of work done in current period only	$ 1	$ 1

18-30 (cont'd)

SOLUTION EXHIBIT 18-30C

Step 4: Summarize Total Costs to Account For, and Assign These Costs to Units Completed, Units Spoiled and Units in Ending Work in Process Using the Weighted-Average Method Cleaning Department of Alston Company for May

	Direct Materials			Conversion Costs			Total Production Costs
	Equivalent Units (1)	Cost per Equivalent Unit (2)	Total Costs (3)=(1)×(2)	Equivalent Units (4)	Cost per Equivalent Unit (5)	Total Costs (6)=(4)×(5)	(7)=(3)+(6)
Panel A: Total Costs to Account For							
Work in process, beginning							
(from Solution Exhibit 18-30B)	1,000	$1	$ 1,000	800	$1	$ 800	$ 1,800
Work done in current period only							
(from Solution Exhibit 18-30B)	9,000		9,000	8,000		8,000	17,000
To account for	10,000	$1*	$10,000	8,800	$1†	$8,800	$18,800
Panel B: Assignment of costs							
Good units completed and transferred out							
(7,400 units):							
Costs before adding normal spoilage	7,400‡	$1	$ 7,400	7,400‡	$1	$7,400	$14,800
Normal spoilage	740‡	$1	740	740‡	$1	740	1,480
(A) Total costs of good units transferred out			8,140			8,140	16,280
(B) Abnormal spoilage	260‡	$1	260	260‡	$1	260	520
(C) Work in process, ending	1,600‡	$1	1,600	400‡	$1	400	2,000
(A)+(B)+(C) Accounted for	10,000		$10,000	8,800		$8,800	$18,800

*Weighted-average cost per equivalent unit of direct materials = Total costs of direct materials divided by total equivalent units of direct materials
= $10,000 ÷ 10,000 = $1.

†Weighted-average cost per equivalent unit of conversion costs = Total conversion costs divided by total equivalent units of conversion costs
= $8,800 ÷ 8,800 = $1.

‡From Solution Exhibit 18-30A.

18-32 (35 min.) Weighted-average method, Milling Department.

Solution Exhibit 18-32A calculates the equivalent units of work done for each cost element; Solution Exhibit 18-32B presents computations of the cost per equivalent unit of beginning inventory and of work done in the current period for each cost element under the weighted-average method; Solution Exhibit 18-32C presents a summary of total costs to account for and assigns these costs to units completed, normal spoilage, abnormal spoilage, and to units in ending work in process using the weighted-average method.

SOLUTION EXHIBIT 18-32A
Steps 1 and 2: Summarize Output in Physical Units and Compute Equivalent Units
Milling Department of Alston Company for May

| | (Step 1) | (Step 2) Equivalent Units | | |
| | Physical | | | |
Flow of Production	Units	Transferred-in Costs	Direct Materials	Conversion Costs
Good units completed and transferred out during current period	6,000	6,000	6,000	6,000
Normal spoilage[†]	300			
300 × 100%; 300 × 100%; 300 × 100%		300	300	300
Abnormal spoilage[‡]	100			
100 × 100%; 100 × 100%; 100 × 100%		100	100	100
Work in process, ending[§]	4,000			
4,000 × 100%; 4,000 × 0%; 4,000 × 25%		4,000	0	1,000
Total accounted for	10,400	10,400	6,400	7,400
Deduct work in process, beginning[≠]	3,000			
3,000 × 100%; 3,000 × 0%; 3,000 × 80%		3,000	0	2,400
Started during current period	7,400			
Work done in current period only		7,400	6,400	5,000

[†] Normal spoilage is 5% of good units transferred out: 5% × 6,000 = 300 units; Degree of completion of normal spoilage in this department: transferred-in costs, 100%; direct materials, 100%; conversion costs, 100%.

[‡] Degree of completion of abnormal spoilage in this department: transferred-in costs, 100%; direct materials, 100%; conversion costs, 100%.

[§] Degree of completion in this department: direct materials, 100%; conversion costs, 25%.

[≠] Degree of completion in this department: direct materials, 100%; conversion costs, 80%.

18-32 (cont'd)

SOLUTION EXHIBIT 18-32B
Step 3: Compute Equivalent Unit Costs:
Milling Department of Alston Company for May

	Transferred-in Costs	Direct Materials	Conversion Costs
Equivalent unit costs of beginning work in process			
Work in process, beginning (given)	$ 6,450	—	$2,450
Divide by equivalent units in beginning work in process (from Solution Exhibit 18-32A)	÷ 3,000	—	÷2,400
Cost per equivalent unit of beginning work in process	$ 2.15	—	$ 1.021
Equivalent unit costs of work done in current period only			
Costs added in current period (given)	$16,280	$ 640	$4,950
Divide by equivalent units of work done in current period (from Solution Exhibit 18-32A)	÷ 7,400	÷6,400	÷5,000
Costs per equivalent unit of work done in current period only	$ 2.20	$ 0.10	$ 0.99

18-32 (cont'd)

SOLUTION EXHIBIT 18-32C

Step 4: Summarize Total Costs to Account for, and Assign These Costs to Units Completed, Units Spoiled, and Units in Ending Work in Process Using the Weighted-Average Method Milling Department of Alston for May

	Transferred-in Costs			Direct Materials			Conversion Costs			Total Production Cost
	Equivalent Unit	Cost per Equivalent Unit	Total Costs	Equivalent Unit	Cost per Equivalent Unit	Total Costs	Equivalent Unit	Cost per Equivalent Unit	Total Costs	
	(1)	(2)	(3)=(1)×(2)	(4)	(5)	(6)=(4)×(5)	(7)	(8)	(9)=(7)×(8)	(10)=(3)+(6)+(9)
Panel A: Total Costs to Account For										
Work in process, beginning (from Solution Exhibit 18-32B)	3,000	$2.15	$ 6,450	—	—	—	2,400	$1.021	$2,450	$ 8,900
Work done in current period only (from Solution Exhibit 18-32B)	7,400	$2.20	16,280	6,400	$0.10	$640	5,000	$0.99	4,950	21,870
To account for	10,400	$2.19#	$22,730	6,400	$0.10*	$640	7,400	$1.00†	$7,400	$30,770
Panel B: Assignment of Costs										
Good units completed and transferred out (6,000 units): Costs before adding normal spoilage	6,000‡	$2.19	$13,113	6,000‡	$0.10	$600	6,000‡	$1.00	$6,000	$19,713
(A) Normal spoilage	300‡	2.19	656	300‡	0.10	30	300‡	1.00	300	986
(B) Total costs of good units tranfd			13,769			630			6,300	20,699
(C) Abnormal spoilage	100‡	$2.19	219	100‡	$0.10	10	100‡	$1.00	100	329
Work in process, ending	4,000‡	2.19	8,742	0‡	0.10	0	1,000‡	1.00	1,000	9,742
(A)+(B)+(C) Accounted for	10,400		$22,730	6,400		$640	7,400		$7,400	$30,770

#Weighted-average cost per equivalent unit of transferred-in costs = Total transferred-in costs divided by total equivalent units of transferred-in costs
= $22,730 ÷ 10,400 = $2.19

*Weighted average costs per equivalent unit of direct materials = Total direct materials costs divided by total equivalent units of direct materials
= $640 ÷ 6,400 = $0.10

†Weighted-average cost per equivalent unit of conversion costs = Total conversion costs divided by total equivalent units of conversion costs
= $7,400 ÷ 7,400 = $1

‡From Solution Exhibit 17-32A.

18-34 (20-25 min.) **Job-cost spoilage and scrap.**

1. (a) Materials Control $ 600
   Manufacturing Department Overhead Control   800
        Work in Process Control $1,400
        (650 + 500 + 250 = 1,400)

   (b) Accounts Receivable $1,250
        Work in Process Control $1,250

2. (a) The clause does not specify if the 1% calculation is to be based on the input cost ($26,951 + $15,076 + $7,538) or the cost of the good output before the "1% normal spoilage" is added.

   (b) If the inputs are used to determine the 1%:

        $26,951 + $15,076 + $7,538 = $49,565

   1% of $49,565 = $495.65 or $496, rounded. Then the entry to leave the $496 "normal spoilage" cost on the job, remove the salvageable material, and charge manufacturing overhead would be:

   Materials Control $ 600
   Manufacturing Department Overhead Control   304
        Work in Process Control $ 904
   ($800 spoilage minus $496 = $304 spoilage
   cost that is taken out of the job;
   $600 salvage value plus $304 = $904; or
   $1,400 minus $496 = $904)

   If the outputs are used to determine the 1%:

        $26,951 − $650 = $26,301
        15,076 − 500 = 14,576
        7,538 − 250 =   7,288
        $49,565 $48,165

Then, $48,165 × 1% = $481.65 or $482, rounded. The journal entry would be:

Materials Control $ 600
Manufacturing Department Overhead Control   318
     Work in Process Control $918

18-36 (30 min.) **Job costing, scrap.**

1. Materials Control   7,000
        Materials-Related Manufacturing Overhead Control   7,000
    (To record scrap common to all jobs at the time it is
    returned to the storeroom)

2. Cash or Accounts Receivable   7,000
        Materials Control   7,000
    (To record sale of scrap from the storeroom)

3. A summary of the manufacturing costs for HM3 and JB4 before considering the value of scrap are as follows:

	HM3		JB4		Total Costs
	Cost per Unit (1)	Total Costs (2)=(1) × 20,000	Cost per Unit (3)	Total Costs (4)=(3) × 10,000	(5)=(2)+(4)
Direct materials	$10	$200,000	$15	$150,000	$350,000
Direct manufacturing labour	3	60,000	4	40,000	100,000
Materials-related manufacturing overhead (20% of direct materials)	2	40,000	3	30,000	70,000
Other manufacturing overhead (200% of direct manufacturing labour)	6	120,000	8	80,000	200,000
Total	$21	$420,000	$30	$300,000	$720,000

The value of scrap generated during March of $7,000 will reduce materials-related manufacturing overhead costs by $7,000 from $70,000 to $63,000. Materials-related manufacturing overhead will then be allocated at 18% of direct materials costs ($63,000 ÷ 350,000 = 0.18).

The revised manufacturing cost per unit would then be:

	HM3		JB4		Total Costs
	Cost per Unit (1)	Total Costs (2)=(1) × 20,000	Cost per Unit (3)	Total Costs (4)=(3) × 10,000	(5)=(2)+(4)
Direct materials	$10.00	$200,000	$15.00	$150,000	$350,000
Direct manufacturing labour	3.00	60,000	4.00	40,000	100,000
Materials-related manufacturing overhead (20% of direct materials)	1.80	36,000	2.70	27,000	63,000
Other manufacturing overhead (200% of direct manufacturing labour)	6.00	120,000	8.00	80,000	200,000
Total	$20.80	$416,000	$29.70	$297,000	$713,000

18-38 (25-35 min.) **Weighted-average, inspection at 80% completion.**

The computation and allocation of spoilage is the most difficult part of this problem. The units in the ending inventory have passed inspection. Therefore, of the 80,000 units to account for (10,000 beginning + 70,000 started), 10,000 must have been spoiled in June [80,000 − (50,000 completed + 20,000 ending inventory)]. Normal spoilage is 7,000 [0.10 × (50,000 + 20,000)]. The 3,000 remainder is abnormal spoilage (10,000 − 7,000).

Solution Exhibit 18-38A calculates the equivalent units of work done for each cost element. We comment on several points in this calculation:

- Ending work in process includes an element of normal spoilage since all the ending WIP have passed the point of inspection—inspection occurs when production is 80% complete, while the units in ending WIP are 95% complete.

- Spoilage includes no direct materials units because spoiled units are detected and removed from the finishing activity when inspection occurs at the time production is 80% complete. Direct materials are added only later when production is 90% complete.

- Direct materials units are included for ending work in process, which is 95% complete but not for beginning work in process, which is 25% complete. The reason is that direct materials are added when production is 90% complete. The ending work in process therefore contains direct materials units; the beginning work in process does not.

Solution Exhibit 18-38B presents computations of the cost per equivalent unit of beginning inventory and of work done in the current period for each cost element under the weighted-average method.

Solution Exhibit 18-38C presents a summary of total costs to account for and assigns these costs to units completed, normal spoilage, abnormal spoilage, and to units in ending work in process using the weighted-average method. The cost of ending work in process includes the assignment of normal spoilage costs since these units have passed the point of inspection. The costs assigned to each cost element are as follows:

Cost of good units completed and transferred out (including normal spoilage costs on good units)	$1,877,350
Abnormal spoilage	67,710
Cost of ending work in process (including normal spoilage costs on ending work in process)	734,140
Total costs assigned and accounted for	$2,679,200

18-38 (cont'd)

SOLUTION EXHIBIT 18-38A

Steps 1 and 2: Summarize Output in Physical Units and Compute Equivalent Units
Finishing Department of Ottawa Manufacturing for June

| | (Step 1) | (Step 2) Equivalent Units | | |
| | Physical | Transferred- | Direct | Conversion |
Flow of Production	Units	in Costs	Materials	Costs
Good units completed and transferred out during current period	50,000	50,000	50,000	50,000
Normal spoilage on good units[†]	5,000			
5,000 × 100%; 5,000 × 0%; 5,000 × 80%		5,000	0	4,000
Work in process, ending[§]	20,000			
20,000 ×100%; 20,000 × 100%; 20,000 × 95%		20,000	20,000	19,000
Normal spoilage on ending WIP	2,000			
2,000 × 100%; 2,000 × 0%; 2,000 × 80%		2,000	0	1,600
Abnormal spoilage[‡]	3,000			
3,000 × 100%; 3,000 × 0%; 3,000 × 80%		3,000	0	2,400
Total accounted for	80,000	80,000	70,000	77,000
Deduct work in process, beginning[≠]	10,000			
10,000 × 100%; 10,000 × 0%; 10,000 × 25%		10,000	0	2,500
Started during current period	70,000			
Work done in current period only		70,000	70,000	74,500

[†] Normal spoilage is 10% of good units that pass inspection: 10% × 70,000 = 7,000 units; Degree of completion of normal spoilage in this department: transferred-in costs, 100%; direct materials, 0%; conversion costs, 80%.

[‡] Abnormal spoilage = Actual spoilage – Normal spoilage = 10,000 – 5,000 - 2,000 = 3,000. Degree of completion of abnormal spoilage in this department: transferred-in costs, 100%; direct materials, 0%; conversion costs, 80%.

[§] Degree of completion in this department: transferred-in costs, 100%; direct materials, 0%; conversion costs, 95%.

[≠] Degree of completion in this department: transferred-in costs, 100%; direct materials, 100%; conversion costs, 25%.

18-38 (cont'd)

SOLUTION EXHIBIT 18-38B
Step 3: Compute Equivalent Unit Costs:
Finishing Department of Ottawa Manufacturing for June

	Transferred-in Costs	Direct Materials	Conversion Costs
Equivalent unit costs of beginning work in process			
Work in process, beginning (given)	$ 82,900	—	$ 42,000
Divide by equivalent units in beginning work in process (from Solution Exhibit 18-38A)	÷ 10,000	—	÷ 2,500
Cost per equivalent unit of beginning work in process	$ 8.29	—	$ 16.80
Equivalent unit costs of work done in current period only			
Costs added in current period (given)	$647,500	$655,200	$1,251,600
Divide by equivalent units of work done in current period (from Solution Exhibit 18-38A)	÷ 70,000	÷ 70,000	÷ 74,500
Costs per equivalent unit of work done in current period only	$ 9.25	$ 9.36	$ 16.80

18-38 (cont'd)

SOLUTION EXHIBIT 18-38C
Step 4: Summarize Total Costs to Account For, and Assign These Costs to Units Completed, Units Spoiled, and Units in Ending Work in Process Using the Weighted-Average Method, Finishing Department of Ottawa Manufacturing for June

		Transferred-in Costs			Direct Materials			Conversion Costs			Total Production Cost
		Equivalent Units	Cost per Equivalent Unit	Total Costs	Equivalent Units	Cost per Equivalent Unit	Total Costs	Equivalent Units	Cost per Equivalent Unit	Total Costs	
		(1)	(2)	(3)=(1)×(2)	(4)	(5)	(6)=(4)×(5)	(7)	(8)	(9)=(7)×(8)	(10)=(3)+(6)+(9)
Panel A:	**Total Costs to Account For**										
	Work in process, beginning (from Solution Exhibit 18-38B)	10,000	$8.29	$ 82,900	—	—	—	2,500	$16.80	$ 42,000	$ 124,900
	Work done in current period only (from Solution Exhibit 18-38B)	70,000	$9.25	647,500	70,000	$9.36	$655,200	74,500	$16.80	1,251,600	2,554,300
	To account for	80,000	$9.13#	$730,400	70,000	$9.36*	$655,200	77,000	$16.80†	$1,293,600	$2,679,200
Panel B:	**Assignment of Costs**										
	Good units completed and transferred out (50,000 units):										
	Costs before adding normal spoilage	50,000‡	$9.13	$456,500	50,000‡	$9.36	$468,000	50,000‡	$16.80	$ 840,000	$1,764,500
	Normal spoilage	5,000‡	$9.13	45,650	0‡	$9.36	0	4,000‡	$16.80	67,200	112,850
(A)	Total costs of good units transfd			502,150			468,000			907,200	1,877,350
(B)	Abnormal spoilage	3,000‡	$9.13	27,390	0‡	$9.36	0	2,400‡	$16.80	40,320	67,710
(C)	Work in process, ending										
	WIP ending, before normal spoilage	20,000‡	$9.13	182,600	20,000‡	$9.36	187,200	19,000‡	$16.80	319,200	689,000
	Normal spoilage on ending WIP	2,000‡	$9.13	18,260	0‡	$9.36	0	1,600‡	$16.80	26,880	45,140
	Total cost of ending WIP			200,860			187,200			346,080	734,140
(A)+ (B)+ (C)	Accounted for	80,000		$730,400	70,000		$655,200	77,000		$1,293,600	$2,679,200

#Weighted-average cost per equivalent unit of transferred-in costs = Total transferred-in costs divided by total equiv. units of transferred-in costs = $730,400 ÷ 80,000 = $9.13

*Weighted-average cost per equivalent unit of direct materials = Total direct materials costs divided by total equivalent units of direct materials = $655,200 ÷ 70,000 = $9.36

†Weighted-average cost per equivalent unit of conversion costs = Total conversion costs divided by total equivalent units of conversion costs = $1,293,600 ÷ 77,000 = $16.80

‡From Solution Exhibit 17-35A.

19-2   Quality of design measures how closely the characteristics of products or services match the needs and wants of customers. Conformance quality measures whether the product has been made according to design, engineering and manufacturing specifications.

19-4   An internal failure cost differs from an external failure cost on the basis of when the nonconforming product is detected. An internal failure is detected *before* a product is shipped to a customer whereas an external failure is detected *after* a product is shipped to a customer.

19-6   No, companies should emphasize financial as well as nonfinancial measures of quality, such as yield and defect rates. Nonfinancial measures are not directly linked to bottom-line performance but they indicate and direct attention to the specific areas that need improvement. Tracking nonfinancial measures over time directly reveals whether these areas have, in fact, improved over time. Nonfinancial measures are easy to quantify and easy to understand.

19-8   Examples of nonfinancial measures of internal performance are:
1. The number of defects for each product line.
2. Process yield (rates of good output to total output at a particular process).
3. Manufacturing lead time (the time taken to convert direct materials into finished output).
4. Employee turnover (ratio of the number of employees who left the company in a year, say, to the total number of employees who worked for the company in that year).

19-10   No. There is a trade-off between customer-response time and on-time performance. Simply scheduling longer customer-response time makes achieving on-time performance easier. Companies should, however, attempt to reduce uncertainty of arrival of orders, manage bottlenecks, reduce setup and processing time and run smaller batches. This would have the effect of reducing both customer-response time and improving on-time performance.

19-12   No. Adding a product when capacity is constrained and the timing of customer orders is uncertain causes delays in delivering all existing products. If the revenue losses from delays in delivering existing products and the increase in carrying costs of the existing products exceeds the positive contribution earned by the product that was added, then it is not worthwhile to make and sell the new product, despite its positive contribution margin. The chapter describes the negative effects (negative externalities) that one product can have on others when products share manufacturing facilities.

19-14 The four key steps in managing bottleneck resources are:
Step 1: Recognize that the bottleneck operation determines throughput contribution.
Step 2: Search for and find the bottleneck.
Step 3: Keep the bottleneck busy and subordinate all nonbottleneck operations to the bottleneck operation.
Step 4: Increase bottleneck efficiency and capacity.

19-16 (30 min.) **Costs of quality.**

1.   The ratio of each COQ category to revenues for each period is as follows:

Semi-annual Costs of Quality Report Bergen, Inc.
(in thousands)

	6/30/2000		12/31/2000		6/30/2001		12/31/2001	
	(1)	% of Rev. (2) = (1) ÷ 4,120	(3)	% of Rev. (4) = (3) ÷ 4,540	(5)	% of Rev. (6) = (5) ÷ 4,650	(7)	% of Rev. (8) = (7) ÷ 4,510
Prevention costs								
Machine maintenance	$ 215		$ 215		$ 190		$ 160	
Training suppliers	5		45		20		15	
Design reviews	20		102		100		95	
	240	5.8%	362	8.0%	310	6.7%	270	6.0%
Appraisal costs								
Incoming inspection	45		53		36		22	
Final testing	160		160		140		94	
	205	5.0%	213	4.7%	176	3.8%	116	2.6%
Internal failure costs								
Rework	120		106		88		62	
Scrap	68		64		42		40	
	188	4.6%	170	3.7%	130	2.8%	102	2.2%
External failure costs								
Warranty repairs	69		31		25		23	
Customer returns	262		251		116		80	
	331	8.0%	282	6.2%	141	3.0%	103	2.3%
Total quality costs	$ 964	23.4%	$1,027	22.6%	$ 757	16.3%	$ 591	13.1%
Total production and revenues	$4,120		$4,540		$4,650		$4,510	

19-16 (cont'd)

From an analysis of the Cost of Quality Report, it would appear that Bergen Inc.'s program has been successful since

- Total quality costs as a percentage of total revenues have declined from 23.4% to 13.1%.
- External failure costs, those costs signalling customer dissatisfaction have declined from 8% of total revenues to 2.3%. These declines in warranty repairs and customer returns should translate into increased revenues in the future.
- Internal failure costs have been reduced from 4.6% to 2.2% of revenues
- Appraisal costs have decreased from 5.0% to 2.6%. Preventing defects from occurring in the first place is reducing the demand for final testing.
- Quality costs have shifted to the area of prevention where problems are solved before production starts. Maintenance, training, and design reviews have increased from 5.8% of total revenues to 6% and from 25% of total quality costs (240 ÷ 964) to 45.7% (270 ÷ 591). The $30,000 increase in these costs is more than offset by decreases in other quality costs.

Because of improved designs, quality training, and additional pre-production inspections, scrap and rework costs have declined. Production does not have to spend an inordinate amount of time with customer service since they are now making the product right the first time and warranty repairs and customer returns have decreased.

2. To measure the opportunity cost of not implementing the quality program, Bergen Inc. could assume that

- Sales and market share would continue to decline if the quality program had not been implemented and then calculate the loss in revenue and contribution margin.
- The company would have to compete on price rather than quality and calculate the impact of having to lower product prices.

Opportunity costs are not recorded in accounting systems because they represent the results of what might have happened if Bergen had not improved quality. Nevertheless, opportunity costs of poor quality can be significant. It is important for Bergen to take these costs into account when making decisions about quality.

19-18 (30-40 min.) **Costs of quality analysis, nonfinancial quality measures.**

1. and 2.

**Sales, Costs of Quality and Costs of Quality
as a Percentage of Sales for Olivia**

Sales = $2,000 × 10,000 units = $20,000,000

Costs of Quality	Cost (1)	Percentage of Sales (2) = (1) ÷ $20,000,000
Prevention costs		
Design engineering ($75 × 6,000 hours)	$ 450,000	2.25%
Appraisal costs		
Testing and inspection ($40 × 1 hour × 10,000 units)	400,000	2.00%
Internal failure costs		
Rework ($500 × 5% × 10,000 units)	250,000	1.25%
External failure costs		
Repair ($600 × 4% × 10,000 units)	240,000	1.20%
Total costs of quality	$1,340,000	6.70%

**Sales, Costs of Quality and Costs of Quality
as a Percentage of Sales for Solta**

Sales: $1,500 × 5,000 units = $7,500,000

Costs of Quality	Costs (1)	Percentage of Sales (2)=(1)÷$7,500,000
Prevention costs		
Design engineering ($75 × 1,000 hours)	$ 75,000	1.00%
Appraisal costs		
Testing and inspection ($40 × 0.5 × 5,000 units)	100,000	1.33%
Internal failure costs	200,000	2.67%
Rework ($400 × 10% × 5,000 units)		
External failure costs	180,000	2.40%
Repair ($450 × 8% × 5,000 units)		
Estimated forgone contribution margin	210,000	2.80%
on lost sales [($1,500 − $800) × 300]	390,000	5.20%
Total external failure costs		
Total costs of quality	$765,000	10.20%

Costs of quality as a percentage of sales are significantly different for Solta (10.20%) compared with Olivia (6.70%). Ontario spends very little on prevention and appraisal activities for Solta, and incurs high costs of internal and external failures. Ontario follows a different strategy with respect to Olivia, spending a greater percentage of sales on prevention and appraisal activities. The result: fewer internal and external failure costs and lower overall costs of quality as a percentage of sales compared with Solta.

3. Examples of nonfinancial quality measures that Ontario Industries could monitor as part of a total-quality-control effort are
   (a) Outgoing quality yield for each product.
   (b) Returned refrigerator percentage for each product.
   (c) On-time delivery.
   (d) Employee turnover.

19-20 (25 min.) **Quality improvement, relevant costs, and relevant revenues.**

1.   Incremental costs over the next year of choosing the new lens = $50 × 20,000 copiers = $1,000,000.

2.

	Incremental Benefits over the Next Year of Choosing the New Lens
Costs of quality items	
Savings on rework costs	
$1,600 × 300 fewer copiers reworked	$ 480,000
Savings in customer-support costs	
$80 × 200 fewer copiers repaired	16,000
Savings in transportation costs for parts	
$180 × 200 fewer copiers repaired	36,000
Savings in warranty repair costs	
$1,800 × 200 fewer copiers repaired	360,000
Opportunity costs	
Contribution margin from increased sales	
100 × $6,000	600,000
Cost savings and additional contribution margin	$1,492,000

3.   Since the expected benefits of $1,492,000 (requirement 2) exceed the costs of the new lens of $1,000,000 (requirement 1), Photon should introduce the new lens. Note that the opportunity cost benefits in the form of higher contribution margin from increased sales is an important component for justifying the investment in the new lens. The incremental costs of the new lens of $1,000,000 is greater than the incremental savings in rework and repair costs of $892,000. Investing in the new lens is beneficial provided it generates additional contribution margin of, at least, $108,000 ($1,000,000 − $892,000), that is, additional sales of at least $108,000 ÷ $6,000 = 18 copiers.

19-22 (20 min.) **Waiting time, banks.**

1. If the branch expects to receive 40 customers each day and it takes 5 minutes to serve a customer, the average time that a customer will wait in line before being served is:

$$= \frac{\left(\begin{array}{c}\text{Average number}\\\text{of customers}\end{array}\right) \times \left(\begin{array}{c}\text{Time taken to}\\\text{serve a customer}\end{array}\right)^2}{2 \times \left[\begin{array}{c}\text{Available time}\\\text{counter is open}\end{array} - \left[\left(\begin{array}{c}\text{Average number}\\\text{of customers}\end{array}\right) \times \left(\begin{array}{c}\text{Time taken to}\\\text{serve a customer}\end{array}\right)\right]\right]}$$

$$= \frac{[40 \times (5)^2]}{2 \times [300 - (40 \times 5)]} = \frac{(40 \times 25)}{2 \times (300 - 200)} = \frac{1,000}{2 \times 100} = \frac{1,000}{200} = 5 \text{ minutes}$$

2. If the branch expects to receive 50 customers each day and the time taken to serve a customer is 5 minutes, the average time that a customer will wait in line before being served is:

$$= \frac{[50 \times (5)^2]}{2 \times [300 - (50 \times 5)]} = \frac{(50 \times 25)}{2 \times (300 - 250)} = \frac{50 \times 25}{2 \times 50} = \frac{1,250}{100} = 12.5 \text{ minutes}$$

3. If the branch expects to receive 50 customers each day and the time taken to serve a customer is 4 minutes, the average time that a customer will wait in line before being served is:

$$= \frac{[50 \times (4)^2]}{2 \times [300 - (50 \times 4)]} = \frac{(50 \times 16)}{2 \times (300 - 200)} = \frac{50 \times 16}{2 \times 100} = \frac{800}{200} = 4 \text{ minutes}$$

19-24 (15 min.) **Theory of constraints, throughput contribution, relevant costs.**

1.   Finishing is a bottleneck operation. Hence, producing 1,000 more units will generate additional throughput contribution and operating income.

Increase in throughput contribution ($72 – $32) × 1,000	$40,000
Incremental costs of the jigs and tools	30,000
Net benefit of investing in jigs and tools	$10,000

Mayfield should invest in the modern jigs and tools because the benefit of higher throughput contribution of $40,000 exceeds the cost of $30,000.

2.   The Machining Department has excess capacity and is not a bottleneck operation. Increasing its capacity further will not increase throughput contribution. There is therefore no benefit from spending $5,000 to increase the Machining Department's capacity by 10,000 units. Mayfield should not implement the change to do setups faster.

19-26 (15 min.)   **Theory of constraints, throughput contribution, quality.**

1.   Cost of defective unit at machining operation which is not a bottleneck operation is the loss in direct materials (variable costs) of $32 per unit. Producing 2,000 units of defectives does not result in loss of throughput contribution. Despite the defective production machining can produce and transfer 80,000 units to finishing. Therefore cost of 2,000 defective units at the machining operation is $32 × 2,000 = $64,000.

2.   A defective unit produced at the bottleneck finishing operation costs Mayfield materials costs plus the opportunity cost of lost throughput contribution. Bottleneck capacity not wasted in producing defective units could be used to generate additional sales and throughput contribution. Cost of 2,000 defective units at the finishing operation is

Loss of direct materials $32 × 2,000	$ 64,000
Forgone throughput contribution ($72 – $32) × 2,000	80,000
Total cost of 2,000 defective units	$144,000

Alternatively, the cost of 2,000 defective units at the finishing operation can be calculated as the lost revenue of $72 × 2,000 = $144,000. That is, the direct materials costs of $32 × 2,000 = $64,000 and all fixed operating costs in the machining and finishing operations are irrelevant since these costs would be incurred anyway whether a defective or good unit is produced. The cost of producing a defective unit is the revenue lost of $144,000.

19-28 (30 min.) **Quality improvement, relevant costs, and relevant revenues.**

1. By implementing the new method, Tan would incur additional direct materials costs on all the 200,000 units started at the molding operation.

Additional direct materials costs = $3 per lamp × 200,000 lamps $600,000

2. The relevant benefits of adding the new material are:

(a) Increased revenue from selling 30,000 more lamps
$40 per lamp × 30,000 lamps $1,200,000
(b) Additional variable costs incurred in the welding department on the good lamps
$2.50 × 30,000 lamps   (75,000)
Total benefits to Tan of adding new material to improve quality $1,125,000

Note that Tan Corporation continues to incur the same total variable costs of direct materials, direct manufacturing labour, setup labour, and materials handling labour and the same fixed costs of equipment, rent, and allocated overhead that it is currently incurring even when it improves quality. Since these costs do not differ among the alternatives of adding the new material or not adding the new material, they are excluded from the analysis. The relevant benefit of adding the new material is the extra revenue that Tan would get from producing 30,000 good lamps minus the additional variable welding costs it would incur on these lamps in the welding department.

An alternative approach to analyzing the problem is to focus on scrap costs and the benefits of reducing scrap.

The relevant benefits of adding the new material are:

(a) Cost savings from eliminating scrap:

Variable costs per lamp, $19[a] × 30,000 lamps $ 570,000
(b) Additional contribution margin from selling
another 30,000 lamps because 30,000 lamps
will no longer be scrapped:

Unit contribution margin $18.50[b] × 30,000 lamps   555,000
Total benefits to Tan of adding new material to improve quality $1,125,000

[a]Note that only the variable scrap costs of $19 per lamp (direct materials, $16 per lamp and direct manufacturing labour, setup labour, and materials handling labour, $3 per lamp) are relevant because improving quality will save these costs. Fixed scrap costs of equipment, rent, and allocated overhead are irrelevant because these costs will be incurred whether Tan Corporation adds or does not add the new material.

^{b}<u>Unit contribution margin</u>

Selling price		$40.00
Variable costs:		
Direct materials costs per lamp	$16.00	
Molding department variable manufacturing costs		
per lamp (direct manufacturing labour, setup labour, and		
materials handling labour)	3.00	
Welding department variable manufacturing costs per lamp	2.50	
Variable costs		21.50
Unit contribution margin		$18.50

3. On the basis of quantitative considerations alone, Tan should use the new material. Relevant benefits of $1,125,000 exceeds the relevant costs of $600,000 by $525,000.

4. Other nonfinancial and qualitative factors that Tan should consider in making a decision include the effects of quality improvement on:
   (a) Gaining manufacturing expertise that could lead to further cost reductions in the future.
   (b) Enhanced reputation and increased customer goodwill which could lead to higher future revenues through greater unit sales and higher sales prices.
   (c) More worker empowerment and higher employee morale.

19-30 (30-40 min.) **Compensation linked with profitability, on-time delivery, and external quality performance measures; balanced scorecard.**

1.	Jan.-March	April-June	July-Sept.	Oct.-Dec.
Detroit				
Add: Profitability				
2% of operating income	$16,000	$17,000	$14,000	$18,000
Add: On-time delivery				
$10,000 if above 98%	10,000	10,000	0	0
Deduct: Quality				
50% of cost of sales returns	(9,000)	(13,000)	(5,000)	(12,500)
Total: Bonus paid	$17,000	$14,000	$ 9,000	$ 5,500
Los Angeles				
Add: Profitability				
2% of operating income	$32,000	$30,000	$36,000	$38,000
Add: On-time delivery				
$10,000 if above 98%	0	0	0	10,000
Deduct: Quality				
50% of cost of sales returns	(17,500)	(17,000)	(14,000)	(11,000)
Total: Bonus paid	$14,500	$13,000	$22,000	$37,000

2. <u>Operating income as a measure of profitability</u>

Operating income does capture revenue and cost-related factors. However, there is no recognition of investment differences between the two plants. Los Angeles sales are approximately double that of Detroit. This difference gives the Los Angeles plant manager the opportunity to earn a larger bonus due to investment size alone. An alternative approach would be to use return on investment (perhaps relative to the budgeted ROI).

<u>98% on-time benchmark as a measure of on-time delivery performance</u>

This measure does reflect the ability of Pacific-Dunlop to meet a benchmark for on-time delivery. Several concerns arise with this specific measure:

(a) It is a yes-or-no cut-off. A 10% on-time performance earns no bonus, but neither does a 97.9% on-time performance. Moreover, no extra bonus is paid for performance above 98.0%. An alternative is to have the bonus be a percentage of the on-time delivery percentage.

(b) It can be manipulated by management. The Pacific-Dunlop plant manager may quote conservative delivery dates to salespeople in an effort to "guarantee" that the 98% target is achieved.

(c) It reflects performance only relative to scheduled delivery date. It does not consider how quickly Pacific-Dunlop can respond to customer orders.

19-30 (cont'd)

50% of cost of sales returns as a measure of quality

This measure does incorporate one cost that arises with defective goods. However, there are several concerns with its use:

(a) Not all sales returns are due to defective work by the plant manager. Some returns are due to tampering by the customer. Other returns arise from breakage during delivery and installation.

(b) It does not systematically incorporate customer opinion about quality. Not all customers return defective goods.

(c) It ignores important categories of the cost of defective goods. For example, dissatisfied customers may decline to make any subsequent purchases.

3. Most companies use both financial and nonfinancial measures to evaluate performance, sometimes presented in a single report called a balanced scorecard. Using multiple measures of performance enables top management to evaluate whether lower-level managers have improved one area at the expense of others. For example, did the on-time delivery performance of the Detroit plant manager decrease in the October-December period relative to the April-June period because the manager emphasized shipment of high-margin products to increase operating income?

4. If on-time delivery were dropped as a performance evaluation measure, managers will concentrate on increasing operating income and decreasing sales returns but will give less attention to on-time delivery. Consider the following situation. Suppose a manager must choose between (1) delivering a high-margin order that will add to operating income while delaying a number of other orders and adversely affecting on-time performance or (2) delaying the high-margin order and sacrificing some operating income to achieve better on-time performance. What action will the manager take? If on-time performance is excluded as a performance evaluation measure, the manager will almost certainly choose (1). Only if on-time performance is included in the manager's performance evaluation will the manager consider choosing option (2).

19-32 (20-30 min.) **Waiting times, relevant revenues and relevant costs (continuation of 19-31).**

1.   The direct approach is to look at incremental revenues and incremental costs.

Average selling price per order for Y28, which has average operating throughput time of 350 hours	$ 8,000
Variable costs per order	5,000
Additional contribution per order from Y28	3,000
Multiply by expected number of orders	× 25
Increase in expected contribution from Y28	$75,000

Expected loss in revenues and increase in costs from introducing Y28

Product (1)	Expected Loss in Revenues from Increasing Average Manufacturing Lead Times for All Products (2)	Expected Increase in Carrying Costs from Increasing Average Manufacturing Lead Times for All Products (3)	Expected Loss in Revenues Plus Expected Increases in Costs of Introducing Y28 (4) = (2) + (3)
Z39	$25,000.00[a]	$6,375.00[b]	$31,375.00
Y28	–	2,187.50[c]	2,187.50
Total	$25,000.00	$8,562.50	$33,562.50

[a]50 orders × ($27,000 – $26,500)
[b](410 hours – 240 hours) × $0.75 × 50 orders
[c](350 hours – 0) × $0.25 × 25

Increase in expected contribution from Y28 of $75,000 is greater than increase in expected costs of $33,562.50 by $41,437.50. Therefore, SRG should introduce Y28.

19-32 (cont'd)

Alternative calculations of incremental revenues and incremental costs of introducing Y28.

	Alternative 1: Introduce Y28 (1)	Alternative 2: Do Not Introduce Y28 (2)	Relevant Revenues and Relevant Costs (3) = (1) − (2)
Expected revenues	$1,525,000.00[a]	$1,350,000.00[b]	$175,000.00
Expected variable costs	875,000.00[c]	750,000.00[d]	125,000.00
Expected carrying costs	17,562.50[e]	9,000.00[f]	8,562.50
Expected total variable and carrying costs	892,562.50	759,000.00	133,562.50
Expected revenues minus expected costs	$ 632,437.50	$ 591,000.00	$ 41,437.50

[a] $(50 \times \$26,500) + (25 \times \$8,000)$
[b] $50 \times \$27,000$
[c] $(50 \times \$15,000) + (25 \times \$5,000)$
[d] $50 \times \$15,000$

[e] $(50 \times \$0.75 \times 410) + (25 \times \$0.25 \times 350)$
[f] $50 \times \$0.75 \times 240$

2. Introducing Y28 results in an incremental cost of $33,562.50. To break even, we need to earn a total contribution of $33,562.50 over the 25 orders, or a contribution per order of $33,562.50 ÷ 25 = $1,342.50.

Variable costs per order of Y28	$5,000.00
Required contribution to break even	1,342.50
Selling price per dollar of Y28 to break even	$6,342.50

If Y28 sells above $6,342.50 per order, SRG should manufacture and sell Y28. If Y28 sells below $6,342.50 per order, SRG should not manufacture and sell Y28.

19-34 (20 min.) **Theory of constraints, throughput contribution, relevant costs.**

1.   It will cost Columbia $50 per unit to reduce manufacturing time. But manufacturing is not a bottleneck operation, installation is. Therefore manufacturing more equipment will not increase sales and throughput contribution. Columbia Industries should not implement the new manufacturing method.

2.   Additional relevant costs of new direct materials, $2,000 × 320 units $640,000
        Increase in throughput contribution, $25,000 × 20 units $500,000

The additional incremental costs exceed the benefits from higher throughput contribution by $140,000, so Columbia Industries should not implement the new design.

Alternatively, compare throughput contribution under each alternative.

Current throughput contribution is $25,000 × 300 $7,500,000
With the modification, throughput contribution is $23,000 × 320 $7,360,000

The current throughput contribution is greater than the throughput contribution resulting from the proposed change in direct materials. Hence, Columbia Industries should not implement the new design.

3.   Increase in throughput contribution, $25,000 × 10 units $250,000
        Increase in relevant costs $ 50,000

The additional throughput contribution exceeds incremental costs by $200,000 so Columbia Industries should implement the new installation technique.

4.   Motivating installation workers to increase productivity is worthwhile because installation is a bottleneck operation and any increase in productivity at the bottleneck will increase throughput contribution. On the other hand, motivating workers in the manufacturing department to increase productivity is not worthwhile. Manufacturing is not a bottleneck operation, so any increase in output will only result in extra inventory of equipment. Columbia Industries should only encourage manufacturing to produce as much equipment as the installation department needs, not to produce as much as it can. Under these circumstances, it would not be a good idea to evaluate and compensate manufacturing workers on the basis of their productivity.

19-36 (25 min.)   **Quality improvement, Pareto charts, fishbone diagrams.**

1.   Examples of failures in accounts receivable management are:
    (a)   Uncollectible amounts or bad debts.
    (b)   Delays in receiving payments.

2.   Prevention activities that could reduce failures in accounts receivable management include:
    (a)   Credit checks on customers
    (b)   Shipping the correct copier to the customer
    (c)   Supporting installation of the copier and answering customer questions
    (d)   Sending the correct invoice, in the correct amount and to the correct address promptly
    (e)   Following up to see if the machine is functioning smoothly

3.   A Pareto diagram for the problem of delays in receiving customer payments might look like the following:

SOLUTION EXHIBIT 19-36A
Pareto Diagram for Failures in Accounts Receivables at Murray Corporation

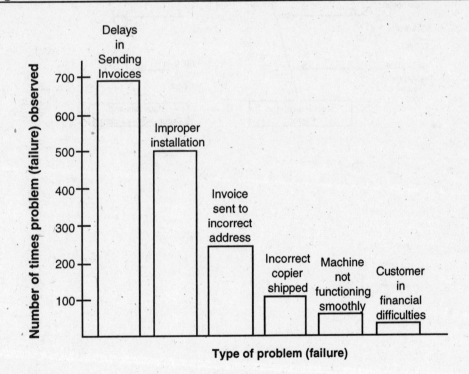

19-36 (cont'd)

A cause-and-effect or fishbone diagram for the problem of delays in sending invoices may appear as follows:

SOLUTION EXHIBIT 19-36B
Cause-and-Effect Diagram for Problem of Delays in Sending Invoices at Murray Corporation

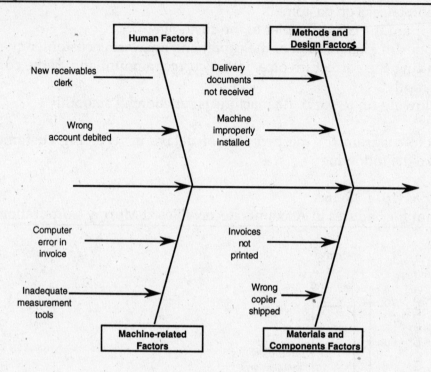

CHAPTER 20
INVENTORY MANAGEMENT, JUST-IN-TIME,
AND BACKFLUSH COSTING

20-2 Five cost categories important in managing goods for sale in a retail organization are:
1. Purchase costs.
2. Ordering costs.
3. Carrying costs.
4. Stockout costs.
5. Quality costs.

20-4 Costs included in the carrying costs of inventory are *incremental costs* for such items as insurance, rent, obsolescence, spoilage, and breakage plus the *opportunity cost* of capital (or required return on investment).

20-6 The steps in computing the costs of a prediction error when using the EOQ decision model are:
Step 1: Compute the monetary outcome from the best action that could have been taken, given the actual amount of the cost input.
Step 2: Compute the monetary outcome from the best action based on the incorrect amount of the predicted cost input.
Step 3: Compute the difference between the monetary outcomes from Steps 1 and 2.

20-8 Just-in-time (JIT) purchasing is the purchase of goods or materials such that a delivery immediately precedes demand or use. Benefits include lower inventory holdings (reduced warehouse space required and less money tied up in inventory) and less risk of inventory obsolescence and spoilage.

20-10 The sequence of activities involved in placing a purchase order can be facilitated by use of the Internet. For example, Cisco is streamlining the procurement process for its customers—e.g., having online a complete price list, information about expected shipment dates, and a service order capability that is available 24 hours a day with e-mail or fax confirmation.

20-12 Obstacles to companies adopting a supply-chain approach include:
*   Communication obstacles—the unwillingness of some parties to share information.
*   Trust obstacles—includes the concern that all parties will not meet their agreed-upon commitments.
*   Information system obstacles—includes problems due to the information systems of different parties not being technically compatible.
*   Limited resources—includes problems due to the people and financial resources given to support a supply-chain initiative not being adequate.

20-14 Traditional normal and standard costing systems use sequential tracking, which is any product-costing method where recording of the journal entries occurs in the same order as actual purchases and progress in production.

Backflush costing omits the recording of some or all of the journal entries relating to the cycle from purchase of direct materials to sale of finished goods. Where journal entries for one or more stages in the cycle are omitted, the journal entries for a subsequent stage use normal or standard costs to work backward to flush out the costs in the cycle for which journal entries were not made.

20-16 (20 min.)   **Economic order quantity for retailer.**

1.   D = 10,000, P = $225, C = $10

$$\text{EOQ} = \sqrt{\frac{2\,DP}{C}} = \sqrt{\frac{2(10,000)\$225}{10}}$$

$$= 670.82$$

$$\cong 671 \text{ jerseys}$$

2.   Number of orders per year $= \dfrac{D}{\text{EOQ}} = \dfrac{10,000}{671}$

$$= 14.90$$

$$\cong 15 \text{ orders}$$

3.   Demand each working day $= \dfrac{D}{\text{Number of working days}}$

$$= \dfrac{10,000}{365}$$

$$= 27.40 \text{ jerseys per day}$$

Purchase lead time = 7 days

Reorder point   = 27.40 × 7

$$= 191.80 \cong 192 \text{ jerseys}$$

20-18 (15 min.) **EOQ for a retailer.**

1. $D = 20,000$, $P = \$160$, $C = 20\% \times \$8 = \$1.60$

$$\text{EOQ} = \sqrt{\frac{2DP}{C}} = \sqrt{\frac{2(20,000)\$160}{\$1.60}} = 2,000 \text{ metres}$$

2. Number of orders per year: $\dfrac{D}{\text{EOQ}} = \dfrac{20,000}{2,000} = 10$ orders

3. Demand each working day $= \dfrac{D}{\text{Number of working days}}$

$\quad\quad\quad\quad\quad\quad\quad\quad\quad\quad\quad = \dfrac{20,000}{250}$

$\quad\quad\quad\quad\quad\quad\quad\quad\quad\quad\quad = 80$ metres per day

$\quad\quad\quad\quad\quad\quad\quad\quad\quad\quad\quad = 400$ metres per week

Purchasing lead time = 2 weeks
Reorder point = $400 \times 2 = 800$ metres

20-20 (20 min.)   **Economic order quantity for retailer, ordering and carrying costs.**

1. $D = 20,000$, $P = \$120$, $C = \$10$

$$\text{EOQ} = \sqrt{\frac{2(20,000)(\$120)}{\$10}}$$

$$= 692.8 \cong 693 \text{ modems}$$

2. $\text{RTC} = \dfrac{DP}{Q} + \dfrac{QC}{2}$

$$= \frac{20,000 \cdot \$120}{692.8} + \frac{692.8 \cdot 10}{2}$$

$$= \$3,464 + 3,464$$
$$= \$6,928$$

3.   Reorder point = $\begin{array}{c}\text{Number of units} \\ \text{sold per} \\ \text{unit of time}\end{array}$ × $\begin{array}{c}\text{Purchase - order} \\ \text{lead time}\end{array}$

$$= \frac{20,000}{360} \times 5$$

$$= 277.78 \cong 278 \text{ modems}$$

20-22 (20 min.)   **JIT production, relevant benefits, relevant costs.**

1.   Solution Exhibit 20-22 presents the annual net benefit of $154,000 to Evans Corporation of implementing a JIT production system.

2.   Other nonfinancial and qualitative factors that Evans should consider in deciding whether it should implement a JIT system include:
   a.   The possibility of developing and implementing a detailed system for integrating the sequential operations of the manufacturing process. Direct materials must arrive when needed for each subassembly so that the production process functions smoothly.
   b.   The ability to design products that use standardized parts and reduce manufacturing time.
   c.   The ease of obtaining reliable vendors who can deliver quality direct materials on time with minimum lead time.
   d.   Willingness of suppliers to deliver smaller and more frequent orders.
   e.   The confidence of being able to deliver quality products on time. Failure to do so would result in customer dissatisfaction.
   f.   The skill levels of workers to perform multiple tasks such as minor repairs, maintenance, quality testing, and inspection.

SOLUTION EXHIBIT 20-22
Annual Relevant Costs of Current Production System and JIT Production System
for Evans Corporation

Relevant Items	Incremental Costs Under Current Production System	Incremental Costs Under JIT Production System
Annual tooling costs	–	$150,000
Required return on investment		
12% per year × $900,000 of average inventory per year	$108,000	
12% per year × $200,000 of average inventory per year		24,000
Insurance, space, materials handling, and setup costs	200,000	140,000[a]
Rework costs	350,000	280,000[b]
Incremental revenues from higher selling prices	–	(90,000)[c]
Total net incremental costs	$658,000	$504,000
Annual difference in favour of JIT production	↑　　$154,000　　↑	

[a]$200,000 (1 – 0.30) = $140,000
[b]$350,000 (1 – 0.20) = $280,000
[c]$3 × 30,000 units = $90,000

20-24 (20 min.) **Backflush costing, two trigger points, materials purchase and sale (continuation of 20-23).**

1.

(a) Purchases of raw materials	Inventory Control	2,754,000	
	Accounts Payable Control		2,754,000
(b) Incur conversion costs	Conversion Costs Control	723,600	
	Various Accounts		723,600
(c) Completion of finished goods	No entry		
(d) Sale of finished goods	Cost of Goods Sold	3,432,000	
	Inventory Control		2,692,800
	Conversion Costs Allocated		739,200
(e) Underallocated or overallocated conversion costs	Conversion Costs Allocated	739,200	
	Costs of Goods Sold		15,600
	Conversion Costs Control		723,600

2.

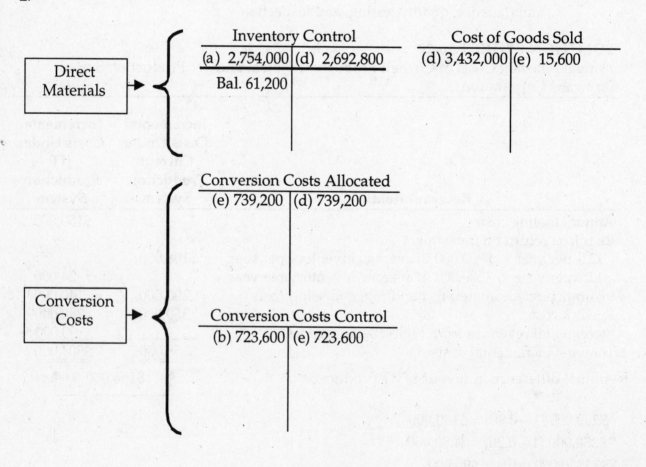

Inventory Control		Cost of Goods Sold	
(a) 2,754,000	(d) 2,692,800	(d) 3,432,000	(e) 15,600
Bal. 61,200			

Direct Materials

Conversion Costs Allocated	
(e) 739,200	(d) 739,200

Conversion Costs Control	
(b) 723,600	(e) 723,600

Conversion Costs

20-26 (30 min.) **Effect of different order quantities on ordering costs and carrying costs, EOQ.**

1. A straightforward approach to this requirement is to construct the following table for different purchase-order quantities.

D: Demand	26,000	26,000	26,000	26,000	26,000
Q: Order quantity	300	500	600	700	900
Q/2: Average inventory in units	150	250	300	350	450
D/Q: Number of purchase orders	86.67	52	43.33	37.14	28.89
(D/Q) × P: Annual ordering costs	$6,240	$3,744	$3,120	$2,674	$2,080
(Q/2) × C: Annual carrying costs	1,560	2,600	3,120	3,640	4,680
Total relevant costs of ordering and carrying inventory	$7,800	$6,344	$6,240	$6,314	$6,760

$$\uparrow$$
Minimum
Cost

D = 26,000 units
Q = order quantity
P = $72
C = $10.40

$$\text{EOQ} = \sqrt{\frac{2DP}{C}} = \sqrt{\frac{2 \times 26,000 \times \$72}{\$10.40}} = \sqrt{360,000} = 600 \text{ packages}$$

The shape of the total relevant cost function for Koala Blue is relatively flat from order quantities 500 to 700.

2. When the ordering cost per purchase order is reduced to $40:

$$\text{EOQ} = \sqrt{\frac{2 \times 26,000 \times \$40}{\$10.40}} = \sqrt{200,000} = 447.2 \text{ packages} \cong 447 \text{ packages}$$

The EOQ drops from 600 packages to 447 packages when Koalo Blue's ordering cost per purchase order drops from $72 to $40.

20-28 (20-30 min.) **EOQ, cost of prediction error.**

1. EOQ $= \sqrt{\dfrac{2DP}{C}}$

    $D = 2{,}000;\ P = \$40;\ C = \$4 + (10\% \times \$50) = \$9$

    EOQ $= \sqrt{\dfrac{2(2{,}000)\$40}{\$9}} = 133.333$ tires $\simeq$ 133 tires

    TRC $= \dfrac{DP}{Q} + \dfrac{QC}{2}$ where Q can be any quantity, including the EOQ

    $= \dfrac{2{,}000 \times \$40}{133.3} + \dfrac{133.3 \times \$9}{2} = \$600 + \$600 = \$1{,}200$

    If students used an EOQ of 133 tires (order quantities rounded to the nearest whole number),

    TRC $= \dfrac{2{,}000 \times \$40}{133} + \dfrac{133 \times \$9}{2} = \$601.5 + \$598.5 = \$1{,}200.$

    Sum of annual relevant ordering and carrying costs equal $1,200.

2. The prediction error affects C, which is now:

    $C = \$4 + (10\% \times \$30) = \$7$

    $D = 2{,}000,\ P = \$40,\ C = \$7$

    EOQ $= \sqrt{\dfrac{2(2{,}000)\$40}{\$7}} = 151.186$ tires $\simeq$ 151 tires

20-28 (cont'd)

The cost of the prediction error can be calculated using a three-step procedure:

Step 1: Compute the monetary outcome from the best action that could have been taken, given the actual amount of the cost input.

$$TRC = \frac{DP}{Q} + \frac{QC}{2}$$

$$= \frac{2{,}000 \times \$40}{151.186} + \frac{151.186 \times \$7}{2}$$

$$= \$529.15 + \$529.15 = \$1{,}058.30$$

Step 2: Compute the monetary outcome from the best action based on the incorrect amount of the predicted cost input.

$$TRC = \frac{DP}{Q} + \frac{QC}{2}$$

$$= \frac{2{,}000 \times \$40}{133.333} + \frac{133.333 \times \$9}{2}$$

$$= \$600 + \$600 = \$1{,}200$$

Step 3: Compute the difference between the monetary outcomes from Step 1 and Step 2:

	Monetary Outcome
Step 1	$1,058.30
Step 2	1,200.00
Difference	$ (141.70)

The cost of the prediction error is $141.70.

Note: The $20 prediction error for the purchase price of the heavy-duty tires is irrelevant in computing purchase costs under the two alternatives because the same purchase costs will be incurred whatever the order size.

Some students may prefer to round off the EOQs to 133 tires and 151 tires respectively. The calculations under each step in this case follows:

Step 1: $TRC = \dfrac{2{,}000 \cdot \$40}{151} + \dfrac{151 \cdot \$7}{2} = \$529.80 + \$528.50 = \$1{,}058.30$

Step 2: $TRC = \dfrac{2{,}000 \cdot \$40}{133} + \dfrac{133 \cdot \$9}{2} = \$601.50 + \$598.50 = \$1{,}200.00$

Step 3: Difference $= \$1{,}058.30 - \$1{,}200.00 = \$141.70$

20-30 (20 min.)   **Supply-chain analysis, company viewpoints.**

1. The major benefits to adopting a supply-chain approach include:

   a. Overall reduction in inventory levels across the supply chain:
      - "receiving better information has allowed us to forecast and reduce inventory levels ..."
      - "The inventory levels are lower ... by not overstocking the warehouses"

   b. Fewer stockouts at the retail level.

   c. Reduced manufacturing of items not subsequently demanded by retailers:
      - "You produce only what you need"
      - "We have less waste by not overstocking the warehouses"

   d. Lower manufacturing costs due to better production scheduling and fewer expedited orders:
      - "We can fine tune our production scheduling"

These benefits can both increase revenues (fewer stockouts) and decrease costs (lower manufacturing costs, lower holding costs, and lower distribution costs).

2. Key obstacles to a manufacturer adopting a supply-chain approach are:

   a. Communication obstacles—includes the unwillingness of some parties to share information.

   b. Trust obstacles—includes the concern that all parties will not meet their agreed-upon commitments.

   c. Information system obstacles—includes problems due to the information systems of different parties not being technically compatible.

   d. Limited resources—includes problems due to the people and financial resources given to support a supply-chain initiative not being adequate.

20-32   (20 min.)   Backflush, two trigger points, materials purchase and sale (continuation of 20-32).

1.

(a) Purchases of raw materials	Inventory Control Accounts Payable Control	550,000	550,000

(b) Incur conversion costs	Conversion Costs Control
	    Various Accounts
	    (such as Accounts Payable)
	    Payable Control and Wages
		440,000	440,000

(c) Completion of finished goods	No entry		

(d) Sale of finished goods	Cost of Goods Sold
	    Inventory Control
	    Conversion Costs Allocated
		900,000	500,000
			400,000

(e) Underallocated
    or overallocated
    conversion costs
	Conversion Costs Allocated
	Cost of Goods Sold
	    Conversion Costs Control
		400,000
		40,000
			440,000

2.

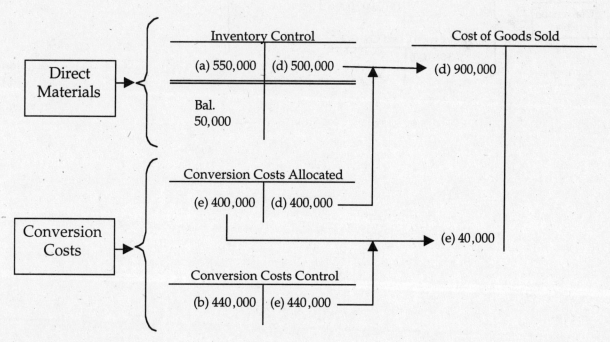

20-34 (20–25 min.) **Backflush costing and JIT production.**

1.

(a) Purchases of raw material	Inventory: Raw and In-Process Control	5,300,000	
	Accounts Payable Control		5,300,000
(b) Incur conversion costs	Conversion Costs Control	3,080,000	
	Various Accounts		3,080,000
(c) Completion of finished goods	Finished Goods Control	8,200,000	
	Inventory: Raw and In-Process Control		5,200,000
	Conversion Costs allocated		3,000,000
(d) Sale of finished goods	Cost of Goods Sold	7,872,000	
	Finished Goods Control		7,872,000

2.

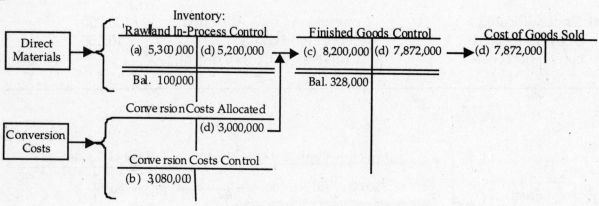

20-36 (20-25 min.) **Backflush, two trigger points, completion of production and sale (continuation of 20-34 and 20-35).**

1.

(a) Purchases of raw materials	No entry		
(b) Incur conversion	Conversion Costs Control	3,080,000	
	Various Accounts		3,080,000
(c) Completion of finished goods	Finished Goods Control	8,200,000	
	Accounts Payable Control		5,200,000
	Conversion Costs Allocated		3,000,000
(d) Sale of finished goods	Cost of Goods Sold	7,872,000	
	Finished Goods Control		7,872,000
(e) Underallocated or overallocated conversion costs	Conversion Costs Allocated	3,000,000	
	Cost of Goods Sold	80,000	
	Conversion Costs Control		3,080,000

2.

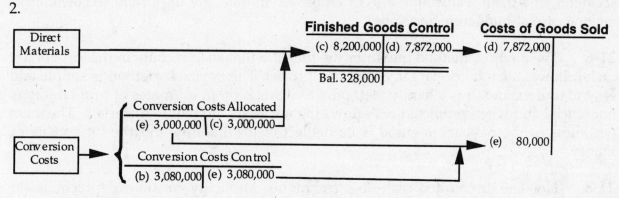

The $328,000 ending balance of Finished Goods Control consists of the 8,000 units of finished goods units in inventory at the standard cost of $41 per unit. Since the first trigger point is at the completion of production, the $100,000 of direct materials on hand (as shown in solution to Problem 20-34) are not recorded as inventory. In this version, in backflush costing, direct materials purchases are recorded only when finished goods are produced.

3.   The key difference between the accounting in Problem 20-34 and the accounting here is the absence of the Inventory: Raw and In-Process Control account. As a result, at the end of June, $100,000 of direct materials purchased but not yet manufactured into finished units have not been entered into the Inventory Control account. (Direct materials purchased is $5,300,000.) This variation of backflush costing is suitable for a production system that has virtually no direct materials inventory and minimum work-in-process inventories. It is less feasible otherwise.

CHAPTER 21
CAPITAL BUDGETING AND COST ANALYSIS

21-2 The six stages in capital budgeting are:

1. An *identification stage* to distinguish which capital expenditure projects will accomplish organization objectives.
2. A *search stage* that explores several potential capital expenditure investments that will achieve organization objectives.
3. An *information-acquisition stage* to consider the consequences of alternative capital investments.
4. A *selection stage* to choose projects for implementation.
5. A *financing stage* to obtain project financing.
6. An *implementation and control* stage to put the project in motion and monitor its performance.

21-4 No. Only quantitative outcomes are formally analyzed in capital-budgeting decisions. Many effects of capital-budgeting decisions, however, are difficult to quantify in financial terms. These nonfinancial or qualitative factors, for example, the number of accidents in a manufacturing plant, or employee morale, are important to consider in making capital-budgeting decisions.

21-6 The payback method measures the time it will take to recoup, in the form of net cash inflows, the total dollars invested in a project. The payback method is simple and easy to understand. It is a handy method when precision in estimates of profitability is not crucial and when predicted cash flows in later years are highly uncertain. The main weakness of the payback method is its neglect of profitability and the time value of money.

21-8 No. The discounted cash-flow techniques implicitly consider depreciation in rate of return computations; the compound interest tables automatically allow for recovery of investment. The net initial investment of an asset is usually regarded as a lump-sum outflow at time zero.

21-10 No. If managers are evaluated on the accrual accounting rate of return, they may not use the NPV method for capital-budgeting decisions. Instead, managers will choose investments that maximize the accrual accounting rate of return.

21-12 Four critical success factors that managers focus on when controlling job projects are (a) scope (b) quality (c) time schedule and (d) costs.

21-14 Exercises in compound interest.

The answers to these exercises are printed after the last problem, at the end of the chapter.

21-16 (30 min.) **Comparison of approaches to capital budgeting.**

The table for the present value of annuities (Appendix C, Table 4) shows: 10 periods at 14% = 5.216

1. Payback period $= \dfrac{\$110,000}{\$28,000} = 3.93$ years

2. Net present value
$$= \$28,000(5.216) - \$110,000$$
$$= \$146,048 - \$110,000 = \$36,048$$

3. Internal rate of return:

   $110,000 = Present value of annuity of $28,000 at X% for 10 years, or what factor (F) in the table of present values of an annuity (Appendix C, Table 4) will satisfy the following equation.

   $\$110,000 = \$28,000F$

   $$F = \dfrac{\$110,000}{\$28,000} = 3.929$$

On the ten-year line in the table for the present value of annuities (Appendix C, Table 4) find the column closest to 3.929; 3.929 is between a rate of return of 20% and 22%.

   Interpolation can be used to determine the exact rate:

	Present Value Factors	
20%	4.192	4.192
IRR rate	—	3.929
22%	3.923	—
Difference	0.269	0.263

Internal rate of return $= 20\% + \left[\dfrac{0.263}{0.269}\right](2\%)$

$$= 20\% + (0.978)(2\%) = 21.96\%$$

4. Accrual accounting rate of return based on net initial investment:

Net initial investment	$= \$110,000$
Estimated useful life	$= 10$ years
Annual straight-line depreciation	$= \$110,000 \div 10 = \$11,000$

Accrual accounting rate of return $= \dfrac{\$28,000 - \$11,000}{\$110,000}$

$$= \dfrac{\$17,000}{\$110,000} = 15.46\%$$

21-18 (20-30 min.) **Net present value, internal rate of return, sensitivity analysis.**

1a.   The table for the present value of annuities (Appendix D) shows:
16 periods at 14%   = 3.88

Net present value = $40,000 (3.889) – $120,000

= $155,560 – $120,000 = $35,560

1b.   Internal rate of return:
· $120,000 =   Present value of annuity of $40,000 at X% for 6 years, or what factor (F) in the table of present values of an annuity (Appendix C, Table 4) will satisfy the following equation.

$120,000 = $40,000F

$$F \quad = \frac{\$120,000}{\$40,000} = 3.0$$

On the six-year line in the table for the present value of annuities (Appendix D), find the column closest to 3.0; 3.0 is between a rate of return of 24% and 26%.

Interpolation is necessary:

	Present Value Factors	
24%	3.020	3.020
IRR rate	—	3.000
26%	2.885	—
Difference	0.135	0.020

$$\text{Internal rate of return} \quad = 24\% + \left[\frac{0.020}{0.135}\right](2\%)$$

$$= 24\% + (0.148)(2\%) \; = \; 24.30\%$$

2.   Let the minimum annual cash savings be $X.
Then we want $X (3.889)   = $120,000

$$X \quad = \frac{\$120,000}{3.889} \quad = \quad \$30,856$$

Johnson Corporation would want annual cash savings of at least $30,856 for the net present value of the investment to equal zero. This amount of cash savings would justify the investment in financial terms.

3.   When the manager is uncertain about future cash flows, the manager would want to do sensitivity analysis, a form of which is described in requirement 2. Calculating the minimum cash flows necessary to make the project desirable gives the manager a feel for whether the investment is worthwhile or not. If the manager were quite certain about the future cash-operating cost savings, the approaches in requirement 1 would be preferred.

21-20 (30 min.)   **Payback and NPV methods, no income taxes.**

1. a. Payback measures the time taken to recoup, in the form of expected future cash flows, the net investment in a project. Payback emphasizes the early recovery of cash as a key aspect of project ranking. Some managers argue that this emphasis on early recovery of cash is appropriate if there is a high level of uncertainty about future cash flows. Projects with shorter paybacks give the organization more flexibility because funds for other projects become available sooner.

Strengths

- Easy to understand
- One way to capture uncertainty about expected cash flows in later years of a project (although sensitivity analysis is a more systematic way)

Weaknesses

- Fails to incorporate the time value of money
- Does not consider a project's cash flows after the payback period

b.
Project A

Outflow, $200,000
Inflow, $50,000^1 + $50,000^2 + $50,000^3 + $50,000^4

Payback = 4 years

Project B

Outflow, $190,000

Inflow, $40,000^1 + $50,000^2 + $70,000^3 + $\dfrac{\$30,000^4}{\$75,000}$

Payback = $3 + \dfrac{\$30,000}{\$75,000}$ = 3.4 years

Project C

Outflow, $250,000

Inflow, $75,000^1 + $75,000^2 + $60,000^3 + $\dfrac{\$40,000^4}{\$80,000}$

Payback = $3 + \dfrac{\$40,000}{\$80,000}$ = 3.5 years

21-20 (cont'd)

Project D

Outflow, $210,000
Inflow, $75,000(Year 1) + $75,000(Year 2) + $60,000(Year 3)

Payback = 3 years

2. Solution Exhibit 21-22 shows the following ranking:

	NPV
1. Project C	$27,050
2. Project B	$25,635
3. Project D	$(3,750)
4. Project A	$(19,750)

3. Using NPV, Project C is the preferred project despite its having the longest payback. Project C has sizable cash inflows after the payback period. Nonfinancial qualitative factors should also be considered. For example, are there differential worker safety issues across the projects? Are there differences in the extent of learning that can benefit other projects? Are there differences in the customer relationships established with different projects that can benefit Cording Manufacturing in future projects?

SOLUTION EXHIBIT 21-20

Sketch of Relevant Cash Flows

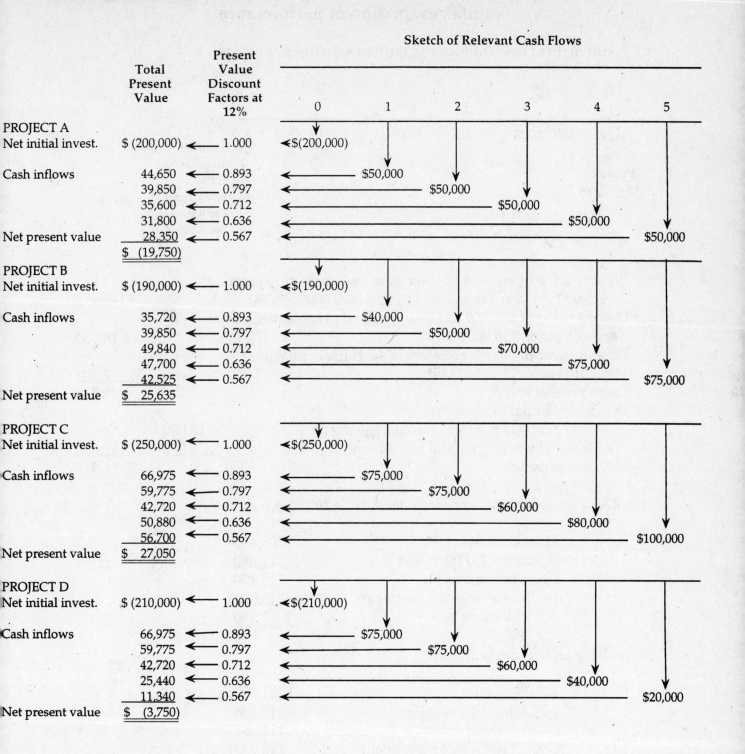

	Total Present Value	Present Value Discount Factors at 12%	0	1	2	3	4	5
PROJECT A								
Net initial invest.	$ (200,000) ← 1.000		◄$(200,000)					
Cash inflows	44,650 ← 0.893			$50,000				
	39,850 ← 0.797				$50,000			
	35,600 ← 0.712					$50,000		
	31,800 ← 0.636						$50,000	
Net present value	28,350 ← 0.567							$50,000
	$ (19,750)							
PROJECT B								
Net initial invest.	$ (190,000) ← 1.000		◄$(190,000)					
Cash inflows	35,720 ← 0.893			$40,000				
	39,850 ← 0.797				$50,000			
	49,840 ← 0.712					$70,000		
	47,700 ← 0.636						$75,000	
	42,525 ← 0.567							$75,000
Net present value	$ 25,635							
PROJECT C								
Net initial invest.	$ (250,000) ← 1.000		◄$(250,000)					
Cash inflows	66,975 ← 0.893			$75,000				
	59,775 ← 0.797				$75,000			
	42,720 ← 0.712					$60,000		
	50,880 ← 0.636						$80,000	
	56,700 ← 0.567							$100,000
Net present value	$ 27,050							
PROJECT D								
Net initial invest.	$ (210,000) ← 1.000		◄$(210,000)					
Cash inflows	66,975 ← 0.893			$75,000				
	59,775 ← 0.797				$75,000			
	42,720 ← 0.712					$60,000		
	25,440 ← 0.636						$40,000	
	11,340 ← 0.567							$20,000
Net present value	$ (3,750)							

21-22 (21-30 min.) **DCF, accrual accounting rate of return, working capital, evaluation of performance.**

1a. A summary of cash inflows and outflows (in thousands) are:

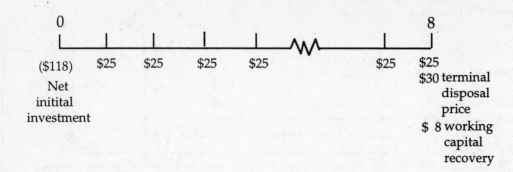

Present value of annuity of savings in cash operating costs ($25,000 per year for 8 years at 14%): $25,000 × 4.639	$115,975
Present value of $30,000 terminal disposal price of machine at end of year 8: $30,000 × 0.351	10,530
Present value of $8,000 recovery of working capital at end of year 8: $8,000 × 0.351	2,808
Gross present value	129,313

Deduct net initial investment:

Special-purpose machine, initial investment	$110,000	
Additional working capital investment	8,000	118,000
Net present value		$ 11,313

1b.   Use a trial and error approach. First, try a 16% discount rate:

$25,000 × 4.344	$108,600
($30,000 + $8,000) × .305	11,590
Gross present value	120,190
Deduct net initial investment	(118,000)
Net present value	$ 2,190

Second, try an 18% discount rate:

$25,000 × 4.078	$101,950
($30,000 + $8,000) × .266	10,108
Gross present value	112,058
Deduct net initial investment	(118,000)
Net present value	$ (5,942)

21-22 (cont'd)

By interpolation:

Internal rate of return $= 16\% + \left(\dfrac{2,190}{2,190 + 5,942}\right)(2\%)$

$= 16\% + (.269)(2\%) = 16.54\%$

2. Accrual accounting rate of return based on net initial investment:

Net initial investment $= \$110,000 + \$8,000$
$= \$118,000$

Annual depreciation
($110,000 - \$30,000) \div 8$ years $\quad = \quad \$10,000$

Accrual accounting rate of return $\quad = \dfrac{\$25,000 - \$10,000}{\$118,000} = 12.71\%$

3. If your decision is based on the DCF model, the purchase would be made because the net present value is positive, and the 16.54% internal rate of return exceeds the 14% required rate of return. However, you may believe that your performance may actually be measured using accrual accounting. This approach would show a 12.71% return on the initial investment, which is below the required rate. Your reluctance to make a "buy" decision would be quite natural unless you are assured of reasonable consistency between the decision model and the performance evaluation method.

21-24 (20-30 min.)   **Payback, net present value, relevant costs, sensitivity analysis.**

All amounts are in thousands.

1. Old cash flow: Cash revenues, $120 – Cash costs, $124 $ (4)
    New cash flow: 10% of $80   8
    Expected increase in recurring operating
       cash flows for 10 years $12

2. Initial machine investment $64
    Deduct current disposal price of old equipment   (4)
    Net initial investment $60

    Payback period: $60 ÷ $12 = 5 years

3. NPV of cash inflows and outflows (in thousands):

End of Year	Total Present Value	Present Value Discount Factor at 14%	0	1	9	10
				Sketch of Relevant Cash Flows		
1. Initial machine investment			$(64)			
2. Current disposal price of old equipment			$ 4			
Net initial investment	$(60.00) ←	1.00 ←	$(60)			
3. Recurring operating cash flows	62.40 ←	5.20 ←		$12 ◄————————————		$12
4. Terminal disposal price of machine	1.35 ←	0.27 ◄————————————				$ 5
Net present value	$ 3.75					

21-9

21-24 (cont'd)

4.   Let X = Annual gross vending machine receipts.

$$(.10X + \$4)(5.20) + \$1.35 = \$60$$
$$0.52X + \$20.80 = \$60 - \$1.35$$
$$0.52X = \$58.65 - \$20.80 = \$37.85$$
$$X = \$37.85 \div 0.52$$
$$= \$72.788 \text{ (or } \$72,788)$$

Proof:

$\$72,788 \times 10\%$	$ 7,278.80
Add	4,000.00
Total	11,278.80
Multiply by	5.20
Total	58,650.00
Disposal price, $5,000 × 0.27	1,350.00
Total	60,000.00
Deduct investment	(60,000.00)
Difference	$ 0

Note: Both the book value and the amortization on the old equipment are irrelevant.

21-26 (40 min.)   **NPV and customer profitability, no income taxes.**

1.

Homebuilders	2000	2001	2002	2003	2004	2005
Revenues (5%)*	$45,000	$47,250	$49,612	$52,093	$54,698	$57,433
COGS (4%)*	22,000	22,880	23,795	24,747	25,737	26,766
Op. Costs (4%)*	10,000	10,400	10,816	11,249	11,699	12,167
Total costs	32,000	33,280	34,611	35,996	37,436	38,933
Cash flow						
from operations	$13,000	$13,970	$15,001	$16,097	$17,262	$18,500
Kitchen						
Revenues (15%)*	$325,000	$373,750	$429,812	$494,284	$568,427	$653,691
COGS (4%)*	180,000	187,200	194,688	202,476	210,575	218,998
Op. Costs (4%)*	75,000	78,000	81,120	84,365	87,740	91,250
Total costs	255,000	265,200	275,808	286,841	298,315	310,248
Cash flow						
from operations	$ 70,000	$108,550	$154,004	$207,443	$270,112	$343,443
Subdivision						
Revenues (8%)*	$860,000	$928,800	$1,003,104	$1,083,352	$1,170,020	$1,263,622
COGS (4%)*	550,000	572,000	594,880	618,675	643,422	669,159
Op. Costs (4%)*	235,000	244,400	254,176	264,343	274,917	285,914
Total costs	785,000	816,400	849,056	883,018	918,339	955,073
Cash flow						
from operations	$75,000	$112,400	$154,048	$200,334	$251,681	$308,549

*Annual increases given in question.

2.

		Homebuilders		Kitchen		Subdivision	
		Cash Flow		Cash Flow		Cash Flow	
	P.V. Factor	from	Present	from	Present	from	Present
Year	for 10%	Operations	Value	Operations	Value	Operations	Value
2001	0.909	$13,970	$12,699	$108,550	$98,672	$112,400	$102,172
2002	0.826	15,001	12,391	154,004	127,207	154,048	127,244
2003	0.751	16,097	12,089	207,443	155,790	200,334	150,451
2004	0.683	17,262	11,790	270,112	184,486	251,681	171,898
2005	0.621	18,500	11,488	343,443	213,278	308,549	191,609
			$60,457		$779,433		$743,374

Customer NPVs

Homebuilders	$ 60,457
Kitchen Constructors	779,433
Subdivision Erectors	743,374

21-26 (cont'd)

3. Assume the 20% discount is given in 2001

	2000	2001	2002	2003	2004	2005
Revenues (5%)	$325,000	$260,000[a]	$273,000[b]	$286,650[b]	$300,982[b]	$316,031[b]
Total costs (4%)	255,000	265,200	275,808	286,841	298,315	310,248
Cash flow from operations	$ 70,000	$ (5,200)	$ (2,808)	$ (191)	$ 2,667	$ 5,783

[a] 20% price discount
[b] 5% annual increase

Net present value:

Year	P.V. Factor at 10%	Cash Flow from Operations	Present Value
2001	0.909	$(5,200)	$(4,727)
2002	0.826	(2,808)	(2,319)
2003	0.751	(191)	(143)
2004	0.683	2,667	1,822
2005	0.621	5,783	3,591
			$(1,776)

The 20% discount and reduced subsequent annual revenue reduces the NPV from $779,433 to ($1,776). This is a drop of $781,209 in NPV.

Christen should consider whether the price discount demanded by Kitchen need be met in full to keep the account. The implication of meeting the full demand is that the account is minimally profitable at best. An equally serious concern is whether Christen's other two customers will demand comparable price discounts if Kitchen's full demands are met. The consequence would be very large reductions in the NPVs of all its customers.

Christen should also consider the reliability of the growth estimates used in computing the NPVs. Are the predicted differences in revenue growth rates based on reliable information? Many revenue growth estimates by salespeople turn out to be overestimates or occur over a longer time period than initially predicted.

21-28 (30 min.) Special order, relevant costs, capital budgeting.

1. Relevant cash inflow from accepting the special order

	Relevant Cash Flows	
	Per Car (1)	Total (2)=(1) × 100,000
Incremental revenues (cash inflows)	$50	$5,000,000
Incremental costs (cash outflows)		
Neon paint	6	600,000
Boxes	3	300,000
Direct manufacturing labour	8	800,000
Total incremental costs	17	1,700,000
Net incremental benefit	$33	$3,300,000

Notes

(a) The costs of plastic cars are irrelevant because these cars have already been purchased and so entail no incremental cash flow.

(b) Vat depreciation is irrelevant because it is a past cost.

(c) Allocated plant manager's salary is irrelevant because it will not change whether or not the special order is accepted.

(d) Variable marketing costs are not deducted because they will not be incurred on the special order.

(e) Fixed marketing costs are irrelevant because they will not change whether or not the special order is accepted.

If it must offer the same $50 price to its other customers, Toys Inc. will lose cash flow of $9 × 130,000 = $1,170,000 per year for 4 years from its existing customers.

Note that whatever incremental costs Toys incurs on sales to its existing customers is irrelevant. These costs would continue to be incurred whether Toys prices the cars at $50 or $59. You can verify that Toys generates positive contribution margin at a price of $50 and so should continue to sell to its existing customers.

21-28 (cont'd)

From Appendix D, the present value of a stream of $1,170,000 payments for 4 years discounted at 16% is $1,170,000 × 2.798 = $3,273,660.

The net relevant benefit of accepting the special order is $3,300,000 – $3,273,660 = $26,340. Therefore, Toys, Inc. should accept the special order.

2.   Let the dollar discount from the current $59 price offered to existing customers be $X

Then $X (130,000) (2.798) =   3,300,000

$$X = \frac{3,300,000}{(130,000)(2.798)} = \$9.0724$$

At a price of $49.9276 ($59 – $9.0724) per car to its existing customers, Toys would just be indifferent between accepting and rejecting Tiny Tot's special order.

21-30 (25 min.) **Capital budgeting, computer-integrated manufacturing, sensitivity.**

1. The net present value analysis of the CIM proposal follows. We consider the differences in cash flows if the machine is replaced. All values in millions.

		Relevant Cash Flows	Present Value Discount Factors at 14%	Total Present Value
1.	Initial investment in CIM today	$(45)	1.000	$(45.000)
2a.	Current disposal price of old production line	5	1.000	5.000
2b.	Current recovery of working capital ($6 – $2)	4	1.000	4.000
3.	Recurring operating cash savings $4[1] each year for 10 years	4	5.216	20.864
4a.	Higher terminal disposal price of machines ($14 – $0) in year 10	14	0.270	3.780
4b.	Reduced recovery of working capital ($2 – $6) in year 10	(4)	0.270	(1.080)
Net present value of CIM investment				$(12.436)

On the basis of this formal financial analysis, Dynamo should not invest in CIM—it has a negative net present value of $(12.436) million.

[1]Recurring operating cash flows are as follows:

Cost of maintaining software programs and CIM equipment	$(1.5)
Reduction in lease payments due to reduced floor-space requirements	1.0
Fewer product defects and reduced rework	4.5
Annual recurring operating cash flows	$4.0

2. Requirement 1 only looked at cost savings to justify the investment in CIM. Burns estimates additional cash revenues net of cash operating costs of $3 million a year as a result of higher quality and faster production resulting from CIM.

From Appendix D, the net present value of the $3 million annuity stream for 10 years discounted at 14% is $3 × 5.216 = $15.648. Taking these revenue benefits into account, the net present value of the CIM investment is $3.212 ($15.648 – $12.436) million. On the basis of this financial analysis, Dynamo should invest in CIM.

21-30 (cont'd)

3. Let the annual cash flow from additional revenues be $X. Then we want the present value of this cash flow stream to overcome the negative NPV of $(12.436) calculated in requirement 1. Hence,

$$X (5.216) = 12.436$$

$$X = \$2.384 \text{ million}$$

An annuity stream of $2.384 million for 10 years discounted at 14% gives an NPV of $2.384 × 5.216 = 12.436 (rounded).

4.

		Relevant Cash Flows	Present Value Discount Factors at 14%	Total Present Value
1.	Initial investment in CIM today	$(45)	1.000	$(45.000)
2a.	Current disposal price of old production line	5	1.000	5.000
2b.	Current recovery of working capital ($6 – $2)	4	1.000	4.000
3a.	Recurring operating cash savings $4 each year for 5 years	4	3.433	13.732
3b.	Recurring cash flows from additional revenues of $3 each year for 5 years	3	3.433	10.299
4a.	Higher terminal disposal price of machines ($20 – $4) in year 5	16	0.519	8.304
4b.	Reduced recovery of working capital ($2 – $6) in year 5	(4)	0.519	(2.076)
	Net present value of CIM investment			$ (5.741)

The use of too short a time horizon such as 5 years biases against the adoption of CIM projects. Before finally deciding against CIM in this case, Burns should consider other factors including

(a) Sensitivity to different estimates of recurring cash savings or revenue gains.

(b) Accuracy of the costs of implementing and maintaining CIM.

(c) Benefits of greater flexibility that results from CIM and the opportunity to train workers for the manufacturing environment of the future.

(d) Potential obsolescence of the CIM equipment. Dynamo should consider how difficult the CIM equipment would be to modify if there is a major change in CIM technology.

(e) Alternative approaches to achieving the major benefits of CIM such as changes in process or implementation of just-in-time systems.

(f) Strategic factors. CIM may be the best approach to remain competitive against other low-cost producers in the future.

CHAPTER 22
CAPITAL BUDGETING: A CLOSER LOOK

22-2 Yes. To apply a consistent set of regulations and to provide for implementation of government initiatives, the federal government has implemented its own system of capital cost allowance (CCA). The Income Tax Act (ITA) does not permit a company to deduct amortization expense in determining taxable income but rather a company is allowed to deduct CCA. Therefore, the accounting amortization method will have no effect on taxes payable.

22-4 The total project approach calculates the present value of *all* cash outflows and inflows associated with each alternative. The incremental approach analyzes only those cash outflows and inflows that differ between alternatives.

22-6 No. Income taxes also affect the cash-operating flows from an investment and the cash flows from current and terminal disposal of machines in the capital-budgeting decision. When a company has positive cash-operating flows, income taxes reduce the cash flows available to the company from these sources.

22-8 The *real rate of return* is the rate of return required to cover only investment risk. This rate is made up of two elements: (a) a risk-free element and (b) a business-risk element. The *nominal rate of return* is the rate of return required to cover investment risk and the anticipated decline, due to inflation, in general purchasing power of the cash that the investment generates. This rate is made up of two elements: (a) the real rate of return and (b) an inflation element.

The *nominal rate of return* and the *real rate of return* are related as follows:

$$\text{Nominal rate} = [(1 + \text{Real rate})(1 + \text{Inflation rate})] - 1$$

22-10 The chapter outlines five approaches used to recognize risk in capital budgeting:

1. Varying the required payback time.
2. Adjusting the required rate of return.
3. Adjusting the estimated future cash flows.
4. Sensitivity ("what-if") analysis.
5. Estimating the probability distribution of future cash inflows and outflows for each project.

22-12   No. Discounted cash-flow analysis applies to both profit-seeking and nonprofit organizations. Nonprofit organizations must also decide which long-term assets will accomplish various tasks at the least cost. Nonprofit organizations incur an opportunity cost of funds.

22-14   NPV and IRR will not always rank projects identically. Different rankings occur when projects have unequal lives or unequal initial investments. The difference arises because the IRR method assumes a reinvestment rate equal to the indicated rate of return for the shortest-lived project. NPV assumes that funds can be reinvested at the required rate of return.

22-16 (15-20 min.) **Multiple choice.**

1. (a)

Before-tax annual cash flow	$10,000
Amortization ($30,000 ÷ 6)	(5,000)
Net income before tax	5,000
Income tax expense	2,000
Accounting income	$ 3,000

After-tax accrual accounting rate of return = $3,000 ÷ 30,000 = 10%

2. (b)

Year	CCA	Tax Shield	Operating-Cash Flows	Total Cash Flows	Cummulative Cash Flows
1	$ 3,000	$ 1,200	$10,000	$11,200	$11,200
2	5,400	2,160	10,000	12,160	23,360
3	4,320	1,728	10,000	11,728	35,088

Payback period = 2 + ((30,000 – 23,360)/11,728) = 2.6 years

3. (b)

	Relevant Cash Flows	Present-Value Discount Factors at 15%	Total Present Value
Initial investment	$(30,000)	1.000	$(30,000)
Recurring after-tax operating savings*	6,000	3.785	22,710
Tax shield from CCA**	6,405	1.000	6,405
Net present value			$ (885)

*10,000 × (1 – 0.40) = 6,000

**(30,000 × 0.4) × (0.20/(0.20 + 0.15)) × (2 + 0.15)/2(1 + 0.15)) = 6,405

4. (b) Only one payment will be made which 5 years later must yield $30,000. Therefore, deduct the value of an annuity of four payments from the value of an annuity of five payments:

$$3.353 - 2.856 = 0.497$$

Note that 3.353 – 2.856 = 0.497 is the present value of a cash outflow of $1 occurring at the end of period 5. Alternatively stated, $1 is the future value of $0.497 invested five years ago. Therefore, to have $30,000 now, we need to invest its present value 5 years ago discounted at 15% equal to:

$$\$30,000 \times 0.497 = \$14,910$$

22-18 (40 min.) **Total project versus differential approach, income taxes.**

(a) Total Project Approach

Replace machine

	Relevant Cash Flows	Present-Value Discount Factors at 14%	Total Present Value
Initial new machine investment	$(63,000)	1.000	$(63,000)
Disposal of old machine	29,000	1.000	29,000
Recurring after-tax cash operating costs*	(28,000)	2.322	(65,016)
Tax shield from CCA**	5,632	1.000	5,632
Net Present Value			$(93,384)

*$40,000 \times (1 - 0.3) = 28,000$

**$((63,000 - 29,000) \times 0.3) \times (0.2/(0.2 + 0.14)) \times ((2 + 0.14)/((2(1 + 0.14))) = 5,632$

Keep machine

	Relevant Cash Flows	Present-Value Discount Factors at 14%	Total Present Value
Disposal of old machine at end of useful life	$6,000	0.675 2.322	$4,050
Recurring after-tax cash operating costs*	(42,000)		(97,524)
Tax shield from CCA**	(1,059)	0.675	(715)
Net Present Value			$(94,189)

*$60,000 \times (1 - 0.3) = 42,000$

**$(-6,000 \times 0.3) \times (0.2/(0.2 + 0.14)) = -1,059$

Net present value different in favour of replacement. $805

(b) Differential Approach

	Relevant Cash Flows	Present-Value Discount Factors at 14%	Total Present Value
Initial new machine investment	$ (63,000)	1.000	$ (63,000)
Disposal of old machine	29,000	1.000	29,000
Recurring after-tax cash operating savings*	14,000	2.322	32,508
Tax shield from CCA	5,632	1.000	5,632
Difference in terminal value	(6,000)	0.675	(4,050)
Tax shield lost from terminal value	1,059	0.675	715
Net Present Value			$ 805

*$(60,000 - 40,000) \times (1 - 0.3) = 14,000$

22-20 (40 min.) **Project risk, required rate of return.**

<u>Drilling equipment project</u>

1.

		Relevant Cash Flows	Present-Value Discount Factors at 12%	Total Present Value
1.	Initial drilling equipment investment	$(1,000,000)	1.000	$(1,000,000)
2.	Tax shield rated by CCA*	191,822	1.000	191,822
3.	Recurring cash-operating flows	$ 370,000		
	Additional income taxes at 30%	(111,000)		
	Recurring after-tax cash-operating flows each year for 5 years (excl. amort. effects)	$ 259,000	3.605	933,695
	Net present value			$ 125,517

*$(1,000,000 \times 0.3) \times (0.25/(0.25 + 0.12)) \times ((2 + 0.12)/2(1 + 0.12)) = 191,822$

<u>Production equipment project</u>

	Relevant Cash Flows	Present-Value Discount Factors at 12%	Total Present Value
Initial production equipment investment	$ (800,000)	1.000	$(800,000)
Tax shield created by CCA*	153,475	1.000	153,475
Recurring operating cash flows**	210,000	3.037	637,770
Net Present Value			$ (8,755)

*$(800,000 \times 0.3) \times (0.25/(0.25 + 0.12)) \times ((2 + 0.12)/2(1 + 0.12)) = 153,475$
**$300,000 \times (1 - 0.3) = 210,000$

At a 12% discount rate for both projects, the drilling equipment project has the higher NPV and would be preferred.

2.   We calculate the NPV of the high-risk drilling equipment project assuming a required rate of return of 18%.

		Relevant Cash Flows	Present-Value Discount Factors at 18%	Total Present Value
1.	Initial drilling equipment investment	$(1,000,000)	1.000	$(1,000,000)
2.	Tax shield created by CCA*	$ 161,006	1.000	161,006
3.	Recurring cash-operating flows	$ 370,000		
	Additional income taxes at 30%	(111,000)		
	Recurring after-tax cash-operating flows each year for 5 years (excl. amort. effects)	$ 259,000	3.127	809,893
	Net present value			$ (29,101)

*$(1,000,000 \times 0.3) \times (0.25/(0.25 + 0.18)) \times ((2+0.18)/2(1 + 0.18)) = 161,006$

22-20 (cont'd)

The lower-risk production equipment project for the refinery discounted at 12% has an NPV of $8,755 (requirement 1) that is greater than the NPV of $(29,101) for the higher-risk drilling equipment project for oil exploration discounted at 18%.

3. Esso should favour the investment in the production equipment for the refinery because it has a positive NPV. It should not invest in the drilling equipment because this project has a negative NPV when discounted at the risk adjusted 18% required rate of return.

22-22 (25 min.) Inflation and nonprofit institution, no tax aspects.

1.   The university official calculated the following NPV using the 18.8% discount rate and real cash-operating savings.

Year	Relevant Cash-Operating Savings in Real Dollars as of 12-31-2000 (1)	Present-Value Discount Factors at 18.8% (2)	Present Value of Cash Flows (3) = (1) × (2)
2001	$1,000	0.842	$ 842
2002	1,000	0.709	709
2003	1,000	0.596	596
2004	1,000	0.502	502
2005	1,000	0.423	423
Present value of recurring cash-operating savings			3,072
Net initial investment			3,500
Net present value			$ (428)

On the basis of these calculations, the university official would reject the proposal to invest in the photocopying machine. This approach is incorrect because it discounts real cash flows using a nominal discount rate. I would redo the analysis after restating the real cash savings into nominal cash savings as shown below.

Year	Relevant Cash-Operating Savings in Nominal Dollars (1)	Present-Value Discount Factors at 18.8% (2)	Present Value of Nominal Cash Flows (3) = (1) × (2)
2001	$1,000 × 1.10 = $1,100	0.842	$ 926
2002	1,000 × (1.10)^2 = 1,210	0.709	858
2003	1,000 × (1.10)^3 = 1,331	0.596	793
2004	1,000 × (1.10)^4 = 1,464	0.502	735
2005	1,000 × (1.10)^5 = 1,611	0.423	681
Present value of recurring cash-operating savings			3,993
Net initial investment			3,500
Net present value			$ 493

22-22 (cont'd)

The net present value using nominal cash flows and a nominal rate of return is positive, $493. Eastern University should invest in the photocopying machine on the basis of financial considerations.

2a.   The real rate of return required by Eastern University can be computed using the following relationship:

$$(1 + \text{real rate}) = \frac{1 + \text{nominal rate}}{1 + \text{inflation rate}} = \frac{1 + 0.188}{1 + 0.10} = \frac{1.188}{1.10} = 1.08$$

Real rate of return required   =   0.08 or 8%

2b.   The net present value using real operating cash savings and real rates of return are as follows:

Year	Relevant Cash-Operating Savings in Real Dollars as of 12-31-2000	Present-Value Discount Factors at 8% (2)	Present Value of Real Cash Flows (3) = (1) × (2)
1	$1,000	0.926	$ 926
2	1,000	0.857	857
3	1,000	0.794	794
4	1,000	0.735	735
5	1,000	0.681	681
Present value of recurring cash-operating savings			3,993
Net initial investment			3,500
Net present value			$ 493

3.   Requirements 1 and 2 when correctly done give the same NPV of $493. Consistency is key in capital budgeting. Requirement 1 uses nominal cash flows and nominal rates of return. Requirement 2 uses real cash flows and real rates of return. Both are valid approaches.

22-8

22-24 (20-30 min.) **Comparison of projects with unequal lives.**

1. Internal rate of return

Project 1

Let F = Present-value factor of $1 at X% received at the end of 1 year, Appendix C, Table 2

$$\$10,000 = \text{PV of \$12,000 at X\% to be received at the end of year 1}$$

$$F = \frac{\$10,000}{\$12,000} = 0.833$$

$$\text{IRR} = 20\%$$

Project 2

Let F = Present-value factor of $1 at X% received at the end of year 4, Appendix C, Table 2

$$\$10,000 = \text{PV of \$17,500 at X\% to be received at the end of year 4}$$

$$F = \frac{\$10,000}{\$17,500} = 0.571$$

The internal rate of return can be calculated by interpolation:

	Present-Value Factors for $1 Received after 4 years	
14%	0.592	0.592
IRR rate	–	0.571
16%	0.552	–
Difference	0.040	0.021

$$\text{IRR rate: } 14\% + \left(\frac{0.021}{0.040}\right)(2\%) = 15.05\%$$

Project 1 is preferable to Project 2 using the IRR criterion.

2. Net present value

Project 1:

Gross present value = PV of $12,000 at 10% to be received at the end of year 1
= $12,000 (0.909) = $10,908
Net present value = $10,908 – $10,000 = $908

22-9

Project 2:

Gross present value = PV of $17,500 at 10% to be received at the end of year 4
                      = $17,500 (0.683)   = $11,952.50

Net present value   = $11,952.50 − $10,000 = $1,952.50

Project 2 is preferable to Project 1 using the net present-value criterion.

3. This problem contrasts the implied reinvestment rates of return under the internal rate of return and net present-value methods. Where the economic lives of mutually exclusive projects are unequal, this clash of reinvestment rates may give different conclusions under the two methods. This result occurs because the internal rate of return method assumes that the reinvestment rate is at least equal to the computed rate of return on the project. The net present-value method assumes that the funds obtainable from competing projects can be reinvested at the rate of the company's required rate of return. Comparisons follow:

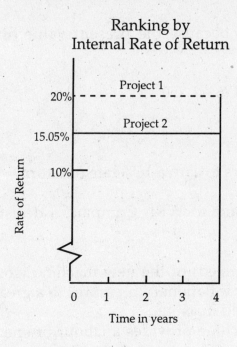

Ranking by
Internal Rate of Return

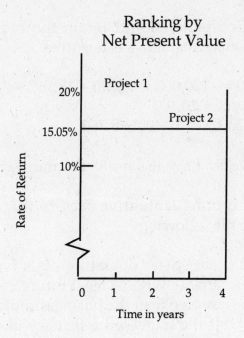

Ranking by
Net Present Value

Assumption: Project 1 funds can be reinvested at 20% over the life of the shorter-lived project.

Assumption: Project (1) funds can be reinvested at 10%, the required rate of return.

22-26 (40 min.) **Replacement of a machine, income taxes, sensitivity.**

1.

	Relevant Cash Flows	Present-Value Discount Factors at 16%	Total Present Value
Initial machine investment	$ (120,000)	1.000	$ (120,000)
Proceeds from disposal of old machine	40,000	1.000	40,000
Tax shield created by CCA*	18,167	1.000	18,167
Recurring operating savings**	11,400	2.798	31,897
Proceeds from disposal of machine***	13,000	0.552	7,176
Lost tax shield because of disposal****	(3,171)	0.552	(1,750)
Net Present Value			$ (24,510)

*$((120,000 - 40,000) \times 0.4) \times (0.25/(0.25 + 0.16)) \times ((2 + .16)/(2(1 + 0.16))) = 18,167$

**$300,000 \times (0.2 - 0.14) \times (1 - 0.4) + (15,000 - 14,000)0.6 = 11,400$

***$20,000 - 7,000 = 13,000$

****$(-13,000 \times 0.4) \times (0.25/(0.25 + 0.16)) = -3,171$

WRL Company should retain the old equipment because the present value of the incremental cash flows is negative.

2. $0 = -120,000 + 40,000 + 18,167 + 2.798atcs + 7,176 - 1,750$
$atcs = 20,160$
$20,160 - 11,400 = 8,760$

WRL would have to save $8,760 more after-tax dollars to earn a 16% rate of return.

3.   The nonquantitative factors that are important to WRL Company's decision include the following:

(a) The lower operating costs (variable and fixed) of the new machine would enable WRL to meet future competitive or inflationary pressures to a greater degree than the business could using the old machine.

(b) If the increased efficiency of the new machine provides a labour or energy cost savings, then additional increases in these costs in the future would make the new machine more attractive.

(c) Maintenance and servicing of both machines should be reviewed in terms of reliability of the manufacturer and the costs.

(d) Potential technological advances in machinery over the next four years should be evaluated.

(e) Space requirements for the new machine should be reviewed and compared with the space requirements of the present equipment to determine if more or less space is required.

22-28 (35 min.) Capital budgeting, inventory changes.

1. A schedule of relevant cash flows follows:

Sketch of Relevant Cash Flows

	Year 0	Year 1	Year 2	Year 3	Year 4
Acquire machines	($109,200)				
Sales					
6,000 × $25		$150,000			
6,200 × $25			$155,000		
7,700 × $24				$184,800	
3,100 × $22					$68,200
Manufacturing Costs					
7,000 × $12		(84,000)			
6,500 × $13			(84,500)		
6,500 × $14				(91,000)	
3,000 × $15					(45,000)
Marketing, distribution & customer service costs					
6,000 × $3		(18,000)			
6,200 × $3			(18,600)		
7,700 × $3				(23,100)	
3,100 × $3					(9,300)
Disposal of machine					18,000
Taxes (see schedule)		(18,540)	(13,165)	(14,914)	(7,425)
Net cash flow after tax	($109,200)	$ 29,460	$ 38,735	$ 55,786	$ 30,275

	Year 1	Year 2	Year 3	Year 4
Sales	$150,000	$155,000	$184,800	$ 68,200
COGS*	72,000	79,600	106,500	46,400
Mkt, Dist. & Cust. serv.	18,000	18,600	23,100	9,300
CCA	13,650	23,888	17,916	8,937
Taxable income	$ 46,350	$ 32,912	$ 37,284	$ 3,563
Tax Rate	40%	40%	40%	40%
Taxes	$ 18,540	$ 13,165	$ 14,914	$ 1,425

*Year 1: 6,000 × 12 = 72,000

Year 2: (1,000 × 12) + (5,200 × 13) = 79,600

Year 3: (1,300 × 13) + (6,400 × 14) = 106,500

Year 4: (100 × 14) + (3,000 × 15) = 46,400

2.

	Relevant Cash Flows	Present- Value Discount Factors at 16%	Total Present Value
Year 0	$ (109,200)	1.000	$ (109,200)
Year 1	29,460	0.862	25,395
Year 2	38,735	0.743	28,780
Year 3	55,786	0.641	35,759
Year 4	30,275	0.552	16,712
Remaining CCA tax shield*	6,539	0.476	3,113
Net Present Value			$ 558

$*((109,200 - 13,650 - 23,888 - 17,916 - 8,937 - 18,000) \times 0.4) \times (0.25 / (0.25 + 0.16)) = 6,539$

22-30 (40 min.) **Mining, income taxes inflation, sensitivity analysis.**

1.   Annual cash flow (Years 1-5)

Revenue ($350 × 4,800[a])		$1,680,000
Cash-operating costs		
Variable costs ($100 × 4,800)	480,000	
Technicians ($110,000)	110,000	
Maintenance	50,000	
Total cash-operating costs		640,000
Recurring cash-operating flows		1,040,000
Additional income taxes at 40%		416,000
Recurring after-tax cash-operating flows		
each year for 5 years (excl. amort. effects)		$624,000

Year	CCA	Tax Shield	Operating Cash Flows	Total Cash Flows	Cummulative Cash Flows
1	$450,000	$180,000	$624,000	$804,000	$ 804,000
2	765,000	306,000	624,000	930,000	1,734,000
3	535,500	214,200	624,000	838,200	2,572,200
4	374,850	149,940	624,000	773,940	3,346,140

Payback period = 3 + ((3,000,000 − 2,572,200)/773,940) = 3.55 years

2.   The net present value of VanDyk Enterprises' proposed acquisition of the extraction equipment is $60,745, as shown in the following calculation:

	Relevant Cash Flows	Present-Value Discount Factors at 12%	Total Present Value
Initial equipment investment	$ (3,000,000)	1.000	$ (3,000,000)
Recurring cash-operating savings*	624,000	3.605	2,249,520
Tax shield created by CCA**	811,225	1.000	811,225
Net Present Value			$ 60,745

*1,040,000 × (1 − 0.4) = 624,000

**((3,000,000 × 0.4) × 0.3/(0.3 + 0.12)) × ((2 + 0.12) (2(1 + 0.12))) = 811,125

3.   In order for VanDyk Enterprises' acquisition of the extraction equipment to break even from a net present-value perspective, the revenue per ounce of gold must be at least $344.15, calculated as follows.

0	=	−3,000,000 + 811,225 + 3.605os
os	=	607,150
607,150	=	(4,800 × (rev − 100) − 110,000 − 50,000) × (1 − 0.4)
rev	=	344.15

Therefore the minimum revenue per ounce is $344.15.

22-30 (cont'd)

4.   Under the assumptions given here, requirement 2 has already calculated NPV using nominal cash flows and nominal rates of return. It has already taken inflationary effects into consideration. Hence no new calculations are necessary. The after-tax net present value is $60,745 as calculated in requirement 2. Some students may question whether the assumptions specified in requirement 4 are appropriate since despite the 2% inflation per year, the revenues and cash-operating costs are assumed to be the same each year for the 5 years. There is no inconsistency here. Despite the 2% increase in general price levels, the specific revenues per ounce of gold and the specific cash-operating costs in this industry could well be the same either because of contractual reasons or because of the general economic conditions of supply and demand.

22-32 (40 min.) **Ranking projects.**

1. <u>Project B</u>

Let F = Present-value factor for an annuity of $1 for 10 years in Appendix C, Table 4

$$\$100,000 = \$20,000\ F$$
$$F = 5.000 \text{ for ten-year life}$$

The internal rate of return can be calculated by interpolation:

	Present-Value Factors for Annuity of $1 for 10 years	
14%	5.216	5.216
IRR	–	5.000
16%	4.833	–
Difference	0.383	0.216

$$\text{IRR} = 14\% + \left(\frac{0.216}{0.383}\right)(2\%) = 15.1\%$$

<u>Project C</u>
$$\$200,000 = \$70,000\ F$$

Let F = Present-value factor for an annuity of $1 for 5 years in Appendix C, Table 4

$$F = 2.857 \text{ for five-year life}$$

The internal rate of return can be calculated by interpolation:

	Present-Value Factors for Annuity of $1 for 5 years	
22%	2.864	2.864
IRR	–	2.857
24%	2.745	–
Difference	0.119	0.007

$$\text{IRR} = 22\% + \left(\frac{0.007}{0.119}\right)(2\%) = 22.1\%$$

22-32 (cont'd)

Project D

$200,000 = PV of a four-year annuity of $200,000 per year deferred five years

Trial and error:

	At 18%	At 20%	At 22%
$1 per year for 4 years	2.690	2.589	2.494
Multiply by $200,000, the total value of the annuity	$538,000	$517,800	$498,800
Multiply by the present value of $1 five years hence	0.437	0.402	0.370
PV of annuity in arrears	$235,106	$208,156	$184,556

$$IRR = 20\% + \left(\frac{\$208,156 - \$200,000}{\$208,156 - \$184,556}\right)(2\%)$$

$$= 20\% + \left(\frac{\$8,156}{\$23,600}\right)(2\%) = 20.7\%$$

Ranking of Projects

Rank	Project	IRR	Initial Investment
1	C	22.1%	$200,000
2	D	20.7	200,000
3	B	15.1	100,000
4	A	14.0	100,000
5	E	12.6	200,000
6	F	12.0	50,000

2. Budget limit:

$500,000	$550,000	$650,000
C	C	C
D	D	D
B	B	B
	F	A
		F

3. Ranking by net present value, discounting at 16%:

Rank	Project	Net Present Value
1	D	$ 66,370
2	C	29,180
3	B	(3,340)
4	F	(3,384)
5	A	(13,170)
6	E	(35,965)

22-32 (cont'd)

Because 16% is the implicit reinvestment rate, these rankings are different from the rankings made on the basis of internal rates of return in requirement 1.

Computations

Project D

PV of $200,000 per year for four years at 16% = $200,000 (2.798)	$559,600
It is in arrears five years, so PV = $559,600 (0.476)	266,370
Net initial investment	(200,000)
Net present value	$ 66,370

Project C

PV of $70,000 per year for five years at 16% = $70,000 (3.274)	$229,180
Net initial investment	(200,000)
Net present value	$ 29,180

Project B

PV of $20,000 per year for ten years at 16% = $20,000 (4.833)	$ 96,660
Net initial investment	(100,000)
Net present value	$ (3,340)

Project F

PV at 16%:		
	$23,000 × 0.862	$ 19,826
	20,000 × 0.743	14,860
	10,000 × 0.641	6,410
	10,000 × 0.552	5,520
	Total PV	46,616
Net initial investment		(50,000)
Net present value		$ (3,384)

Project A

PV of annuity of $20,000 for 15 years	= $20,000 × 5.575	$111,500
Deduct deferral of 2 years	= 20,000 × 1.605	(32,100)
PV of annuity in arrears		79,400
PV of $10,000 due in 2 years	= 10,000 × 0.743	7,430
Total PV		86,830
Net initial investment		(100,000)
Net present value		$ (13,170)

22-32 (cont'd)

Project E

PV of annuity of $50,000 for 10 years	= $50,000	×	4.833	$241,650
Deduct deferral of 3 years	= 50,000	×	2.246	(112,300)
PV of annuity in arrears				129,350
PV of $30,000 due in 3 years	= 30,000	×	0.641	19,230
PV of $15,000 due in 2 years	= 15,000	×	0.743	11,145
PV of $ 5,000 due in 1 year	= 5,000	×	0.862	4,310
Total PV				164,035
Net initial investment				(200,000)
Net present value				$ (35,965)

4. Other influential factors include:

   (a) The risk linked with a given proposal may prompt management to judge it more or less attractive than other proposals that promise a comparable internal rate of return.

   (b) Future investment opportunities may affect the current relative attractiveness of alternative proposals. For example, if management expects that in five years hence the best available alternatives will bring less than 20%, Project D (which promises an internal rate of return of 20.7% for 9 years) may be preferable to Project C (which promises 22.1% for 5 years). However, if future opportunities are expected to bring equal or higher internal rates of return, a shorter-lived project may be more attractive, even though a longer-lived project may yield a higher rate of return. Thus, if a choice must be made now between E and F, Project F (12.0% for 4 years) may be chosen instead of Project E (12.6%, but it locks in capital for 10 years and necessitates a much larger investment).

22-34 (40-50 min.) **Ethics, discounted cash-flow analysis.**
1.

	Relevant Cash Flows	Present-Value Discount Factors at 12%	Total Present Value
Initial equipment investment	$ (900,000)	1.000	$ (900,000)
Initial working capital investment	(200,000)	1.000	(200,000)
Tax shield created by CCA*	207,191	1.000	207,191
Cash flow from canceling lease**	(19,200)	1.000	(19,200)
Additional working capital investment	(200,000)	0.797	(159,400)
Recurring rent cash flow forgone***	(28,800)	4.111	(118,397)
Recurring operating cash flows****			1,200,448
Market research and sales promotion cash flows*****	(192,000)	0.893	(171,456)
Recovery of working capital	400,000	0.507	202,800
Proceeds from disposal of equipment	300,000	0.507	152,100
Lost tax shield from disposal******	(72,973)	0.507	(36,997)
Net Present Value			$ 157,089

*$(900,000 \times 0.36) \times (0.25/(0.25 + 0.12)) \times ((2 + 0.12)/(2(1 + 0.12))) = 207,191$

**$-30,000 \times (1 - 0.36) = -19,200$

***$-45,000 \times (1 - 0.36) = -28,800$

****Recurring after-tax cash-operating flows

Year (1)	Cash-Operating Flows (2)	After-Tax Cash-Operating Flows (3) = 0.64 × (2)	Present-Value Discount Factors at 12%	Total Present Value
1	$400,000	$256,000	0.893	$ 228,608
2	400,000	256,000	0.797	204,032
3	600,000	384,000	0.712	273,408
4	600,000	384,000	0.636	244,224
5	600,000	384,000	0.567	217,728
6	100,000	64,000	0.507	32,448
				$1,200,448

*****$-300,000 \times (1 - 0.36) = -192,000$

******$(-300,000 \times 0.36) \times (0.25/(0.25 + 0.12)) = -72,973$

Dudley should launch the new household product because investing in the product has a positive net present value.

2.

	Relevant Cash Flows	Present-Value Discount Factors at 12%	Total Present Value
Initial equipment investment	$ (1,150,000)	1.000	$ (1,150,000)
Initial working capital investment	(200,000)	1.000	(200,000)
Tax shield created by CCA*	264,744	1.000	264,744
Cash flow from canceling lease**	(19,200)	1.000	(19,200)
Additional working capital investment	(200,000)	0.797	(159,400)
Recurring rent cash flow forgone***	(28,800)	4.111	(118,397)
Recurring operating cash flows (see above)			1,200,448
Market research and sales promotion cash flows****	(192,000)	0.893	(171,456)
Recovery of working capital	400,000	0.507	202,800
Proceeds from disposal of equipment	300,000	0.507	152,100
Lost tax shield from disposal*****	(72,973)	0.507	(36,997)
Net Present Value			$ (35,358)

$$*(1,150,000 \times 0.36) \times (0.25/(0.25 + 0.12)) \times ((2 + 0.12)/(2(1 + 0.12))) = 264,744$$

$$**{-30,000} \times (1 - 0.36) = -19,200$$

$$***{-45,000} \times (1 - 0.36) = -28,800$$

$$****{-300,000} \times (1 - 0.36) = -192,000$$

$$*****(-300,000 \times 0.36) \times (0.25/(0.25 + 0.12)) = -72,973$$

The overall NPV of the project would then be $(35,358). Griffey is unhappy with Chen's revised analysis because the NPV of the project is now negative, possibly leading to the project being rejected. He would like to resume production in the plant, and reemploy his friends who had been laid off earlier. There is also the possibility that Griffey may be hired as a consultant by the new plant management after he retires next year.

Considering the ethical issues, Andrew Chen should evaluate Eric Griffey's directives as follows:

(a) Chen should present complete and clear reports and recommendations after appropriate analyses of relevant and reliable information. Griffey does not wish the report to be complete or clear, and has provided some information which is not totally reliable.

(b) Chen should not disclose confidential information outside of the organization; but it also appears that Griffey wants to refrain from disclosing information to senior management that it should know about.

(c) In evaluating Griffey's directive as it affects Chen, Chen has an obligation to communicate unfavourable as well as favourable information and professional judgments or opinions.

The responsibility to communicate information fairly and objectively, as well as to disclose fully all relevant information that could reasonably be expected to influence an intended user's understanding of the reports and recommendations presented, is being hampered. Management will not have the full scope of information they should have when they are presented with the analysis.

Andrew Chen should take the following steps to resolve this situation:

- Chen should first investigate and see if Dudley Company has an established policy for resolution of ethical conflicts and follow those procedures.
- If this policy does not resolve the ethical conflict, the next step would be for Chen to discuss the situation with his supervisor, Griffey, and see if he can obtain resolution. One possible solution may be to present a "base case" and sensitivity analysis of the investment. Chen should make it clear to Griffey that he has a problem and is seeking guidance.
- If Chen cannot obtain a satisfactory resolution with Griffey, he could take the situation up to the next layer of management, and inform Griffey that he is doing this. If this is not satisfactory, Chen should progress to the next, and subsequent, higher levels of management until the issue is resolved (i.e., the president, Audit Committee, or Board of Directors).
- Chen may want to have a confidential discussion with an objective advisor to clarify relevant concepts and obtain an understanding of possible courses of action.
- If Chen cannot satisfactorily resolve the situation within the organization, he may resign from the company and submit an informative memo to an appropriate person in Dudley (i.e., the president, Audit Committee, or Board of Directors).

CHAPTER 23
CONTROL SYSTEMS, TRANSFER PRICING, AND MULTINATIONAL CONSIDERATIONS

23-2 To be effective, management control systems should be (a) closely aligned to an organization's strategies and goals, (b) designed to fit the organization's structure and the decision-making responsibility of individual managers, and (c) able to motivate managers and employees to put in effort to attain selected goals desired by top management.

23-4 The chapter cites five benefits of decentralization:
1. Creates greater responsiveness to local needs.
2. Leads to quicker decision making.
3. Increases motivation.
4. Aids management development and learning.
5. Sharpens the focus of managers.

The chapter cites four costs of decentralization:
1. Leads to suboptimal decision making.
2. Results in duplication of activities.
3. Decreases loyalty toward the organization as a whole.
4. Increases costs of gathering information.

23-6 No. A transfer price is the price one subunit of an organization charges for a product or service supplied to another subunit of the same organization. The two segments can be cost centres, profit centres, or investment centres. For example, the allocation of service department costs to production departments that are set up as either cost centres or investment centres is an example of transfer pricing.

23-8 Transfer prices should have the following properties. They should
1. promote goal congruence,
2. promote a sustained high level of management effort,
3. promote a high level of subunit autonomy in decision making.

23-10 Transferring products or services at market prices generally leads to optimal decisions when (a) the intermediate market is perfectly competitive, (b) interdependencies of subunits are minimal, and (c) there are no additional costs or benefits to the corporation as a whole in using the market instead of transacting internally.

23-12 Reasons why a dual-pricing approach to transfer pricing is not widely used in practice include:
1. The manager of the division using a cost-based method does not have sufficient incentives to control costs.
2. This approach does not provide clear signals to division managers about the level of decentralization top management wants.
3. This approach tends to insulate managers from the frictions of the marketplace.

23-14 Yes. The general transfer-pricing guideline specifies that the minimum transfer price equals the additional *outlay costs* per unit incurred up to the point of transfer *plus* the *opportunity costs* per unit to the supplying division. When the supplying division has idle capacity, its opportunity costs are zero; when the supplying division has no idle capacity, its opportunity costs are positive. Hence the minimum transfer price will vary depending on whether the supplying division has idle capacity or not.

23-16 (25 min.) **Decentralization, responsibility centres**.

1. The manufacturing plants in the Manufacturing Division are cost centres. Senior management determines the manufacturing schedule based on the quantity of each type of lighting product specified by the sales and marketing division and detailed studies of the time and cost to manufacture each type of product. Manufacturing managers are accountable only for costs. They are evaluated based on achieving target output within budgeted costs.

2a. If manufacturing and marketing managers were to directly negotiate the prices for manufacturing various products, Quinn should evaluate manufacturing plant managers as profit centres—revenues received from marketing minus the costs incurred to produce and sell output.

2b. Quinn Corporation would be better off decentralizing its marketing and manufacturing decisions and evaluating each division as a profit centre. Decentralization would encourage plant managers to increase total output to achieve the greatest profitability, and motivate plant managers to cut their costs to increase margins. Manufacturing managers would be motivated to design their operations according to the criteria that meet the marketing managers' approval, thereby improving cooperation between manufacturing and marketing.

Under Quinn's existing system, manufacturing managers had every incentive not to improve. Manufacturing managers' incentives were to get as high a cost target as possible so that they could produce output within budgeted costs. Any significant improvements could result in the target costs being lowered for the next year, increasing the possibility of not achieving budgeted costs. By the same line of reasoning, manufacturing managers would also try to limit their production so that production quotas would not be increased in the future. Decentralizing manufacturing and marketing decisions overcomes these problems.

23-18 (35 min.) **Multinational transfer pricing, effect of alternative transfer-pricing methods, global income tax minimization.**

1. This is a three-country, three-division transfer pricing problem with three alternative transfer-pricing methods. Summary data in Canadian dollars are:

China Plant

Variable costs:	1,000 Yuan ÷ 8 Yuan per $ = $125 per subunit
Fixed costs:	1,800 Yuan ÷ 8 Yuan per $ = $225 per subunit

South Korea Plant

Variable costs:	240,000 Won ÷ 800 Won per $ = $300 per unit
Fixed costs:	320,000 Won ÷ 800 Won per $ = $400 per unit

Canadian Plant

Variable costs:	= $100 per unit
Fixed costs:	= $200 per unit

Market prices for private label sale alternatives:
China Plant: 3,600 Yuan ÷ 8 Yuan per $ = $450 per subunit
South Korea Plant: 1,040,000 Won ÷ 800 Won per $ = $1,300 per unit

The transfer prices under each method are:

(a) Market price
  • China to South Korea   = $450 per subunit
  • South Korea to Canadian Plant = $1,300 per unit

(b) 200% of full costs
  • China to South Korea
      2.0 ($125 + $225) = $700 per subunit
  • South Korea to Canadian Plant
      2.0 ($700 + $300 + $400) = $2,800 per unit

(c) 300% of variable costs
  • China to South Korea
      3.0 ($125) = $375 per subunit
  • South Korea to Canadian Plant
      3.0 ($375 + $300) = $2,025 per unit

23-18 (cont'd)

	Method A Internal Transfers at Market Price	Method B Internal Transfers at 200% of Full Costs	Method C Internal Transfers at 300% of Variable Costs
1. CHINA DIVISION			
Division revenues per unit	$ 450	$ 700	$ 375
Deduct :			
Division variable costs per unit	125	125	125
Division fixed costs per unit	225	225	225
Division operating income per unit	100	350	25
Income tax at 40%	40	160	10
Division net income per unit	$ 60	$ 190	$ 15
2. SOUTH KOREA DIVISION			
Division revenues per unit	$1,300	$2,800	$2,025
Deduct:			
Transferred-in costs per unit	450	700	375
Division variable costs per unit	300	300	300
Division fixed costs per unit	400	400	400
Division operating income per unit	150	1,400	950
Income tax at 20%	30	280	190
Division net income per unit	$ 120	$1,120	$ 760
3. CANADIAN DIVISION			
Division revenues per unit	$3,200	$3,200	$3,200
Deduct:			
Transferred-in costs per unit	1,300	2,800	2,025
Division variable costs per unit	100	100	100
Division fixed costs per unit	200	200	200
Division operating income per unit	1,600	100	875
Income tax at 30%	480	30	262.5
Division net income per unit	$ 1,120	$ 70	$ 612.5

23-18 (cont'd)

2.   Division net income:

	Market Price	200% of Full Costs	300% of Variable Cost
China Division	$ 60	$ 190	$ 15.00
South Korea Division	120	1,120	760.00
Canadian Division	1,120	70	612.50
User Friendly Computer Inc.	$1,300	$1,380	$1,387.50

User Friendly will maximize its net income by using the 300% of variable cost, transfer-pricing method. This is because the 300% of full cost method sources most income in the country with the lower income tax rates.

23-20 (30 min.)   **Effect of alternative transfer-pricing methods on division operating income.**

1.

	Internal Transfers at Market Prices Method B	Internal Transfers at 110% of Full Costs Method A
MINING DIVISION		
Revenues:		
$90, $66^1 × 400,000 units	$36,000,000	$26,400,000
Deduct:		
Division variable costs:		
$52^2 × 400,000 units	20,800,000	20,800,000
Division fixed costs:		
$8^3 × 400,000 units	3,200,000	3,200,000
Division operating income	$12,000,000	$ 2,400,000
METALS DIVISION		
Revenues:		
$150 × 400,000 units	$60,000,000	$60,000,000
Deduct:		
Transferred-in costs:		
$90, $66 × 400,000 units	36,000,000	26,400,000
Division variable costs:		
$36^4 × 400,000 units	14,400,000	14,400,000
Division fixed costs:		
$15^5 × 400,000 units	6,000,000	6,000,000
Division operating income	$ 3,600,000	$13,200,000

[1]$66 = $60 × 110%

[2]Variable cost per unit in Mining Division = Direct materials + Direct manufacturing labour + 75% of Manufacturing overhead = $12 + $16 + 75% × $32 = $52

[3]Fixed cost per unit = 25% of Manufacturing overhead = 25% ×$32 = $8

[4]Variable cost per unit in Metals Division = Direct materials + Direct manufacturing labour + 40% of Manufacturing overhead = $6 + $20 + 40% × $25 = $36

[5]Fixed cost per unit in Metals Division = 60% of Manufacturing overhead = 60% × $25 = $15

23-20 (cont'd)

2.   Bonus paid to division managers at 1% of division operating income will be as follows:

	Method B Internal Transfers at Market Prices	Method A Internal Transfers at 110% of Full Costs
Mining Division manager's bonus (1% × $12,000,000; 1% × $2,400,000)	$120,000	$ 24,000
Metals Division manager's bonus (1% × $3,600,000; 1% × $13,200,000)	36,000	132,000

The Mining Division manager will prefer Method A (transfer at market prices) because this method gives $120,000 of bonus rather than $24,000 under Method B (transfers at 110% of full costs). The Metals Division manager will prefer Method B because this method gives $132,000 of bonus rather than $36,000 under Method A.

3.   Brian Jones, the manager of the Mining Division will appeal to the existence of a competitive market to price transfers at market prices. Using market prices for transfers in these conditions leads to goal congruence. Division managers acting in their own best interests make decisions that are also in the best interests of the company as a whole.

Jones will further argue that setting transfer prices based on cost will cause Jones to pay no attention to controlling costs since all costs incurred will be recovered from the Metals Division at 110% of full costs.

23-22 (25 min.)   **General guideline, transfer price range.**

1.   If the Screen Division sells screens in the outside market, it will receive, for each screen, the market price of the screen minus variable marketing and distribution costs per screen = $110 – $4 = $106. The incremental cost of manufacturing each screen is $70. The Screen Division is operating at capacity. Hence, the opportunity cost per screen of selling the screen to the Assembly Division rather than in the outside market is the contribution margin the Screen Division would forgo if it transferred screens internally rather than sold them in the outside market.

Contribution margin per screen = $106 – $70 = $36.

Using the general guideline,

$$\text{Minimum transfer price per screen} = \text{Incremental costs per screen up to the point of transfer} + \text{Opportunity costs per screen to the selling division}$$

That is,   Minimum transfer price per screen = $70 + $36 = $106

2.   If the two division managers were to negotiate a transfer price, the range of possible transfer prices is between $106 and $112 per screen. As calculated in requirement 1, the Screen Division will be willing to supply screens to the Assembly Division only if the transfer price equals or exceeds $106 per screen.

If the Assembly Division were to purchase the screens in the outside market, it will incur a cost of $112, the cost of the screen equal to $110 plus variable purchasing costs of $2 per screen. Hence, the Assembly Division will be willing to buy screens from the Screen Division only if the price does not exceed $112 per screen. Within the price range of $106 and $112 per screen, each division will be willing to transact with the other. The exact transfer price between $106 and $112 will depend on the bargaining strengths of the two divisions.

23-24 (30 min.) **Multinational transfer pricing, goal congruence (continuation of 23-23).**

1.   After tax operating income if Mornay Company sold all 1,000 units of Product 4A36 in Canada is

Revenues, $600 × 1,000 units	$600,000
Full manufacturing costs, $500 × 1,000 units	500,000
Operating income	100,000
Income taxes at 40%	40,000
After-tax operating income	$ 60,000

From requirement 1, Mornay Company's after-tax operating income if it transfers 1,000 units of Product 4A36 to Austria at full manufacturing cost and sells the units in Austria is $112,000. Therefore Mornay should sell the 1,000 units in Austria.

2.   Transferring Product 4A36 at the full manufacturing cost of the Canadian Division minimizes import duties and taxes (requirement 2), but creates zero operating income for the Canadian Division. Acting autonomously, the Canadian Division manager would maximize division operating income by selling Product 4A36 in the Canadian market which results in $60,000 in after-tax division operating income as calculated in requirement 3, rather than by transferring Product 4A36 to the Austrian division at full manufacturing cost.

3.   The minimum transfer price at which the Canadian Division manager acting autonomously will agree to transfer Product 4A36 to the Austrian division is $600 per unit. Any transfer price less than $600 will leave the Canadian Division's performance worse than selling directly in the Canadian market. Since the Canadian Division can sell as many units of Product 4A36 in the Canadian market, there is an opportunity cost of transferring the product internally.

This transfer price will result in Mornay Company as a whole paying more import duties and taxes than the answer to requirement 2 as calculated below:

CANADIAN DIVISION

Revenues, $600 × 1,000 units	$600,000
Full manufacturing costs	500,000
Division operating income	100,000
Division income taxes at 40%	40,000
Division after-tax operating income	$ 60,000

AUSTRIAN DIVISION

Revenues, $750 × 1,000 units`	$750,000
Transferred in costs, $600 × 1,000 units	600,000
Import duties at 10% of transferred-in price, $60 × 1,000 units	60,000
Division operating income	90,000
Division income taxes at 44%	39,600
Division after-tax operating income	$ 50,400

Total import duties and income taxes at transfer prices of $500 and $600 per unit for 1,000 units of Product 4A36 follow:

		Transfer Price of $500 per Unit (Requirement 2)	Transfer Price of $600 per Unit
(a)	Canadian income taxes	$ 0	$ 40,000
(b)	Austrian import duties	50,000	60,000
(c)	Austrian income taxes	88,000	39,600
		$138,000	$139,600

The minimum transfer price that the Canadian division manager acting autonomously would agree to results in Mornay Company paying $1,600 in additional import duties and income taxes.

A student who has done the calculations shown in requirement 2 can calculate the additional taxes from a $600 transfer price more directly as follows:

Every $1 increase in the transfer price per unit over $500 results in additional import duty and taxes of $0.016 per unit

So a $100 increase ($600 − $500) per unit will result in additional import duty and taxes of $0.016 × 100 = $1.60

For 1,000 units transferred, this equals $1.60 × 1,000 = $1,600

23-26 (5 min.) **Transfer-pricing problem (continuation of 23-25).**

The company as a whole would benefit in this situation if C purchased from outside suppliers. The $15,000 disadvantage to the company as a whole by purchasing from the outside supplier would be more than offset by the $30,000 contribution margin of A's sale of 1,000 units to other customers.

Purchase costs from outside supplier, 1,000 units × $135		$135,000
Deduct variable cost savings, 1,000 units × $120		120,000
Net cost to company as a whole by buying from outside		$ 15,000
A's sales to other customers, 1,000 units × $155		$155,000
Deduct:		
Variable manufacturing costs, $120 × 1,000 units	$120,000	
Variable marketing costs, $5 × 1,000 units	5,000	
Variable costs		125,000
Contribution margin from selling A to other customers		$ 30,000

23-28 (30-40 min.) **Pricing in imperfect markets (continuation of 23-27).**

An alternative presentation, which contains the same numerical answers, can be found at the end of this solution.

1.   Potential contribution from external intermediate
      sale is $1,000 \times (\$195 - \$120)$ $75,000
     Contribution through keeping price at $200 is
      $800 \times \$80$.   <u>64,000</u>
     Forgone contribution by transferring 200 units   <u>$11,000</u>

Opportunity cost per unit to the supplying division by transferring internally:

$$\frac{\$11,000}{200} = \$55$$

Transfer price = $120 + $55 = $175

An alternative approach to obtaining the same answer is to recognize that the incremental or outlay cost is the same for all 1,000 units in question. Therefore, the total revenue desired by A would be the same for selling outside or inside.

Let X equal the transfer price at which Division A is indifferent between selling all units outside versus transferring 200 units inside
$$1,000 \ (\$195) \ = \ 800 \ (\$200) + 200X$$
$$X \ = \ \$175$$

The $175 price will lead to the correct decision. Division B will not buy from Division A because its total costs of $175 + $150 will exceed its prospective selling price of $300. Division A will then sell 1,000 units at $195 to the outside; Division A and the company will have a contribution margin of $75,000. Otherwise, if 800 units were sold at $200 and 200 units were transferred to Division B, the company would have a contribution of $64,000 plus $6,000 (200 units of final product × $30), or $70,000.

A comparison might be drawn regarding the computation of the appropriate transfer prices between the preceding problem and this problem:

$$\begin{matrix} \text{Minimum} \\ \text{transfer price} \end{matrix} = \begin{pmatrix} \text{Additional } incremental \text{ costs} \\ \text{per unit incurred up} \\ \text{to the point of transfer} \end{pmatrix} + \begin{pmatrix} Opportunity \text{ costs} \\ \text{per unit to} \\ \text{Division A} \end{pmatrix}$$

Perfect markets: = $120 + (Selling price – Outlay costs per unit)
                  = $120 + ($200 – $120) = $200

$$\text{Imperfect markets:} \quad = \$120 + \frac{\text{Marginal revenues} - \text{Outlay costs}}{\text{Number of units transferred}}$$

$$= \$120 + \frac{\$35,000^a - \$24,000^b}{200} = \$175$$

a Marginal revenues of Division A from selling 200 units outside rather than transferring to Division B
= ($195 × 1,000) − ($200 × 800) = $195,000 − $160,000 = $35,000.

b Incremental (outlay) costs incurred by Division A to produce 200 units
= $120 × 200 = $24,000.

Therefore, selling price ($195) and marginal revenues per unit ($175 = $35,000 ÷ 200) are not the same.

The following discussion is optional. These points should be explored only if there is sufficient class time:

Some students will erroneously say that the "new" market price of $195 is the appropriate transfer price. They will claim that the general guideline says that the transfer price should be $120 + ($195 − $120) = $195, the market price. This conclusion assumes a perfect market. But here there are imperfections in the intermediate market. That is, the market price is <u>not</u> a good approximation of alternative revenue. If a division's sales are heavy enough to reduce market prices, marginal revenue will be less than market price.

It is true that <u>either</u> $195 or $175 will lead to the correct decision by B in this case. But suppose that B's variable costs were $120 instead of $150. Then B would buy at a transfer price of $175 (but not at a price of $195, because then B would earn a negative contribution of $15 per unit [$300 − ($195 + $120)]. Note that if B's variable costs were $120, transfers would be desirable:

Division A contribution is:
800 × ($200 − $120) + 200 ($175 − $120) = $75,000
Division B contribution is:
200 × [$300 − ($175 + $120)]   =   1,000
Total contribution $76,000

Or the same facts can be analyzed for the company as a whole:

Sales of intermediate product,
800 × ($200 − $120)   = $64,000
Sales of final products,
200 × [300 − ($120 + $120)]   =   12,000
Total contribution $76,000

23-28 (cont'd)

If the transfer price were $195, B would not accept the transfer and would not earn any contribution. As shown above, Division A and the company as a whole will earn a total contribution of $75,000 instead of $76,000.

2. (a) Division A can sell 900 units at $195 to the outside market and 100 units to Division B, or 800 at $200 to the outside market and 200 units to Division B. Note that, under both alternatives, 100 units can be transferred to Division B at no opportunity cost to A.

    Using the general guideline, the minimum transfer price of <u>the first 100 units</u> [901-1,000] is:

    $$TP_1 = \$120 + 0 = \$120$$

    If Division B needs 100 additional units, the opportunity cost to A is not zero, because Division A will then have to sell only 800 units to the outside market for a contribution of $800 \times (\$200 - \$120) = \$64,000$ instead of 900 units for a contribution of $900 (\$195 - \$120) = \$67,500$. Each unit sold to B in addition to the first 100 units has an opportunity cost to A of $(\$67,500 - \$64,000) \div 100 = \$35$.

    Using the general guideline, the minimum transfer price of <u>the next 100 units</u> [801-900] is:

    $$TP_2 = \$120 + \$35 = \$155$$

    Alternatively, the computation could be:

Increase in contribution from 100 more units, $100 \times \$75$	$7,500
Loss in contribution on 800 units, $800 \times (\$80 - \$75)$	4,000
Net "marginal revenue"	$3,500 ÷100 units = $35

    (Minimum) transfer price applicable to first 100 units
    offered by A is $120 + $0   = $120 per unit
    (Minimum) transfer price applicable to next 100 units
    offered by A is $120 + ($3,500 ÷ 100)   = $155 per unit
    (Minimum) transfer price applicable to next 800 units   = $195 per unit

    (b) The manager of Division B will not want to purchase more than 100 units because the units at $155 would decrease his contribution ($155 + $150 > $300). Because the manager of B does not buy more than 100 units, the manager of A will have 900 units available for sale to the outside market. The manager of A will strive to maximize the contribution by selling them all at $195.

This solution maximizes the company's contribution:

$$900 \times (\$195 - \$120) \quad = \quad \$67,500$$
$$100 \times (\$300 - \$270) \quad = \quad \underline{\quad 3,000}$$
$$\underline{\$70,500}$$

which compares favourably to:

$$800 \times (\$200 - \$120) \quad = \quad \$64,000$$
$$200 \times (\$300 - \$270) \quad = \underline{\quad 6,000}$$
$$\underline{\$70,000}$$

ALTERNATIVE PRESENTATION (by James Patell)

1. Company Viewpoint

a: Sell 1,000 outside at $195		b: Sell 800 outside at $200, transfer 200	
Price	$195	Transfer price	$200
Variable costs	120	Variable costs	120
Contribution	$ 75 × 1,000 = $75,000	Contribution	$ 80 × 800 = $64,000

Total contribution given up if transfer occurs[*]
= $75,000 − $64,000 = $11,000

On a per-unit basis, the relevant costs are:

$$\text{Incremental costs to point of transfer} + \text{Opportunity costs to Division A of transfer} = \text{Transfer price}$$

$$\$120 + \frac{\$11,000}{200} = \$175$$

By formula, costs are:

$$\begin{bmatrix} \text{Incremental costs} \\ \text{to point} \\ \text{of transfer} \end{bmatrix} + \begin{bmatrix} \text{Lost opportunity to} \\ \text{sell 200 at \$195, for} \\ \text{contribution of \$75} \end{bmatrix} - \begin{bmatrix} \text{Gain when 1st 800} \\ \text{sell at \$200} \\ \text{instead of \$195} \end{bmatrix}$$

$$= \quad \$120 + \frac{200 \cdot \$75}{200} - \frac{[(\$200 - \$195) \cdot 800]}{200}$$

$$= \quad \$120 + \$75 - \$20 \ = \ \$175$$

[*]Contribution of $30 per unit by B is not given up if transfer occurs, so it is not relevant here.

2. (a) At most, Division A can sell only 900 units and can produce 1,000. Therefore, at least 100 units should be transferred, at a transfer price no less than $120. The question is whether or not a second 100 units should be transferred.

Company Viewpoint

a: Sell 900 outside at $195		b: Sell 800 outside at $200, transfer 100	
Transfer price	$195	Transfer price	$200
Variable cost	120	Variable cost	120
Contribution	$ 75 × 900 = $67,500	Contribution	$ 80 × 800 = $64,000

Total contribution forgone if transfer of 100 units occurs
= $67,500 − $64,000 = $3,500 (or $35 per unit)

$$\begin{matrix} \text{Incremental costs to} \\ \text{point of transfer} \end{matrix} + \begin{matrix} \text{Opportunity costs to} \\ \text{Division A of transfer} \end{matrix} = \text{Transfer price}$$

$$\$120 \quad + \quad \$35 \quad = \quad \$155$$

(b) By formula:

$$\begin{bmatrix} \text{Incremental costs} \\ \text{to point} \\ \text{of transfer} \end{bmatrix} + \begin{bmatrix} \text{Lost opportunity to} \\ \text{sell 100 at \$195, for} \\ \text{contribution of \$75} \end{bmatrix} - \begin{bmatrix} \text{Gain when 1st 800} \\ \text{sell at \$200} \\ \text{instead of \$195} \end{bmatrix}$$

$$= \quad \$120 + \frac{100 \cdot \$75}{100} - \frac{[(\$200 - \$195) \cdot 800]}{100}$$

$$= \quad \$120 + \$75 - \$40 = \$155$$

Transfer Price Schedule (minimum acceptable transfer price)

Units	Transfer Price
0-100	$120
101-200	$155
201-1,000	$195

23-30 (30 min.)   **Goal congruence problems with cost-plus transfer-pricing methods, dual-pricing methods.**

1.   Two examples of goal congruence problems are:
   (a)   Division managers using an outside supplier when Oceanic Products' operating income is maximized by buying from an internal division.
   (b)   Division managers selling to an outside purchaser when it is better for Oceanic Products to further process internally.

2.   <u>Transfers to buying divisions at market price</u>
   Harvesting Division to Processing Division   = $1.00 per kilogram of raw tuna
   Processing Division to Marketing Division   = $5.00 per kilogram of
                                                               processed tuna

   <u>Transfers out to selling divisions at 150% of full costs</u>
   Harvesting Division to Processing Division
           = 1.5 ($0.20 + $0.40) = $0.90 per kilogram of raw tuna
   Processing Division to Marketing Division
           = 1.5 [($1.00 × 2)* + $0.80 + $0.60] = $5.10 per kilogram
               of processed tuna

*The transferred-in cost is $1.00 per kilogram of raw tuna. It takes two kilograms of raw tuna to produce one kilogram of tuna fillets.

   <u>Tuna Harvesting Division</u>
Division revenues: $0.90 × 1,000	$ 900
Division variable costs: $0.20 × 1,000	200
Division fixed costs: $0.40 × 1,000	400
Division total costs	600
Division operating income	$ 300

   <u>Tuna Processing Division</u>
Division revenues: $5.10 × 500	$2,550
Transferred-in costs: $1.00 × 1,000	1,000
Division variable costs: $0.80 × 500	400
Division fixed costs: $0.60 × 500	300
Division total costs	1,700
Division operating income	$ 850

   <u>Tuna Marketing Division</u>
Division revenues: $12 × 300	$3,600
Transferred-in costs: $5 × 500	2,500
Division variable costs: $0.30 × 300	90
Division fixed costs: $0.70 × 300	210
Division total costs	2,800
Division operating income	$ 800

23-30 (cont'd)

3.
	Division Operating Income
Tuna Harvesting Division	$ 300
Tuna Processing Division	850
Tuna Marketing Division	800
Oceanic Products	$1,950

The overall company operating income from harvesting 1,000 kilograms of raw tuna and its further processing and marketing is $2,000 (see Problem 23-29, requirement 1).

A dual transfer-pricing method entails using different transfer prices for transfers into the buying division and transfers out of the supplying division. There is no reason why the sum of division operating incomes should equal the total company operating income.

4.   Problems which may arise if Oceanic Products uses the dual-transfer pricing system include:

(a)   It may reduce the incentives of the supplying division to control costs since every $1 of cost of the supplying division is transferred out to the buying division at $1.50. It may also reduce the incentives of the supplying divisions to keep abreast of market conditions.

(b)   A dual transfer-pricing system does not provide clear signals to the individual divisions about the level of decentralization top management seeks.

23-32 (30-40 min.) **Multinational transfer pricing and taxation.**

1.   Anita Corporation and its subsidiaries' operating income if it manufactures the machine and sells it in Brazil or in Switzerland follows:

	If Sold in Brazil	If Sold in Switzerland
Revenue	$1,000,000	$950,000
Costs		
Manufacturing costs	500,000	500,000
Transportation and modification costs	200,000	250,000
Total costs	700,000	750,000
Operating income	$ 300,000	$200,000

Anita Corporation maximizes operating income by manufacturing the machine and selling it in Brazil.

2.   Anita Corporation will not sell if the transfer price is less than $500,000—its outlay costs of manufacturing the machine.

The Brazilian subsidiary will not agree to a transfer price of more than $800,000. At a price of $800,000, the Brazilian subsidiary's incremental operating income from purchasing and selling the milling machine will be $0 ($1,000,000 − $200,000 − $800,000).

The Swiss subsidiary will not agree to a transfer price of more than $700,000. At a price of $700,000, the Swiss subsidiary's incremental operating income from purchasing and selling the milling machine will be $0 ($950,000 − $250,000 − $700,000).

Any transfer price between $700,000 and $800,000 will achieve the optimal actions determined in requirement 1. For prices in this range, Anita Corporation will be willing to sell, the Brazilian Corporation willing to buy, and the Swiss subsidiary not interested in acquiring the machine.

Where within the range of $700,000 to $800,000 that the transfer price will be set depends on the bargaining powers of the Anita Corporation and the Brazilian subsidiary managers. Anita Corporation's main source of bargaining power comes from the threat of selling the machine to the Swiss subsidiary. If the transfer price is set at $700,000, then

Anita's operating income, $700,000 − $500,000	$200,000
Brazilian subsidiary's operating income, $1,000,000 − $700,000 − $200,000	$100,000
Overall operating income of Anita and subsidiaries	$300,000

Note that the general guideline could be used to derive the minimum transfer price.

$$\text{Minimum transfer price} = \begin{pmatrix} \text{Additional } \textit{incremental} \text{ costs} \\ \text{per unit incurred up} \\ \text{to the point of transfer} \end{pmatrix} + \begin{pmatrix} \textit{Opportunity} \text{ costs} \\ \text{per unit to the} \\ \text{supplying division} \end{pmatrix}$$

$$= \$500{,}000 + \$200{,}000 = \$700{,}000$$

Anita's opportunity cost of supplying the machine to the Brazilian subsidiary is the $200,000 in operating income it forgoes by not supplying the machine to the Swiss subsidiary. Note that competition between the Brazilian and Swiss subsidiaries means that the transfer price will be at least $700,000.

3. Consider the optimal transfer prices that can be set to minimize taxes (for Anita and its subsidiaries) (a) for transfers from Anita to the Brazilian subsidiary and (b) for transfers from Anita to the Swiss subsidiary.

(a) Transfers from Anita to the Brazilian subsidiary should "allocate" as much of the operating income to Anita as possible, since the tax rate in Canada is lower than in Brazil for this transaction. Therefore, these transfers should be priced at the highest allowable transfer price of $700,000 to minimize overall company taxes.

Taxes paid:

Anita, 0.40 ($700,000 – $500,000)	$ 80,000
Brazilian subsidiary, 0.60 ($1,000,000 – $700,000 – $200,000)	60,000
Total taxes paid by Anita Corporation and its subsidiaries on transfers to Brazil	$140,000

After-tax operating income:

Anita, ($700,000 – $500,000) – $80,000	$120,000
Brazilian subsidiary ($1,000,000 – $700,000 – $200,000) – $60,000	40,000
Total after-tax operating income for Anita Corporation and its subsidiaries on transfers to Brazil	$160,000

(b) Transfers from Anita to the Swiss subsidiary should "allocate" as little of the operating income to Anita as possible, since the tax rate in Canada is higher than in Switzerland for this transaction. Therefore, these transfers should be priced at the lowest allowable transfer price of $500,000 to minimize overall company taxes.

Taxes paid:

Anita, 0.40 ($500,000 – $500,000)	$ 0
Swiss subsidiary, 0.15 ($950,000 – $500,000 – $250,000)	30,000
Total taxes paid by Anita Corporation and its subsidiaries on transfers to Switzerland	$30,000

23-32 (cont'd)

After-tax operating income		
Anita,($500,000 − $500,000) − $0	$	0
Swiss subsidiary ($950,000 − $500,000 − $250,000) − $30,000		170,000
Total net income for Anita Corporation and its subsidiaries on transfers to Switzerland		$170,000

From the viewpoint of Anita Corporation and its subsidiaries together, overall after-tax operating income is maximized if the machine is transferred to the Swiss subsidiary (after-tax operating income of $170,000 versus after-tax operating income of $160,000 if the machine is transferred to the Brazilian subsidiary). Note that the corporation and its subsidiaries trade off the lower overall before-tax operating income achieved by transferring to the Swiss subsidiary with the lower taxes that result from such a transfer. Hence (a) the equipment should be manufactured by Anita and (b) it should be transferred to the Swiss subsidiary at a price of $500,000.

4.   As in requirement 2, the Brazilian subsidiary would be willing to bid up the price to $800,000, while the Swiss subsidiary would only be willing to pay up to $700,000. Anita Corporation acting autonomously would like to maximize its own after-tax operating income by transferring the machine at as high a transfer price as possible. As in requirement 2, the price would end up being at least $700,000. Since the taxing authorities will not allow prices above $700,000, the transfer price will be $700,000. At this transfer price, the Swiss subsidiary makes zero operating income and will not be interested in the machine. Hence Anita Corporation will sell the machine to the Brazilian subsidiary at a price of $700,000.

The answer is not the same as in requirement 3 since, acting autonomously, the objective of each manager is to maximize after-tax operating income of his or her own company rather than after-tax operating income of Anita Corporation and its subsidiaries as a whole. Goal congruence is not achieved in this setting.

Can the company induce the managers to take the right actions without infringing on their autonomy? This outcome is probably not going to be easy.

One possibility might be to implement a dual pricing scheme in which the machine is transferred at cost ($500,000), but under which Anita Corporation is credited with after-tax operating income earned on the machine by the subsidiary it ships the machine to (in this example, $170,000 of net income earned by the Swiss subsidiary). A negative feature of this arrangement is that the $170,000 of after-tax operating income will be "double counted" and recognized on the books of both Anita Corporation and the Swiss subsidiary.

Another possibility might be to evaluate the managers on the basis of overall after-tax operating income of Anita Corporation and its subsidiaries. This approach will induce a more global perspective, but at the cost of inducing a larger noncontrollable element in each manager's performance measure.

23-34 (40–50 min.) **Transfer pricing, utilization of capacity.**

1.

	Super-chip	Okay-chip
Selling price	$60	$12
Direct materials	2	1
Direct manufacturing labour	28	7
Contribution margin per unit	$30	$ 4
Contribution margin per hour ($30 ÷ 2; $4 ÷ 0.5)	$15	$ 8

Because the contribution margin per hour is higher for Super-chip than for Okay-chip, CIC should produce and sell as many Super-chips as it can and use the remaining available capacity to produce Okay-chip.

The total demand for Super-chips is 15,000 units, which would take 30,000 hours (15,000 × 2 hours per unit). CIC should use its remaining capacity of 20,000 hours (50,000 – 30,000) to produce 40,000 Okay-chips (20,000 ÷ 0.5).

2. Options for manufacturing process-control unit

	Using Circuit Board	Using Super-chip
Selling price	$132	$132
Direct materials	60	2
Direct manufacturing labour (Super-chip)	0	28
Direct manufacturing labour (Process-control unit)	50	60
Contribution margin per unit	$ 22	$ 42

Overall Company Viewpoint

Alternative 1:   No Transfer of Super-chips

Sell 15,000 Super-chips at contribution margin per unit of $30	$450,000
Transfer 0 Super-chips	0
Sell 40,000 Okay-chips at contribution margin per unit of $4	160,000
Sell 5,000 Control units at contribution margin per unit of $22	110,000
Total contribution margin	$720,000

Alternative 2:   Transfer 5,000 Super-chips to Process-Control Division. These Super-chips would require 10,000 hours to manufacture, leaving only 10,000 hours for the manufacture of 20,000 Okay-chips (10,000 ÷ 0.5)

Sell 15,000 Super-chips at contribution margin per unit of $30	$450,000
Transfer 5,000 Super-chips to Process-Control Division	0
Sell 20,000 Okay-chips at contribution margin per unit of $4	80,000
Sell 5,000 Control units at contribution margin per unit of $42	210,000
Total contribution margin	$740,000

23-34 (cont'd)

CIC is better off transferring 5,000 Super-chips to the Process-Control Division.

3.   For each Super-chip that is transferred, two hours of time (labour capacity) are given up in the Semiconductor Division, and, in those two hours, four Okay-chips could be produced, each contributing $4.

$$\begin{array}{ccc} \text{Minimum transfer price} \\ \text{per Super-chip} \end{array} = \begin{array}{c} \text{Incremental cost} \\ \text{per unit to} \\ \text{the point of transfer} \end{array} + \begin{array}{c} \text{Opportunity cost per} \\ \text{unit for the} \\ \text{Semiconductor Division} \end{array}$$

$$= \$30 + \$16$$

$$= \$46 \text{ per unit}$$

If the selling price for the process-control unit were firm at $132, the Process-Control Division would accept any transfer price up to $50 ($60 price of circuit board − $10 incremental labour cost if Super-chip used).

However, consider what happens if the transfer price of Super-chip is set at, say, $49, and the price of the control unit drops to $108. From CIC's viewpoint:

	Using Circuit Board	Using Super-chip
Selling price	$108	$108
Direct materials	60	49
Direct manufacturing labour	50	60
Contribution margin per hour	$ −2	$ −1

Process-Control Division will not produce any control units. From the company's viewpoint, the contribution margin on the control unit if the Super-chip is used is:

Selling price	$108
Direct materials	2
Direct manufacturing labour (Super-chip)	28
Direct manufacturing labour (process-control unit)	60
Contribution margin per unit	$ 18

The contribution margin per unit from producing Super-chips for the process-control unit exceeds the contribution margin of $16 from producing 4 Okay-chips, each yielding a contribution margin of $4 per unit. Hence the Semiconductor Division should transfer 5,000 Super-chips as the following calculations show:

Alternative 1—No transfer (and, therefore, no sales of process-control units)

Sell 15,000 Super-chips at contribution margin per unit of $30	$450,000
Sell 40,000 Okay-chips at contribution margin per unit of $4	160,000
	$610,000

23-34 (cont'd)

Alternative 2—Transfer 5,000 Super-chips.

Sell 15,000 Super-chips at contribution margin per unit of $30	$450,000
Sell 20,000 Okay-chips at contribution margin per unit of $4	80,000
Sell 5,000 control units at contribution margin per unit of $18	90,000
	$620,000

Therefore, if the price for the control unit is uncertain, the transfer price must be set at the minimum acceptable transfer price of $46.

4.   For a transfer of any amount between 0 and 10,000 Super-chips (which require 2 hours each to produce), the opportunity cost is the production of Okay-chips (which require 1/2 hour each). In this range, the relevant costs are equal to the transfer price of $46 established in part 3.

If more than 10,000 Super-chips are transferred, the opportunity cost becomes the sale of Super-chips on the outside market. Now the minimum transfer price per Super-chip becomes

Incremental cost per Super-chip up to the point of transfer + Opportunity cost per Super-chip to the Semiconductor Division = $30 + ($60 − $30) = $60, the market price.

At this transfer price, it is cheaper for the Process-Control Division to buy the circuit board for $60, since $10 of additional direct manufacturing labour cost is saved.

The Semiconductor Division should at most transfer 10,000 Super-chips.

Internal Demand	Transfer
0-10,000	$46
10,000-25,000	60

CHAPTER 24
PERFORMANCE MEASUREMENT, COMPENSATION, AND MULTINATIONAL CONSIDERATIONS

24-2 The five steps in designing an accounting-based performance measure are:
1. Choosing the variable(s) that represents top management's financial goal(s).
2. Choosing definitions of the items included in the variables in Step 1.
3. Choosing measures for the items included in the variables in Step 1.
4. Choosing a target against which to gauge performance.
5. Choosing the timing of feedback.

24-4 Yes. Residual income is not identical to ROI. ROI is a percentage with investment as the denominator of the computation. Residual income is an absolute amount in which investment is used to calculate an imputed interest charge.

24-6 Definitions of investment used in practice when computing ROI are:
1. Total assets available.
2. Total assets employed.
3. Working capital (current assets minus current liabilities) plus other assets.
4. Stockholders' equity.

24-8 Special problems arise when evaluating the performance of divisions in multinational companies because
   (a) The economic, legal, political, social, and cultural environments differ significantly across countries.
   (b) Governments in some countries may impose controls and limit selling prices of products.
   (c) Availability of materials and skilled labour, as well as costs of materials, labour, and infrastructure may differ significantly across countries.
   (d) Divisions operating in different countries keep score of their performance in different currencies.

24-10 Moral hazard describes contexts in which an employee is tempted to put in less effort (or report distorted information) because the employee's interests differ from the owner's and because the employee's effort cannot be accurately monitored and enforced.

24-12 Measures of performance that are superior (measures that change significantly with the manager's performance and not very much with changes in factors that are beyond the manager's control) are the key to designing strong incentive systems in organizations. When selecting performance measures the management accountant must choose those performance measures that change with changes in the actions taken by managers. For example, if a manager has no authority for making investments, then using an investment-based measure to evaluate the manager imposes risk on the manager and provides little information about the manager's performance. The management accountant might suggest evaluating the manager on the basis of costs, or costs and revenues, rather than ROI.

24-14 When employees have to perform multiple tasks as part of their jobs, incentive problems can arise when one task is easy to monitor and measure while the other task is more difficult to evaluate. Employers want employees to intelligently allocate time and effort among various tasks. If, however, employees are rewarded on the basis of the task that is more easily measured, they will tend to focus their efforts on that task and ignore the others.

24-16 (30 min.) **Return on investment; comparisons of three companies.**

1.   The separate components highlight several features of return on investment not revealed by a single calculation:
   (a)   The importance of investment turnover as a key to income is stressed.
   (b)   The importance of revenues is explicitly recognized.
   (c)   The important components are expressed as ratios or percentages instead of dollar figures. This form of expression often enhances comparability of different divisions, businesses, and time periods.
   (d)   The breakdown stresses the possibility of trading off investment turnover for income as a percentage of revenues so as to increase the average ROI at a given level of output.

2.   (Filled-in blanks are in bold face.)

	Companies in Same Industry		
	A	B	C
Revenue	$1,000,000	$ 500,000	$10,000,000
Income	$ 100,000	$ 50,000	$ 50,000
Investment	$ 500,000	$5,000,000	$ 5,000,000
Income as a % of revenue	10%	10%	0.5%
Investment turnover	2.0	0.1	2.0
Return on investment	20%	1%	1%

Income and investment alone shed little light on comparative performances because of disparities in size between Company A and the other two companies. Thus, it is impossible to say whether B's low return on investment in comparison with A's is attributable to its larger investment or to its lower income. Furthermore the fact that Companies B and C have identical income and investment may suggest that the same conditions underlie the low ROI, but this conclusion is erroneous. B has higher margins but a lower investment turnover. C has very small margins (1/20th of B) but turns over investment 20 times faster.

I.M.A. Report No. 35 (p. 35) states:

"Introducing revenues to measure level of operations helps to disclose specific areas for more intensive investigation. Company B does as well as Company A in terms of income margin, for both companies earn 10% on revenues. But Company B has a much lower turnover of investment than does Company A. Whereas a dollar of investment in Company A supports two dollars in revenues each period, a dollar investment in Company B supports only ten cents in revenues each period. This suggests that the analyst should look carefully at Company B's investment. Is the company keeping an inventory larger than necessary for its revenue level? Are receivables being collected promptly? Or did Company A acquire its fixed assets at a price level that was much lower than that at which Company B purchased its plant?"

24-3

24-16 (cont'd)

"On the other hand, C's investment turnover is as high as A's, but C's income as a percentage of revenue is much lower. Why? Are its operations inefficient, are its material costs too high, or does its location entail high transportation costs?"

"Analysis of ROI raises questions such as the foregoing. When answers are obtained, basic reasons for differences between rates of return may be discovered. For example, in Company B's case, it is apparent that the emphasis will have to be on increasing turnover by reducing investment or increasing revenues. Clearly, B cannot appreciably increase its ROI simply by increasing its income as a percent of revenue. In contrast, Company C's management should concentrate on increasing the percent of income on revenue."

24-18 (10-15 min.) ROI and RI.

$$\text{ROI} = \frac{\text{Operating income}}{\text{Investment}}$$

$$\text{Operating income} = \text{ROI} \times \text{Investment}$$

[No. of menhirs sold (Selling price – Var. cost per unit)] – Fixed costs = ROI × Investment

Let X = minimum selling price per unit to achieve a 20% ROI

1. $10,000 (X – \$300) – \$1,000,000 = 20\% (\$1,600,000)$
$$10,000X = \$320,000 + \$3,000,000 + \$1,000,000 = \$4,320,000$$
$$X = \$432$$

2. $10,000 (X – \$300) – \$1,000,000 = 15\% (\$1,600,000)$
$$10,000X = \$240,000 + \$3,000,000 + \$1,000,000 = \$4,240,000$$
$$X = \$424$$

24-20 (25 min.) **Financial and nonfinancial performance measures, goal congruence.**

1.   Operating income is a good summary measure of short-term financial performance. By itself, however, it does not indicate whether operating income in the short run was earned by taking actions that would lead to long-run competitive advantage. For example, Summit's divisions might be able to increase short-run operating income by producing more product while ignoring quality or rework. Harrington, however, would like to see division managers increase operating income without sacrificing quality. The new performance measures take a balanced scorecard approach by evaluating and rewarding managers on the basis of direct measures (such as rework costs, on-time delivery performance, and sales returns). This motivates managers to take actions that Harrington believes will increase operating income now and in the future. The nonoperating income measures serve as surrogate measures of future profitability.

2.   The semi-annual installments and total bonus for the Charter Division are calculated as follows:

Charter Division Bonus Calculation
For Year Ended December 31, 2000

January 1, 2000 to June 30, 2000

Profitability	(0.02) ($462,000)	$ 9,240
Rework	(0.02 × $462,000) – $11,500	(2,260)
On-time delivery	No bonus – under 96%	0
Sales returns	[(0.015 × $4,200,000) – $84,000] × 50%	(10,500)
Semi-annual installment		(3,520)
Semi-annual bonus awarded		$ 0

July 1, 2000 to December 31, 2000

Profitability	(0.02) ($440,000)	$ 8,800
Rework	(0.02 × $440,000) – $11,000	(2,200)
On-time delivery	96% to 98%	2,000
Sales returns	[(0.015 × $4,400,000) – $70,000] × 50%	(2,000)
Semi-annual installment		6,600
Semi-annual bonus awarded		$ 6,600
Total bonus awarded for the year		$ 6,600

The semi-annual installments and total bonus for the Mesa Division are calculated as follows:

Mesa Division Bonus Calculation
For Year Ended December 31, 2000

January 1, 2000 to June 30, 2000

Profitability	(0.02) ($342,000)	$ 6,840
Rework	(0.02 × $342,000) – $6,000	0
On-time delivery	Over 98%	5,000
Sales returns	[(0.015 × $2,850,000) – $44,750] × 50%	(1,000)
Semi-annual bonus installment		$10,840
Semi-annual bonus awarded		$10,840

July 1, 2000 to December 31, 2000

Profitability	(0.02) ($406,000)	$ 8,120
Rework	(0.02 × $406,000) – $8,000	0
On-time delivery	No bonus—under 96%	0
Sales returns	[(0.015 × $2,900,000) – $42,500] which is greater than zero, yielding a bonus of	3,000
Semi-annual bonus installment		$11,120
Semi-annual bonus awarded		$11,120
Total bonus awarded for the year		$21,960

3.   The manager of the Charter Division is likely to be frustrated by the new plan as the division bonus is more than $20,000 less than the previous year. However the new performance measures have begun to have the desired effect—both on-time deliveries and sales returns improved in the second half of the year while rework costs were relatively even. If the division continues to improve at the same rate, the Charter bonus could approximate or exceed what it was under the old plan.

The manager of the Mesa Division should be as satisfied with the new plan as with the old plan as the bonus is almost equivalent. However, there is no sign of improvements in the performance measures instituted by Harrington in this division; as a matter of fact, on-time deliveries declined considerably in the second half of the year. Unless the manager institutes better controls, the bonus situation may not be as favourable in the future. This could motivate the manager to improve in the future but currently, at least, the manager has been able to maintain his bonus without showing improvements in the areas targeted by Harrington.

Ben Harrington's revised bonus plan for the Charter Division fostered the following improvements in the second half of the year despite an increase in sales
- increase of 1.9 percent in on-time deliveries.
- $500 reduction in rework costs.
- $14,000 reduction in sales returns.

However, operating income as a percent of sales has decreased (11 to 10 percent).

The Mesa Division's bonus has remained at the status quo as a result of the following effects
- increase of 2.0 percent in operating income as a percent of sales (12 to 14 percent).
- decrease of 3.6 percent in on-time deliveries.
- $2,000 increase in rework costs.
- $2,250 decrease in sales returns.

This would suggest that there needs to be some revisions to the bonus plan. Possible changes include:

- increasing the weights put on on-time deliveries, rework costs, and sales returns in the performance measures while decreasing the weight put on operating income.
- a reward structure for rework costs that are below 2 percent of operating income that would encourage managers to drive costs lower.
- reviewing the whole year in total. The bonus plan should carry forward the negative amounts for one six-month period into the next six-month period incorporating the entire year when calculating a bonus.
- developing benchmarks, and then giving rewards for improvements over prior periods and encouraging continuous improvement.

24-22 (25 min.) **RI, EVA.**

1.

	Truck Rental Division	Transportation Division
Total assets	$650,000	$950,000
Current liabilities	120,000	200,000
Investment (Total assets – current liabilities)	530,000	750,000
Required return (12% × Investment)	63,600	90,000
Operating income before tax	75,000	160,000
Residual income (Optg inc. before tax – Reqd. return)	11,400	70,000

2. After-tax cost of debt financing = $(1 - 0.4) \times 10\% = 6\%$
    After-tax cost of equity financing = 15%

$$\text{Weighted average cost of capital} = \frac{\$900,000 \times 6\% + 600,000 \times 15\%}{\$900,000 + 600,000} = 9.6\%$$

Required return for EVA 9.6% × Investment (9.6% × $530,000; 9.6% × $750,000)	$50,880	$72,000
Operating income after tax 0.6 × operating income before tax	45,000	96,000
EVA (Optg inc. after tax – Reqd. return)	(5,880)	24,000

3. Both the residual income and the EVA calculations indicate that the Transportation Division is performing better than the Truck Rental Division. The Transportation Division has a higher residual income ($70,000 versus $11,400) and a higher EVA [$24,000 versus $(5,880)]. The negative EVA for the Truck Rental Division indicates that on an after-tax basis the division is destroying value—the after-tax economic return from the Truck Rental Division's assets is less than the required return. If EVA continues to be negative, Burlingame may have to consider shutting down the Truck Rental Division.

24-24 (20 min.) **Multinational performance measurement.**

1. Canadian Division's 2000 ROI $= \dfrac{\$1,200,000}{\$8,000,000} = 15\%$

2. Swedish Division's 2000 ROI in kronas $= \dfrac{6,552,000 \text{ kronas}}{42,000,000 \text{ kronas}} = 15.6\%$

3. Convert total asset into dollars at December 31, 1999 exchange rate, the rate prevailing when assets were acquired (6 kronas = $1)

$$42,000,000 \text{ kronas} = \frac{42,000,000 \text{ kronas}}{6 \text{ kronas per dollar}} = \$7,000,000$$

Convert operating income into dollars at the average exchange rate prevailing during 2000 when operating income was earned equal to

$$\frac{6,552,000 \text{ kronas}}{6.5 \text{ kronas per dollar}} = \$1,008,000$$

$$\text{Comparable ROI for Swedish Division} = \frac{\$1,008,000}{\$7,000,000} = 14.4\%$$

The Swedish Division's ROI calculated in kronas is helped by the inflation that occurs in Sweden in 2000. Inflation boosts the division's operating income. Since the assets are acquired at the start of the year on 1-1-2000, the asset values are not increased by the inflation that occurs during the year. The net effect of inflation on ROI calculated in kronas is to use an inflated value for the numerator relative to the denominator. Adjusting for inflationary and currency differences negates the effects of any differences in inflation rates between the two countries on the calculation of ROI. After these adjustments, the Canadian Division shows a higher ROI than the Swedish Division.

1(a) An evaluation of the three proposals to compensate Marks, the general manager of the Dexter Division follows:

(i) Paying Marks a flat salary will not subject Marks to any risk, but will provide no incentives for Marks to undertake extra physical and mental effort.

(ii) Rewarding Marks only on the basis of Dexter Division's ROI would motivate Marks to put in extra effort to increase ROI because Marks' rewards would increase with increases in ROI. But compensating Marks solely on the basis of ROI subjects Marks to excessive risk, because the division's ROI depends not only on Marks's effort but also on other random factors over which Marks has no control. For example, Marks may put in a great deal of effort, but despite this effort, the division's ROI may be low because of adverse factors (such as high interest rates, or a recession) which Marks cannot control.

To compensate Marks for taking on uncontrollable risk, AMCO must pay him additional amounts within the structure of the ROI-based arrangement. Thus, compensating Marks only on the basis of performance-based incentives will cost AMCO more money, on average, than paying Marks a flat salary. The key question is whether the benefits of motivating additional effort justify the higher costs of performance-based rewards.

Furthermore, the objective of maximizing ROI may induce Marks to reject projects that, from the viewpoint of the organization as a whole, should be accepted. This would occur for projects that would reduce Marks' overall ROI but which would earn a return greater than the required rate of return for that project.

(iii) The motivation for having some salary and some performance-based bonus in compensation arrangements is to balance the benefits of incentives against the extra costs of imposing uncontrollable risk on the manager.

1(b) Marks's complaint does not appear to be valid. The senior management of AMCO is proposing to benchmark Marks' performance using a relative performance evaluation (RPE) system. RPE controls for common uncontrollable factors that similarly affect the performance of managers operating in the same environments (for example, the same industry). If business conditions for car battery manufacturers are good, all businesses manufacturing car batteries will probably perform well. A superior indicator of Marks' performance is how well Marks performed relative to his peers. The goal is to filter out the common noise to get a better understanding of Marks' performance. Marks' complaint will only be valid if there are significant differences in investments, assets and the business environment in which AMCO and Tiara operate. Given the information in the problem, this does not appear to be the case.

2.   Superior performance measures change significantly with the manager's performance and not very much with changes in factors that are beyond the manager's control. If Marks has no authority for making capital investment decisions, then ROI is not a good measure of Marks' performance—it varies with the actions taken by others rather than the actions taken by Marks. AMCO may wish to evaluate Marks on the basis of operating income rather than ROI.

ROI, however, may be a good measure to evaluate Dexter's economic viability. Senior management at AMCO could use ROI to evaluate if the Dexter Division's income provides a reasonable return on investment, regardless of who has authority for making capital investment decisions. That is, ROI may be an inappropriate measure of Marks' performance but a reasonable measure of the economic viability of the Dexter Division. If, for whatever reasons, bad capital investments, weak economic conditions, etc., the Division shows poor economic performance, as computed by ROI, AMCO management may decide to shut down the division even though they may simultaneously conclude that Marks performed well.

3.   There are two main concerns with Marks' plans. First, creating very strong sales incentives imposes excessive risk on the sales force, because a salesperson's performance is affected not only by his or her own effort, but also by random factors (such as a recession in the industry) that are beyond the salesperson's control. If salespersons are risk averse, the firm will have to compensate them for bearing this extra uncontrollable risk. Second, compensating salespersons only on the basis of sales creates strong incentives to sell, but may result in lower levels of customer service and sales support (this was the story at Sears auto repair shops where a change in the contractual terms of mechanics to "produce" more repairs caused unobservable quality to be negatively affected). Where employees perform multiple tasks, it may be important to "blunt" incentives on those aspects of the job that can be measured well (for example, sales) to try and achieve a better balance of the two tasks (for example, sales and customer service and support). In addition, the division should try to better monitor customer service and customer satisfaction through surveys, or through quantifying the amount of repeat business.

24-28 (25 min.)   **Historical-cost and current-cost ROI measures.**

1.

	City Plaza	South Station	Central Park
$\dfrac{\text{Operating income}}{\text{Investment at historical cost}}$	$\dfrac{\$90,000}{\$300,000} = 30.0\%$	$\dfrac{\$120,000}{\$500,000} = 24.0\%$	$\dfrac{\$60,000}{\$240,000} = 25.0$
$\dfrac{\text{Operating income}}{\text{Investment at current cost}}$	$\dfrac{\$90,000}{\$600,000} = 15.0\%$	$\dfrac{\$120,000}{\$700,000} = 17.1\%$	$\dfrac{\$60,000}{\$450,000} = 13.3$

2.   Using investments at historical cost as the denominator, City Plaza has the highest ROI and South Station the lowest. Using investment at current cost as the denominator, South Station has the highest ROI and Central Park the lowest.

The choice of an appropriate measure depends on how Nobillo Corporation judges the performance of its convenience stores.

If Nobillo uses a single benchmark (say, 16%) in judging the performance of each store, the current cost measure will promote comparability among stores that were bought at different times or in areas with different real estate markets. Historical cost will give rise to differences in ROI among convenience stores that are unrelated to differences in operating efficiency. For example, in times of rising prices, the oldest store (City Plaza) will have a lower historical cost investment level than the newest store (South Station) for comparable amounts of square feet of store space in comparable locations. The current cost differences of the investment in the City Plaza and South Station stores, for example, are much smaller than the differences in historical costs, due largely to the different time periods in which the two stores were build. A drawback of current cost is that current cost estimates are difficult to obtain.

If Nobillo tailors the performance benchmark for each convenience store in its budgeting process, then the choice of a specific investment measure is less contentious. For example, if historical cost is used, the budgeted ROI benchmark for the South Station store could be, say, 25% whereas the budgeted ROI benchmark for the City Plaza store could be, say, 30%. Another benefit of tailoring the budget to each manager is that more incentives are provided to managers who are put in charge of poorly performing stations or stations in highly competitive markets.

24-30 (40-50 min.) **Evaluating managers, ROI, value-chain analysis of cost structure.**

1.

	$\dfrac{\text{Revenues}}{\text{Total Assets}}$ ×	$\dfrac{\text{Operating Income}}{\text{Revenues}}$ =	$\dfrac{\text{Operating Income}}{\text{Total Assets}}$
Computer Power			
1999	1.111	0.250	0.278
2000	0.941	0.125	0.118
Peach Computer			
1999	1.250	0.100	0.125
2000	1.458	0.171	0.250

Computer Power's ROI has declined sizably from 1999 to 2000, largely because of a decline in operating income to revenues. Peach Computers' ROI has doubled from 1999 to 2000, in large part due to an increase in operating income to revenues.

2.

Business Function	Computer Power		Peach Computer	
	1999	2000	1999	2000
Research and development	12.0%	6.0%	10.0%	15.0%
Design	5.0	3.0	2.0	4.0
Production	34.0	40.0	46.0	34.0
Marketing	25.0	33.0	20.0	23.0
Distribution	9.0	8.0	10.0	8.0
Customer Service	15.0	10.0	12.0	16.0
Total costs	100.0%	100.0%	100.0%	100.0%

24-30 (cont'd)

Business functions with increases/decreases in the % of total costs from 1999 to 2000 are:

	Computer Power	**Peach Computer**
Increases	Production Marketing	Research and development Design Marketing Customer service
Decreases	Research and development Design Distribution Customer service	Production Distribution

Computer Power has decreased expenditures in several key business functions that are critical to its long-term survival—notably research and development and design. These costs are discretionary and can be reduced in the short run without any short-run effect on customers, but such action is likely to create serious problems in the long-run.

3.   Based on the information provided, Provan is the better candidate for president of User Friendly Computer. Both Computer Power and Peach Computer are in the same industry. Provan has headed Peach Computer at a time when it has considerably outperformed Computer Power:

(a)   The ROI of Peach Computer has increased from 1999 to 2000 while that of Computer Power has decreased.
(b)   The computer magazine has increased the ranking of Peach Computer's main product, while it has decreased the ranking of Computer Power's main product.
(c)   Peach Computer has received high marks for new products (the lifeblood of a computer company), while Computer Power new-product introductions have been described as "mediocre."

24-32 (20-30 min.)   **Division manager's compensation, risk sharing, incentives (continuation of 24-31).**

1.   Consider each of the three proposals that the management of Mason Industries is considering:

a.   *Compensate Grieco on the basis of a fixed salary without any bonus.*
Paying Grieco a flat salary will not subject Grieco to any risk, but will provide no incentives for Grieco to undertake extra physical and mental effort.

b.   *Compensate Grieco on the basis of division residual income (RI).*
The benefit of this arrangement is that Grieco would be motivated to put in extra effort to increase RI because Grieco's rewards would increase with increases in RI. But compensating Grieco largely on the basis of RI subjects Grieco to excessive risk, because the division's RI depends not only on Grieco's effort but also on random factors over which Grieco has no control. Grieco may put in a great deal of effort, but the division's RI may be low because of adverse factors (high interest rates, recession) that the manager cannot control. For example, general market conditions will influence Grieco's revenues and costs.

To compensate Grieco for taking on uncontrollable risk, Mason Industries must pay her additional amounts within the structure of the RI-based arrangement. Thus, only using performance-based incentives costs Mason more money, on average, than paying a flat salary. The key question is whether the benefits of motivating additional effort justify the higher costs of performance-based rewards.

c.   *Compensate Grieco using other companies that also manufacture go-carts and recreational vehicles as a benchmark.*

The benefit of benchmarking or relative performance evaluation is to cancel out the effects of common noncontrollable factors that affect a performance measure. Taking out the effects of these factors provides better information about management performance. However, benchmarking and relative performance evaluation are effective only when similar noncontrollable factors affect each of the companies in the benchmark group. If this is the case, as it appears to be here, benchmarking is a good idea. If, however, the companies in the benchmark group are not exactly comparable because, for example, they have other areas of business that cannot be separated from their go-cart and recreational vehicle business, or they operate under different market conditions, benchmarking may not be a good idea. If the noncontrollable factors are not the same, then comparing the RI of Grieco's division to the RI of the other companies will not provide useful relative performance evaluation information.

24-32 (cont'd)

2.   Mason should use a compensation arrangement that includes both a salary component and a bonus component based on residual income. The motivation for having some salary and some performance-based bonus in Grieco's compensation is to balance the benefits of incentives against the extra costs of imposing uncontrollable risk on the manager. If similar noncontrollable factors affect the performance of the benchmark companies that also manufacture and sell go-carts and recreational vehicles, I would recommend that the bonus be based on the JSD's residual income relative to the residual income earned by the benchmark companies.

24-34 (20-30 min.)   **Division manager's compensation (continuation of 24-31).**

Consider each of the three proposals that Rupert Prince is considering:

1.   <u>Compensate managers on the basis of Division ROI.</u>

The benefit of this arrangement is that managers would be motivated to put in extra effort to increase ROI because managers' rewards would increase with increases in ROI. But compensating managers largely on the basis of ROI subjects the managers to excessive risk, because each division's ROI depends not only on the manager's effort but also on random factors over which the manager has no control. A manager may put in a great deal of effort, but the division's ROI may be low because of adverse factors (high interest, recession) that the manager cannot control.

To compensate managers for taking on uncontrollable risk, Prince must pay them additional amounts within the structure of the ROI-based arrangement. Thus, using mainly performance-based incentives will cost Prince more money, on average, than paying a flat salary. The key question is whether the benefits of motivating additional effort justify the higher costs of performance-based rewards. The motivation for having some salary and some performance-based bonus in compensation arrangements is to balance the benefits of incentives against the extra costs of imposing uncontrollable risk on the manager.

Finally, rewarding a manager only on the basis of division ROI will induce managers to maximize the division's ROI even if taking such actions are not in the best interests of the company as a whole.

2.   <u>Compensate managers on the basis of companywide ROI.</u>

Rewarding managers on the basis of companywide ROI will motivate managers to take actions that are in the best interests of the company rather than actions that maximize a division's ROI.

A negative feature of this arrangement is that each division manager's compensation will now depend not only on the performance of that division manager but also on the performance of the other division managers. For example, the compensation of Ken Kearney, the manager of the Newspaper Division, will depend on how well the managers of the Television and Film studios perform, even though Kearney himself may have little influence over the performance of these divisions. Hence compensating managers on the basis of company-wide ROI will impose extra risk on each division manager.

24-34 (cont'd)

3. <u>Compensate managers using the other divisions' average ROI as a benchmark</u>.
The benefit of benchmarking or relative performance evaluation is to cancel out the effects of common noncontrollable factors that affect a performance measure. Taking out the effects of these factors provides better information about a manager's performance. What is critical, however, for benchmarking and relative performance evaluation to be effective is that similar noncontrollable factors affect each division. It is not clear that the same noncontrollable factors that affect the performance of the Newspaper Division (cost of newsprint paper, for example) also affect the performance of the Television and Film studios divisions. If the noncontrollable factors are not the same, then comparing the ROI of one division to the average ROI of the other two divisions will not provide useful information for relative performance evaluation.

A second factor for Prince to consider is the impact that benchmarking and relative performance evaluation will have on the incentives for the division managers of the Newspaper, Television and Film studios Divisions to cooperate with one another. Benchmarking one division against another means that a division manager will look good by improving his or her own performance, or by making the performance of the other division managers look bad.